The U. S. Media and Yugoslavia, 1991–1995

R

The U.S. Media and Yugoslavia, 1991–1995

James J. Sadkovich

PRAEGER

Westport, Connecticut
London

Library of Congress Cataloging-in-Publication Data

Sadkovich, James J., 1945–
     The U.S. media and Yugoslavia, 1991–1995 / James J. Sadkovich.
          p.   cm.
     Includes bibliographical references (p.   ) and index.
     ISBN 0-275-95046-8 (alk. paper)
     1. Yugoslav War, 1991–   —Press coverage—United States.
     2. Yugoslav War, 1991–   —Mass media and the war.   3. Yugoslav War,
     1991–   —Foreign public opinion, American.   4. War in mass media.
     I. Title.
     DR1313.7.P73S23   1998
     949.703—dc21   97-19233

British Library Cataloguing in Publication Data is available.

Library of Congress Catalog Card Number: 97-19233
ISBN: 0-275-95046-8

First published in 1998

Praeger Publishers, 88 Post Road West, Westport, CT 06881
An imprint of Greenwood Publishing Group, Inc.

Printed in the United States of America

The paper used in this book complies with the
Permanent Paper Standard issued by the National
Information Standards Organization (Z39.48-1984).

10 9 8 7 6 5 4 3 2 1

For James and William

Contents

Preface

This study took too long to write and it remains incomplete.

I wish it were otherwise.

I have spent the past three years abroad, with brief forays back to the States. Happily, the importance of the American media, CD-ROM, and Internet have made it possible to tap into everything from the *New York Times* to television transcripts. If one is a newsaholic (I am not), it is even possible to watch CNN on a regular basis. I wrote this study to make some sense of why the U.S. media did the job it did covering Yugoslavia's dissolution. To a considerable extent, I have done that, at least for myself, and I hope for others as well.

Although I prefer to work alone, a habit picked up in archives and libraries as a graduate student, I had a good deal of help from my students, who have scoured periodicals and newspapers for articles about Yugoslavia and then provided me with summaries regarding frequency of sources, bias, point of view, and use of language. This took a bit of time to organize, but has allowed me to spend my time more efficiently this past year. I could not have managed without them. So many have helped that I cannot name them all, so I hope they will all understand that I am also thinking of them when I thank Aliya Belgybaeva, Sokol Cano, Bogdan Cosmaciuc, Borbala Deak, Yordan Milev, Maria Spirova, Boryana Stilianova, Nickolay Stoianov, and Nadia Tisheva for their help and their perceptive comments.

Encouragement from Stjepan Meštrovič and Norman Cigar picked up my spirits when they sagged in the face of so much reading in so many different areas. Comments by Branka Magaš and Ivo Banac have improved the final manuscript. Mildred Vasan's confidence in me overcame my doubts that I could do this, and Nita Romer's patience allowed me the extra time to finish as much as I have. I am indebted to those I talked to at PBS and CNN for helping me orient myself in their universe, and to Hugh Fullerton for looking at an early draft. I am greatly indebted to my friends and my students here for helping me survive the American University in Bulgaria (AUBG).

The University of Southern Mississippi gave me a small grant to buy transcripts, and AUBG has provided some money for books and student help. I did not seek more funding because in the beginning I was merely satisfying my curiosity, and as the project developed time seemed better spent reading and writing. I hope the final product repays the efforts of those who have helped me along, and that the reader will come away with a better understanding of things Yugoslav and a deeper appreciation of how the media shape our realities.

Whatever errors in interpretation and fact may exist are, of course, all mine, but at this point I can only regret them.

Finally, I should note that my roots are Croatian, but I was raised American. Whatever nationalism exists is therefore very diluted, and I have tried to be as critical of Tudjman and Croatia as my data led me to be. The story of Yugoslavia's dissolution is not a fairy tale, but there are gradations of guilt and enormous differences in responsibility. All I ask is that the reader approach my work and the media with both an open mind and a critical eye. That is what is important.

James J. Sadkovich
Blagoevgrad, 7 April 1997

Introduction: Approaching the Media

All theories on the media are limited, convenient ways of organizing and understanding data, the intellectual equivalent of maps, tools, and weapons. Every theoretical approach is artificial and entails risks. To adopt the acritical, descriptive, "morally cretinous" approach of the Popular Culture Association is to reflect and fetishize the media. But to defamiliarize the familiar and destabilize existing power relations by taking the critical, analytic, sociological approach of Marshall McLuhan and the Frankfurt School has led to plausible elitist theories that have little relevance outside the classroom. Yet there seems little choice—you can adore the media or you can debunk them.[1]

Both approaches have been used by insiders who focus on personal experiences and technique, and by outsiders who extrapolate process and intention from the media's products. Insiders have an intimate understanding of the media's processes and realities, but they tend to superfluous detail, have difficulty maintaining a critical distance from colleagues and contacts, balance on a shaky theoretical scaffolding, and base generalizations on anecdotal evidence. Outsiders can be cool and analytic, but are often superficial, lack contact with those in the media, have a weak grasp of process, use overly elaborate theoretical models, and generalize from narrow studies.[2]

Edward Herman and Noam Chomsky are examples of outsiders, Norman Isaacs of an insider. Whether owing to ideological assumptions or to their different status, they offer different explanations regarding the media view of life. Herman and Chomsky believe that the media, as institutions integrated into and protective of the status quo, construct reality and manufacture consent.[3] Isaacs discerns various "gatekeepers" who define news like "automatons" and display a "schizophrenic streak" as they reconcile the dictates of duty with the need to make profits. All three are critical of the media's performance, but Isaacs traces its deficiencies to structural flaws and contradictions that are economic, personal, and apolitical, not to processes that are integrated and consciously ideological.[4]

Herbert Gans and Mark Fishman temporarily became insiders, but wrote as outsiders, relying on their professional training to maintain an analytical distance from their subjects. Both contributed crucial concepts to media criticism: Gans the idea that news is made as a result of professional constraints and assumptions, Fishman that the beat largely determines what can be reported.[5]

Ben Bagdikian has translated his years of experience in the media into biting critiques. Like Isaacs, he is uncomfortable with the creation of commercial chains and the deformities to which the media lend themselves.[6] Keith Tester, John Fiske, Douglas Kellner, David L. Paletz, and Robert M. Entman are among the better-known media critics. Their approaches are ideologically sophisticated and focus on technique and the products generated by the media.[7]

My approach is that of an outsider who consumes news and is consumed and confused by it. I am more interested in understanding what the media produce than how or why they do so; my theoretical scaffolding is eclectic and more than a little bit improvised. I hope to achieve something closer to an essay than a monograph, on the order of the works by Martin A. Lee and Norman Solomon, or Ron Powers's irreverent analysis of newscasters.[8] I have tried to read as much of the printed media as time has allowed, to watch what television has been available with a critical eye, and to listen to National Public Radio with some attention. Because transcripts do not convey the feel of newscasts, and I have limited access to the electronic media, the weakest sections of this study have to do with television and radio, especially radio, which I usually listened to while doing something else—paying it its due as a hot medium.

I have used media and communications theories to explain why reporters interviewed accused war criminals in much the same way that they questioned members of an American football team. Part of the explanation is simply that the media need celebrities so desperately that they will create them if they do not exist.[9] I have also made forays into legal texts on international law, human rights, and genocide that helped me understand why reporters preferred to interview accused war criminals rather than plow through monographs on war crimes.

Three assumptions regarding the media struck me as useful: the idea that there are gatekeepers and filters controlling the flow of information through the media to their audiences; the view that the audience reads the media texts and transforms them in the process; and the belief that newsworkers can only maintain their jobs and rise within news organizations if they unconsciously accept the dominant ideologies of the corporation and mainstream society.[10]

Distinguishing an attentive public from the general public, and opinion makers from policy makers, helps clarify who makes and who uses the news and for what ends. Diplomats use the media to mold domestic and foreign public opinion, and to signal other governments and negotiate with them. But official sources are so diverse and prolific that what information reaches the top is digested and bland. So media have little effect on existing policies, although diplomats justify and explain those policies by using the media.[11]

Most academic theories—and almost all radical and postmodern theories—agree that media influence our perceptions of reality by shaping and defining events and issues for us. Not only is each medium its own message as well as the content of another medium, but the media construct their own realities and present them as news, in the process filtering information, shaping attitudes, and manufacturing consent. Disagreement begins when one places the media in their cultural matrices.[12]

There is no consensus as to whether media realities are consciously or unconsciously intended to maintain the status quo, whether their representations are so different from alternative realities that they are essentially distorted and false, or whether the audience can regain control of their minds and their lives by reshaping mediated realities through active interaction with the news, instinctively or as scholarly observers.[13] But most agree that the media's shaping of reality depends on the sources consulted and the conventional devices used to report news. The media produce culture, but they are also part of a culture that distorts their assumptions about, and perceptions of, what might be termed absolute reality. This was obvious in the case of the U.S. media and the breakup of Yugoslavia. Prior assumptions about Slavs in general, and Yugoslavia and its history in particular, determined reporting, influenced editorial positions, and otherwise distorted reporters' grasp of reality and acted as filters on their mediation of events and personalities. The media's version of reality then shaped the perceptions and influenced the actions of their audiences.

The process was not a simple one-way indoctrination imposed on a passive public. The news is part of a larger cybernetic loop that includes stereotypes current in U.S. culture, official news releases by governments and other organizations with access to the media, academic monographs and journals dealing with foreign policy, works on history and politics, and simple prejudice.[14] The media played the role of mediator for the public, but they were hardly in a position to shape reality absolutely, because most realities had already been heavily mediated by the time they reached the editorial desks of the major media organizations. The output of the media influenced such phenomena as opinion polls, and these in turn influenced policy makers, who themselves had influenced the media positions that had influenced the polls in the first place. In short, a given culture is incapable of being anything other than what it is, and its perceptions of reality are uniquely its own.[15]

Information is generated by politicians and bureaucrats and the reporters covering them, but then spin doctors and pundits recast it as expert commentary, academic monograph, popular entertainment, and personal prejudice, thereby influencing the positions and perceptions of the politicians and bureaucrats and affecting the assumptions and receptivity of reporters and their audiences to the messages of the politicians and bureaucrats (assuming they are contained in some relatively undiluted form, such as interviews or sound bites).

Media, their sources, and their audiences form a single porous, seamless conduit on which information moves like figures on an Escher drawing. It is difficult to decide whether one is analyzing the container or the content; whether the views are those of the source, the reporter, the audience, or some combination of all three; or where source, medium, and audience begin and end. The flow of information changes so rapidly and is so unpredictable that the only constants are the complexity and uncertainty of the media's products.[16]

When I first began to look at the media carefully, my impression was that they were doing a poor job of reporting Yugoslavia's breakup and the conflicts that followed. Now I am not so sure. It is easy to criticize the media, but works on Yugoslavia and Bosnia by the journalists Mark Thompson and Noel Malcolm are as good as, if not better than, the painfully pedantic products of many of my colleagues. Moreover, the more I read on the media, the more I was struck by the similarities between my profession and their craft. Both journalists and academics are salaried professionals working in bureaucracies. Both have an illusory autonomy. Both use words to tell stories derived from real sources. Both strive to be fair and objective. Both are biased. And both hate to admit their shortcomings.

That said, as an "academic" (a.k.a. a critical intellectual) and as a citizen (a condition that demands an informed interest in public affairs) I have both a right to demand that the media serve their function of informing me and a duty to criticize them when they fail to do so. Unlike Baudrillard's audience, who may be content simply to be entertained before the lights go out, those of us in the academic elite are in positions that carry an obligation to think, speak, and write critically about society. That so few of us have done so with regard to the media is undoubtedly owing to our own occupational deformities, which tend to seal us in ever smaller and tighter intellectual boxes. Nonetheless, the media shape our behavior and frame our attitudes through their depiction of reality just as surely as teachers mold their students' minds through the choice of texts and as surely as politicians control their constituents' lives through their use of government office; if the media are immune from scrutiny and criticism, they will become as corrupt as any closed system—political, administrative, educational, or entertainment—that feels itself privileged and above those it purports to serve.[17]

Perhaps I am more critical than I need be, so it is worth noting that most of my information comes from the media, which have done a mixed rather than a poor job in this instance. If saying that the media short-circuited the ethical and moral sensibilities of their audiences seems an extreme statement that lets the audience off the hook, I am echoing Tester, for whom "media significance means moral insignificance."[18]

Something about the media tends to transform their audiences into amoral voyeurs, but exactly how the numbing of social conscience occurs is unclear. That Americans are inured to violence from childhood may have helped us accept what happened as something inevitable and of little concern to us, and even to find the whole business rather boring and tedious after a while.[19] If Arnold Schwarzenegger is just the Cisco Kid with automatic weapons, Radovan Karadžić is just Huey Long with an accent.

The crisis itself and the ideologies that fueled and shaped it are of only peripheral importance to me, so I will deal with them only to compare the media's realities to their alternatives. But it is worth stressing that if Balkan nationalisms and their consequences seemed archaic, with their medieval symbols and long-dormant hatreds, computers and public relations made them as alike and as different from their precursors as ethnic cleansing from genocide.[20]

I will look at the period from the outbreak of hostilities in July 1991 to their abrupt termination by the Dayton peace agreements in December 1995, but not systematically or in detail. Like a beat reporter, I will pay special attention to the "critical stages"—the years 1991 and 1995—because during those periods, as Balkan neonationalists captured state bureaucracies and military organizations and implemented a politic that combined military aggression with genocide, the West imposed a peace that ended one of the longest-running action serials in modern European history. In 1995, the media hailed peace, often uncritically, but in 1991 they failed to present events so that the general public and policy makers could place the efforts of Yugoslavia's constituent nationalities to obtain separate states in a social, economic, and political

framework that would allow them to understand why Belgrade's policies resulted in military aggression and mass slaughter, and then react
appropriately.

The media bore considerable responsibility for the failure of Americans as a people and a polity to formulate viable political responses to
the new realities reshaping the Balkans, and to act and react ethically
and morally. We sporadically lost interest in the conflict, although
revelations about Serbian contributions to the British Conservative
Party, the West's cynical behavior regarding Srebrenica, and the indictments for war crimes handed down by the World Court have kept
interest in the region alive.[21] It is therefore worth a look at the nature of
the media and at the quantity, quality, and distribution of media coverage of the crisis.

One reason the media cannot make things clear to their audience lies
in techniques and technologies that numb us by absorbing and shaping
our individual and collective minds, in the process making us vicarious
action-seekers and voyeurs to unreal, televised images. McLuhan believed that we live our lives according to mythic concepts, a proposition
familiar to those who have read Vico or the literature on nationalism
and fascism, which exploited technology and myth.[22] He concluded
that hot media, like newspapers and photographs, tend to preclude
empathy and participation by overwhelming the consumer with data.
The more coverage, the less impact, because the nervous system shuts
down when exposed to too many stimuli. We numb ourselves and make
ourselves apathetic and dull to avoid experiencing too much emotion,
too much involvement. "The price of eternal vigilance," McLuhan
warned, "is indifference." Yet if to "behold" a medium is to "become"
it, then other questions must be raised beyond theories dealing with
technique, text, and technology.[23]

Media perform certain tasks poorly because of their culture, which
includes the history that they know. The media are trapped within their
own textual universe—news becomes reality, and as it accumulates, it
is transformed into history. But selection is neither careful nor systematic, so media history is haphazard and unchecked for chronological
context and accuracy. It is also amazingly simplistic, because when style
became information, truth became a commodity and news a series of
simple-minded and meaningless issues such as "who won?" So the
media are a wonderful conduit for myth and propaganda, especially
when a particular piece of information, like Croatia's "fascist" past,
seems relevant and is repeatedly used as a news peg, a story frame, or
an explanation.[24]

The process holds true for what appear to be real histories. Few
reporters have the leisure to read systematically or carefully, and like
anyone who is not an expert in a field, they tend to read what is easily

available and digestible.[25] Books like Kaplan's *Balkan Ghosts* and Rebecca West's Yugoslav opus became fundamental to all news stories on Yugoslavia, the informational matrix in which those who had read them grounded and shaped their perceptions of reality. That Kaplan knew Greece best or that West reflected the views of a racist, pro-Serbian culture was of little concern to the uncritical reader, but such observations were crucial to understanding tendencies and frames in the media, such as the repeated contrast of Croatia's genocidal fascist past to Serbia's heroic, pro-Allied record. Such matrices framed and filtered reality and led to bizarre assertions, like Susan Woodward's claim that Croatian *Gastarbeiters* in Germany had more influence not because they outnumbered Serbian *Gastarbeiters*, but because they had more "fascist" organizational experience.[26]

To identify the media's matrices involves both a critique of the media and of academic and scholarly sources. This is particularly true for such quasi-academic publications as *Foreign Affairs*, whose commentaries and analyses are written by academics and insiders, but aimed at both specialist and nonspecialist audiences. It is also useful to include such academic journals as *Slavic Studies*, the widely read organ of the American Association for the Advancement of Slavic Studies, because it forms part of the informational matrix that has been consistently pro-Serbian and anti-Croatian.[27]

Finally, it is necessary to discuss alternative histories of Yugoslavia to balance widely distributed works, such as those by Alex Dragnich, because most people in the media and most consumers of the media will not realize that Dragnich is a Serbian nationalist and a member of the Serbian King's Court—small bytes of information as crucial to assessing his version of historical reality as noting that the bulk of his sources are Serbian.

NOTES

1. Douglas Kellner, *Media Culture: Cultural Studies, Identity and Politics between the Modern and the Postmodern* (London: Routledge, 1995), 24–33, uses a "multiperspective" approach. Keith Tester, *Media, Culture, and Morality* (London: Routledge, 1994), 3–76, sees cultural studies as suffering from their mode of address, selection of objects to study, and national focus. He concludes that they have failed to resolve the "problem of fetishization of everyday life" to the extent that they have accepted the separation of the media from their social and cultural contexts and have failed to do much more than *describe* the media and their audiences. David Lazere, "Introduction," in *American Media and Mass Culture: Left Perspectives* (Berkeley: University of California Press, 1987), 1–6, questioned whether structuralism and deconstruction are radical, given the speed with which the academy absorbed them. Todd Gitlin, *The Whole World Is Watching: Mass Media in the Making and Unmaking of the New Left* (Berkeley: University of California Press, 1980), 249–59.

2. Leo Bogart, *Press and Public: Who Reads What, When, Where, and Why in American Newspapers* (Hillsdale, NJ: Lawrence Erlbaum Associates, 1981), xii, thought academic studies on communications theory useful but frustrating, because they lacked "statistically satisfying conclusions." He oversaw studies at the Newspaper Advertising Bureau from 1960 to 1980. Philip Gaunt, *Choosing the News: The Profit Factor in News Selection* (Westport, CT: Greenwood Press, 1990), 139, limited himself to suggesting the use of content analysis, observation, and surveys for further research—a typical academic conclusion.

3. Edward S. Herman and Noam Chomsky, *Manufacturing Consent: The Political Economy of the Mass Media* (New York: Pantheon, 1988), xii–xv; Edward S. Herman, "Media in the U.S. Political Economy," in John Downing et al., *Questioning the Media: A Critical Introduction* (London: Sage, 1990), 75–77. Because the media internalize constraints imposed by the market, the government, and the system of private ownership, they are self-censoring. Challenges to the system's basic premises are excluded automatically, and the media proffer a propaganda that is so subtle and credible, it seems natural. Dissent and inconvenient facts are ignored or domesticated by being explained within ideologically acceptable contexts.

4. Norman Isaacs, *Untended Gates: The Mismanaged Press* (New York: Columbia University Press, 1986), 2, 11, 42, 90, 217–21, thinks newsrooms are mismanaged because those in control have limited perspectives and lack broad-gauged training—both occupational or professional deformities. He believes that the profit motive precludes ethical behavior, and that corporate chains reduce the autonomy of local editors because editorial policies are decided at regional or national levels. Ethics and good reporting thus give way to the "ability to play the game."

5. Herbert J. Gans, *Deciding What's News: A Study of CBS Evening News, NBC Nightly News, Newsweek, and Time* (New York: Pantheon, 1979), and Mark Fishman, *Manufacturing the News* (Austin: University of Texas Press, 1980, 1990).

6. Ben H. Bagdikian, *The Media Monopoly* (Boston: Beacon Press, 1983), passim.

7. John Fiske, *Television Culture* (New York: Methuen & Co., 1991); Kellner, *Media Culture, op.cit.*, and *The Persian Gulf TV War* (Boulder: Westview, 1992); David L. Paletz and Robert M. Entman, *Media, Power, Politics* (New York: The Free Press, 1981); and Tester, *Media, op. cit.*

8. Ron Powers, *The Newscasters* (New York: St. Martin's, 1977); Martin A. Lee and Norman Solomon, *Unreliable Sources: A Guide to Detecting Bias in News Media* (Secaucus, NJ: Carol Publishing Group, 1990).

9. Gitlin, *The Whole World*, 155–57.

10. Herman, "Media," 78–87, for a summary of filters used by the media. For texts, Tester, *Media*, passim, and Fiske, *Television Culture*, passim.

11. Yoel Cohen, *Media Diplomacy: The Foreign Office in the Mass Communications Age* (London: Frank Cass, 1986), 3–5, 21–32, 43–97.

12. Marshall McLuhan, *Understanding Media: The Extensions of Man* (New York: Mentor, 1964), 21–27. Vincent Moscow, "Introduction: Information in the Pay-per Society," in V. Moscow and J. Wasko, *The Political Economy of Information* (Madison: University of Wisconsin Press, 1988), 3–17, for information as a commodity and the use of electronic technologies to control information and monitor consumer choices and work-place performance.

13. Tester, *Media Culture*, 57–80, for the audience and dialogue.

14. McLuhan, *Understanding Media*, 21, thought that all cultures and periods have their "favorite model of perception and knowledge" that they tend "to prescribe for everybody and everything." Also Cohen, *Media Diplomacy*, 21–35.

15. McLuhan, *Understanding Media*, 35, cites Jung, who noted that Romans were slaves because they were surrounded by slaves. Tester, *Media Culture*, 14–15, defines "culture" as social relationship on a day-to-day basis, and texts that make sense of the world in accordance with certain conventions. It is what we produce every day to help us make sense of a world that is without inherent form or meaning.

16. The flow of information is carefully managed and "produced" by "information workers" who are wage earners working for large commercial organizations. Dan Schiller, "How to Think about Information," in Moscow and Wasko, *The Political Economy of Information*, 27–41.

17. Bagdikian, *Media Monopoly*, xiv, considers the mass media "the authority . . . for what is true and false, what is reality and what is fantasy, what is important and what is trivial." He sees "no greater force in shaping the public mind."

18. Tester, *Media Culture*, 3, 101–30; also Mark Thompson, *A Paper House: The Ending of Yugoslavia* (New York: Vintage, 1992), 326–27.

19. McLuhan, *Understanding Media*, 31–33. Assigning guilt is difficult in contemporary society because we are aware that technologies affect mind, not "at the level of opinions or concept," but by gradually and effortlessly altering "sense ratios or patterns of perception"—so we "become what we behold." For the impact of television violence on audiences, see Lee and Solomon, *Unreliable Sources*, 238–39, and George Comstock, Steven Chaffee, Natan Katzman, Maxwell McCombs, and Donald Roberts, *Television and Human Behavior* (New York: Columbia University Press, 1978), 387–477.

20. Anthony D. Smith, *Theories of Nationalism* (New York: Harper and Row, 1971), and Louis L. Snyder, *Varieties of Nationalism: A Comparative Study* (Hinsdale, IL: The Dryden Press, 1976); John Breuilly, *Nationalism and the State* (Chicago: University of Chicago Press, 1993); Leo Kuper, *Genocide: Its Political Use in the Twentieth Century* (New Haven: Yale University Press, 1982); and Norman Cigar, *Genocide in Bosnia: The Policy of Ethnic Cleansing* (College Station, TX: Texas A&M University Press, 1995).

21. Elizabeth Neuffer, "The Ghost of Srebrenica," *Boston Globe*, 19 May 1996, and Tim Kelsey and David Leppard, "Serbs Gave Tories £100,000," *Sunday Times*, both from Bosnia Internet Forum.

22. George L. Mosse, *The Nationalization of the Masses: Political Symbolism and Mass Movements in Germany from the Napoleonic Wars through the Third Reich* (New York: New American Library, 1965), esp. the chapters on the aesthetics of politics, national monuments, and public spectacles for the use of sacred space, ritual, and myth to mobilize people politically. As he notes in his conclusion, "Large numbers of people today may still share those basic longings for wholeness and the need to objectify which seem an integral part of humanity. There is, even in our own time, a longing for the totality of life which is closely related to myth and symbol. Politics and life must penetrate each other, and this means that all forms of life become politicized."

23. McLuhan, *Understanding Media*, 38–39, 43, 55–56; and Daniel Pick, *War Machine: The Rationalisation of Slaughter in the Modern Age* (New Haven, CT: Yale University Press, 1993), passim.

24. Stuart Ewen, *All Consuming Images: The Politics of Style in Contemporary Culture* (New York: Basic Books, 1984), 25–27, 259–65; Jasmina Kuzmanović, "Media: The Extension of Politics by Other Means," in Sabrina Petra Ramet and Ljubiš S. Adamovich, *Beyond Yugoslavia: Politics, Economics, and Culture in a Shattered Community* (Boulder, CO: Westview, 1995), 94–95. Both Croats and Serbs quickly learned to name the enemy. Croats were "Tudjman's black legions" and "Ustaša forces," whereas their own troops were "defenders" and "reserve forces." Serbs were "chetniks" and the Jugoslavenska Narodna Armija (JNA) an "occupation force." As a result, there were disconcerting reports of "defenders" from a small village having "encircled" a major city.

25. Obviously, this is a generalization that needs to be challenged. Yet, in her interview with Judy Woodruff of *MacNeil/Lehrer*, Shirley Biagi noted that "Woodruff's IN box is piled with reference materials—*Washington Dossier, The New York Times, The Atlantic* and *Ms.* magazine" (emphasis added). Woodruff saw the difficulties of becoming an instant expert and thought the best solution was to consult local reporters. The consequences of doing so in Yugoslavia are obvious. Shirley Biagi, *NewsTalk II: State-of-the-Art Conversations with Today's Broadcast Journalists* (Belmont, CA: Wadsworth Publishing Co., 1987), 40, 44.

26. Woodward's matrix is apparent in her choice of sources and in her belief that World War II can be understood by seeing Croatians as fascists and Serbians as pro-Allied partisans. This dichotomy made Serbian fears of a resurgent Croatian fascist state credible and led Woodward to see Croatians as so duplicitous that she accused them of provoking almost every Serbian or JNA attack, including the shelling of Dubrovnik. Susan L. Woodward, *Balkan Tragedy: Chaos and the Dissolution of Yugoslavia after the Cold War* (Washington, DC: Brookings Institution, 1995), 24–25, 148–49, 159–60, 164, 170, 182.

27. My own experience with this review suggests intentional selection of pieces that were pro-Serbian and anti-Croatian. Although the journal published Dragnich's polemical rejection of the term "Serbian hegemony," the editor refused even to consider a scholarly rebuttal. Alex Dragnich, "The Anatomy of a Myth: Serbian Hegemony," *Slavic Review* (1991), and J. Sadkovich, "Serbian Hegemony Revisited, or Blaming the Perpetrator, Not the Victim," *Association of Croatian Studies Bulletin* (Oct. 1992). The journal has published articles by Robert M. Hayden, whose bias is apparent in his praise of Woodward's book and his "Nationalism in Former Yugoslavia," *Slavic Review* (1992), 671–72, in which he cites Tudjman out of context to demonstrate that the Croat leader approved "the inevitability of final solutions," and Gale Stokes, John Lampe, Dennison Rusinow, and Julie Mostov, "Instant History: Understanding the War of Yugoslav Succession," *Slavic Review* (1996), esp. 143, 146–47, and 157–58, for a cynical approach to the war, praise for the works by Woodward and by Silber and Little, and defense of Misha Glenny and Slavenka Drakulić.

Media Elites and Their Audiences

WHO ARE THE MEDIA?

Dissemination of international news in the American media is largely done through three wire services (AP, UPI, Reuters), three newspapers (the *New York Times*, the *Washington Post*, the *Los Angeles Times*), and two television stations (CNN and WTN/UPITN). AP alone has 3,000 U.S. clients, and its correspondents send 200,000 words daily to its New York foreign bureau. The American media include hundreds of popular outlets, scores of scholarly publications, and subscription services on the Internet.[1]

The amount of information available is staggering. It is impossible to survey all of it, much less do so in a comprehensive manner. So I have sampled major outlets, especially print and televised media. This seemed a feasible approach. It also seemed appropriate—an eclectic methodology for an eclectic media universe.

The nature of the media is elusive, but it is useful to see them as filters managed by gatekeepers who recast reality in ways congruent with the attitudes of those who control the political and economic levers of the country. That they should do so is not surprising. They are part of national and local power structures, and their elites tend to live and work near those structures in places like New York, Washington, London, and Paris. If Daniel Patrick Moynihan considered the press corps a frustrated elite, Michael Novak thought he could see most of their leading members from his office window in midtown Manhattan.[2]

Lichter, Rothman, and Lichter's preconceptions led them to view those working in the media as a liberal elite in much the same way that

Chomsky and Herman saw them as staunch supporters of the status quo. Organizations to the right and the left of the political spectrum have kept a critical eye on the media in the United States. The best known and best financed are AIM (Accuracy in the Media), a conservative organization founded in 1969, and its counterpart on the left, FAIR (Fairness and Accuracy in Reporting), created in 1987.[3]

Newspapers do more analysis and TV more spot news, but reporters for both get their information on foreign affairs from government officials and employees of think tanks and universities with ties to the government. Sam Donaldson called reporters "blood brothers" to the establishment, and many have been linked to the CIA. Pat Ellis believed that the executive branch sets the foreign policy agenda, and one reporter believed that even if they know "that government facts are not facts but lies," they tend to support their government. If Walter Friedenberg did not think that journalists take the government's word as "sacred writ," sometimes it is the only writ.[4]

At both local and national levels, beats predispose reporters to use official sources and ignore others; because journalists are reluctant to offend their sources, hearsay becomes truth and leaks can be used to manage those who show their gratitude by reporting them. Those reporters closest to power cannot therefore challenge the system. As Walter Karp put it, "the most esteemed journalists are precisely the most servile."[5]

Reporters may question government officials if they perceive a "national interest" to be at stake or official versions of reality conflict sharply with interpretations of important politicians, prestigious academics, or prominent think tanks.[6] If reporters do their job well, they inevitably alienate some elites, notably government officials and military officers.[7] But initially, they were not likely to do so over the Balkans, because their own knowledge was limited, academics and think-tank employees reinforced official policies, the region was marginal, and no American interests seemed in play.

The media are part of a feedback loop that includes their sources, their audience, and themselves. They mediate information from their sources, they define what is newsworthy, and they distribute it in the form of news. The audience then mediates and legitimates by consuming the news and feeding it back in various ways, including public opinion surveys. Raw material from sources is thus processed by journalists, consumed by the public, analyzed by pollsters, and recycled by political advisers.[8]

Journalists have the power to publicize events and actors, but sources and advertisers can exert political, ideological, and economic pressure on the media. Public officials can complain to news and corporate executives, threaten to hurt the firm economically, investigate, bring suit, and appeal to the public. Interest groups can write letters, call press conferences, and organize public meetings. Everyone tries to influence reporters, and marketing considerations have led to mindless "happy" news. But direct censorship is rare. The most effective censors are peers, immediate superiors, advertisers, affiliates, and parent firms. Journalists practice self-censorship and look askance at those who rock the boat.[9]

Threats and coercion are seldom used because reporters reflect conventional ideas and preclude pressure by giving in on their own terms and cooperating with those in power. Pressure prompts them to appeal to the First Amendment and their status as a fourth estate serving the public's right to know. But they prefer to avoid problems by a prudent choice of sources and objective reporting. They do not ask embarrassing questions about the system, and if their values have evolved since the more liberal 1960s, John Chancellor's observation that most are "members of the extreme center" still seems valid. Most are middle or upper middle class and center-of-the-road—liberal on social issues, but conservative on economic questions.[10]

Journalists help to shape perceptions and realities, but their social status and self-image mirror those of professionals and midlevel managers, so they tend to fit reality into categories shared by other middle-class professionals. They report on the upper and lower ends of national social, economic, and political hierarchies, but like their audiences, journalists come from the middle sectors. In other words, manufacturing and consuming news is a middle-class activity and a middle-class passion.[11]

Journalists are trained to compile, not analyze, information. They assure credibility by keeping their opinions moderate, ignoring unbelievable news, using authoritative sources, and selecting evidence acceptable to their editors and the public. Their judgments about reality are stereotyped, and their assumptions and comprehension tend to coincide, giving them what Gans labeled a para-ideology that shapes the news in a very basic way. They are neither wise men nor particularly interested in analyzing events. They do want to be where the action is, and many like being part of the action. They are therefore also players and insiders.[12]

Bureaucracies are key mediators of reality, because journalists depend on officials and consider them well-informed, authoritative sources. By providing information that is accessible, easily digestible, and unlikely to result in libel suits, they give invisible subsidies to news organizations, which in turn promote, publicize, and legitimate their benefactors. If their data are accepted as factual and "official" is a synonym for "competent," then those outside official structures can be ignored.[13]

In short, most journalists support the status quo. A bare majority in Lichter's study were liberal; journalists like George Will and William Safire are both influential and conservative, and critics like Kellner view the mainstream media as accomplices of the system. Certainly the media are not the apolitical fourth estate that they claim to be, and neither the elite nor those in the trenches are above politics or economics. If the bloated salaries of national anchormen predispose them to support the system, a more modestly paid hometown reporter who criticized local elites would have a short career.[14]

Yet if journalists depend on sources with whom they share an interest in existing social, economic, cultural, and political systems, they work in a profession whose values include an objective search for and representation of the truth. They are thus caught in a dilemma whose horns are formed by the values of their profession and those of their sources. How vigorously they defend their professional purity seems proportionate to the compromises demanded by their job, which continually sully that purity.[15]

Journalists are not a homogeneous group socially or economically. They are stratified according to income and educational levels, and local journalists lack the power of their national colleagues who are often graduates of elite universities and can participate in the formulation of policy. Whether they can be objective is another question, because Washington's revolving door creates an elite with common bonds, points of view, and contacts. Like all elites, it insulates itself from nonelite sectors of society, tends to support the status quo that assures its privileges, and values conventional wisdom. Journalists have most in common with elites in business, government, and academe. The news thus reflects the demographics of the reporters, not of American society.[16]

Although journalists distinguish columnists from those reporting hard news, their work is also routinized, stylized, and bureaucratic. News hierarchies stretch from corporate and news executives through top editors, producers, and senior editors to reporters and researchers. Power is exercised through budgets, personnel decisions, general policy, and story selection. Senior editors set the tone and oversee the production process. Journalists share work habits, attitudes, dress, and a desire to please their editors. Their freedom is conditioned by factors like seniority, and if they are jealous of their autonomy, they complain if neglected by their superiors.[17]

Depictions of reporters as hard-nosed investigators are misleading. The news is a business where profits are primary and prestigious beats and sources confer power and position on reporters. In such a world, the investigative reporter is doubly handicapped: he is unprofitable and he risks embarrassing powerful people and institutions. It is safer for reporters to run in packs, interview the powerful respectfully, and write commentaries that appeal to the well-heeled members of their audience.[18]

If journalism is a "subjective pursuit, tempered and shaped by the political conditions and cultural traditions of the particular societies where it is practiced," then in the United States it must bear a capitalist imprint. News gathering is centralized to keep costs low, and survival depends on selling advertising space and paying decent dividends to shareholders. But advertising brings blandness and monopoly, and bottom-line managers seek to please the advertiser, not inform the public.[19]

Few media outlets are any longer family concerns. Most are owned by corporations and share the structures and mentalities of large business bureaucracies. They tend to protect corporate power and hamper the public's ability to understand the forces that shape their world. The media may appear value-free, but they serve the interests of business and government, or in Bagdikian's terminology, "authorities" and "personalities."[20]

Corporate media sell the news less to the public than to advertisers, and they cut costs to increase profits. Television and newspapers hire and fire staff based on the programming hours and news columns that can profitably be broadcast or printed, not on the news available or the community's need to know. Print media cut back investigative reporting and hard news in favor of features and fluff, and broadcast media use standard shots and sequences and "rip and read" wire service reports. Because news media are understaffed and journalists overworked, they cannot search out news.[21]

Both Isaacs and Gans believed that a struggle was inevitable between journalists impatient with commercial restraints and corporations intent on maximizing profits. Yet to change how news is gathered and distributed risks loss of audience, increased pressure from the powerful, and higher costs. Organizational constraints also favor caution and conformity. In other words, media change only when society changes.[22]

Changes are usually cosmetic, like those of the 1970s, when the addition of photos and features made serious news weeklies resemble *People* magazine. Reporters and editors have been socialized to accept the routines of their profession and their particular organization.[23] News organizations seem to constrain imagination and promote conformity more than they encourage excellence or foster creativity. There is little incentive to depart from stereotypic interpretations, and beat reporters seek out opposing points of view among competent sources. If not subject to a "party line," reporters are constrained by corporate policy, routine, and structure.[24]

Those who discerned a liberal media elite were both right and wrong. There is an elite, but it is neither liberal nor homogeneous. The process of news gathering puts reporters in certain places, gives them access to some sources and not others, predisposes them to certain concepts and certain ways of perceiving the world, and leads them to create a world congruent with their culture. The result is a shared vision of the world.[25] Christopher Hitchens may be a nudge, but he appeared on ABC or PBS and did his bit, and Alexander Cockburn of *The Nation* may be to the left, but he was no better informed on Yugoslavia than A. M. Rosenthal of the *New York Times*.

WHO IS THE AUDIENCE AND WHAT DOES IT DO?

Defining the audience is not easy, public opinion is a slippery term, and different methodologies yield different answers regarding audiences and their relationship to the media.[26] Yet media coverage is shaped by the need to appeal to certain audiences, whether the average American who watches the three major networks, the college-educated viewers of CNN, the conservative readers of *The National Review,* or the radical who buys *The Nation.*[27]

Media seek to expand their audiences, and mass advertising and technology have created media monopolies just as mass production and technology did political and economic monopolies. But if media are both commercial and intellectual monopolies, the term "mass" is misleading, because they try to appeal to those with the money to buy the products their advertisers are hawking.[28]

If audiences seem to prefer human interest stories to analysis, a sizeable number of people crave hard national and international news. But what the audiences get often depends less on their political and cultural, than on their consumer, preferences. Just as political and business elites set the agenda for public debate, advertising influences the media, which in turn set the context for public debate by framing questions so that certain data are available while others are not.[29]

By deciding what is newsworthy, the media determine what information is available to an audience. What is not reported is as important as what is reported, because selection of news items limits an audience's ability to grasp and respond to events and issues. The media create discontent, but they also contain and channel it, and the audience ultimately approves the actions of the elite and affirms the system as a whole, merely by paying attention or, more exactly, by merely paying attention.[30]

Rather than defamiliarizing the familiar and destabilizing the social order, the media stabilize the social order by familiarizing the unfamiliar. By treating the Gulf War as a football game or the Bosnian conflict as a tribal conflict, they make them topics for conversation and reassure the public that they are immune to such exotic events. Middle-class audiences readily accept news that reflects their values, and those in the lower-class audiences seeking to become middle class do so as well.[31]

Because most Americans had little interest in or knowledge of the history, culture, and fate of the peoples who populated Yugoslavia, the media could reflect official policies and allow war criminals as much time to argue their case as they did the victims of aggression to make their accusations. Reporters sought to be objective, but they often reflected a utilitarian mélange of parochial American and cynical British interests and perspectives.[32]

Journalists can influence both policy makers and audiences, but most of us are spectators at a spectacle, eavesdroppers on conversations between policy makers and journalists. As spectators we learn our roles and what pose to strike; as eavesdroppers we seem to be the final arbiters of what the news really means. But most of us evidently ignore substance to focus on style (i.e., how someone speaks or what they look like), and Kellner rejects the concept of an audience that confers meaning and ridicules the theory that audiences struggle to overcome an ideological hegemony as fetishism.[33] Half of us read columnists loyally, but we have little respect for journalists and only a sporadic and superficial interest in foreign affairs. We are an "inadvertent audience" who ingest the news whole, like a Twinkie.[34]

Those fond of the linear thinking in books have been alarmed that the public seems to prefer TV's surrealistic vision of reality to the print media's smorgasbord of hard news.[35] The public's apparent indifference to the news caused Richard Harwood to complain that in its reporting on Bosnia the press had played the role envisioned by the Founding Fathers, but the average American had not paid attention. Deployment of U.S. troops to Bosnia had piqued the public's interest, but a Times-Mirror poll found only 9 percent of the public had followed events in Bosnia "closely." Harwood assumed the public was uninterested because we were not directly involved in Bosnia, a faraway place populated by strangers. He concluded that an informed public opinion simply did not exist.[36]

Of course, to blame the audience is to reject the media's role in preventing it from following the news and thinking about it coherently. Yet the media's tendency to personalize events and issues, to pay more attention to culturally and geographically proximate elites, and to present only the surface of things precludes complexity and analysis.[37] Summaries of polls sampling political attitudes mislead, because they test an uninformed public, whose lower and middle classes make up the majority of respondents and are the most adversely affected by the media. Audiences are diverse, and polls, like journalists, can ask the wrong questions.[38]

The question is not how many followed the conflict in Bosnia, but how many bother to follow the news at all. In the 1970s TV news was watched mostly by people over fifty who were well or poorly educated. Even then, the focus was on local affairs, and twice as many men watched sitcoms as news. Given how few people watch TV news, how many newspaper items compete for a reader's attention, and how quickly and totally we block out items that are not of interest, 9 percent was a fairly high figure.[39]

Journalists see themselves as representative, but see no need for their audience to be represented. They mix disdain with resignation for those uninterested in the news, dislike "sensation seekers," and are uneasy with "would-be intellectuals" who make them feel inferior. They seem happiest with audiences they have invented.[40]

Lichter concluded that journalists usually champion social underdogs and criticize authorities, and they can be ambivalent regarding business. While Chet Huntley chided his colleagues for being too hard on business, he insisted that "the free-enterprise, capitalist or profit system is not part of the Constitution" and "the sole purpose and function of business" is the "satisfaction of the consumer, not profit." Their most important audience seems to be their sources, and they themselves were active players during the Gulf War and the conflict in Bosnia.[41]

Journalists attract audiences by telling useful stories in clear, simple prose, with heroes, villains, and victims. Their stories shock and panic, but they seek to preserve the social order by keeping certain realities from the audience. So war footage is sanitized, and politically acceptable stereotypes are common.[42]

Because the media tell stories that are intuitive and anti-intellectual, they preclude rather than further discourse. Television journalists and pundits mug at the camera, shout at one another, answer inane questions with rehearsed witticisms, and offer slogans as analysis, assuming that people do not want serious news and informed discussion. But unlike pundits, "ordinary citizens" are less interested in the "game of politics" than such realities as paying taxes and scrounging scholarships.[43]

Standard electronic news sources and news services homogenize news content and editorial style, but audiences are increasingly fragmented. Specialized publications, cable TV, and the Internet segregate rather than integrate audiences. Different media texts carry different meanings that audiences change as they view or read them, so they often have unintended and contradictory effects.[44]

Television's polysemic texts have multiple meanings but serve limited social interests because they circulate some meanings and exclude others. This appears to be true of all media. Not even the underground press could escape such conventions as the need for personalities, and cyberpunk remains quintessential American fantasy. Media provide sites where reporters and readers seek and control meaning. Because reading a text is an acquired interactive skill and a creative social practice, readers can learn to resist certain meanings, reject the control sought by journalists, and expand the meanings of texts.[45]

Yet Tester cautions that while audiences can engage in dialogues with media texts, they do not necessarily do so. In the case of Yugoslavia's dissolution, reporters like David Rieff and Roy Gutman, columnists like Anthony Lewis and William Safire (hardly a matched set), and special-interest groups needed three to five years to prompt a counterreading to the official text of the conflict. The lag occurred because existing policies are always difficult to change, and events in Yugoslavia overwhelmed analysis. Policies explain events, so by covering certain events journalists superimpose leaders (like Owen) and structures (like the peace process) over the public's perception of reality. Issues are not hard news and take second place to events, which are easier to report. So debate is limited and political alternatives narrowed.[46]

Media texts are not obvious because they use the codes of sources, actors, and reporters. Ginzburg showed how codes work by using an inquisitor and an accused heretic. The inquisitor used one code, the accused another, but only the former's account reaches the historian, who brings a third to his reading of the record. The reader of the historian's account may have a fourth. By then little is left of the accused's account. If one substitutes the Yugoslavs for the accused, the ubiquitous UN/NATO/U.S. official for the inquisitor, and the reporter for the historian, then it is clear that the audience receives codes, not objective accounts, especially since neither diplomatic nor media images are real.[47]

Of course, audiences are no more aware of deciphering texts than most reporters are of encoding them. Yet Novak's working man resented journalists who enforce their version of reality because by doing so, they validate one culture and trash another.[48] Elite codes are simply not congruent with blue-collar common sense, even if they help to shape it.

If news is political soap opera and much of the world invisible to the media, much of the media are invisible to the average American, overwhelmed with data filtered through a media prism that reduces them to so many bytes of information scattered across a vast field of electronic signals and computer-generated print, from CNN, PBS, and NPR to the dailies, weeklies, and special-interest publications that make up the media.[49] The perception that the media are biased is inaccurate only if they are considered as a unit. But most of us receive only a few bytes of the data carried by the media and lack the time to obtain enough bytes to get a complete view of the world. This is why studies confine themselves to a specific sector, a small number of publications, or a short time span. Nor can most of us critique the media, because the values and techniques that inform news coverage, from media logic to visual grammar, are arcane concepts to most of us.

When Lord Owen and others used the media to justify policy and define issues within narrow parameters, it was hard to find multiple meanings in their texts. Routine news simply limits political consciousness. Politically and socially sterile, the news replaces a "coherent view of politics" with "personal melodramas carefully strained of explicit political and social significance."[50]

It is a nice irony that the proliferation of news outlets, easy access to news with the advent of CNN and C-SPAN, and sophisticated technologies have homogenized news content and editorial styles, and, with C-SPAN, forced viewers to become sophisticated editors. We can choose between bland news whose conformity to a dominant ideology prescribes alternatives and a mud-slide of raw news whose lack of organization leaves us buried under heaps of useless information.

SOURCES, EXPERTS, AND CHARLATANS

Sources are the basis of the process because they select and encode information for reporters and editors.[51] Reporters prefer sources who allow them to meet their deadlines with credible information. They also like powerful sources whose status rubs off on those reporters with access to them. Inaccessible sources simply do not exist. All sources spruce up when reporters are around, so that what the reporter sees is often both rehearsed and misleading.[52]

Which sources reporters encounter depends on whether they are specialists on a beat or generalists on assignment. Beats can be geographical (Sarajevo), organizational (the United Nations), or topical (diplomacy), and most prefer a beat's predictability to a general assignment's uncertainties. Sources can manipulate beat reporters because they develop symbiotic relationships with them; they can manage generalists because their knowledge of any given subject is rudimentary. All reporters follow packs in pursuit of certain sources and check with their colleagues to reduce uncertainty regarding sources.[53] But if journalists are themselves experts and sources, they often ignore the information that their colleagues publish. Reports by America's newspaper of record were fairly objective during 1991, but those covering the crisis did not seem to cooperate. What one reporter knew in January, another had forgotten by June. An editorial policy that seemed to reflect shifts in the posture of the American government, and the opinions expressed by columnists and guest editorials, further confused matters.

Beats and locations of reporters seemed to constrain what and how they reported, and there were few beat reporters in Yugoslavia in 1991. Many who hurried there as the country was collapsing were generalists in need of local guides, and their stories reflected the guides they found and the packs they followed. In general, pack journalism misplaces resources, wastes energy, and distorts information. As Judy Woodruff noted, "Everybody goes out and reports the same thing, which is very little." This was true in Yugoslavia, where Belgrade and Sarajevo became the loci of most reports and UN officials the sources usually cited.[54]

The crisis in Yugoslavia began in the 1980s, but analysts and reporters were unprepared, because, like Helsinki Watch, they were preoccupied with the repression of Albanians in the Kosovo region, an event that coincided with the emergence of Slobodan Milošević and an aggressive Serbian neonationalism. All were major threats to Yugoslavia's political integrity.[55] But crucial economic issues were poorly covered, and partisan scholarship compounded the defects of the media's early reporting.[56]

Chuck Sudetic was crucial to shaping perceptions because he was the main source of hard news for the *New York Times,* which also published several op-ed pieces and ran articles by Stephen Engelberg, David Binder, Alan Riding, Celestine Bohlen, Craig Whitney, Stephen Kinzer, and John Tagliabue. Binder reported from Washington and Belgrade, Riding and Whitney from Luxembourg, Bohlen from Zagreb, and Tagliabue from Belgrade. Engelberg and Sudetic traveled a lot. None demonstrated a deep understanding of Yugoslav economics, history, or politics; all reflected the biases of their sources.

Sudetic's reports helped to validate a number of assumptions and rationalizations. Among them were the beliefs that the Serbs were physically threatened by the creation of a Croatian state because only Croats had a fascist past and longed to resurrect it; that Croatia's Serbs lived in two areas where they constituted an overwhelming majority and had a right to secede from Croatia; that Yugoslavia's political dissolution and the subsequent war were a single phenomenon; that Zagreb and Ljubljana were largely to blame for the course events took; and that the conflict was a civil war whose genocidal nature derived from a South Slav (a.k.a. Balkan) history steeped in enmity and bathed in blood.

In January 1991, Sudetic reported that the Serbian government had saved Serbian industry by illegally appropriating $1.86 billion (18.3

billion dinars) from the national banks, with which Milošević was closely associated. Yet in April, Engelberg blamed all the republics for Yugoslavia's fiscal crisis. Ramet later concluded that Milošević had used the money to buy the Serbian electorate.[57] Sudetic implied that violence and an inability to live together plague South Slavs when he wrote that there were growing fears that a "serious exchange of fire [could] unleash a cycle of violence in Yugoslavia's frayed patchwork of quarrelsome peoples with different languages and religions."[58] He reported that the Yugoslav Minister of Defense did not "dispute" the right of Croatia and Slovenia to secede, but had warned that secession would lead to "civil war." By reporting the minister's claim that both were acting "in the direct service of some foreign factors," Sudetic prepared the ground for later accusations of Vatican plots and German efforts to break up Yugoslavia.[59]

In May, he balanced his report of an RTV broadcast of a JNA film accusing Croatia's Defense Minister, Martin Špegelj, of buying weapons and preparing for a "merciless civil war" by noting that the Croat had denounced it as a "Stalinist calumny." The film had used subtitles to complement a corrupt soundtrack, and so was suspect, but its authenticity was less important than the JNA's arming of Croatia's Serbs and its disarming of Croatian territorial defense forces. Yet Sudetic referred to Serbs in Croatia as "rebels" and "vigilantes." Such labels were as misleading as the film, which disconcerted the West, stirred up Serbs, and gave the JNA an excuse to order Špegelj's arrest on the eve of talks with the Croatian government.[60]

When the failure of the talks appeared to seal Yugoslavia's fate, Sudetic reported that Croatia and Slovenia wanted an EC model, the JNA favored a centralized state, and Milošević would accept a confederation if all Serbs were included in a Serbian state. He did not note that Milošević's demands would have eviscerated Bosnia and Croatia, nor that the Serbian leader had already trashed Yugoslavia's 1974 constitution. Both Belgrade and the JNA were justifying their use of force against Croatia and Bosnia by claiming the "right" of all Serbs to live in a Serbian state and accusing Croatia of being a neofascist state whose government was plotting genocide against its Serbian minority and working with the Vatican and Germany to break up Yugoslavia—supposedly the latest in a history of attacks on Serbia by the Papacy, the Comintern, Nazis, Muslims, Masons, the United States, and Tito.[61]

In May, Bohlen and Engelberg saw the Serbs as provoking the Croats, but Sudetic reported Serb charges without comment, thus lending some credibility to efforts to rationalize Serbian actions, just as John Tagliabue's reports from Belgrade helped to rationalize the JNA's use of force. Noting that the army would take "decisive military action" that might lead to "civil war," he implied that the federal government had been constrained to resort to military action because Slovenia and Croatia were not "willing to halt carrying out steps toward independence" and "radical Croatian separatists" had attacked "the villages of Mirkovci and Osijek, Serbian strongholds." This was somewhat misleading, because Zagreb and Ljubljana had offered plans to save Yugoslavia, and with 90,828 Croats and 28,582 Serbs, Osijek was not exactly a village or a Serbian stronghold.[62]

Nor was Sudetic more accurate. Depicting the JNA's halting advance into Slovenia as a "blitz," he reported that Slovenes had "eased their nerves with beer and plum brandy" at the local café, but "appeared firm . . . in their resolve to resist" what "they insisted on calling an occupation by a foreign army instead of a civil war." The proper term, of course, was "civil war." The following day he reported that in an attempt "to ease the country away from the edge of civil war," the Prime Minister [sic], Stipe Mesić, had ordered the JNA back to its barracks in the "breakaway republic of Slovenia" where Slovenian Territorial Defense Forces had "surrounded" the army, a neat trick against an army conducting a blitz.[63]

In fact, there was neither blitz nor civil war. The JNA was backed up along the roads or trapped in its barracks. Tagliabue, who denied that the army was "a Serbian tool," reported that Serbs interpreted Mesić's order to return to barracks as a humiliating insult to the "Serbian soldier." A Croat was thus to blame for the JNA's failure, and, by making General Kadijević "a bitter foe" of Milošević, Tagliabue absolved the latter of responsibility for the JNA's actions. "Wounded and angry" following their lackluster performance, JNA commanders urged the "secessionist republic" to "stop harassing army units."[64]

Evidently, fighting in Slovenia and "an increasingly effective war" by Croatia's Serbs were merely what Tagliabue termed "civil strife," because Sudetic and Engelberg thought "civil war" likely only if Tudjman and Kučan, both "former communists," joined forces after JNA forces, supposedly acting on their own, had fired on a crowd in Zagreb. Even so, Tagliabue believed that civil strife had shredded "the authority of the Central government," collapsed the Serbian "center," and left Mesić "detested" by the JNA and "helpless." Upset at the "useless sacrifice of Serbian sons" in Slovenia, Serbs wanted their army redeployed to "defend" Serbs in Croatia and Bosnia. While Berlin and Vienna pressed for recognition of Croatia and Slovenia on the basis of the 1975 Helsinki Accords, Washington warned that doing so would only lead to "civil war" in Yugoslavia, and some worried that "civil wars" resulting from a highly contagious "separatist virus" might explode into a dangerous pan-European civil war.[65]

Although Sudetic reported Stipe Mesić's remark that Milošević wanted to create a Greater Serbia, he implied that the referendum in

Croatia had been invalid and cast the Serbs as heroic figures.[66] Few saw the JNA's occupation of Croatia as aggression, but the war there was very much the JNA's conflict. Cigar has shown that the organization was overrated, and Almond mused that the West—helped by John (Jovan) Zametica, the International Institute for Strategic Studies in London, and the PEW Trust—"conjured up the historical myth of the invincible Serbian peasant soldier." In 1991, of course, the mythic peasant soldier should have been superfluous, because the JNA could field 1,850 main battle tanks, 500 armored personnel carriers (APCs), 2,000 pieces of towed and self-propelled artillery, 489 fixed-wing combat aircraft, and 165 armed helicopters. Of these, about 800 tanks and APCs, 4,000 guns and mortars, and 36,000 troops were deployed near Croatia. Against this, Croatia could initially pit only 34,000 policemen and guardsmen.[67]

By the time that the war had ended in Croatia, Sudetic, Zametica, and a number of other experts and reporters had elaborated rationalizations for Serbian aggression and genocide. Germany was cast as the villain for supporting the Croats, who were depicted as predatory neofascists, even after the Serbs had destroyed Vukovar, shelled Dubrovnik, and cleansed the Krajina of Croats.[68] Dennison Rusinow, Gale Stokes, Bogdan Denitch, William Pfaff, Lenard Cohen, and others have contributed more scholarly apologies for Serbian actions, often by attacking Croatians as fascist or Bosnians as unreasonable and intractable, even though Serb nationalists had refused to tolerate Croatians and Bosnian Muslims, and the Serbian government and the JNA had armed and trained the local populations in Croatia and Bosnia and then incited them to rebellion and terrorism.[69]

Initially incomplete and inaccurate, information was subsequently distorted by the reporters, news shapers, spin doctors, columnists, commentators, and analysts who created a world of convenient and reassuring stereotypes.[70] The rise of what Soley calls news shapers coincided with the use of sound bites and visuals in campaigns, and the erosion of analysis by discussions of a candidate's style and ranking in the polls. Networks replaced lost bureaus with news shapers who were often employees of conservative think tanks, GOP consultants, or economists from large business firms. Ostensibly nonpartisan experts, most news shapers depend on the media for their expert status and on institutions with an ideological agenda for their livelihood. Like Lichter's media elite, they are a self-contained group, isolated geographically and socially. They talk to and cite each other, and they subscribe to a conventional wisdom that reinforces the status quo.[71]

Reporters shape information by prompting sources to view events in certain ways. Because they saw Croats and Muslims as unconventional or unimportant groups, journalists treated them as irrelevant or partisan. Their preferred sources sought to manage, not examine or explain, events in Yugoslavia, so they fed the media politically safe and analytically unsophisticated information. News was filtered through official, often anonymous, sources and experts. The UN, EC, and United States all used spin doctors.[72]

To the extent that news shapers objectify and reify reality according to their ideological preconceptions, the audience becomes passive, depoliticized, frustrated, dysfunctional, and angry. Thirty years ago, Novak thought workers right to resent the media's appropriation of reality, and Fallows recently warned that the antics of pundits "jeopardize the credibility of everything that journalists do." In short, the noise created by experts and pundits makes it hard for viewers and readers to make sense of the news.[73]

If audiences felt like eavesdroppers on conversations between experts and journalists, that was because they often were. The viewer watching Kissinger discuss events in Bosnia with Jim Lehrer or Charlayne Hunter-Gault was privy to a conversation between Council on Foreign Relations (CFR) members. If consensus seemed easy, that was not surprising. Washington and CFR elites are interlocked and reinforce one another's views. Dan Rather, Tom Brokaw, David Brinkley, William F. Buckley, Daniel Schorr, Marvin Kalb, and A. M. Rosenthal are all CFR members. Reporters understandably prefer the views of CFR members and D.C. elites to those of less prestigious and less conventional sources, even those better qualified to discuss foreign affairs and policy.[74]

Many experts were employees of consulting firms or think tanks, and most were familiar to reporters. Among those employed by Kissinger's influential consulting group that shaped both policy and the news on Yugoslavia were William Hyland, Lawrence Eagleburger, and Brent Scowcroft. When he left to become Secretary of State in 1988, Eagleburger got $250,000 in severance to add to his $660,000 in salary that year. Because much of this was earned working for Serbian firms, Patrick Glynn perceived a conflict of interest when Eagleburger began to formulate and implement American policy on the Balkans.[75]

Most guests on news shows are members of government, large corporations, political parties, or think tanks.[76] Shows like *The MacNeil-Lehrer Newshour* presented the crisis in the Balkans through deferential interviews with newsmakers like David Owen, Lawrence Eagleburger, and Cyrus Vance, who were rarely challenged but often addressed by pompous and irrelevant titles.[77] Whether Eagleburger was beholden to Belgrade was less important than whether, by deferring to his person during interviews, journalists helped him to promote his views as authoritative because they were unwilling to act as devil's advocates or unable to challenge gaps in reasoning and knowledge they did not even know existed.[78]

Not only were Western newsmakers treated with deference and sympathy, so were accused war criminals like Radovan Karadžić. In July 1995, after reports that Serbians had massacred Srebrenica's defenders, Stephen Kinzer humanized the Serbs by visiting Pale and interviewing Karadžić's daughter. He noted that Pale had "been condemned around the world for savagery and ethnic chauvinism," but the headline—"In Stronghold, Serbs Cite Dread of Muslim Rule"—implied that Serbs were beleaguered and fearful. His Serbian sources claimed that they were "desperate for someone to do something to bring this all to an end," but as "prisoners of history" they had "no alternative to war" because Muslims and Croats had "always" committed genocide against them.[79] By balancing abstract condemnation of Pale with personal Serb points of view, Kinzer effectively invited his reader to sympathize with Bosnia's Serbs, echoing reports by Chuck Sudetic, David Binder, and Stephen Engelberg four years earlier.[80]

Like them, Kinzer was an expert because he was where the action was. Among the experts who were not, but still shaped the news, were Washington's usual suspects including a new category, the former State Department employee. The first to make the news was George Kenney, who resigned on 25 August 1992 to protest the State Department's failure to tell the truth and the U.S. government's refusal to act. He claimed that "more than twenty" colleagues believed that only Western miliary intervention could resolve the crisis, but that in the "highly politicized" State Department internal debate was "stifled" and "professional standards" moot. Younger officers focused on policy, older ones on their careers, and no one dealt with crises "on the scale of Yugoslavia." Denouncing a system that made lying to Congress obligatory, he called for "a healthy debate on the Yugoslav crisis."[81]

Kenney's dissent gradually gave way to opinions congruent with those of the State Department, the Pentagon, and the White House. When he argued in December 1994 that lifting the arms embargo on the Bosnians would have "brutal consequences," he echoed the *New York Times,* which had earlier published an essay by an anonymous author who had supported the embargo by arguing that what was needed was "not to introduce new weaponry but to find ways of reducing the vast arsenals already there."[82]

Although such arguments ignored the reality that the vast arsenals were largely in Serbian hands, many experts supported the embargo because they perceived the massacre in Bosnia as the most recent installment of an age-old struggle among the region's savage tribes. Even those who saw the struggle as recent shared the second assumption.

David Binder, who filed his stories from Belgrade and Washington, knew that Serb-Croat animosities were "of recent origin," but he blamed the Croats for them. He believed that the "majority of Croats" had fallen "under the spell of narrow nationalists demanding a separate state," led by Ante Pavelić, an "avowedly fascist leader." Supported by Fascist Italy, Pavelić's Ustaša "terrorists" had "murdered" the Serbian king and the "majority" of the 350,000 Serbs killed during the war. Serbian Chetniks had "retaliated against Croats wherever they could," and partisans killed 100,000 Croats after the war ended. Now, fifty years later, "nationalist animosities" were "focused once more on the Krajina, home of 600,000 Serbs."[83]

Such displays of expertise were disarming and inaccurate. About 150,000 Serbs lived in the "Krajina," the rest scattered throughout Croatia. To excuse Serbian atrocities as retaliation was as disingenuous as claiming that only Croatia had collaborated during the war and that only Croatians had fallen under the spell of ultranationalists in the interwar period. King Alexander's dictatorship displayed marked fascist characteristics; the Serbian prime minister, Milan Stojadinović, reviewed his strutting greenshirts in Belgrade in 1939; and the Serbians had several fascist organizations, including SRNAO and Ljotić's followers.[84] Cohen's book on wartime Serbia details Serbian collaboration with the Nazis, and Magaš noted that of 55,000 Jews killed in the war, 24,000 perished in Serbia, where 79,000 died in concentration camps, just 6,000 less than in Croatia.[85] More accurate data were available in 1991, but most instant experts and some academics used and diffused flawed histories.

Some did so unconsciously, others intentionally. In a piece in the *New York Times*, Aleksandar Nenadović, former editor of Serbia's *Politika*, argued that despite evidence of "modern civilization," like fast food, in Yugoslavia reason succumbed to "tribal animosities" and passion, leading to "fears, hatreds, threats, clashes, shootings, killings." Yugoslavia, an "infantile democracy" suffering "a poisonous nationalistic euphoria," was becoming Lebanon, owing to efforts by Serbs, Croats, "and many of the rest" to "topple" the federal government. Nenadović urged talk and "compromises." He did not mention that Serbs had provoked and manipulated the crisis, nor that to blame everyone was to exculpate the Serbs. Although Nenadović was a Serb and *Politika* one of the four pillars of Milošević's regime, the *Times* presented him as a former U.S. correspondent for "the leading Yugoslav daily."[86]

Like Nenadović, Flora Lewis was an expert by dint of being a journalist, in her case a "senior columnist" for the *New York Times*. From Paris she could hear the "shouting match among Yugoslavia's ethnic rivals becoming a shooting match." With "minorities in too many places" and nationalists "choking themselves with history" (which could "be made to prove any point"), the Yugoslavs clearly needed help to overcome their tendency to read history and shoot one another. Lewis saw the crisis as a test case with far-reaching implications, and she thought the Conference on Security and Cooperation in Europe (CSCE), whose "basic principle" was that borders not be changed by force, should force everyone to calm down. But the CSCE had ignored appeals by Croatia and Slovenia to settle the crisis by negotiation, and it was not complexity that had caused the JNA to support aggressive Serbian nationalism.[87]

A British "war artist," Peter Howson, became an instant expert by visiting Bosnia twice, each time for three weeks. He expressed his opinions in paintings, including one of a Croat raping a Muslim. Britain's Imperial War Museum found his work of dubious value, but Howson believed rape was "a symbol of Bosnia's plight." If so, it was odd to show a Croat raping a Muslim, given that by 1994 it was clear that Serbs had systematically used rape to terrorize Muslims and Croats.[88]

Thomas Friedman, another columnist who helped shape opinion, traveled to Belgrade in 1991 to report on James Baker's visit. According to Friedman, Baker could not persuade the "feuding leaders of Yugoslavia's six republics" to maintain a unitary state. Worried that Yugoslavia's dissolution "could have some very tragic consequences" there and "in Europe" and concerned lest history repeat itself, Baker declared that America would "welcome" a "federal restructuring" of the country. But, like "its European allies," it would refuse recognition and economic aid to republics that went their own way.[89]

Friedman missed the green light Baker had given the JNA, but Peter Millionig, a "foreign agent representing Slovenia," did not. Millionig appealed to principle and economic self-interest, not history or realpolitik, by arguing that the Slovenes had a right to independence because they had been exploited by Serbia after 1918 and helped the Croats to carry Serbia and the "other poor southern republics" after 1945. But Baker had refused to recognize Slovenia, and it was not clear that Bush's "new world order" would guarantee democracy in Yugoslavia.[90]

The following day, the *Times* published Srdja Popović, "a human rights lawyer" and publisher of *Vreme*, "an independent news weekly." The paper had introduced Millionig as a lobbyist, but presented Popović as a neutral professional. Popović ridiculed Yugoslavia's "immature and irresponsible nations" for playing "Balkan poker" just "to impress onlookers." Ante Marković was "mature," but surrounded "by unruly adolescent republics" trying to become adults by inventing symbols and "real borders," a dangerous activity because most conflicts had "started over symbols." He singled out the Croats for refusing to "admit their defeat under the Axis flag" and their "crimes against the

Serbs," and he called for the international community to keep Croats and other immature South Slavs from setting "the European house" on fire.[91]

The *Times* balanced Popović with Michael Scammell, a Russian literature professor at Cornell and "a frequent visitor to Yugoslavia." He saw the "Serbian" government's "brutal suppression of Albanians in Kosovo" as evidence it was "wedded to violence," and he chided Washington for sacrificing basic principles of freedom, democracy, and independence to "Serbian blackmail." He saw Slovenia and Croatia as having "bent over backward to avoid proclaiming outright independence" and "secession," and he condemned Serbia as an authoritarian anachronism. Recalling the U.S. failure to support Poland in 1953, Hungary in 1956, Czechoslovakia in 1968, and the Baltic republics in 1991, he urged Washington to "get it right this time."[92]

Two years later, Warren Christopher, whose expert status derived from his position as Secretary of State, announced on the *MacNeil-Lehrer Newshour* that Washington could do nothing because all groups in Yugoslavia were consumed by "ancient hatreds." Boutros Boutros-Ghali, whose expertise came with his position as head of the UN, compared tribal wars in Rwanda and Burundi to the crisis in Bosnia; Henry Kissinger, who combined academic, government, and lobbying expertise, asserted on *Nightline* that South Slavs had been fighting each other for "a thousand years," a neat trick since they had their hands full fighting Venetians, Byzantines, Magyars, and Turks.[93]

Among the anonymous experts was the U.S. official who wrote an op-ed piece for the *New York Times* in May 1993. The official ruled out air strikes against Serb positions, given Europe's lack of support, and opposed lifting the embargo, because the "challenge in Bosnia [was] not to introduce new weaponry but to find ways of reducing the vast arsenal already there." The anonymous wise person pronounced "safe havens" a "promising approach" and urged sanctions against Croatia for using regular army troops in Bosnia, where they were "holding down front-line positions against Serb fighters" and "terrorizing civilians in Mostar and central Bosnia."[94] Evidently, using irregular forces, like Chetniks, would have been acceptable.

John Newhouse, who summarized diplomatic gossip for the *New Yorker*'s readers, made a similar argument when he asserted that eastern Europe was "a cat's cradle of ethnic and national groups that are recovering their past," an area where "nationalism, ethnic passions, and capricious behavior" torment the inhabitants.[95] Misha Glenny, whose studied objectivity gave the impression that all sides shared the blame for the war, concluded that lifting the arms embargo in 1994 "would have cemented a ruthless military alliance between the Serbs and Croats." He argued that the war was not "exclusively a matter of Serb aggression," because Serbs could not have undone a Bosnian state that was never "viable." What Glenny neglected to mention was that it was not viable because the West had imposed an arms embargo on Bosnia while Serbia and the JNA had incited, armed, and trained its Serbs.[96]

An influential commentator on Bosnia, owing to his position as a former editor of the *New York Times,* A. M. Rosenthal did not hide his pro-Serbian, anti-Muslim bias. He argued that 49 percent of Bosnia was not a "decent share" for the Serbs who made up 32 percent of its population, and he insisted that lifting the arms embargo would merely lead to endless war in the Balkans.[97]

The *Times* also published Anthony Lewis, whose expertise was conferred by having a regular column and who was highly critical of U.S. and UN policies. He condemned the accommodating posture adopted by the UN commander, General Sir Michael Rose, and censured the United States and NATO for allowing the slaughter to continue. Yet he could see "only two honorable choices" for the West—either massive military intervention supported by air strikes or a message to the Bosnian Muslims that they were on their own.[98] Of course, there was a third choice: lifting the embargo and allowing both Bosnians and Croats to fight on a level battlefield.

David Gompert, a former government official, tried a fourth. Because Britain, France, Russia, and the UN opposed a "heavy bombing campaign," he called for a "sustained economic and informational war" to "topple" the "archvillain" of the Balkans, "Milošević, Inc."[99] Why this would have worked against Bosnian Serbs supplied through Romania, Macedonia, Greece, Albania, Bulgaria, and Serbia is not clear when it was not even tried against Iraq. Only the straw man of a heavy bombing campaign, set up to justify doing nothing, was likely to topple.

But it was clear that Bosnia was on its own after the West rejected proposals to lift the arms embargo and refused to take energetic military action against the Serbs. Instead, the West put its faith in a flawed negotiating process and Slobodan Milošević, who was supplying Bosnia's Serbs, leading Stanley Hoffman, an expert from Harvard's Center for European Studies, to dismiss the arms embargo as "a fiasco" and note that without a "credible threat of armed force," negotiations become appeasement. The West should have used force to "press" the Serbs to conclude a "fair deal" with Bosnia, but the United States and "its obstinately appeasing allies" had placated the Serbs, who had gained 70 percent of Bosnia thanks to the JNA's help. As in 1938, the great powers had chosen peace over honor, but peace had eluded them, leaving them only dishonor.[100]

Others thought the West had tried to do too much. Richard Betts argued in *Foreign Affairs* that both limited intervention and impartial intervention can work, but when combined they result in "years of military stalemate, slow bleeding, and delusionary diplomatic hag-gling." By adopting both policies in Bosnia, the West became an unwit-ting accomplice to "slow-motion savagery."[101]

However, if most observers agreed that the West's failure to act against Serbian aggression had resulted in disaster, few saw an alterna-tive to the use of force by the West; that option was precluded because most saw the situation as too politically unstable and too unpredictable to risk committing combat troops.[102] Some who advocated using force, like Warren Zimmerman, former U.S. ambassador to Yugoslavia, thought it should have been used to deter aggression in 1991–92, not to reverse it later.[103]

Other experts rationalized Serbian actions by accusing Croats and Muslims of the same, attacking the Western media as biased, distorting history, and misrepresenting recent events. Peter Brock, an American journalist, excoriated the Western media as anti-Serbian, and Darko Tanaskovič, of Belgrade's Oriental Institute, claimed that Muslims threatened Serbs. Both authors published in *Mediterranean Quarterly*, a journal distinguished for its pro-Serbian bias.[104]

Misha Glenny, who wrote for publications like *Foreign Affairs* and the *New York Review of Books*, implied that Croats and Muslims were responsible for the breakup of Yugoslavia and the subsequent geno-cide. Typical was his observation that in 1991 "the Slovene weasel, the Croat marten, and the Serbian jackal" began "scratching one another's eyes out" in their rush to devour Yugoslavia's carcass, a metaphorical assertion that everyone was responsible. Tudjman was thus as guilty for being "insensitive" to Serbian demands as Milošević was for attacking Croatia, and Glenny implied that Serbian actions were understandable given Croatian insensitivity and the potential Muslim threat to Serbdom.[105]

Like Glenny, Max Primorac engaged in a reporting style similar to that typical of the literature of fact.[106] Concerned that comparisons of Yugoslavia to Lebanon, Northern Ireland, and Vietnam were intended "to blunt public pressure for intervention," he argued that air strikes against lines of communication and military targets were feasible. So he urged the West to "repel the aggressor" and echoed Croat and Bosnian positions by insisting they could defeat the Serbs themselves if the embargo was lifted. He criticized Eagleburger for creating "a one-sided slaughter" by letting the Yugoslavs "exhaust themselves"; he wondered how Richard Cheney could claim it was "unclear" who the enemy might be and how Brent Scowcroft could insist Bosnia was a "civil war" after Washington had recognized Sarajevo and condemned Belgrade for aggression; and he ridiculed Bush for depicting the crisis as a "hiccup," a "skirmish," and a "quagmire."[107]

Primorac was not an expert guest on television and radio, perhaps because his point of view conflicted with the official line purveyed by the media's stock experts, perhaps because his message that the Bosnians felt "betrayed" by the West was too uncomfortable for prime-time television viewers. But David MacKenzie, a Canadian who became an expert by commanding UNPROFOR forces, was invited to partici-pate in the domestic "debate" over U.S. foreign policy. The major networks carried his remarks while he was in Sarajevo, and he later appeared on various talk shows. His claim that thirty-seven German divisions had been unable to defeat the Serbs and his accusations that the Muslims had shelled their own people to get media attention were duly carried by the major media and resonated for months because they were congruent with those from other sources. Easily refuted, his re-marks suggested that those who viewed UNPROFOR as favoring the Serbs were correct to do so.[108]

In July 1995, R. Jeffrey Smith reported a disingenuous spin on the Bosnian conflict from U.S. officials who insisted that the Serbian seizure of Srebrenica and Žepa did *not* mean that Bosnia was losing the war, because Bosnians were "better organized, better trained, better equipped" than at any time before, thanks to the help of Iran, Malaysia, Pakistan, Turkey, Saudi Arabia, and the Persian Gulf states. The loss of two strategically located safe areas had apparently not altered the "military balance," because the Bosnian Serbs were suffering from battle fatigue, too few recruits, and decreasing support from Serbia. Smith's sources sought both to excuse the UN for failing to protect safe areas unable to defend themselves and to insinuate that Bosnia, sup-plied by fanatical Muslim states, could have done so.[109]

Unable to understand the conflict's course, the media and the experts they consulted could not foresee its ending. In late July, the *New York Times* reported that the West might pull its peacekeeping forces out of Bosnia, even though "the Serb war machine" continued to "roll forward implacably." Like *Time* magazine, the newspaper considered Mladić to be controlling events, and Serbia and the United States to be the main players. Because Srebrenica's fall was "an immense public humiliation" for the West, the paper suggested that it should either "admit failure or decide to confront the Serbs."[110] The West did nothing, but a week later the Croats drove the Serbs out of the Krajina and joined the Bosnians to roll them back in Bosnia.

NOTES

1. William A. Hachten, *The World News Prism: Changing Media of International Communication* (Ames: Iowa State University Press, 1992), 38, 42–53. Also influential are Agence France Presse, TASS, Deutsches Press Agentur (DPA), Kyodo News

Service, and Xinhua News Agency. Newer agencies include PANA (Pan African News Agency) and CANA (Caribbean News Agency). The media in Serbia, Croatia, and Bosnia were largely state-controlled, with the exceptions of Serbia's *Vreme*, B-92, and Studio B, Slovenia's *Mladina*, and Croatia's *Danas*, *Globus*, *Slobodna Dalmacija*, *Novi list*, *Feral Tribune*, and Radio 101. Jasmina Kuzmanović, "Media," and Sabrina Ramet, "The Yugoslav Crisis and the West," in Ramet and Adamovich, *Beyond Yugoslavia*, 84–97, 458–68, and Article 19, *Forging War: The Media in Serbia, Croatia and Bosnia-Hercegovina* (Avon: Bath Press, 1994), passim, for a detailed study of the media.

2. Hachten, *World News Prism*, 53; Michael Novak, "Why the Working Man Hates the Media," in John C. Merrill and Ralph D. Barney, *Ethics and the Press: Readings in Mass Media Morality* (New York: Hastings House, 1976), 108.

3. Isaacs, *Untended Gates*, 99–136, saw a need for watchdogs. S. Robert Lichter, Stanley Rothman, and Linda S. Lichter, *The Media Elite* (Bethesda, MD: Adler & Adler, 1986), 294, saw the media elite as a homogeneous professional group whose members are cosmopolitan, well-off, and indifferent to religion; come from the northern or northeastern United States; hold liberal values; and display symptoms of alienation but accept capitalism and reject the Left.

4. Paletz and Entman, *Media*, 217–19; Hachten, *World News Prism*, 42, 128–29, for Kalb's remarks on the "compromising ties" between the press and government; Lee and Solomon, *Unreliable Sources*, 17, for Donaldson. It is not clear that when print journalists found their way to TV in the 1970s, only the dim ones did so, but, as one reporter told Isaacs, *Untended Gates*, 182, in television you don't have to know how to spell. Michael J. Robinson, "Reflections on the Nightly News," in Richard P. Adler, ed., *Understanding Television: Essays on Television as a Social and Cultural Force* (New York: Praeger, 1981), 340–44, and Chet Huntley, "A Disturbing Arrogance in the Press," in Merrill and Barney, *Ethics and the Press*, 145. Landrum R. Bolling, ed., *Reporters under Fire: U.S. Media Coverage of Conflicts in Lebanon and Central America* (Boulder, CO: Westview Press, 1985), 151, 154. John Newhouse commented on the availability of "authoritative sources" in "Diplomatic Round (Yugoslavia)," *New Yorker*, 24 August 1992, 143.

5. Paletz and Entman, *Media*, 20; Lee and Solomon, *Unreliable Sources*, 18–19; Fishman, *Manufacturing the News*, 44, 83, 138–40; Kellner, *Media Culture*, 201–4; and Cohen, *Media Diplomacy*, 15–16, 33, 54, 70–72.

6. A striking example was the turnabout by Walter Cronkite after the Tet Offensive in 1968, apparently owing to his wounded pride. Gitlin, *The Whole World*, 206–9.

7. Comstock et al., *Television*, 135–40; and Richard Halloran, "Soldiers and Scribblers," in Loyd J. Matthews, ed., *Newsmen and National Defense: Is Conflict Inevitable?* (Washington, DC: Brassey's, 1991), 40–56. Most people trusted television news and found it credible in the mid-1970s, with the exception of military officers. Huntley, "A Disturbing Arrogance," 145–48, decried the antibusiness, prolabor bias of his colleagues.

8. Hachten, *World News Prism*, 98–99. Information elites read publications like *Time* and *Newsweek*, which had circulations of 5.5 and 3.2 million, respectively, in 1991, including about 500,000 and 300,000 in Europe.

9. Gans, *Deciding What's News*, 78–81, 249–66; Bagdikian, *Media Monopoly*, 87, 158–62, 223; Bogart, *Press and Public*, 251–54; Isaacs, *Untended Gates*, 34–35; and Ralph

D. Barney, "The Ways of the Corruptors," in Merrill and Barney, Ethics and the Press, passim. "Scholarly" reviews like the Columbia Journalism Review are taken seriously.

10. Gitlin, The Whole World, 203, for media manipulation of the cybernetic loop; Gans, Deciding What's News, 204–16, 268–76. Chet Huntley, "A Disturbing Arrogance," observed that the media followed mainstream opinion. Merrill listed six types of bias: attributive, adjectival, adverbial, contextual, photographic, and outright opinion.

11. For Gans, Deciding What's News, 284–85, "News is about the economic, political, social, and cultural hierarchies we call nation and society." Lichter et al., Media Elite, 26–31, 35–36, noted that even liberals favored free enterprise and deregulation in the mid-1970s.

12. Gans, Deciding What's News, 196–203; Fishman, Manufacturing the News, 32, 139–40, defines ideology as a scheme for interpreting a factual domain containing procedures for not knowing certain things; Kellner, Media Culture, 61, thinks it characterizes, labels, divides, and orders into hierarchies by creating binary opposition with I/it am/is as the norm, and all others as deviant; Werner J. Severin and James W. Tankard, Jr., Communications Theories: Origins, Methods, Uses (New York: Longman, 1988), 37–47, 62–64; Paletz and Entman, Media, 14.

13. Fishman, Manufacturing the News, 76–120, 151–52; Herman and Chomsky, Manufacturing Consent, 20–25; Isaacs, Untended Gates, 212–15, for libel suits, especially Sharon's suit against Time and Westmoreland's against CBS.

14. Halloran, "Soldiers and Scribblers," 49; Kellner, Media Culture, 201; Bagdikian, Media Monopoly, 207; Fishman, Manufacturing the News, 135–38. Reporters accept official accounts as fact and "repair" flawed bureaucratic procedures, hardly the actions of free-thinking rebels.

15. Novak, "Why the Working Man Resents," 114.

16. Gans, Deciding What's News, 248, 257–59; Novak, "Why the Working Man Resents," 112; Lawrence C. Soley, The News Shapers: The Sources Who Explain the News (Westport, CT: Praeger, 1992), 20–21, 139–44. Robin Wright, Leslie Gelb, Jeane Kirkpatrick, and David Gergen have used the revolving door. A long apprenticeship is necessary if one lacks the right pedigree. Roughly 80 percent of all reporters earned over $30,000 in the 1980s, 80 percent were male, and 94 percent white. Dan Rather, the anchor for CBS, earned $2.3 million a year, and George Wills, an influential "news shaper," well over a million.

17. Lichter et al., The Media Elite, 23, 122. Gans, Deciding What's News, 94–107. The top brass protect the organization's commercial and political interests, but policy is ad hoc. Editors, not corporate executives, were supervising stories in the late 1970s.

18. Paletz and Entman, Media, 10–13, 19; Fishman, Manufacturing the News, 140–55. Kellner, Media Culture, 212–13, considers the media "money machines seeking ratings and profits."

19. Bagdikian, Media Monopoly, 235, 239–44. Hachten, World News Prism, xx, 16–25, assumes that all media are controlled, and the most independent are those "situated in a free enterprise capitalist economy, enjoying the same autonomy as other private business enterprises."

20. Gaye Tuchman, Making News: A Study in the Construction of Reality (New York: The Free Press, 1978), 168–69; Bagdikian, Media Monopoly, ix, xv–xvii, 4–24, 132–33, 181–82. About fifty corporations control 25,000 media "voices," including 1,700 dailies and 11,000 magazines.

21. Gitlin, *The Whole World*, 264; Fishman, *Manufacturing the News*, 146–49; Bogart, *Press and Public*, 263–69; and Tuchman, *Making News*, 16, 19–20, 124–27.

22. Gans, *Deciding What's News*, 247–50, 285–90; Bagdikian, *Media Monopoly*, 233.

23. Various writers have made this point, including Novak, "Why the Working Man Resents," 109–10; Bogart, *Press and Public*, 150–52; and Gore Vidal, who argued in *The Nation* (1991) that to succeed, reporters and editors had to have, or adopt, certain attitudes and biases.

24. Bagdikian, *Media Monopoly*, 37–38; Gaunt, *Choosing the News*, 63–65; and Fishman, *Manufacturing the News*, 109–27, 139–49, for an investigation. Mark Schulman, "Control Mechanisms inside the Media," in John Downing et al., *Questioning the Media*, 121–22, notes those who reject the dominant ideology are soon unemployed; Denis McQuail, *Media Performance: Mass Communication and the Public Interest* (Newbury Park: Sage, 1992), 184–95, on objective coverage.

25. Bagdikian, *Media Monopoly*, ix–xiv, 37–38, 44–46. Halloran, "Soldiers and Scribblers," 41–42, 49, thought the media elite a myth.

26. Lester Markel, *What You Don't Know Can Hurt You: A Study of Public Opinion and Public Emotion* (New York: Quadrangle, 1972), 1–56; Bogart, *Press and Public*, 111–12; Muriel Cantor, "Audience Control," in Horace Newcomb, ed., *Television: The Critical View* (New York: Oxford University Press, 1987), 361–79. The media satisfy five types of needs: (1) cognitive, (2) affective, (3) societally integrative, (4) personally integrative, and (5) escapist.

27. Bagdikian, *Media Monopoly*, 111–31. The *New Yorker*'s editor, William Shawn, could ignore advertisers because he published a magazine for a select audience, but the commercial aspect remained. Bagdikian argues that newspapers target audiences based on their ability to consume. Peripheral publications like *The Nation* make no secret of their biases, but seem to believe that revealing their agenda makes them morally superior to the less forthright mainstream media. Both ignore those who do not share their ideologies, but seem sensitive to criticism from those who do, especially if they advertise.

28. Bagdikian, *Media Monopoly*, 111–30, 140–57; Kellner, *Media Culture*, 211–13. Advertising destroys competition and allows the media to ignore parts of the community and replace serious news with fluff.

29. Bogart, *Press and Public*, 113–14, 126–28; Denis McQuail, *Media Performance*, 219–21; Bagdikian, *Media Monopoly*, 139, 180. Readers want hard news; the trend to features and soft news was due to advertising and editorial decisions.

30. Newsworthiness is determined through "negotiations" between various newsworkers, including the reporter and his editors. Tuchman, *Making News*, x, 12; Paletz and Entman, *Media*, 242–43, 249; Kellner, *Media Culture*, 211; Todd Gitlin, *The Whole World*, 243–45, 271. Because it is vulnerable to framing of events, the audience helps journalists support the established order. Social conflict and criticism of the system are reported, but in ways that reinforce the conventional values and elite definitions of social order.

31. Kellner, *Media Culture*, 211–15; Bogart, *Press and Public*, 128; Madeleine Albright's comments on *This Week with David Brinkley*, 25 April 1993. In a 1977 survey, half of the respondents said they talked current events, a fifth talked politics.

32. Gaunt, *Choosing the News*, passim, for summaries of recent studies. He suggests that selection of news in regional papers in France, Britain, and the United States is governed by factors that tend to maximize profits, but include such

intangible variables as the public's image of journalism and the journalists' image of themselves.

33. Halloran, "Soldiers and Scribblers," 44–47, thought the audience decided whether the news was slanted and whether it was bad or good, but it is not clear that the audience *can* decide. Kellner, *Media Culture*, 259; Ewen, *All Consuming Images*, 260–61.

34. Bogart, *Press and Public*, 129, 132; Robinson, "Reflections on the Nightly News," 324–28, for the "Inadvertent Audience." Hachten, *World News Prism*, 7, 75–76, saw more audience "involvement and participation," but ignored its passive nature. Sarkesian, "Soldiers, Scholars, and the Media," 68, noted that a 1986 Gallup Poll sampling public confidence regarding ten major institutions found more people trusted the military (63 percent) than the press (37 percent) or TV (27 percent). Peter Stoler, *The War against the Press: Politics, Pressure and Intimidation in the 80s* (New York: Dodd, Mead, 1986), 3–5, concluded the public thought the press rude, intrusive, and uncivilized. He cited a poll showing a drop in public confidence in the press from 29 percent to 13.7 percent from 1976 to 1983.

35. Novak, "Why the Worker Resents," 114; Robinson, "Reflections," 323; Comstock et al., *Television*, 135–40. Neil Postman, "The Teaching of the Media Curriculum," in Lazere et al., *American Media*, 422–23, blamed TV for short attention spans and saw the "electronic information environment" as "fundamentally hostile to conceptual, segmented, linear modes of expression." So we are forgetting how to cut and dress language to create meaning and getting lost in a polysemic forest of images.

36. Richard Harwood, "And Still a Mystery to Most of Us," *Washington Post*, 5 June 1995; Bogart, *Press and Public*, 158–59. Most papers devote between 9.5 percent and 11.5 percent of their space to international affairs.

37. Cohen, *Media Diplomacy*, 45; McQuail, *Media Performance*, 215–17; Claus Mueller, "Class as the Determinant of Political Communication," in Lazere et al., *American Media*, 435–36; Herman, "Media," 75–77. Gatekeepers prefer personalities; news values stress the personal, the elite, and the negative; and the media simplify events and issues by personalizing them. Functional ignorance makes it hard to make rational choices; appeals to emotion, use of metaphors, and superficial coverage block thought.

38. Emotion, fear, and prejudice make polls hard to read, and public opinion is often "unreasoning, volatile, [and] impulsive." The latter is the perfect vehicle for demagogues, the former impact public policy. Markel, *What You Don't Know*, esp. 41–46.

39. Comstock et al., *Television*, 113–40; Bogart, *Press and Public*, 156–57, 204–10. Only 7 percent of the men between eighteen and forty-nine years old watched the news, but 14 percent tuned in to weekend sports and sitcoms.

40. Gans, *Deciding What's News*, 236–41; Isaacs, *Untended Gates*, 136.

41. Lichter et al., *Media Elite*, 72–86, 114–17; Chet Huntley, "A Disturbing Arrogance," 146–48; Gail Evans, telephone interview, 19 July 1993.

42. Gans, *Deciding What's News*, 241–46.

43. James Fallows, "Why Americans Hate the Media," *The Atlantic Monthly* (February 1996), 50; Kellner, *Media Culture*, 76. Bagdikian, *Media Monopoly*, 111–13. The public may want serious news, but even the *New Yorker* had problems after

losing those eighteen to forty-nine years old, who found its articles too serious, too political, and too long.

44. Armand Mattelart and Jean-Marie Piemme, "Twenty-three Guidelines for Political Debate on Communications in Europe," *The Critical Communications Review* (1984), II, 214–16; Gaunt, *Choosing the News*, 71–72; Kellner, *Media Culture*, 80, 226, 231–43, 260.

45. Kellner, *Media Culture*, 316; Gitlin, *The Whole World*, 164; Gaunt, *Choosing the News*, 116; Fiske, *Television Culture*, 14–20. Discourse is an extensive language in the broadest sense, both a social act and a power relationship. Texts have three foci: the formal qualities and flow of the programs, the intertextual relationship with other media and with the self, and the readers and process of reading.

46. Cohen, *Media Diplomacy*, 62–63; Tuchman, *Making News*, 139, 156.

47. History is linguistically conditioned and language historically conditioned, and, like events, temporal and cultural, so it is not what it seems. Cohen, *Media Diplomacy*, 48; Carlo Ginzburg, *Clues, Myths, and the Historical Method* (Baltimore, MD: Johns Hopkins University Press, 1989), 156–64; Reinhart Koselleck, "Linguistic Change and the History of Events," *Journal of Modern History* (1989), 649, 659.

48. Novak, "Why the Working Man Resents," 110–11.

49. Annabelle Sreberny-Mohammadi, "U.S. Media Covers the World," in *Questioning the Media*, 297–305. News and soap opera merge in soft pieces like *Frontline*'s "Romeo and Juliet in Sarajevo," PBS, 10 May 1994.

50. Fisher, *Manufacturing the News*, 138; Bagdikian, *Media Monopoly*, 208.

51. Severin and Tankard, *Communications Theories*, 5, 37–47. The basic communications model posits a source that selects information and codes it in a message that a transmitter (the journalist) recodes and sends as a signal along a channel (newspaper, TV, radio) to a receiver (reader, viewer, listener) who decodes. Gatekeepers complicate the process. If the source is a UN official and the transmitter a stringer, reporters and editorial gatekeepers create noise and limit information before the information is picked up, recoded and sent by the local evening news to viewers who must decode it.

52. Gans, *Deciding What's News*, 57, 117–27, 281–82; Soley, *News Shapers*, 24–25; Tuchman, *Making News*, 112; Paletz and Entman, *Media*, 219–21; Lichter et al., *Media Elite*, 294–96. Reporters structure reality by selecting sources who share their attitudes and social class and tend to adopt the outlook of their sources and frame their questions in terms of the sources' world.

53. Gans, *Deciding What's News*, 89–90, 131–45, noted that 78 percent of the sources for domestic and foreign news used by the *New York Times* and the *Washington Post* were public officials, and that both journalists and their audience are usually ignorant of their subject. Hachten, *World News Prism*, 150–53. Obstacles to gathering news abroad include authoritarian regimes, ethnocentrism and racism, perishable news, a parochial point of view, and a tendency to pander to the public.

54. Soley, *News Shapers*, 20–21; Tester, *Media*, 86–88; Biagi, *NewsTalk*, 45–46. At one point more money was being spent on media coverage of the famines in Ethiopia and Somalia than on relief efforts.

55. Mark Almond, *Europe's Backyard War: The War in the Balkans* (Toronto: Mandarin, 1994), 184–206; Cigar, *Genocide*, 22, 43, 73–80; Sabrina Ramet, "Serbia's Slobodan Milosević: A Profile," *Orbis* (1991); Dijana Pleština, "Democracy and Nationalism in Croatia: The First Three Years," in Ramet and Adamovich, *Beyond*

Yugoslavia; Helsinki Watch, *Violations of the Helsinki Accords: Yugoslavia* (Washington, DC, November 1986), *Increasing Turbulence: Human Rights in Yugoslavia* (Washington, DC, October 1989), and *Yugoslavia: Crisis in Kosovo* (Washington, DC: March 1990).

56. For partisan scholarship, Woodward, *Balkan Tragedy*; Gale Stokes, *The Walls Came Tumbling Down: The Collapse of Communism in Eastern Europe* (New York: Oxford University Press, 1993), 218–52; Dennison Rusinow, "The Avoidable Catastrophe," in Ramet and Adamovich, Beyond Yugoslavia. For rebuttals to Serbian positions, including the 1986 SANU memorandum, Branka Magaš, *The Destruction of Yugoslavia: Tracking the Break-up 1980–92* (New York: Verso, 1993), 49–73; and Matthew Meštrović and Radovan Latković, *The Croatian Response to the Serbian National Program* (Saddle River, NJ: The Croatian National Congress, 1988).

57. Chuck Sudetic, 10, 22 January 1991, and Stephen Engelberg, 20 April, 12 May 1991, *New York Times*. Sabrina P. Ramet, *Balkan Babel: Politics, Culture, and Religion in Yugoslavia* (Boulder, CO: Westview, 1992), 45–46, saw the diversion as theft; Lenard J. Cohen, *Broken Bonds: The Disintegration of Yugoslavia* (Boulder, CO: Westview, 1993), 198, reduced the figure to $1.46 billion and labeled it "unauthorized appropriation"; Woodward, *Balkan Tragedy*, ignored the incident.

58. *New York Times*, 22, 25 January 1991; Banac's remarks on the negative image of the region portrayed by Ivo Andrić and Robert Kaplan in Rabia Ali and Lawrence Lifschultz, *Why Bosnia? Writings on the Balkan War* (Stony Creek, CT: The Pamphleteer's Press, 1993), 163–64.

59. Sudetic, *New York Times*, 25 January 1991; Susan Woodward, *Balkan Tragedy*, 159–60, 183–98.

60. Sudetic, *New York Times*, 22, 26, 31 January, 1, 2, 9 April 1991; Reuters, *New York Times*, 18 January, 1 February 1991. For Špegelj, Slaven Letica, *Obećana zemlja: Politički antimemoari* (Rijeka: Biblioteka Ex Ungue Leonem, 1992), 198–228; Almond, *Backyard War*, 214; Marko Milivojević, "The Armed Forces of Yugoslavia: Sliding into War," in Ramet and Adamovich, *Beyond Yugoslavia*, 76–79; Alan F. Fogelquist, *The Breakup of Yugoslavia, International Policy, and the War in Bosnia-Hercegovina* (Los Angeles, CA: Institute of South Central European and Balkan Affairs, 1993), 10; Magaš, *Destruction of Yugoslavia*, 264–74. A.P., *New York Times*, 21 January 1991, could still describe Croatia's crest (a red-and-white checkerboard) as a historic, not an Ustaša, symbol.

61. Reuters, *New York Times*, 10 February 1991; Sudetic, *New York Times*, 14 February 1991; Almond, *Backyard War*, 185–87; Thompson, *Forging War*, 75–83, 100–11. The Serbs had used similar foreign plots to divert domestic attention in the 1920s and 1930s. See James J. Sadkovich, *Italian Support for Croatian Separatism, 1927–1937* (New York: Garland, 1987), 194–227, and "The Use of Political Trials to Repress Croatian Dissent, 1929–1934," *Journal of Croatian History* (1987–88), passim.

62. John Tagliabue, "Yugoslavia's Army Issues Ultimatum to Rebel Republic," *New York Times*, 30 June 1991, noted that "Belgrade television tends to be pro-Serbian," a serious understatement; John Kraljic, *Belgrade's Strategic Designs on Croatia* (Washington, DC: Croatian Democracy Project, 1991), for numbers.

63. Sudetic, *New York Times*, 30 June, 1 July 1991, and editorial, 16 May 1991. Ante Marković, who had no domestic political support, was prime minister; Stipe Mesić, then an HDZ member, was head of the federal presidency. See Stipe Mesić, *Kako je srušena Jugoslavia* (Zagreb: Mislav Press, 1994), passim.

64. Tagliabue, "An Army Besieged," *New York Times*, 1, 2 July 1991, portrayed Adžić as "a fiercely pro-Serb officer." General Kolsek, the Slovene commander in Slovenia, was replaced by General Avramović, a Serb.

65. Articles by Sudetic, Binder, Engelberg, and Tagliabue, *New York Times*, 3 July 1991. Bogdan Denitch, *Ethnic Nationalism: The Tragic Death of Yugoslavia* (University of Minnesota Press, 1994), esp. 72–73, repeatedly referred to the conflict as a "civil war" and Croatia's "rebel Serb minority."

66. Sudetic, *New York Times*, 19, 20, 21 May 1991; Cohen, *Broken Bonds*, 211–13, misrepresented the results of referenda in Croatia, noting that 93 percent of the 84 percent who voted in the "Croatian" referendum approved Croatian independence, while 99.8 percent of those voting in the "Krajina" wanted Serbian independence. He did not mention that only Serbs were allowed to vote in the Krajina where so many Serbs from Serbia voted that there were more votes than voters. See Ramet, *Balkan Babel*, 43.

67. Norman Cigar, "The Serbo-Croatian War," *Journal of Strategic Studies* (1994), 308–13, and "War Termination and Croatia's War of Independence: Deciding When to Stop," *Journal of Croatian Studies* (1991–92), 129; Almond, *Backyard War*, 224–25, 294–95. Despite having absorbed half of the budget and having a nominal strength of some 200,000, the JNA's morale and fighting quality were low and its MiGs and armor poorly utilized. Martin Špegelj, "The Disposition of Former Yugoslavia's Military in the Northwest Theater on the Eve of the Conflicts in Slovenia and Croatia," *Journal of Croatian Studies* (1991–92/1995), 64–67, believed the Croats overestimated their ability to get an agreement with Serbia and the international community's readiness to help the new states.

68. Articles by Engelberg, Tagliabue, Sudetic, Binder, *New York Times*, 3 July 1991. The accompanying pictures were sympathetic to the JNA; Reuters, *New York Times*, 2 July 1991. Thompson, *Forging War*, 112. Zametica became an adviser to Pale after leaving the UK.

69. *Why Bosnia?*, 275, 286–99; Mihailo Crnobrnja, *The Yugoslav Drama* (Montreal: McGill-Queen's University Press, 1994); Denitch, *Ethnic Nationalism*, 12, 51–52; William Pfaff, "Invitation to War," *Foreign Affairs* (Summer 1993); Rusinow in Ramet and Adamovich, *Beyond Yugoslavia*; Stokes, *The Walls Came Tumbling Down*, 218–52.

70. Typical was *This Week with David Brinkley*, 25 April 1993, which began with reports by Jack Smith and Tony Birtley, went to interviews with Radovan Karadžić, Madeleine Albright, and Muhammed Sacirbey and ended with the program's news shapers who discussed . . . Russia.

71. Soley, *News Shapers*, 2–6, 10–41, 146–47. Political commercials averaged 42.3 seconds in 1968, 9.8 in 1988; visuals increased 300 percent. Of the ninety news shapers making the rounds of NPR, PBS, and the major networks, thirty-four dominated. Republicans outnumbered Democrats on television two to one. AEI employees logged 142 appearances on *The MacNeil-Lehrer Newshour* (January 1982 to October 1990), employees of Brookings eighty-two, those from Carnegie seventy-two. David Gergen, the CFR's Rob Levgold, and the Heritage Foundation's Norm Ornstein were typical news shapers. Regularly presented as a scholar, Ornstein had few scholarly publications.

72. Magaš, *The Destruction of Yugoslavia*, xv, xvii, 232, 255–56, 351; Soley, *The News Shapers*, 24; Fishman, *Manufacturing the News*, 131.

73. Noise is anything that interrupts information flows and undermines redundancy. Reification is extreme objectification, which presents social, ecological, and economic phenomena as outside human control. It confuses concepts, abstract relationships, and theoretic assumptions with concrete reality, that is, things that are subject to manipulation (or may not exist at all) are presented as concrete objects. Severin and Tankard, *Communications Theories*, 46; Novak, "Why the Working Man Resents," passim; Fallows, "Why Americans Hate," 64; Soley, *News Shapers*, 25–27.

74. Soley, *News Shapers*, 74–83, notes that the CFR canvases the media and both supplies and legitimizes experts. CFR membership in effect precertifies sources.

75. Soley, *News Shapers*, 85–94, 151; Patrick Glynn, "Yugoblunder," *New Republic*, 24 February 1992. ABC hired Kissinger in 1983 to select experts. In 1989, he joined a CBS board dominated by CFR members.

76. Lee and Solomon, *Unreliable Sources*, 298; Herman and Chomsky, *Manufacturing the News*, 60–63, 107, 112, 118–25; Gitlin, *The Whole World*, 152.

77. Miffed newsmakers can refuse future invitations to appear on shows that depend on their ability to book powerful people to attract middle-class audiences. Juan Señor, who managed European coverage for *MacNeil-Lehrer*, briefed those being interviewed—after they had gone through the equivalent of a screen test. Telephone interview, 16 July 1993.

78. Glynn, "Yugoblunder." Reporters interview each other more often than academics, but both depend on government officials and the media. The rare independent point of view seems both idiosyncratic and iconoclastic.

79. Stephen Kinzer, "In Stronghold, Serbs Cite Dread of Muslim Rule," *New York Times*, 1 July 1995. A July 1992 survey by the Serbian publication *Borba* found that 20.5 percent of their sample believed the artillery shelling Sarajevo was Serbian, but 38.4 percent thought it was Muslim and/or Croatian; 39.3 percent did not know. Sabrina P. Ramet, *Social Currents in Eastern Europe: The Sources and Consequences of the Great Transformation* (Durham, NC: Duke University Press, 1995), 481.

80. For Binder and Engelberg, *New York Times*, 3 March, 4, 10–14 April 1991.

81. George Kenney, "Truth as a Policy Casualty," and editorial, "George Kenney, Down the Memory Hole," *Washington Times*, 7 October 1992; "Sarajevo 911," *Washington Post*, 15 October 1992.

82. George Kenney, "Ending Bosnia's Endgame," *New York Times*, 1 December 1994; *New York Times*, 20 May 1993; and Peter Jennings, "Bosnia: Land of the Demons," *ABC*, 18 March 1993.

83. David Binder, "The Serbs and Croats: So Much in Common, Including Hate," *New York Times*, 16 May 1991.

84. Milan Stojadinović, *Tri godine vlade dr. Milana M. Stojadinovića* (Belgrade, 1939); and James J. Sadkovich, "Il regime di Alessandro in Iugoslavia: 1929–1934. Un'interpretazione," *Storia contemporanea* (Feb. 1984), and "Terrorism in Croatia, 1929–1934," *East European Quarterly* (March 1988).

85. Philip J. Cohen, *Serbia's Secret War: Propaganda and the Deceit of History* (College Station, TX: Texas A&M University Press, 1996); and Magaš, *The Destruction of Yugoslavia*, 314–15. About 85,000 died in concentration camps in Croatia, including 18,000 Jews at Jasenovac; 79,000 died in Bosnia-Herzegovina. Most of the 237,000 partisans and 209,000 collaborators who died in combat, died in the NDH. Serbia saw little fighting after 1941.

86. The other three pillars were the Orthodox Church, the Serbian Academy of Arts and Sciences, and the JNA. Magaš, *The Destruction of Yugoslavia*, 262; and Aleksandar Nenadović, "Serbia, Croatia, Chaos," *New York Times*, 21 May 1991. Thompson saw Nenadović as a "veteran liberal."

87. Flora Lewis, "How to Stop a Civil War," *New York Times*, 31 May 1991.

88. Peter Millership, "Art World Flinches at Brutal Vision of Bosnia," *Reuters*, 9 October 1994; and Amnesty International, *Bosnia-Herzegovina: Rape and Sexual Abuse by Armed Forces* (London: January 1993).

89. Thomas L. Friedman, "Baker Urges End to Yugoslav Rift," *New York Times*, 22 June 1991.

90. Peter Millionig, "After 7 Centuries, Slovenia Is Free," *New York Times*, 26 June 1991.

91. Srdja Popović, "Psychodrama in Yugoslavia," *New York Times*, 27 June 1991. Like Thompson, Denitch, Rusinow, and others, Popović was what might be termed a Yugoslav nationalist, making him anti-Croatian, and both critical and tolerant of the Serbs, who are seen as the "core" of the Yugoslav state.

92. Michael Scammell, "What Price Yugoslavia," *New York Times*, 2 July 1991.

93. "MacNeil-Lehrer Newshour," *PBS*, 5 April 1993; "Nightline," 22 April 1993; Boutros Boutros-Ghali, "Genocide: When Will We Ever Learn?" *International Herald Tribune*, 6 April 1995.

94. The piece echoed so many of the arguments put forward by Nora Beloff and other pro-Serbian propagandists that its authorship was questionable. "End the War in Bosnia—Peacefully," *New York Times*, 20 May 1993.

95. Newhouse, "The Diplomatic Round," 60, 71.

96. Misha Glenny, "Yugoslavia: The Great Fall," *New York Review of Books*, 23 March 1995, 62–63.

97. A. M. Rosenthal, "On My Mind: Lighting Bosnia's Fire," *New York Times*, 23 December 1994, and "For America's Worth," *New York Times*, 15 September 1995.

98. Anthony Lewis, "Abroad at Home: Shame, Eternal Shame," *New York Times*, 2 December 1994.

99. David Gompert, "How to Defeat Serbia," *Foreign Affairs* (July–August, 1993) 33, 43.

100. Stanley Hoffman, "What Will Satisfy Serbia's Nationalists?" *New York Times*, 4 December 1994.

101. Richard K. Betts, "The Delusion of Impartial Intervention," *Foreign Affairs* (1994), 20–33.

102. Like Laura Silber and Allan Little, *The Death of Yugoslavia* (London: Penguin/BBC Books, 1996), a military analyst concluded this at *A Symposium on the Question of Multilateral Military Intervention*, University of North Carolina at Chapel Hill, 13–14 April 1993. Because the Pentagon saw *all* sides as potential enemies, it was reluctant to act.

103. Warren Zimmerman, *International Herald Tribune*, 13 March 1995.

104. Peter Brock, "'Greater Serbia' vs. the Greater Western Media," *Mediterranean Quarterly* (1995) 6(1), and Darko Tanasković, "Religion and Human Rights," *Mediterranean Quarterly* (1995).

105. Misha Glenny, *The Fall of Yugoslavia: The Third Balkan War* (New York: Penguin, 1992), esp. 163–84, and his pieces in *New York Review of Books*, esp. "Yugoslavia: The Great Fall," 56.

106. Ronald Weber, *The Literature of Fact: Literary Nonfiction in American Writing* (Athens, OH: Ohio University Press, 1980), 3. Literary nonfiction is reporting in which "the writer tries to draw together the conflicting roles of observer and maker, journalist and artist," using "selection, arrangement, emphasis, and other literary devices" to impose significant themes.

107. Max Primorac, "Serbia's War/Out of the Ruble," *National Review,* 14 September 1992, 48.

108. ABC, CBS, NBC, 31 August 1992. Timothy L. Francis, Letter, *Washington Post,* 14 August 1992, noted that the Germans never had more than 24 divisions in the Balkans, with the wartime average 14.1.

109. R. Jeffrey Smith, "Bosnian Forces Capturing Territory from Serbs, Intelligence Indicates," *Washington Post,* 21 July 1995.

110. *New York Times,* 24 July 1995; *Time,* 24 July 1995.

2

Realities and Values

PARADIGMATIC REALITIES

Some social science models suggest that social organization determines our construction of reality. If so, institutions like the media must use conventional depictions of reality within accepted paradigms. If institutional structures generate and inculcate norms in individuals, then the group dominates and most meaning is institutional meaning. There is no creativity, only convention. Even if institutions merely create norms, we use their rules to construct meanings that are interpretive, pretheoretic, subjective, and conventionally creative. The news is then a series of stories, or media events, produced through an institutional process that uses cultural resources and negotiations among those involved in its construction.[1] In short, to make news is to construct reality and provide the basis for social action.

But reality is too solid a word to describe the news, because if there is an absolute reality out there, the media cannot discern it or convey it to its audiences; news stories are not determined by their importance or any objective reality, but by whether journalists can sell them in a profession where competition for airtime and newshole is fierce. Raw news is unformed and subject to interpretation via selection, editing, structuring, and presentation. As Paletz and Entmann put it, "To edit is to interpret, to speak is to define, to communicate is to structure reality." They see the media as perpetuating an illusion of objectivity and conveying the credibility and legitimacy of the existing order and of the media itself.[2]

Like historians, journalists belong to a discipline that uses empirical inquiry, concepts, and methods. They jealously guard their right to use their instincts to decide what's news, and they manage to describe an inchoate reality by dividing events into hard, soft, spot, developing, and continuing news. Hard news is extremely perishable and needs to be used immediately. Soft news is not timely, so it can be used anytime—it keeps. Spot news is unscheduled, but can become a developing story, and continuing news can be prescheduled. Ordinarily, only truly dramatic events upset the normal routine and assumptions of news-workers.[3] The discovery of detention camps in Bosnia did so, but like other events in the Balkans, it was quickly routinized and made amenable to conventional modes of reporting.

Because the media have difficulty dealing with the unfamiliar, they routinize it or make it over into soft news. Confronted by unfamiliar and uncomfortable political events in the Balkans, they latched onto such things as rape in Bosnia and the shelling of Mostar's Old Bridge, both easy to report.[4] Typical were Slavenka Drakulić's essays, which appeared in both *The Nation* and the *New York Times.* As with much soft news, her essays focused as much on her inner journey as on outer realities. In her piece on the destruction of Mostar's Old Bridge, which she had never seen, she wrote, "When I remember what is no longer there, I feel a spasm in my stomach, a knot in my throat. I feel death lurking in its absence." Unable to say who had destroyed the bridge, she reported that "The Muslims are accusing the Croats, the Croats are accusing the Muslims." But she doubted that it mattered. "The question is not who shelled and demolished it," she wrote. "The question is: What kind of people do not need that bridge?" It is, obviously, a rhetorical question, as rhetorical as her answer: people who are "barbarians."[5]

There is no absolute standard of what is important or what constitutes reality, and journalists perceived it as having various voices—Serb, Croat, and Muslim. They preferred concrete events like the destruction of a flour mill to abstract questions like self-determination; if different media employed different techniques, subjective elements were inherent in news coverage by all media.[6]

Because highlights (deviations from the norm) sell, they shape stories that become highlights of highlights, and a minor personality or a minor event can become a major story. The media create myths by transforming reality into images (and vice versa), by selective repetition, and by reporting designed to escalate confrontation and violence. Because journalists tend to believe their myths and fail to see the patterns that they create, they delve beneath the surface of things only when attracted by a particularly odd or obviously missing bit of data.[7]

In Yugoslavia, reporters played up tensions between Izetbegović and Abdić; they amplified differences between Croats and Muslims, assumed conspiracies between Tudjman and Milošević, and focused on rape and ethnic cleansing. All of these were good stories and easier to deal with than discussing the internal structure of the Bosnian political process or the Croatian polity, both complex stories hard to describe simply.

If journalists shape the world by the way in which they organize their rounds, conduct their interviews, and write their stories, news organizations objectify social meanings and produce rules and procedures to justify their actions. News becomes an ahistorical theoretical account of reality in which journalists are circumscribed by their own unconscious ideologies. Unaware that they are engaged in creating self-fulfilling prophecies and shoring up the status quo, they cannot challenge institutions and social structures. So they tend to follow, not lead. As a former editor of the *New York Times* put it, if you're "an Establishment institution, whenever your natural community changes its opinion, then naturally you will too."[8] In Yugoslavia, this meant following the lead of events and of various UN, NATO, and local officials and officers.

Because to categorize is to theorize, journalists have an ideology that preinterprets the world for them. So they often tell the same stories, and mutual expectations discourage innovation. *USA Today* may be newsprint aping TV, but different media do not really compete. However, *Time* does contend with *Newsweek* to attract those who buy news magazines. News media do not collude, but they do copy each other, and stories in the *New York Times,* which sets professional standards for all media, regularly crop up elsewhere.[9]

When journalists tell stories, they base them on assumptions about reality and values that they share with the society in general, and their profession and socioeconomic groups in particular. Objectivity thus becomes more theoretical than real. This is also true for the critic, who often merely compares his assumptions and values to those of the media.[10]

Most reporters consciously strive to be objective, but it is clear from the reporting on Yugoslavia that those in the media, whether in the field in Bosnia or behind an editorial desk in the States, brought their full complement of stereotypes and assumptions with them when they processed the raw data and reworked the semifinished products of news reporting. Bias often seemed to overcome reality, and compromise often led to distortion, however unintended or well intentioned.

BUREAUCRATIC VALUES

The United States has been training journalists in universities since the turn of the century, when Missouri and Columbia set up journalism programs. There are now around 300 departments, but fewer than 100 are accredited and only a handful are first-rate. For the 90,000 students majoring in journalism, it is still the workplace that creates the social order in which they will live, inculcates the meanings that they will share, and leads them to report the news they report in the way they do. It is in the newsroom that journalists absorb the values of their profession as they learn the techniques of their trade.[11]

Journalists work in bureaucracies with hierarchies, routines, rules, and procedures. Because most learn their trade while working for news organizations, their concepts of professionalism serve the interests and further the ends of the organization and the status quo. Their work routines limit their reporting to routine realities and generate routine news stories, which reflect and confirm the system that created them.[12]

Journalists use routine to make reality manageable. How they do so depends on the individual, the organization, the event, and the technology available. Education also plays a part. Isaacs thought that without a broad liberal arts education and catholic interests, reporters could not grasp their subject, and gatekeepers could not perform well.[13] The most common routine is the beat, a ritual that guarantees credible and accessible sources who deliver short, easy-to-cut stories that can be slotted with a minimum of effort.

The newspaper in Fishman's study devoted two-thirds of its manpower to beats. These were assigned by an editor, and each had a history, an object to report, a social setting, and a daily round of sources. Each beat had identifiable phases that allowed the reporter to transform "an amorphous something into a determinate sequence of events." When there were inconsistencies in the phases or a social type was out of place, the reporter either filled in what was missing or conducted an investigation.[14] But if beat reporters know what to look for, few journalists had a Balkan beat in 1991, and reporters and pundits with little or no expertise ended up shaping Yugoslav realities for the American public.

If lack of familiarity with the Balkans made it harder for the media to get the facts straight, doing so was not crucial because accuracy does not always have priority in journalism. Manipulation of data is arbitrary, and there are few checks on raw data. Although researchers can challenge facts, their low status bars them from questioning assumptions or generalizations by reporters and policy makers; if anyone can suggest a story, editors usually determine story selection, design, and production. A complex system of controls thus assures direction from the top.[15] Because the easiest stories to do are those that can be anticipated, press conferences got more coverage than events in Yugoslavia.

If organizational structure determines what is covered, deadlines and commercial constraints limit most reports to basic description. Efficiency has priority, and review and control overwhelm objectivity, making the news both historical and debatable.[16]

Reporters make sense of the world by using conventions to construct meanings; they create and control controversy by intermingling facts and sources, and they use quotes to protect themselves from libel suits and to distance themselves from events. They prefer hard news, because it needs little checking or thought, and they are under a subtle pressure to reinforce official positions. Major networks accept government guidelines, editors kill stories that might disturb the public order, and corporate and media executives occasionally exert pressure.[17]

But pressure is usually not needed, because the skills that journalists develop to find and check sources help to keep them within the system. When Fishman's reporters checked their stories, they used competent sources, common frames of reference, and consensual data. They never left nor seriously challenged the bureaucracies providing their data. If the news is a prism that breaks an object into multiple images, it is a prism with few facets.[18]

The effects of routine and pressure are compounded by a tendency to forget history and to ignore process. A journalist is interested in the new, in reporting the reinvention of the wheel, not understanding why it was necessary or what makes it work. Sociologists divide external reality into social processes and historians examine process over time, but journalists see external reality as "disparate and independent events, each of which is new and can therefore be reported as news."[19] By being ahistorical, journalists rediscovered World War II, but they were incapable of understanding the event, so they tended to parrot what their biased sources told them. The result was a lot of bad history.

Nor was this surprising. The media have difficulty gaining perspective and performing analysis because they cover events on a daily basis and operate in real time.[20] Lack of analytic perspective is obvious in television newscasts, which seem real only because they occur in real time. However, taped coverage is much more common than live coverage, and often presented without proper warning; news is carefully choreographed and edited. Even spontaneous talk shows are rehearsed. Everything on the tube is so artificial, so ephemeral, and so abstracted from the real world that it forms an altogether different reality in the same way that the media form a distinct culture not accessible and often unfathomable to outsiders. Indeed, for Cecelia Tichi, TV has itself become a separate environment. To some extent, this is true of media in general, making comprehensiveness difficult and sustained analysis nearly impossible.[21]

ETHICS?

For most people the words "media" and "ethics" are dubious partners. Isaacs thought journalists suffered from "intellectual diabetes," despite having formulated their first code of ethics in 1910. He believed ombudsmen were needed to point out both errors and conflicts of interest in the media. Yet most journalists are quick to defend their profession as ethical and to present themselves as professionals trying hard to live up to the highest standards of ethical behavior. Richard Halloran believed that journalists strive to meet standards that transcend the individual, the organization, and the profession.[22] Still, what is bad or special-interest journalism to some can be enlightened and moral reporting to others; the concept and practice of professionalism is at odds both with the First Amendment, which confers individual, not corporate, rights, and with free speech, which cannot be controlled by organizations.[23]

Defining morality is difficult, but the definition given by Klaidman and Beauchamp is useful. They saw morality as a cultural, not an individual, virtue that supports social stability and preserves human decency. Olen would add that the real test of morality is whether the journalist fulfills his tacit contract with the consumer of news. Fairness is an effort to strike a balance between conflicting interests and tell stories that are balanced, accurate, and complete. Objectivity is an effort to present the news without preference, but can conflict with fairness because balance is simple weighing, and reality often has more than two sides.[24] To be fair in Yugoslavia would have meant regularly presenting at least ten different points of view: the Serbs in Belgrade, Pale, and Knin; the Croats in Zagreb and Mostar; the Bosnians in Sarajevo and Velika Kladuša; and the UN, United States, and NATO. To be objective meant to present unbiased reports in ways that furthered understanding by the audience.

The media have no moral obligation to report views that are uninformed, silly, or tendentiously partisan. But they must give those accused of foul play a chance to reply; they should not pander to morbid curiosity; they should correct their errors promptly, completely, and publicly; they should not whimsically invade the privacy of individuals; and they must maintain a dialogue with the public. These are not easy tasks, especially given the nature of some media.[25] Determining accuracy is hard, few stories are ever complete, and objectivity needs credible sources, especially in Yugoslavia, where it was hard to disentangle propaganda from fact and where the victims had less access to the media than the victimizers.

Given that journalists are often generalists and reflect biases common to their profession and their social class, what is absurd and uninformed to them may be quite accurate and objective to members of their audience. Moreover, deadlines and other constraints endemic to the media make completeness a chimera chased only by the most idealistic, and journalists tend to rely on familiar sources.[26] In Yugoslavia, reporters depended on sources who were accessible and spoke English. Doing so prejudiced coverage toward UN officials, and this helped the Serbs, given the pro-Serbian and anti-Croatian attitudes of London and Paris and UN officials like Akashi and MacKenzie.

Completeness involves comparison, and the media performed very badly in Yugoslavia, in part because they have such a poor collective memory, in part because they reflected official sources and policy. Coverage was both uninformed and biased, reflecting the media's superficial grasp of history and their ritual treatment of current affairs. Coverage also reflected the media's tendency to hew to the official line, to apply a double standard to human rights violations, to ignore criminal actions by our friends, and to promote groups sponsored by the American government.[27] Most news from Yugoslavia reflected official policy reinforced by ignorance, not enlightened professional ethics. In 1983 the media condemned the Soviets for shooting down a Korean aircraft, but in 1988 they sought to explain the American downing of an Iran airliner. In Yugoslavia, the media condemned Croatians for having been Ustaša and being nationalists, but sought to explain Serbian behavior by stressing putative Croatian and Muslim insensitivity to Serbs.

Bias is not necessarily ideological, partisan, or even consistent over time. It is often unconscious, and most reporters strive to avoid bias by not letting their values or those of their superiors distort or slant the news.[28] Faulty information and insufficient knowledge are often the culprits, but the media's easy acceptance of the official line during the Yugoslav conflict raises serious questions regarding their coverage of human rights in general.[29]

Reporters usually check information from sources and give the accused an opportunity to reply, but they failed to do so during the Yugoslav crisis. They regularly reported information without checking it, they repeated partisan accounts, and they ignored other explanations. Because most sources were Serbian politicians and military leaders or Western officials and officers, reporting tended to be biased. Efforts at historical explanation only made things worse, because most reporters lacked the time and knowledge to construct nonpartisan historical accounts. Instead they relied on a few works in English, notably those by West, Djilas, Glenny, and Kaplan—all biased toward Serbs or against Croats and Muslims.[30]

Journalists generally embrace objectivity as a practical defense against critics. They see themselves as detached observers who strive to remain uninvolved, both to protect their credibility and to sell their product. Such attitudes seem to make them America's last real positivists. But although the doctrine of objectivity and pressures to conform drive people with strong belief systems from the mainline media to special-interest publications, these forces still have considerable, if oblique, influence. Nor did many reporters and publications appear to be objective when it came to reporting on events in Yugoslavia. Like *The Nation's* Hitchens, the *New York Times's* Rosenthal tended to see Croats and Muslims as inconvenient troublemakers; Pfaff, Huntington, and others muddied the intellectual waters with simplistic theories in publications like *Foreign Affairs*.[31]

Why this was so is not clear, but may have been owing to the ethnocentric assumptions basic to foreign reporting. Because we assume that there is an ethnic hierarchy descending from First World to Third World, and we believe that values like democracy and capitalism are universally valid, it was hard to fit the Balkans—with their tribes, villages, religions, and Slavic physiognomy—into an American frame.[32] The pictures of peasant Slavs, as opposed to city dwellers, increased the foreignness of the region and the exotic nature of the conflict. But a stroll through Zagreb or Dubrovnik reveals few peasants, save near the market. Assumptions about the Balkans were reinforced by such images. To the extent that reports and images were conflicting or congruent, the public was misled in any number of directions.[33]

If news reports are not supposed to express opinion, in reality they carry the opinions of both the sources and the journalists. As a result, factual statements are often presented as if they were values and can be found embedded in evaluative statements, whereas value statements are inherent in the selection of facts. Because all judgments are value-driven and because value-laden stories may be descriptive, the criteria on which selection is based become crucial. Assuming that all reporters and all news are biased, Klaidman and Beauchamp concluded that only if the general public "find fault" with the press or a journalist is aware of lying does a problem exist. Olen essentially agreed, noting that ethical norms depend on what consumers expect of a news outlet and whether they consider it to be trustworthy.[34]

Such ethical fudging may be the best that journalists can manage, because the nature of the media seems to make some bias inevitable. Among the factors that distort presentation of the news are cultural phenomena, structures and techniques specific to the medium, and repressive governments that strive to protect their image abroad and control information at home. The media usually transmit the viewpoints of the official culture, and the best a journalist can do is to remain skeptical of his biases and those of his sources. To speak of ethics therefore seems almost naive.[35]

But this seems too convenient. Isaacs, a practicing journalist, insisted that ethical performance is possible if a journalist is accountable and strives for accuracy, balance, fairness, compassion, objectivity, and depth of coverage. He cited Supreme Court Justice Potter Stewart, who drew a distinction "between what we have a right to do and what is the right thing to do."[36] Thomas Griffiths, a former editor of *Life* magazine, came to the conclusion that to be aware of one's biases was to act professionally and therefore ethically. Like a juror, the reporter must render an impartial verdict by separating personal beliefs when performing the task at hand. Is fairness, not objectivity, then the goal, with skepticism as journalism's primary virtue?[37]

Evidently not. Bagdikian considered fairness a chimera and thought objectivity, dismissed by Gitlin as a nineteenth-century artifact, a concept that limited news to official versions of events. Nat Hentoff, who has impeccable credentials as a civil libertarian, concluded that the fairness doctrine had a chilling effect on the media, although he did not go as far as Novak and Tuchman, who considered taking sides inevitable and even desirable. The latter saw objectivity as learning as much as possible about the topic and bias as exercising judgment. Bagdikian saw balance as illusory, and Gitlin saw it as undercutting a radical critique. Larry Gross rejected both balance and objectivity—myths with consequences—in favor of allowing marginalized groups and minorities to speak for themselves.[38] In other words, objectivity, fairness, and balance may be professional norms, but they are not practical guidelines; in Yugoslavia, the most marginalized groups—the Muslims and Croats—rarely spoke.

Rather, the media indulge in con games. Among those listed by Lee and Solomon are misleading headlines, dishonest use of statistics, presentation of assertion as fact, editorials that contradict the news stories they accompany, and simple exaggeration.[39] Loaded language is hard to pick up, and if repeated often enough, it becomes true. Repeated references to South Slavs as savage tribes, to Croats as fascists, and to Bosnians as Muslim-led made it hard to imagine a democratic Croatia, a secular Bosnia, or a civilized Yugoslavia.

Reporters also regularly publish unattributed assertions and use unnamed sources to express opinions unacceptable in straight reporting. Long assignments abroad, beats, and the use of unnamed sources lead to "localitis," a "buddy-type of conflict of interest," and manipulation of journalists by sources. Stenographic reporting of the official line hides bias, as does the use of photos to discredit or lessen the impact of a story, for example, picturing a Serbian mother mourning her son next to a story about Serbian genocide against Muslims in Bosnia. Passive phrases hide actors, euphemisms confuse meaning, and surface details replace content; polls restrict and guide discussion rather than clarify issues.[40]

Even if they wish to be totally ethical, reporters are subject to pressure and manipulation, including the use of both coercion and reasoned argument. Ultimately, they are not responsible to their audience, but to their employers, their sources, and the subjects of their stories. So they regularly withhold information and present the doubtful as factual or the factual as doubtful.[41] As a result, the public has learned to distrust and dislike the news media.

Too many journalists have become "ignorant, arrogant and point-lessly adversarial" pundits who see politics as a game. Some, like Fred Barnes, seem to have a hard time drawing a "line between news and fun," and others, like Morton Kondracke, seem to believe that what they are doing is neither writing nor thought. The antics of journalists on talk shows like *Crossfire* and the *McLaughlin Group* make Tom Brokaw "cringe"; Peter Jennings and Mike Wallace demonstrated such a lack of morals that a USMC colonel could only express his "utter contempt" for them on the PBS show *Ethics in America*; and pundits prove unable to predict much of anything. If the public still tunes in, it does not expect much, except a little entertainment.[42]

Thirty years ago, Aldous Huxley found the tendency to reduce complex political issues to comments on personality upsetting but inevitable as the media abandoned the search for truth in favor of consulting motivation specialists versed in the art of selling. For Ron Powers, the "biggest heist of the 1970s was the five o'clock news," spirited nimbly away from the journalists by salesmen who then sold it to the eighteen- to forty-nine-year-old age group. It was in the elevation of the anchor-man to stardom that TV news finally debased itself. Personalities like Cronkite and Brinkley became symbols for their network's "collective persona" and the news became a coat of arms.[43]

Efforts to impose ethics, like the 1959 Fairness Doctrine for TV, have backfired; their commitment to professionalism makes it difficult for reporters to see that they are responsible for the consequences of their actions. Hvistendahl drew a useful distinction between microethics, which stress the obligation to inform the public of the day's happenings, write balanced stories, and raise the media mirror to reality, and macroethics, which stress the impact of events on everybody, realize that the mirror is raised selectively, and attempt to put stories in a global context.[44] In Bosnia, the mirror was raised by official fiat and too many reporters and editors merely did their job. Gutman and Rieff, whose moral outrage informed their reporting, were exceptions.

Given the trend toward concentration of media and control of information flows, some have argued that the Western media have colonized the Third World where the First World promotes its own interests over those of poorer states. The concept has led to some bizarre arguments, such as that put forward by Fareed Zakaraia, who accused anyone outraged at genocide in Bosnia of racism because they were concerned only with the deaths of white Europeans.[45] More accurate would be the observation that Balkan Muslims and Croatian Catholics were marginal groups who had difficulty influencing how they were represented in media that tended to repeat official versions of reality.

Journalists present themselves as ethical and wax eloquent over their role as a fourth estate guarding the republic, but such a pose seems disingenuous. Lyndon Johnson dismissed reporters as "puppets" who "respond to the pull of the most powerful strings." Tom Wicker saw dependence on official sources as a serious weakness, and Bill Moyers believed that the bulk of television news was "unfortunately, whatever the government says is news." Ted Koppel covered up the U.S. role in Laos in 1969–71; Leslie Gelb and his brother, Bernard, used the revolving media-government door; Tom Braden, the "left-winger" on CNN's *Crossfire,* worked for the CIA; the *Washington Times* was established in 1982 by Sun Myung Moon's Unification Church; and even the venerable *New York Times* has had the CIA vet its articles. According to Jeff Gralnick, former executive producer of ABC *World News Tonight,* television news was never a "watchdog," it was merely a front page.[46]

Nor was television alone. In the late 1970s only 14 percent of the public had confidence in TV news, but not many more—22 percent— had faith in the print media. If newspaper editors shared common professional values and displayed a certain confidence in their readers, the public was not inclined to return the compliment.[47] If the media have ethics, they appear to be situational and conventional. Reporters may be pros, but they are not necessarily moral, nor trusted by their audiences.

DOMESTIC AND FOREIGN NEWS FRAMES

If news is an institutional method of distributing information to consumers, foreign news should be tailored for the U.S. consumer using domestic themes. The media cover the same kinds of people and activities abroad as at home, but foreign coverage has shorter stories, clearer priorities, and more overt meanings. All news frames are essentially domestic or adjusted to appeal to a domestic audience, even if a fifth of the nightly news on the major networks is devoted to foreign affairs. Whether foreign news has a sharper focus is debatable. There is little inclination to question sources like the State Department, most journalists lack the expertise to judge and edit wire service items on foreign affairs, and there is less reason to be scrupulous because the audience recognizes errors in local coverage more readily than in foreign.[48]

Even during the 1960s, a period in which Vietnam dominated domestic politics, foreign news got a relatively small percentage of airtime and magazine space. Coverage then focused on areas and events that somehow affected the United States and its citizens, including American actions abroad, political conflict and protest relevant to the cold war or race relations, and disasters affecting U.S. citizens. The media reported the excesses of dictators to underscore the moderation of the U.S. system, much as it compared Balkan savagery to American civility.[49]

If editors at home prefer an American angle to foreign news, reporters overseas are hampered by shortages of time, knowledge, and labor. Consequently, foreign news reporting is inconsistent, haphazard, and narrowly defined or recast as domestic news.[50] Reporting on Yugoslavia focused first on the United States and its NATO allies, then on the Serbs, who were the equivalent to the Communists, followed by a supporting cast of Croats, Muslims, and UN officials. What is striking is how much coverage, both in the popular media and in academic publications, was "Serbo-centric," with the opinions and feelings of Serbs primary.

Because foreign coverage stresses revolutions, coups, mass murder, and natural catastrophes, the average American tends to view life abroad as more dangerous than life in the United States, foreigners as more intractable and irrational, and the area beyond our borders as a no-man's-land. No viable alternatives to the United States seem to exist. Ignorance is multiplied and turned back on itself as simple catchphrases, stereotypes, and prejudices are recycled at increasing rates while news stories heat up, rather like money circulating in the economy. This was especially true for eastern Europe, which was largely ignored before 1989. Even the experts were befuddled.[51]

During the cold war the media focused on the failures and shortcomings of the Communist bloc and used heroic dissidents as symbols of the political and human failure of Communism, but ignored or dismissed similar dissidents in the United States. The media reflected the priorities of U.S. foreign policy in its reporting, and this robbed conflicts abroad of political content and invalidated challenges to the established order at home.[52] During Yugoslavia's breakup, the media also followed the lead of official sources, and reporters quickly picked up Owen's refrain that arming the Muslims would have escalated the level of violence (rather than allow the victims of aggression to defend themselves) and that the priority was peace (no matter how unjust or soiled).[53] Coverage of political issues was denatured or biased toward those favoring a return to order—any order.

As Yugoslavia came unglued, anti-Arab and anti-Muslim reporting permeated the U.S. media, with Saddam Hussein the very symbol of evil in 1991. Americans were therefore primed to see Bosnian Muslims as a problem and to sympathize with Serbian dissidents identified by reporters and prominent academics, whether anti-Croatians like Drašković or the liberals close to the magazine *Vreme*. Able to find only Serb dissidents in Croatia and Bosnia, journalists reporting from Yugoslavia's capital, Belgrade, added these to the Serbian sources and ideas readily available in the former capital. While this seemed to hurt some Serbian political leaders, it gave the Serbs center stage and salvaged their image as a nation, and sympathetic coverage of Serbian nationalists in Bosnia and Croatia left the impression that both states were less democratic than Serbia. The result was a tendency to give the Serbs the benefit of the doubt, but to savage the Croatians, whose Catholicism was also a disadvantage, and to distrust the Bosnians, who were cast as potential fundamentalists, cousins to Yasser Arafat, Saddam Hussein, and Muammar Gaddafy.[54]

Whether reporting reflected the prejudices of America's elites, they certainly shaped coverage of the Yugoslav crisis. They served as the media's sources, and only after they began to argue did doubts appear in the media. The debate over whether to mount air strikes against Serbian positions and lift the arms embargo on Bosnia were discussions among elites on how best to pursue shared goals. It was tactical and practical, not strategic or ethical. As with Vietnam, the media reflected elite convictions that U.S. foreign policy is honorable, U.S. interests deserve protection, and revolutionary change is undesirable. We are the good guys, "constantly taken by surprise in a world we are trying to help but don't quite understand."[55] Our opposition to secession by Slovenia and Croatia, our humanitarian aid, and our involvement in the Dayton peace conference were congruent with such beliefs, even if they also masked our tacit support for Belgrade in 1991 and excused our failure to act decisively before 1995.

Because the media's short memory made them parochial and ethnocentric, they viewed events in the Balkans as discrete actions in time and space, but sought connections to recent events like the Gulf War or familiar themes like the Vietnam syndrome, which were used as news pegs or frames.[56] By seeking links to the immediate past, the media tried to fit Yugoslavia's breakup into a cluster of historic myths and a bogus peace process. They were both predisposed and encouraged to repeat, rather than examine, their first assumptions about events in the Balkans.

A fine example of this was provided by Russell Baker, who described his test drive of a Yugo in a June 1995 piece in the *New York Times*. The humorist, who seemed unaware that the car was produced on license from FIAT, mused that anyone "capable of building the Yugo" was "obviously never going to care much for the things Americans consider important." After driving the diminutive Yugo, he decided that the Balkans were an "untractable political mess," a region populated by "barbarians" who took "obvious delight in killing each other." What the column lacked in wit, it made up for in ethnic clichés.[57]

But then, the column was a "wholehearted embrace of the irrational." More subtle, if equally fantastic, was A. M. Rosenthal's assertion that Bosnians are Serbians or Croatians, divided not by origin, but by "history, religion, nationalism, and the hatreds bred of them." This is as plausible as the theory that current neonationalisms are merely long-suppressed ethnic hatreds dating back centuries, a claim that Ramet dismissed as a "chauvinistic theory about chauvinism."[58] Ethnicity is a slippery concept. It is not easy to define a nationality, nor to decide when a minority becomes a people with a right to be a nation.[59]

Yet the media depicted the war in Yugoslavia as an ethnic conflict, a phenomenon that the U.S. media relegated to a separate category in the 1960s.[60] Operating in an atmosphere of persistent racial tension, the U.S. media are sensitive to ethnicity. They were disposed to view the Yugoslavia crisis as ethnic, and then encouraged to do so by those who noted that the literal translation of the Serbian-Croatian word *pleme* means "tribe," and that Croatians and Serbians have various words for "nation." By 1993, the *New York Times* was worried that America might be the next Bosnia.[61]

Meštrović, Letica, and Goreta have described an alternate to the simple concept that ethnic conflict is endemic to the Balkans. Basing themselves on Dinko Tomašić, Emil Durkheim, and R. N. Bellah, they have perceived a clash of two civil religions in Yugoslavia—a Croatian-Slovenian variant based on universal, peaceful values, and a Serbian-Montenegrin variant grounded in the violent culture of the Dinaric Mountains. They also posit an increase in anomie, the growth of self-seeking and passion to compensate for weakening regulatory social mechanisms, as a necessary condition for the unleashing of these forces. Communism's collapse created an ideological and emotional void, leading some to seek refuge in "past tradition" and "Western institutions," and leading an insecure and aggressive Serbian culture to attack its neighbors.[62]

By viewing the conflict as one between civil religions the model helps to explain why the Serbians systematically waged war against civilians and destroyed cultural monuments. But the media saw only an ethnic conflict, partly because they were under the illusion that history had ended. The West had apparently won the cold war and Francis Fukuyama confidently proclaimed that history was indeed over. But nationalism and tradition endure; only the forms they assume vary. Serbian nationalism is not bad per se, but its present form expresses the values of a particularly violent form of Slavic culture.[63]

Fukuyama's analysis failed. His definition of democracy as free elections was disingenuous, his confusion of economic and political liberalism misleading. Only if one accepts the presuppositions of Hegel does Fukuyama's stress on a monocausal theory of human behavior based on striving for esteem make sense. His theory is essentially capitalist philosophy dressed up as history, and as the nineteenth-century historian Jacob Burckhardt observed, history coordinates, philosophy subordinates. So such theories "degenerate into histories of civilizations." Of course, one need not be a philosopher to assume that "our time is the consummation of all time, or very nearly so," and that "the whole past may be regarded as fulfilled in us, while it, with us, existed for its own sake, for us, and for the future."[64] One can also be a journalist, or a government analyst.

If history has not ended, neither has ideology, and the media have an ideology, similar to Kuhn's dominant paradigm in the sciences or Gouldner's domain assumptions in sociology. It is unconscious and flexible. In the 1970s it was right-liberal or left-conservative and reformist. Since then the media have shifted toward conservative and even reactionary positions on social problems, foreign policy, and the economy.[65] They were thus unlikely to challenge the assertion that lacking vital interests in Bosnia, the United States should not spend lives or treasure to stop genocide or punish aggression.

Journalists ground their reporting and their analyses in conventional wisdom. They want to be clever analysts and engaging storytellers who are witness to exciting events and acquainted with powerful people. The contest for power, not issues, qualifications, or ideology, counts. Slaves to the "tyranny of the immediate," journalists lust after the here and now, the ephemeral moment. They want to be where the action is, and they confuse events with history, action with meaning.[66]

The media covered the Yugoslav crisis as if it were a succession of horse races. They reported who was winning, not why the races were being run, and what the pedigrees of the horses were, not how they had been bred. They interviewed spectators and players, but never examined the motives of the jockeys and their employers. Journalists objectively reported what Karadžić said about ethnic cleansing, just as they had the body counts enumerated by military spokesmen in Vietnam. The internal politics of Croatia, Bosnia, Serbia, and Slovenia were of no interest. All that mattered was whether certain forms existed—an opposition in Serbia, fascist organizations in Croatia, or mujahedeen volunteers in Bosnia.

In Yugoslavia, the media seem to have sought out individuals and political groups that were similar to the upper-class and upper-middle-class sectors of society in the United States.[67] They found them in *Vreme* and its editor, not in Croatia's *Globus*. They paid little attention to social structure, but they spent a great deal of time discussing leaders like Tudjman and Milošević, who came to embody and symbolize values, issues, and groups. In a sense, the media created the Yugoslav leaders, just as they had SDS leaders in the 1960s.[68]

Owing to their unsophisticated approach to ideology, journalists see conflicts as temporary and amenable to resolution.[69] They therefore focused on efforts to resolve the crisis rather than on the social, economic, and political realities underlying it, and they viewed the warring parties as irrational. Ironically, such biases made the media ineffective. Presenting the crisis as the result of irrational ethnic hatred endemic to the area undercut reports and images of genocide. If everyone was guilty, no one was guilty, and if the problem was endemic and chronic, no one could resolve it except the Yugoslavs, and they refused to do so.

It is also worth noting Goffman's concept of *vicarious action*. We live in a safe and boring society but still crave action. The media help by manufacturing and distributing vicarious experience, and during the Yugoslav crisis we participated vicariously in a continuing drama with no risk to ourselves, complete with heroes, villains, and character contests. The latter helped "to massage our morality," so we continued to watch the serial drama of ethnic cleansing unfold until it was abruptly canceled in 1995. Goffman's comments on the consequences of looking for where the action is clearly have ramifications for media coverage of the conflicts in Yugoslavia:[70]

> Looking for where the action is, one arrives at a romantic division of the world. On one side are the safe and silent places, the home, the well-regulated role in business, industry, and the professions; on the other are all those activities that generate expression, requiring the individual to lay himself on the line and place himself in jeopardy during a passing moment. It is from this contrast that we fashion nearly all our commercial fantasies. It is from this contrast that delinquents, criminals, hustlers, and sportsmen draw their self-respect. Perhaps this is payment in exchange for the use we make of the ritual of their performance.

If the Balkans is where the action was and the United States is a gigantic home, then the Yugoslavs had the roles of hero, villain, and victim forced on them by media whose main interest was in selling the news.

That, of course, is a cynical view of reality.

Yet one wonders if a victim makes any noise if a reporter is not present. If events are defined as action and only the media can make them real by recording them, so long as ethnic cleansing was not recorded, it did not exist. Questions regarding the definition of reality then become something more than academic speculation, as do queries as to whether there are perhaps a historical time that exists in the print media and a real time that permeates TV and other electronic media. Is a "real-life Big Event" definable as accessible to television cameras, interesting and important to gatekeepers, and symbolic of trends that prove what the public is ready to believe?[71]

In reality, victims who died on a weekend, or far from TV minicams, or in a forest deep inside Bosnia made little or no sound, because few journalists worked weekends—or from 7:00 P.M. in the evening to 10:00 A.M. the next morning, or in Bosnia's forests; TV journalists have a window from 10:00 A.M. to 4:00 P.M. when they gather news for the prime-time slot. Journalists stayed in major cities, because access to occupied areas was limited. By limiting access, the Serbians diverted more attention to Croatian and Bosnian territories.[72] As a result, human rights violations and war crimes by Croatians and Bosnians were exaggerated by UN officials and a media anxious for copy, whereas genocide in Serbian areas was not even reported—unless the potential or actual victim was an American.

When the victim was an American, the U.S. media shifted gears and the Serbs scrambled to help. Thousands of dead Slavs and hundreds of dead European peacekeepers and journalists made less of an impression than the plight of one American pilot named O'Grady, shot down over Bosnia by a Serbian missile in June 1995. Coverage of his rescue was excessively patriotic. Typical was a detailed account of a "daring" and "risky daytime" rescue operation that showed the U.S. armed forces to be the world's "finest." Naturally, Clinton declared the "slightly dehydrated and undernourished" O'Grady "an American hero."[73] One of the few discordant voices came from William Safire, who chided the West for creating a Rapid Reaction Force to protect its troops and the media for celebrating the rescue while the Pentagon and CIA feigned ignorance of what was happening to thousands of victims of genocide and the UN and NATO were caving in to Serbian blackmail.[74]

O'Grady was familiar and American—one of our own—and journalists strive for subjects and locales with such symbolic value.[75] Some locales, like Sarajevo, acquired such strong emotional and symbolic charges that they became part of the action, just as scenery on a stage becomes part of the play. Some even had their own personalities. Sarajevo was dangerous and tortured, the Balkans dark, primitive, and mysterious. The night air was different there than it was in Scarsdale and Milwaukee, even if the latter city is home to a lot of Balkan types and their descendants.

Originally, Yugoslavia was too remote and too Balkan to be seen clearly, and few in the media gave it more than a cursory glance. Yugoslavia was not where the action was in early 1991; it was all in the

Middle East, a privileged foreign news area in the U.S. media. When the action came to Slovenia and Croatia, journalists packed their bags and went to report on the action, with little expertise and local stringers or U.S. and UN officials as their guides.

Because our information was limited, domesticated, and denatured, we became postmodern voyeurs imbibing novel events through familiar myths and official opinions, both of which shaped our perceptions of what was happening as surely as our own prejudices and beliefs. We saw violence as natural to the Balkans, rape as a feminist issue, and genocide as understandable behavior for atavistic tribes. Serbian actions were rationalized as paranoia, the West's policy justified as a reasonable means of dealing with intractable natives. Croat and Bosnian resistance to Serbian aggression was an example of unrealistic and uncooperative behavior, and the arms embargo was transformed from a cynical policy that helped the aggressor to a humane tool designed to save lives.

That American culture extols violence as a solution to problems and as a self-justifying act made acceptance of violence abroad easier. Even genocide was not that startling to a culture whose prime-time programs depict the old, the young, and minorities as the usual victims of violence.[76] Because Hollywood had conditioned us to happy endings and because we viewed diplomacy, not force, as the way to resolve conflicts, the real villains became those who rejected peace at any price and instead fought to roll back aggression.

NOTES

1. Gans, *Deciding What's News*, 122–24; Tuchman, *Making News*, 5–6, 12, 168, 189, 194, 206–7; Cohen, *Media Diplomacy*, 49–50; Isaacs, *Untended Gates*, 218. News records and is a product of social reality. Goffman's frames (strips of daily life) help explain how social organization influences events and our involvement in them. Lloyd de Mause, *Foundations of Psychohistory* (New York: Creative Roots, 1982), 172–243, an extreme update of Le Bon and Sighele, believes groups unconsciously generate and sustain fantasies that help them to deal with reality by ignoring or manipulating it.

2. Paletz and Entmann, *Media*, 22, 149–51; Gans, *Deciding What's News*, 90–91. The media socialize people to remain passive while accepting the values and politics of the system and supporting elite goals at home and abroad.

3. Tuchman, *Making News*, 12–16, 46–50, 60–63; Bogart, *Press and Public*, 172. The public likes the unexpected.

4. Tuchman, *Making News*, 135–38. Also Amnesty International, *Bosnia-Herzegovina: Rape and Sexual Abuse*, and Alexandra Stiglmayer, ed., *Mass Rape: The War against Women in Bosnia-Herzegovina* (Lincoln: University of Nebraska Press, 1994).

5. Slavenka Drakulić, *The Balkan Express: Fragments from the Other Side of the War* (New York: HarperCollins, 1993/4), 157–60. Evidently, her sensibilities were so

highly developed, she could even remember, and mourn, a bridge she had never seen, save in photos.

6. Lichter et al., *Media Elite*, 137–38, 296, 301. Severin and Tankard, *Communications Theories*, 62–64, think one can avoid bias by doing stories that report rather than infer or judge.

7. Gans, *Deciding What's News*, 90–93; Gitlin, *The Whole World*, 173–91; Herman, "Media," 85–86. Both media and government can create newsworthy events by making the story into "a major propaganda campaign." Fishman, *Manufacturing the News*, 109–15, for cues to investigate.

8. Tuchman, *Making News*, 195–97 for ideologies; Gitlin, *The Whole World*, 206–7, for citation.

9. Tuchman, *Making News*, 201–5; Ewen, *All Consuming Images*, 266; Gans, *Deciding What's News*, 167–74. Bogart, *Press and Public*, 166–70, 182–87, defines news as word of events and interpretation as developing those events.

10. Lichter et al., *Media Elite*, 112; Gans, *Deciding What's News*, 39–40.

11. Gaunt, *Choosing the News*, 36–46, 123–26; Isaacs, *Untended Gates*, 167–82; Tuchman, *Making News*, 185–88. Personal convictions, attitudes and work habits, socialization, and self-image may be more important than training. Missouri, Northwestern, Columbia, Kansas, and Indiana form the elite. Journalism attracted the bottom of the academic class in the 1980s. A third of those majoring in journalism found work as journalists, but only two-fifths of U.S. journalists majored in the subject.

12. Fishman, *Manufacturing the News*, 3–14; Tuchman, *Making News*, 5, 105; Paletz and Entman, *Media*, 19; Gaunt, *Choosing the News*, 9, for a discussion of the studies of journalists at work. Timothy R. Haight, "The New American Information Order," *The Critical Communications Review* (1984), II, 105–8, thinks that knowledge of how to cooperate is a resource and that determining a pattern of cooperation (division of labor) is an informational battle. If so, then the socialization of journalists should determine both their pattern of work and those they view as acceptable.

13. Isaacs, *Untended Gates*, 17, 178–80, 221; Gaunt, *Choosing the News*, 126–31.

14. Fishman, *Manufacturing the News*, 27–66, 109–15.

15. Isaacs, *Untended Gates*, 58–62. Gans, *Deciding What's News*, 84–87, stresses the functional, rather than formal, nature of roles. Policy makers, top editors, producers, senior editors, section heads, and reporters all stand above writers, filmmakers, researchers, and staff.

16. Gans, *Deciding What's News*, 81–84; Gitlin, *The Whole World*, 266–68.

17. Tuchman, *Making News*, 87, 95, 99; Gans, *Deciding What's News*, 51–52, 58; Gitlin, *The Whole World*, 211–14, 269; Bagdikian, *Media Monopoly*, 223; J. K. Hvistendahl, "An Ethical Dilemma: Responsibility for 'Self-Generating' News," in Merrill and Barney, *Ethics and the Press*, 186–88.

18. Libel laws also limit news coverage. Fishman, *Manufacturing the News*, 120–22; Tuchman, *Making News*, 82–84; Lichter et al., *Media Elite*, 133.

19. Gans, *Deciding What's News*, 167–68; and Tuchman, *Making News*, 177. News limits access, transforms dissent, and tends to legitimize the existing state by eschewing analysis in favor of ahistoricity, the logic of the concrete, and stress on contingency of events, rather than attention to structural necessity.

20. Paletz and Entmann, *Media*, 21. Journalists take a short-term, antihistorical view of events; stress the causal roles of individuals and groups over structural and

impersonal forces; and try to create stories easily understood by their audiences. Even careful analysis can lead to questionable conclusions, such as H. M. Erzenberger's conclusion that "molecular civil wars" like Bosnia have destruction as their only goal and are "about nothing at all." See Paul Levine's review of "Civil War: From L.A. to Bosnia," *The Nation*, 23 January 1995, 103; Hans Magnus Enzensberger, *New York Times*, 16 September 1992.

21. Because television news has evolved its own manners, mores, and techniques, much as diplomatic corps, churches, and academia, it possesses its own "culture." To the extent that this culture does not coincide with those of viewers, the media is seen to be biased or off-the-wall. For discussions of television culture, the "transparency fallacy," the use of "clawback" to neutralize unwelcome news, and discussions of television's conventions, see Fiske, *Television Culture*, esp. 281–307; Adler et al., *Understanding Television*, passim; Cecelia Tichi, *Electronic Hearth: Creating an American Television Culture* (New York: Oxford University Press, 1991). I am indebted to Gail Evans, Stephen Cassidy, and Juan Señor for trying to explain the workings of television news to me.

22. Isaacs, *Untended Gates*, 25–26, 135–65. Halloran, "Soldiers and Scribblers," 43–44, noted that "the finest compliment" one journalist could get from another was to be called a "pro," the worst insult, to be labeled an "amateur." Also Gabe Pressman, Robert Lewis Shayon, and Robert Schulman, "Ethics in Television Journalism," 237–47, and Thomas Griffiths, "A Few Frank Words about Bias," both in Merrill and Barney, *Ethics and the Press*, 216.

23. Jeffrey Olen, *Ethics in Journalism* (Englewood Cliffs, NJ: Prentice-Hall, 1988), 13–24, 29–30. Journalism lacks a required body of knowledge one has to master in order to practice, required degrees, and shared values and standards, despite the code issued by Sigma Delta Chi, the Society of Professional Journalists. Nor are there clients who need to be protected from poor journalists. Olen thinks the marketplace fulfills that function.

24. Stephen Klaidman and Tom L. Beauchamp, *The Virtuous Journalist* (New York: Oxford University Press, 1987), 14–21, 32, 43–47; Olen, *Ethics*, 11.

25. Klaidman and Beauchamp, *Virtuous Journalist*, 46–50; Olen, *Ethics*, 14–25; McQuail, *Media Performance*, 210–13. Completeness can be internal to a given story or external to all stories. Content analysis helps discover the degree of completeness of a given story, but there are no standards regarding how much information is sufficient.

26. Lee and Solomon, *Unreliable Sources*, 30–31.

27. Lee and Solomon, *Unreliable Sources*, 277–85, 305–6, 329, also question the coverage of Pan Am 103, which exploded over Scotland in December 1988. Herman and Chomsky, *Manufacturing Consent*, 42–85, 143–67, for Poland, Central America, and the "Bulgarian conspiracy."

28. For Klaidman and Beauchamp, *Virtuous Journalist*, 60–61, bias is "a value-directed departure from accuracy, objectivity, and balance, not just a distorted presentation of facts." Bias in journalism is "a distorted and unfair judgment or disposition caused by the values of a reporter, editor, or institution." Distortion is causally linked to the values of writers and editors and derives from "irrationality, illusion, prejudice, greed, ambition, and religious fervor" . . . and ignorance.

29. Lee and Solomon, *Unreliable Sources*, 300–3, for problems.

30. Misha Glenny and Aleksa Djilas had regular access to such influential periodical as *The New York Review of Books, Foreign Affairs*, and *The New Republic*. Rebecca West, *Black Lamb and Grey Falcon: A Journey through Yugoslavia* (New York: Viking, 1941/53, and Penguin, 1982); Robert J. Kaplan, *Balkan Ghosts: A Journey through History* (New York: St. Martin's, 1993); Glenny, *The Fall of Yugoslavia, op. cit.*

31. Academics have tended to discard objectivity as a useless concept. *Foreign Affairs* (Summer 1993), for Pfaff and Huntington; Gaunt, *Choosing the News*, 23–24; Gans, *Deciding What's News*, 182–95; Bogart, *Press and Public*, 152. McQuail, *Media Performance*, 184–85, defines objectivity as balance and evenhandedness in presenting various sides of an issue, accurate and realistic reporting, presentation of main, relevant points, separation of fact from opinion, minimizing the reporter's attitudes and opinions, and avoiding slant, rancor, or devious purpose.

32. Gans, *Deciding What's News*, 42–52, saw domestic news informed by six values shared by reporters of foreign news and domestic editors. The values are moderatism, individualism, ethnocentrism, altruistic democracy, responsible capitalism, and small-town pastoralism. Jeremy Turnstall, "Stars, Status, Mobility," in D. Lazere et al., *American Media and Mass Culture*, 121–22. The Anglo-American media confer high status on a "north European physical appearance," create an "ethnic division of labor," and ratify ethnic and racial hierarchies.

33. Larry Gross, John Stuart Katz, and Jay Ruby, *Image Ethics: The Moral Rights of Subjects in Photographs, Film, and Television* (New York: Oxford University Press, 1988), xvii, 3–33, note that ethical problems are political, and working ethics constantly in flux. Especially problematic are questions of privacy, misrepresentation, and consent.

34. Olen, *Ethics*, 11, 24–25. Klaidman and Beauchamp, *Virtuous Journalist*, 62–71, think standards of bias contain "vital cultural assumptions" that give them "legitimacy."

35. Klaidman and Beauchamp, *Virtuous Journalist*, 72–89; Cohen, *Media Diplomacy*, 40–43.

36. Isaacs, *Untended Gates*, 162, 223–24.

37. Griffiths, "A Few Frank Words," 212–17. Schulman, "Control Mechanisms," 119, thinks liberals seek truth via objective reporting, lack of bias, and a presentation of both sides, but a critical observer views objectivity as illusory, truth as a complex cultural tradition with varying interpretations, and bias as an exclusion of those viewpoints common to all systems.

38. Barbara Tuchman, *Practicing History* (New York: Ballantine, 1982), 60–61; Novak, "Why the Working Man Resents," 112; Nat Hentoff, "How 'Fair' Should TV Be?," in Merrill and Barney, *Ethics and the Press*, 251–63; Gitlin, *The Whole World*, 215, 268; Larry Gross, "The Ethics of (Mis)representation," in Gross et al., *Image Ethics*, 191.

39. Lee and Solomon, *Unreliable Sources*, 35–56; Herman and Chomsky, *Manufacturing Consent*, 111.

40. Lee and Solomon, *Unreliable Sources*, 35–56; Isaacs, *Untended Gates*, 50–54, 157–58, 165; Cohen, *Media Diplomacy*, 39, 52–53, 70, 112.

41. Klaidman and Beauchamp, *Virtuous Journalist*, 188–217.

42. James Fallows, "Why Americans Hate the Media," 45–55, 64.

43. Powers, *Newscasters*, 1, 53, 58, and passim; Aldous Huxley, "The Arts of Selling," in Merrill and Barney, *Ethics and the Press*, passim.

44. Pressman et al., "Ethics in Television Journalism," 241–46; Hentoff, "How 'Fair' Should TV Be?," passim; Hvistendahl, "An Ethical Dilemma," 189–91.

45. Ramet, "The Yugoslav Crisis and the West," 460. About 75 percent of all television shows are from the United States, and English has become the international media language. Hachten, World News Prism, 88–89, 95–96, 110, 174–78; Schiller, "Informatics," 12–13; Gross, "Ethics," 188–202, and Jack G. Shaheen, "Perspectives on the Television Arab," in Gross et al., Image Ethics, 203–17.

46. Lee and Solomon, Unreliable Sources, 104–28, 150.

47. Bogart, Press and Public, 181–82.

48. Gans, Deciding What's News, 31, 38, 147–52; Tuchman, Making News, 3–4; Paletz and Entman, Media, 9. Gaunt, Choosing the News, 9; Isaacs, Untended Gates, 180; Bogart, Press and Public, 226–28.

49. Lee and Solomon, Unreliable Sources, 257; Bogart, Press and Public, 158–62, 176–78; Gans, Deciding What's News, 32–38; Paletz and Entman, Media, 216. TV news gives about ten minutes nightly to foreign policy, but that is over 40 percent of its programming; papers devote 9.5 percent to 11.5 percent of their space to foreign affairs.

50. Paletz and Entmann, Media, 215. Gaunt, Choosing the News, 5–7, 13. Constraints on coverage of foreign affairs include lack of commercial sponsorship and lack of information; ownership and circulation; location and technical facilities; and professional values regarding selection, content, and allotment of space.

51. Paletz and Entmann, Media, 220–21, 232–34; Gaunt, Choosing the News, 8; Ramet, Social Currents, 552. AP and UPI tend to focus coverage on conflicts in developing nations. One of the reasons Yugoslav experts proved poor prophets was the academic equivalent of pack journalism. For how it works, see Stephen F. Cohen, Rethinking the Soviet Experience: Politics and History since 1917 (New York: Oxford University Press, 1986).

52. Paletz and Entmann, Media, 225, 231, 246–48. Governments use foreign events to manipulate public opinion and manufacture foreign threats to distract attention from domestic problems.

53. Journalists and academics found it hard to realize that some dissidents had become chauvinists favoring the creation of a Greater Serbia. Branka Magaš, The Destruction of Yugoslavia, 61–72, for her polemical exchange in 1986 with Zaga Golubović, Mihailo Marković, and Ljuba Tadić, all former editors of Praxis; Gale Stokes, ed., From Stalinism to Pluralism: A Documentary History of Eastern Europe since 1945 (New York: Oxford University Press, 1991), 94–106, 102–30.

54. The power of the image should not be underestimated. According to Alex Carey, "Reshaping the Truth: Pragmatists and Propagandists in America," in D. Lazere et al., American Media and Mass Culture, 34–41, the image has replaced the ideal because the pragmatic propagandist emphasizes the consequences of action as crucial. Also Ewen, The All Consuming Image, passim, for the power and ubiquity of images, which leave us with only the surface of things, empty and unhappy.

55. Paletz and Entmann, Media, 214–15; Lee and Solomon, Unreliable Sources, 258, for James Reston's remark.

56. Gans, Deciding What's News, 32–37. Genocidal war and famine are ignored if the areas are unknown in the United States or have little political significance there, as are problems and policies foreign to U.S. experience.

57. Russell Baker, "The Yugo Episode," New York Times, 3 June 1995.

58. A. M. Rosenthal, "How to Succeed in Bosnia," *New York Times*, 6 June 1995; Ramet, *Social Currents in Eastern Europe*, 431–32.

59. Mark H. Maier, *The Data Game: Controversies in Social Science Statistics* (Armonk, NY: M. E. Sharpe, 1991), 17–21; Noel Malcolm, *Bosnia: A Short History* (New York: New York University Press, 1994), 7–12. Given scanty and contradictory evidence, Malcolm concludes only that the Bosnians are the Slavs who live in Bosnia.

60. Gans, *Deciding What's News*, 32–37.

61. *New York Times*, 8 December 1992.

62. Stjepan Meštrović, Slaven Letica, Miroslav Goreta, *Habits of the Balkan Heart: Social Character and the Fall of Communism* (College Station, TX: Texas A & M University Press, 1993), passim.

63. Meštrović et al., *Habits*, esp. 136–38.

64. Francis Fukuyama, *The End of History and the Last Man* (New York: Macmillan, 1992), xi–xxiii, 43–44, 59–70, 337–38. Jacob Burckhardt, *Reflections on History* (Indianapolis, IN: Liberty Fund, 1989), 33–35.

65. Gans, *Deciding What's News*, 68–69; Bogart, *Press and Public*, 130; Paletz and Entmann, *Media*, 196–207, 217–19. The media helped create the conservative mood by encouraging conservatives and discouraging liberals in electoral reporting; setting campaign themes; discouraging liberal and radical voters; and setting public priorities, defining problems, and proposing solutions that precluded other definitions and solutions.

66. Tuchman, *Making News*, 12–16, 121–24, 138; Gans, *Deciding What's News*, 29–30; Lichter et al., *Media Elite*, 109, 128–29, 297. To become news, an issue or event must be sociologically or psychologically pertinent to the reporter's grasp of the world and his practical needs. Journalists appear to value people and institutions that are pragmatic and adaptable, and they see ideology as explicit and political, not implicit and cultural, so they cannot perceive themselves or Americans as ideological.

67. Gans, *Deciding What's News*, 58–61.

68. Gitlin, *The Whole World*, esp. 157 ff.; Gans, *Deciding What's News*, 62–66. While sociology sees leadership as a *role* to be filled, the media see the leader as a particular type of person; sociology sees the group as *selecting* leaders, the media see the group only as following the leader; sociology sees institutions as *generating* leaders, the media see leaders blocked by institutions. The media thus tend to ignore groups, but they reflect their sources and their audiences, which tend to be corporate.

69. Gans, *Deciding What's News*, 25.

70. Erving Goffman, "Where the Action Is," in *Interaction Ritual: Essays on Face-to-Face Behavior* (Garden City, NY: Doubleday, 1967), esp. 262–70.

71. Isaacs, *Untended Gates*, 218. Brian Winston, "The Tradition of the Victim in Griersonian Documentary," in Gross et al., *Image Ethics*, 41–43, noted that factual television replaces analysis with empathy, puts effect over cause, and has little practical impact. Filmmakers and journalists are dominant, victims merely subjects.

72. Tuchman, *Making News*, 39–41. Lichter et al., *Media Elite*, 301; and Roger Cohen, "Ideas & Trends: In Bosnia, the War That Can't Be Seen," *New York Times*, 25 December 1994.

73. Francis X. Clines, "Downed U.S. Pilot Rescued in Bosnia in Daring Raid," *New York Times*, 9 June 1995 and 3 June 1995, for comments that the shooting down of the pilot was an extreme provocation by the Serbs.

74. William Safire, "Break the Siege (Help Bosnia Turn the Tide)," *New York Times*, 15 June 1995.

75. Tuchman, *Making News*, 121–24.

76. George Gerbner, Larry Gross, Michael Morgan, and Nancy Signorielli, "Charting the Mainstream: Television's Contributions to Political Organizations," in Lazere et al., *American Media and Mass Culture*, 441–60.

3

Types

TELEVISION

It seems a puzzle that four years of televised images of dead bodies and distraught refugees left us largely indifferent, our moral sense dulled, our human impulses overloaded and short-circuited. But the puzzle has its logic. Televised images were disconnected, contradictory, and accompanied by stories whose emotional meaning was clear on a primitive level, but whose cognitive meaning was confused and biased toward inaction. Put another way, the medium may be the message, but the image doesn't mean a damn thing. The nature of television and its messages prevented the tube from reporting in a way that would mobilize the public to act. Television news is not a story; it is an open-ended cliff-hanger, incoherent and promiscuous in its choice of images and stories. It is multipurpose addictive entertainment.[1]

Television not only provides entertainment; it is also a medium viewed for itself. Inertia appears to be a major reason for watching the tube, and TV viewing is an activity in which attention is repeatedly given and withdrawn, so one cannot assume that a viewer watches what is on the screen carefully. Edward R. Murrow thought the tube was "being used to distract, delude, and insulate us," and Peter Wood saw it as a dream whose "enormous and powerful content . . . is readily and thoroughly forgotten." If television gives us information about the world, helps us to place ourselves in that world, and entertains us, it also serves a function simply by being watched. It is a light show that eschews historical, linear thinking and explanation in favor of symbolic meaning embedded in images that are often as obtuse as those in a dream.[2]

Wood carries the analogy of television as dream to its logical conclusion, noting that TV replicates Freud's concept of dreamwork, leaving the viewer to interpret the disjointed, trivial, and contradictory images that flit across the crowded screen.[3] Like the dream, TV condenses information by combining, fragmenting, and omitting. It is a visual shorthand whose reading demands that the viewer have adequate prior information. If so, then the only ones capable of linking TV's disjointed images and verbal messages were experts in Yugoslav history and politics, and even they would have been challenged by the speed and segmented nature of TV news because they think like books, in a linear manner, not like TV, whose images appeal to the appositional right side of the brain.[4] Of course, the images are linked by stories that should appeal to the left side too, but the melding of nonlinear images and linear narrative is total and must be assembled by the viewer, who ultimately makes sense of the combination.[5]

To understand the media's coverage of events in Yugoslavia, it was necessary to be an expert in mass communications; and to arrange and transform the information in the media into coherent patterns, one needed to be well versed in things Yugoslav. This was especially true of television, a medium that dramatizes events, replaces one element with another, and constantly shifts accent.[6] A thing can stand for itself, its opposite, or both. The focus may be altogether misleading, meaning is inverted and obfuscated, and even conversation is suspect because it consists of things heard or said by the dreamer, who is both the viewer and the journalist. This is especially true of talk shows, whose format makes them incoherent.[7]

A fine example of incoherence was provided in April 1993 by Dave Marash, who appeared on *Nightline* to tell Ted Koppel how UNPROFOR troops in Croatia had overseen an uneasy peace for eighteen months. He began by showing a Serbian map of Croatia and interviewing two Serbians who blamed the Croatians for the war. He then cut to Osijek to interview the owners of two grocery stores (both solidly middle-class Croats). A brief report on attacks that killed 900 people in Osijek followed, then back to the Serbs and a definition of a Chetnik as a Serbian volunteer and soldier, followed by claims that the Croatians had attacked the Serbs, and a comment by one of the Croatian grocers that Serbs "like to conquer and rule," and the observation that since his friend was a Chetnik, it was just a question of who would shoot first. Who had burned a Serbian's house was not clear, but it was obvious that Serbs could never again live with Croats.[8]

Then Ted broke for about five minutes of commercials.

When he came back, Marash noted that 30 percent of Croatia was under Serbian control and that the 16,000 UNPROFOR troops were impotent because the different sides could not agree. Colonel Miguel Moreno, an Argentine, then noted that Croatia had been ethnically cleansed of Serbs, so the Serb areas had been cleansed of some 230,000 Croats. Tudjman was quoted as complaining that UNPROFOR had not fulfilled its mission, but Bulatović warned that there would be a European war if the Croats "attacked," and a UN official worried that the JNA might participate in a second Serbo-Croatian war—as if it had not won the first for the local Serbs.

Then there was another commercial break.

Marash began again by noting that the Serbs were convinced they could not live with the Croats and held 30 percent of Croatia, which the Croats would try to retake. The UN was not a factor, but the Croats were too weak to go it alone. Ted then asked if the families interviewed were "symbols of the problem," and Marash said, yes, that Drago, the Croat, feared Steva, the Serb, adding that the Serbs could only be beaten if they became overextended, and there was always the danger the Albanians would rebel. But should that happen, the Russians, Greeks, Turks, and others would intervene—and this possibility kept UN officials up nights. So Ted asked if things were getting better or worse, and Dave said, well, worse, because sanctions were hurting the Serbs, who were angry and desperate and, well, would not give up their turf and surrender it to weaker "aggrieved" powers.

And then there was another commercial break.

And what had the viewer learned? That Serbs and Croats hate and fear and loathe one another, and would shoot one another if they got a chance. That no one was to blame. That the whole thing could get out of hand and become a real European problem. That Croats were a weak, aggrieved people who would make trouble if they got the chance. That the Serbs were a really tough, aggressive people who were not about to cave in to pressure. That the Russians and Greeks and Turks were just waiting for a chance to make the affair a pan-European war. And that if you bought the right product you could live happily ever after, or at least look good in the meantime.

That's basically what they learned. Nor had the message changed from February, when Dave told Ted:

> What really sticks is the force of the hatred that is so out of control, in Bosnia particularly, but all throughout Yugoslavia. People nurse grudges over generations. Talk about tragedies of today and you'll hear about the crimes of World War II. And at the elementary school level, children are taught about the conflict between the Muslims and the Christians in the 14th century, and all of those are still open wounds, gaping, bleeding,

hurting and creating, as I say, a hatred that is just beyond anything I've ever experienced.

And lest anyone hope that things might improve, Marash quickly noted—since he had only forty seconds—that "the defining thing about the children of Yugoslavia is that almost all of them don't have their father right now. The hatreds that took away their fathers live, burning very, very hot, in the hearts of these children."[9]

And what did the public learn from that? That the kids would carry on mindless vendettas and mass slaughter.

Nor was *MacNeil-Lehrer,* the thinking person's talk show, better. In April 1993 it carried an amazing, and amusing, bit of theater in which Senator Biden urged that the embargo be lifted, and President Clinton said, "I've done everything I know to do. . . . We obviously have made life more difficult for the people in Serbia," but the use of the U.S. military had "never been ruled in" because the United States could not solve the problem, especially given Serbia's heroic resistance to Nazi Germany, and, well, "It is the most difficult and frustrating problem in the world today." In short, the United States would not take unilateral action. The segment ended appropriately, with a tape of Milošević thanking Clinton for doing nothing.[10]

And what did the thinking person learn from that?

Television seems able to portray only a limited range of emotions because it lacks linear development and nuance. It homogenizes and reduces complex situations, events, and emotions to simple standard items that are almost mythic.[11] But if the news pegs on which the myths are hung are recognizable, TV's product remains the new.[12] Television precludes careful exegesis in favor of simple explanations of group conflict and reality in general. It invokes and evokes, it does not inform or explain.[13]

If television is dream, it also decides what is real. Novak found its artificial reality more substantive than the world from which it was constructed, and its "parade of experts instructing the unenlightened" a symptom of a medium run by a biased, college-educated, economically privileged, cultural elite out of touch with its audience. As the tube creates and idealizes some groups and ideas by focusing on them, it makes others disappear by ignoring them. Because it is a key news source for most Americans, it has seriously distorted our view of reality.[14]

Television is a major socializing agent but its effect on its audience is not reassuring. Heavy viewers appear to be apolitical and see themselves as unable to affect events.[15] Happily, not everyone is a heavy viewer, and for many, turning on the news in the evening is more akin to lighting the hearth than an effort to seek information about the world.

Since different segments of the audience watch the news at different points in their viewing cycles, the impact of news broadcasts differs. Attention is not focused, and reports and discussions of violence, unlike images, may have little impact on viewers reared on a medium in which violence is repeatedly portrayed as a legitimate means to achieve societally approved ends. If viewing justified violence (societally sanctioned vengeance and self-defense) breeds violence, then depicting the Serbs as defending themselves against potential Croatian fascists and Muslim fanatics, or seeking vengeance for what Croatian fascists and Muslim fanatics had reportedly done to their ancestors, should have struck resonant chords in an American public inured to such formulations, and eroded sympathy for the victims of "ethnic cleansing."[16]

American air strikes against Libya in 1986, repeated Israeli retaliations against Palestinian camps and bases in Lebanon and Tripoli for terrorist actions, American-led operations against Iraq in 1991, American invasions of Panama and Grenada in 1988 and 1983, and the domestic bombing of black activists by Philadelphia's mayor were all acceptable uses of violence. The public has been repeatedly asked to accept vengeance (retaliation) and self-defense (loosely defined and often preventive) as rationales for extreme acts of violence by the good guys. How then should it react to a situation in which the bad guys are the Balkan peoples and the good guys the mediators attempting to keep them from killing one another? If not good, the Serbs were not bad either, and if not bad, the Croats were certainly not good. That left the Bosnians, whose victimhood was vitiated by their potential to become Palestinians or Shi'ites.

Given the models put forward by Goffman and Comstock, we would not have expected viewers to act to affect the situation in Yugoslavia because there was neither reason nor opportunity for Americans to act.[17] It is unlikely that many viewers perceived a real opportunity to affect the situation personally, nor was it their place to do so. Or perhaps the distance and low energy of television images lacked the power to move the audience and defined the problem as someone else's responsibility. If the low-key anchor reassured us, the symbiotic link of sound and image befuddled us, and a haphazard, sporadic, illogical presentation confused the functions of the characters.[18]

Even if news reports of ethnic cleansing aroused a desire to act for moral reasons, the desire would have been transitory and dissipated over time, especially if the viewer lacked the appropriate status to intervene and could not find a way to act or displaced the desire to do so by arguing with a colleague, or in some other manner. Viewers could find social acts to substitute for their desire to act to end the slaughter in Bosnia. Whether they were positive would have depended on the repertoire of actions available to a given viewer.[19]

The American public has difficulty acting to correct domestic political problems, and it could not be expected to do so to benefit foreign subjects or agents.[20] Because news reports and opinion pieces were not uniform or hewed to the line that all sides were equally guilty, they created considerable cognitive confusion and undermined whatever lessons the crisis could teach. Moreover, the consequences of acting were negligible for most Americans, the perceived opportunity almost nonexistent, and the possibility of using scapegoats (reporters, diplomats, congressional representatives, and abstract stereotypes of Balkan tribes, including the victims of genocide) to achieve catharsis always available. If the perception that tragic results may follow acting inhibits action, then the reporting on Yugoslavia inhibited action by depicting all sides as guilty and the crisis as the tragic result of centuries of warfare. In effect, the American public was achieving a dubious vicarious catharsis by watching the Balkan equivalent of a classic Greek tragedy or a Slavic version of *Cops*.[21]

Nor is there any reason to assume that the public paid attention or made a serious effort to retain, sort, and order raw information. The medium's nature militated against this, especially given that events in Yugoslavia were like a conventional dramatic series. The public was not encouraged to act, but to turn on the nightly news to catch the next episode of the Balkan soaps or watch one of the talk shows to learn what the political equivalent of film critics had to say. There were rewards for doing so, in the form of entertainment, but no punishment for not acting to end the situation. To act would have been to cancel the series, and good prime-time entertainment is hard to find.[22]

To what extent such a model is useful is up to the reader to decide, just as it was up to the viewer to decide to what extent events in Yugoslavia were real. If the war was a soap, it was one broadcast sporadically, not daily. Viewer interest waxed and waned, and it was hard to follow the plot, especially when the scene shifted from Sarajevo to Washington to Belgrade to Dayton to Geneva, with appropriate shifts in character and story line.[23]

Even had there been a coherent continuity and clearly explained meaning, political action of any sort has a very low salience within the response hierarchy of the American public, a lowly status that the nature of the tube appears to reinforce. Shows like *MacNeil-Lehrer* and the nightly news are to be enjoyed, not treated as calls to action. The information they convey is encrusted with noise and any action to be taken far from clear.

This model also applies to print media. Like them, television newscasts have lead stories, hard news, and features, but the tube mediates reality more than the press, because its coverage is so brief and so stylized.[24] On average, less than three minutes of an hour of taped footage will be broadcast, and these are not necessarily the best three minutes, if for no other reason than that the last three hours before airtime is rushed. When Gans wrote his study of the media in the late 1970s, the news programs of the major networks averaged about 22.5 to 23.0 minutes of film and stories. Most were D.C.-based and concerned with domestic topics; foreign news accounted for only 14 percent of news programs in 1967. By the early 1970s, the three major networks crammed twenty-seven items into thirty minutes, with up to a quarter outside of the United States or on site, and two-thirds originating in the studio.[25]

The amount of airtime is crucial to the impact of a topic or subject, so content analysis fails. It is not a question of what is said, but of who says it and frames it—and how many times they do so.[26] Fairness implies equal access and equal tone and quality of coverage, but this is an ideal never realized. Access is conditioned by social role, economic status, and ideology; the tone and quality of coverage range from bland to enthusiastic and censorious.[27] Fairness implies that all sides have equal access, but this did not occur during Yugoslavia's prolonged dissolution. The negative effects of exclusion were compounded because the three major networks reported the same stories, often picked up from the major wire services and newspapers, especially the *New York Times*, which heavily influenced coverage of foreign affairs by regional and local media. Television was the most mediated because it followed the lead of print media.[28]

The prevalence of "tell stories" on newscasts led Fiske to see TV news as an oral mode of communication. But verbal accounts rely heavily on videotape and they are influenced by a sophisticated visual language that includes such devices as logos. Among the factors that affect presentation of a story are film speed, camera angles, and framing. Both reporters and editors prefer head-on shots at a specific distance. Distorted shots are used only when the subject is bizarre or the newscast seeks to present it that way. Of Hall's distances, TV news uses the far personal, the close social, and the far social. It eschews the public, which tends to diminish, and the intimate, which tends to invade or intimidate. These categories correspond to those used by Fiske, who notes that the extreme close-up indicates villainy or intimacy.[29] Bosnians tended to be shot at a public distance, diplomats close up and personal—and often.

Fiske has written one of the most detailed accounts of television conventions, including an excellent example of how technique shapes message in a discussion of labor and business leaders. He views the TV anchor, whom Paletz and Entmann consider a reassuring figure, as the author of TV news, and he sees filmed segments and interviews as games that invite the audience to contradict and disagree. Because it is highly ritualistic and structured, TV draws attention to its constructive nature through graphics, electronic effects, and conventions specific to it. If soaps deal with fiction and cast reality in a feminist frame, and the news deals with fact and tells masculine stories that impose order on the culture, then Bosnia was both a soap opera and an adventure flick.[30]

Fiske thinks that television uses paradigmatic and syntagmatic semiotic axes to control its texts. The first selects and categorizes, the second combines and recasts as narrative. Newsworthy events must be recent (no more than twenty-four hours old) and concern the elite (those who fill important social roles and are familiar to the audience). They may be negative and surprising. The news is "masculine" in that it is public and complete, and it views events abroad differently than those at home. Yugoslavs suffered from being identified with the Third World, a place of famine, natural disaster, social revolution, and political corruption. This worldview confirms our superiority and enables the media to exaggerate conflict abroad but play it down at home.[31]

If our media reflect our culture by applying a double standard that defines the norm in the Balkans as genocide and political instability, then the ethnic cleansing of masses of Bosnians would be considered normal by most Western observers and reporters. Such an approach would be congruent with the media's depiction of elections and atrocities in U.S. client states differently from those in states perceived as hostile or indifferent to U.S. ideals.[32]

Like fictional TV, the news represents dominant individuals and groups as performing positive actions. Subordinates are deviant and negative; conflict is the norm and has specific functions to help the story along. News stories mediate the real using conventions, and reporters fill in local details for preconceived news stories. Live coverage is used because it validates the transparency fallacy by making stories seem depictions of reality rather than conventional mediations of reality. Yet television remains a filter and its representations of reality are far from transparent. Nor are they objective. Television news has a high modality; it depicts reality in an indicative mood that makes sense of things by embedding data in reassuring contexts. News reports actually discourage analysis and critiques of societal systems to the extent that they imply problems can be solved reasonably.[33]

If this is true, part of the moral paralysis that pervaded the West was due to the media's inability to represent reality in anything but conventional ways. The constant reiteration by the media that peace plans— which were really partition proposals that validated territorial and demographic shifts gained through military action and genocide—were the only way to resolve Yugoslavia's endemic violence left the public frustrated, passive, disappointed, and angry with all of the "warring parties." Feeling guilty because we could not act, we justified inaction by blaming the victims of aggression and genocide. The displacement of past emotions onto current events also left us confused. If Croatia seemed the victim, pity for its plight was neutralized by our empathy for the Serbs, who had suffered under the Croats during World War II.[34]

Disruptive or inconvenient events, like the discovery of Serbian death camps or the stubbornness of Croatian and Bosnian military resistance, were welcomed as surprises, then redefined and explained by reinserting them within the dominant value system, a technique that Hartley and Fiske refer to as clawback. TV masks its construction of news and reinforces the illusion of objectivity and transparency by the apparent authenticity and the immediacy of reports that feature interviews, visual images, and an omniscient and objective news reader who links them all and operates in real time. The apparently instantaneous nature of TV news gives the impression that the events represented are immediate and real, not mediated by the use of numerous conventions and the careful editing of both videotape and newscript.[35] We therefore thought we knew what was happening in Yugoslavia, but we only knew what reporters told us was happening—and that wasn't much, because most could not get to where the action really was.

It is not surprising that some theorists think TV informs less than it inoculates the body politic against dissident and radical voices by mediating and distorting them in the news. The South Slavs were such voices. Their reality depended on how they were portrayed relative to other groups and to each other. By carefully selecting individuals, groups, and events to represent complex realities, and by appealing to common sense and using stereotypes, the media recreated a familiar Balkans.[36] The region again became a synonym for political chaos and assassination that could be resolved only by outside intervention because Balkan peoples are too primitive and hot-blooded to resolve conflict rationally. Resolution thus became our job, and the American public reluctantly concluded that short of a massive intervention by the United States, nothing could be done. When the Western media looked at the Balkans, it applied its codes to signs embedded in eastern European realities. The result was confusion.[37]

Nor were appeals to scholarship or history useful, in part because television blurs the distinction between reality and fiction, in part because TV news engages in a narrative that seeks to reestablish a state of equilibrium and reassure the viewer that resolution is possible only within certain ideological parameters. Television presents events through the actions of individuals and groups, recast as heroes or dangerous characters, whose stories become stock fictions that journalists can then appropriate.[38] The fundamentalist Bosnian Muslims and the neofascist Catholic Croats became Chevalier's *dangerous classes*, and the Serbs, posing as our former allies, enjoyed a benevolent historical stereotype.

The more objective and concrete the news story, the more authoritarian. Because it presents multiple plots and characters, because it repeats and creates the familiar, and because a story's closure is temporary and superficial, the news becomes a "repetition of the problematic," much like fictional soap operas.[39] The difference is that while women watch the soaps, which treat domestic problems, men watch the news, which deals with the real world.

Sharon Sperry's analysis of TV news as narrative reinforces Fiske's observations. The news is the first prime-time show in most locales, and it comprises narratives using the hero plot. There is no analysis because the aim is not to convey meaning or aid understanding, but to engage and hold the audience emotionally. The story is the same as most others during prime time. A small cast of regular characters has a clearly identifiable protagonist, like David Owen, and an obvious antagonist, like the fascist—and usually stupid—Croatian leader, Tudjman, or the devout, but slightly befuddled and occasionally recalcitrant, Izetbegović.[40] There is a conflict and plenty of action, the problem underlying the conflict is identified and resolved, as Milošević reveals himself to be a good guy and the white knight Holbrooke arrives to right matters. The world now returns to normal as good prevails, thanks to the U.S.A.

The problem with such a presentation is that the world is not so orderly, and while the anchorman may appear omniscient, omnipresent, and omnipotent, his studied objectivity frustrates emotions excited by the story by conveying the cognitive realization that nothing has been resolved. The viewer is left impotent and angry. The viewer may know more, but not even his emotional response can be clear-cut, owing to the fast pace of the news, the lack of cues encouraging action, and the attachment of past emotions to current realities. There are just too many conflicting emotions to deal with. So we develop coping strategies, from avoidance to addiction to raw information, to reordering the modality of the news from real to fictive.[41]

Michael Robinson considered a *videomalaise* the result of the introduction of nightly news in the 1950s, because any increase in information creates anxiety and because dependence on TV for news correlated to an individual's confusion and estrangement from the political process. Television created an inadvertent audience within a mass audience at the same time that it weakened the role of the opinion leaders that Katz and Lazerfeld thought mediated the news for the public. If Soley's news shapers have appropriated the latter's role, Fallows's punditocracy has recast politics as farce. The net result has been a feeling of alienation and impotence in the audience.[42]

If information overload trivializes reality and paralyzes the audience, then a major contributor to that paralysis is CNN (Cable News Network), created by Ted Turner in 1980 and now in 53 million American homes and over 100 foreign countries. CNN maintains 18 bureaus abroad and is definitely a player in the international arena. But its news is usually reduced to headlines, and even its segments rarely run more than three minutes.[43]

There is therefore a partial explanation for our easy acceptance of the breakup of Yugoslavia and the subsequent genocide on its territories, despite increasingly frequent television newscasts of emaciated inmates, dead bodies, outraged eyewitnesses, frustrated human rights activists, and concerned politicians and diplomats. Television presented events in the Balkans as a continuing drama about an area of the world far removed from our realities and standards, with stereotyped and depersonalized actors who served as metaphors for realities too complex to analyze participating in a bloody conflict that was a cliché for the region itself. The image of a Balkan peninsula more or less permanently engaged in some form of genocide was reinforced by interviews with official spokesmen, whether U.S. secretaries of state, the head of Pale's government, or UN officials, who mediated reality more than they sought peace and who presented whatever the official line regarding the area might be. Their job was to take care of the mess. Our job was to cheer them on.

Nor would more quality programming on PBS have helped.

Ostentatiously distinct from the commercial channels, PBS and NPR are actually on a short leash because both depend on the government, corporations, and a narrow, middle-class segment of the population for funding. The result is nonrisk programming. *All Things Considered* is decidedly mainstream, with conservative commentators like Cokie Roberts; the *MacNeil Lehrer Newshour* is an insiders' show with a very restricted guest list of the movers and shakers in Washington. Both shows tend to present both sides, not all sides, so both fail the ethical test of completeness. Like many of the talk shows on C-SPAN and PBS, *Washington Week in Review* is boring and unimaginative, a conversation among insiders. In contrast, *The McLaughlin Group* makes a fetish of being aggressively partisan, purposely snide, and inordinately superficial. They do not even attempt to be ethical or balanced, except in the most vulgar meaning of the terms. Funded by GE, the show reflects the extremely conservative agenda of its benefactor.[44]

GE also controls NBC, while the boards of directors of the three major networks are riddled with CEOs and powerful lawyers, as are such publications as the *New York Times* and *Fortune 500*.[45] In other words, it is unlikely that the elites running PBS or NPR would challenge official policies, and *MacNeil-Lehrer* proved one of the most bully pulpits for D.C. officialdom during the conflict.

In March 1994, PBS ran "Sarajevo: The Living and the Dead," which its author hoped would make the anonymous faces in the news real so that we would all feel we had friends in the besieged city. But the show's anecdotal nature invoked pity without purpose; its presentation of the war as routine was a call to resignation, not action. A nurse thought ethnic states stupid; a former literature student could not understand why her friend was shooting people for 500 DM a pop; the chief surgeon at the hospital proclaimed life stronger than death after the birth of a baby; a Serb denounced violence; and a two-year-old corpse was named. The viewer was led to see Sarajevo as a laboratory experiment calculated to demonstrate that anyone could be broken. A main character was killed after marrying his sweetheart, who was left widowed and pregnant. The final image was of a Serb in Serbia learning to walk with a prosthesis and repudiating Karadžić and Mladić.[46]

What had the viewer learned? That the Serbs were also victims of the war? That some Serbian leaders were bad men? That some people were optimists, others resigned pessimists? Without social structure, without politics, there was no context other than the backdrop of the shattered city, tragic and meaningless. Only the personal and the anecdotal remained. The show triggered tears, frustration, and anger, not action.

In May, PBS aired "Romeo and Juliet in Sarajevo," the story of the death of a Muslim girl and her Serbian boyfriend. With vengeance, duplicity, and hatred as themes, drama again overwhelmed meaning. Because hatred was ubiquitous and the lovers died in a no-man's zone, everyone and no one was guilty. The girl's father saw their deaths as proof that love was impotent against those who expressed "love and hatred" through a bullet, and her mother could only hope "that the madness [would] stop."[47]

As drama the show was wonderful. As news, it meant nothing. Perhaps that was the point. Perhaps all efforts to analyze violence are futile. Perhaps we feel impotent and apathetic because we are the mass audience, isolated in our homes, viewing the affairs of the global village but participating in life only as statistics in a poll. We don't feel, we reminisce. Repeated images of death merely dull our moral sense, as Beccaria thought executions did. If the media have become life, life has become "a stylized edited media event" in which journalists hawk dead emotions and current events as used-car salesmen hawk broken-down sedans.[48]

Or perhaps Baudrillard had it right, perhaps the media are "terrorists" who sell "fascination without scruples." Perhaps it doesn't matter. Perhaps the masses don't want meaning and enlightenment, maybe they don't want to be mobilized. Maybe all they want is "to be entertained before they die." If so, then all media is spectacle, and all spectacle is vacuous. "Media significance," as Tester concluded, "means moral insignificance."[49]

In seeing, we forget; in hearing, we ignore; in reading, we find only anecdote.

THE PRESS

It is worth recapitulating what the press and the tube have in common. News is a genre, and both media give current accounts of current events. They do so by using factual description and specialized workers in specialized organizations. Both stress melodramatic accounts and employ similar themes, formulas, and symbols. Both TV and print journalists meet deadlines, both ignore the complex and ambiguous in favor of the concrete and the particular, both share a similar ethos, both tend toward the faddish and the sensational, both mediate the events that they report, and their audiences prefer news to features.[50]

Of the differences between the media, the most basic is that whereas television operates in time, the press exists in space. TV stories contain ten times less information, but they are tighter, more organized, and unified, compared to a newspaper's chaotic pastiche of anecdote and data. TV stations have half the staff of comparable newspapers, and TV news treats the day's events as a whole and is more interpretive than the press. TV mobilizes its audience around a single vision of reality; the press tends to confuse its readers with a smorgasbord of data. TV foists its view of reality on the viewer; the paper allows the reader to create a personal reality by choosing among the items. TV is intensely visual and very personal, while the press is extremely impersonal.[51] TV dictates through redundant entertainment; the press instructs by displaying information. TV neutralizes its reports with noise; the press vitiates meaning by cramming so much unconnected information into its pages that making sense of any given subject over time is almost impossible.

TV and the press complement one another because they approach and report the news differently. Two-thirds of us mix the media, watching TV for a quick news fix, then reading newspapers and magazines for details and interpretation. We use electronic media for spot news of disasters and politics, because they provide easy-to-grasp, pictorial, dramatic accounts. But we go to print media for explanation and background. Newspapers generate the news and bind society together. They are the quintessential urban institution, just as TV is the perfect suburban medium. Because they integrate and carry a variety of specialized items, they are essential to those hooked on the news.[52]

Television, radio, and wire services report events, but newspapers and magazines interpret them by relating them to one another. TV influences by images, newspapers by their editorials, which about a fifth of a newspaper's readers read and approve, with agreement more likely the more remote the issue. Columnists are also powerful, and their opinions probably have as much impact as hard news. Print media are catalysts for conversation, so information and opinions on Yugoslavia were disseminated quickly, and the region's remoteness should have made editorials and columns more convincing.[53]

Television and the press sell a similar product, but they operate under constraints specific to their medium. While the press seeks out dramatic pictures that may be a single individual in a hackneyed pose, TV prefers action film. Format considerations are crucial, especially in TV where deadlines create routine formats. News media use short stories with pictures or film as appendages, even though doing so precludes complexity and reduces reality to story, myth, and legend. Placement is crucial, with stories toward the beginning of a newscast, first page, or main section getting more space and attention.[54]

News weeklies experienced a rapid growth in readership between 1965 and 1975, and by the early 1980s, they were read by 10 million Americans, twice the readership of city magazines like *New York* or *Chicago*, but about the same as *People*, the *Star*, and the *National Enquirer*. Most Americans therefore formed their opinions about Yugoslavia from watching the tube or talking to others. Opinions were similar because there is a lot of redundancy in the system. Like TV, local newspapers and national news magazines reflect the news put out by wire services and published in papers like the *New York Times* and the *Washington Post*.[55]

The dissemination of news by a few newspapers and wire services tends to homogenize its content at the same time that managerial influences have eroded personal and professional values. Agencies serve up similar items in similar ways, and news managers strive to maximize profits by cutting down on luxuries like investigative reporting. The major news services maintain relatively modest staffs, and a large proportion of their reporters are stringers.[56]

Formats tend to be stable. *Time* kept the same format from the early 1920s to the early 1970s, and TV stays with formats that attract audience. When formats do change, it is generally to obtain more audience share. Novelty is important, but is not synonymous with format change. News can be news to both journalists and audiences, and during the 1990s both rediscovered the Balkans. But excessive novelty is risky, and finding a logical framework for stories can be difficult. Consequently, reports of ethnic cleansing were treated gingerly, and Roy Gutman had trouble being heard owing to the excessive novelty of his stories, whose credibility was doubted because they did not fit into the media's current version of reality.[57]

If resistant to change, magazines and newspapers have tinkered with style and format over the past decades, tending to become more like *People* magazine, with emphasis on color pictures, boxes with special features and information, and other concessions to the technology and mentality of the computer age. But their basic layout is still much like that described by Gans in the late 1970s. Magazines print about fifty pages of news columns weekly, with narrative and still pictures. The front of the news magazine still deals with national, international, and business news; foreign news still takes a back seat to domestic; and the back sections are less serious.[58]

Newspapers have changed the mix of hard and soft news as formats shifted to attract audiences in the 1970s, and the percentage of news fluctuated. Domestic coverage still has precedence over foreign affairs, larger papers run more stories on international affairs than smaller ones, and local and state news gets the most attention.[59]

Local newspapers differ from their East and West Coast cousins in the size of their staffs, the percentage of newshole available, and their heavy reliance on the major dailies and the wire services. They display geographic, ethnic, and political biases associated with their readership and their location, and tend to be cosmopolitan if located in cities with sizable ethnic populations, like Chicago or Milwaukee. They are more likely to be owned by a large chain, to lack investigative reporters, and to be under pressure to maximize profits. Foreign stories are stored as soft news, and coverage is as homogenized as that of television.[60]

While national newspapers and magazines exercise a disproportionate influence on other news outlets, local papers have increasingly been taken over by chains, and special-interest publications have multiplied. Think tanks, which measure excellence by the relevance or ideological orthodoxy of a piece, not its intellectual rigor or creative insight, publish in-house journals which serve both to disseminate particular ideological positions and to establish and inflate the scholarly credentials of their employees, who then appear on TV or on the op-ed page of major newspapers as neutral experts.[61] This is also true of academics, whose journals are usually controlled by small groups and whose expertise is proportionate to the timeliness of their work.

Print coverage of events in the former Yugoslavia was more detailed, more sustained, and more analytic than that of the electronic media. While electronic media depend on newsmakers, those very players and officials who Bagdikian believed "issue a high quotient of imprecise and self-serving declarations," print media pay more attention to marginal actors and observers, and do so in more detail, because even the longest newscast has less information than half a newspaper page.

MacNeil-Lehrer ran the risk of becoming a mouthpiece for the current administration, *Nightline* of becoming a forum for a small clique of experts and authorities, and *CNN* of becoming a player in the diplomatic game.[62] All were superficial.

Surprisingly, so were many of the policy and academic journals. *Foreign Affairs*, which was edited by William Hyland, mirrors the opinions of conservative and elite organizations and institutions (CIA, NSC, CSIS, Carnegie Endowment, Kissinger and Associates). The periodical did run several dissident pieces, including criticism of Boyd's piece by such scholars as Norman Cigar. *Foreign Policy*, edited by Charles Maynes, also had elite and conservative ties (Carnegie Endowment, Harvard, IISS). A high percentage of articles in *Foreign Affairs* were by CFR members, an exclusive club of 2,500 that draws a third of its members from the corporate world. It also publishes scholars like Sabrina Ramet, but the main purpose of both publications is to serve as forums for policy discussion. In this sense, they complement the op-ed pages of the *New York Times* and the *Washington Post*.[63]

The *New York Review of Books* regularly published articles on Yugoslavia, most by Misha Glenny, whose bias seems to have reflected that of the periodical. Both the *New Republic* and the *National Review* were more catholic in their coverage, but the former adopted what might be termed a Yugoslav posture that stressed human rights and sought to apply an ideal standard to real events. *The Nation* was frankly anti-Croat and subtly pro-Serbian, an example of extreme Yugoslav nationalism also found in the writings of Bogdan Denitch, who wondered who would protect the rights of Yugoslavs. The *Atlantic* was objective, and *Commentary* and *Commonweal* moral but ambivalent. Publications like *Forbes* and *Fortune* ignored the war, and the news magazines followed the lead of the newspapers. The *New Yorker* provided the best and most varied coverage with pieces by a variety of authors, including Rieff and Newhouse.

No medium and no publication passed the ethical tests of fairness and completeness.

NOTES

1. David Buckingham, *Moving Images: Understanding Children's Emotional Responses to Television* (Manchester: Manchester University Press, 1996), 49, 177–83. Todd Gitlin, "Prime Time Ideology: The Hegemonic Process in Television Entertainment," in Newcomb et al., *Television*, 507–29, for the use of format, formula, slant, and character to control the contents of programming and the responses of the audience; Tester, *Media Culture*, 94, 96–97, for Ignatieff's assertion that images mean nothing. There is no moral message. So a picture of a starving child moves me only to reach for a potato chip.

2. George Comstock, "Television and Human Behavior," and Peter H. Wood, "Television as Dream," in Adler et al., *Understanding Television*, 44, 46, 59–61; Bogart, *Press and Public*, 180; Isaacs, *Untended Gates*, 199; Tester, *Media Culture*, 98–100; Gruneau and Hacket, "The Production of T.V. News," in Downing et al., *Questioning the Media*, 284–85. TV has a highly visual quality, a highly symbolic content, a high degree of wish fulfillment, a high percentage of information that is disjointed and trivial, and materials from recent experience whose use is overt, disguised, and consistent. TV news is a political and advertising institution that tries hard not to offend the public.

3. Wood, "Television as Dream," 57–69. Ted Carpenter saw TV's content as "the stuff of dreams" and its form as "pure dream."

4. Douglas Cater, "Television and Thinking People," and Michael Novak, "Television Shapes the Soul," in Adler, ed., *Understanding Television*, 12–15, 21–22, for problems caused by TV's segmented, rapid, and dense programming. John Fiske and John Hartley, "Bardic Television," in Horace Newcomb, ed., *Television: The Critical View* (New York: Oxford University Press, 1987), 600–5, see TV as "bardic," a mediator of language standing at the center of culture and speaking with an oral, nonliterate voice to integrate the audience and report realities into the dominant culture by using myths expressed as conventions.

5. Tester, *Media Culture*, 96–97; Herbert Zettl, "Television Aesthetics," in Adler et al., *Understanding Television*, 134–38. The format of TV makes all pictures and stories only relatively important, and ephemeral as well, since stories change daily. Sound and images also form a symbiotic relationship that synthesizes meaning.

6. The viewer would also have to understand the visual grammar of television. Arthur Asa Berger, "Semiotics and TV," in Adler et al., *Understanding Television*, 97, 110–15; Gruneau and Hackett, "The Production of T.V. News," 285–86; Todd Gitlin, "Television's Screens: Hegemony in Transition," in Lazere et al., *American Media and Mass Culture*, 245–59.

7. Zettl, "Aesthetics," 130–31, and Berger, "Semiotics," passim. Whether talk shows can be analyzed using semiotics seems dubious because there seem to be no syntagmatic or paradigmatic (oppositional) structures, but they are ideal to the "now" medium.

8. *Nightline*, 6 April 1993.

9. *Nightline*, 4 February 1992, Transcript #3054, Journal Graphics.

10. *MacNeil-Lehrer Newshour*, 6 April 1993, interview with Joseph Biden; tape of Clinton, Milošević, Karadžić.

11. Zettl, "Aesthetics," 130–33; Fiske and Hartley, "Bardic Television," 604–12. TV is well suited for character development, but it lacks stability, soaps must remain unresolved, and resolutions are all simple-minded.

12. Novak, "Television Shapes the Soul," 22–26. Annabelle Sreberny-Mohammadi, "U.S. Media Covers the World," 302–5, sees TV as an ethnocentric medium that deals in cultural mythology and analyzes events abroad in simple stereotypic clichés. Thus coverage of the Iran hostage crisis failed to analyze Shi'ism or discuss Iranian history. Instead, it told a human interest story in which good guys faced down bad guys in a "political soap opera" about a menacing world where Americans needed to stand tall and hang tough. Bosnian coverage was similar.

13. Novak, "Television Shapes the Soul," 21–22, 32–33. Cater, "Television and Thinking People," 14–15, thought TV evokes, but does not inform; he quoted Tony

Schwartz, who saw truth as "a print ethic, not a standard for ethical behavior in electronic communication." Wood, "Television as Dream," 61, believed the tube's "brief and nonlinear visual images invoke—and also evoke—a great wealth of familiar and often current material stored in the viewer's mind."

14. Novak, "Television Shapes the Soul," 26–33, Comstock, "Television and Human Behavior," 43; Bogart, *Press and People,* 115–17. By the 1970s, 83 percent of Americans depended on TV, 68 percent on radio, and 70 percent on the newspapers. Weekdays, 25 percent combined all three as news sources. About 20 percent used TV and papers, 10 percent only TV, and 12 percent only papers.

15. Gerbner et al., "Charting the Mainstream: Television's Contributions to Political Organizations," passim. Tichi, *Electronic Hearth,* 61, sees TV as domesticating reality. The children in Buckingham, *Moving Images,* 185–86, 191–93, saw suffering as sad but inevitable, and were offered no cues by TV regarding how to help.

16. Cater, "Television and Thinking People," 15–16; George Comstock et al., *Television and Human Behavior,* 37–48, 385–92, 440–42. The literature before 1978 indicated that the "null" hypothesis had given way to conclusions that viewing television violence *either* increased aggressiveness *or* a third variable determined the effect of doing so. Buckingham's subjects in *Moving Images,* 197, 201, 240, distinguished fictional from real violence. Desensitized to the former, they were upset by the latter because they could not use cues to deconstruct or shift its modality.

17. Tester, *Media Culture,* 101, thinks TV desensitizes the viewer. "What exactly would Europe be about," he mused, "if it was not able to prevaricate over a response to mass rape in Bosnia." Zettl, "Aesthetics," 132, worried that TV would create a crowd without individuality or judgment, whose collective mind could be easily manipulated.

18. Comstock et al., *Television and Human Behavior,* 393–47; Zettl, "Aesthetics," 133–38; Berger, "Semiotics," 103; Goffman, *Interaction Ritual,* 42–43, 116. Our place in the ritual order was not to act; our proper involvement was to let the diplomats resolve things. Both the United States and American viewers certainly appeared to be trying to save face.

19. Put another way, "The media make us lazy cowards," and ignorant too. In essence, we lose our individuality and we view events in isolation. Tester, *Media Culture,* 108. The public was not informed of the slaughter in Croatia, merely told that ethnic cleansing was occurring. Even "activist" children in Buckingham's *Moving Images,* 191–93, 228–29, felt powerless to affect issues, whether foreign wars or neighborhood crime.

20. It is, of course, possible, especially given polls that indicate the decision not to vote is a decision to protest the system, that viewers simply decide to act by not deciding. Tester, *Media Culture,* 103–4.

21. Buckingham, *Moving Images,* 228–38, suggests that children find shows such as *Crimewatch* and *Cops* "too real" to enjoy, and thus watch them to get information.

22. Tester, *Media Culture,* 101–3. If audiences build up a tolerance to morally outrageous news and become morally exhausted and weary, TV's format trivializes, confuses, and edits out certain data. For the viewer, this means that if the headline is Ethiopia, Ethiopia is a problem. If Bosnia makes headlines, Africa cedes its place in the public conscience to the Balkans. Buckingham, *Moving Images,* 184, 199, 203–4, suggests an ambivalence toward the news and a desire to know all the gory details to cope with reality.

23. Bogart, *Press and Public*, 156–57, notes that the public's interest in all stories waxes and wanes. Buckingham's subjects, *Moving Images*, 181–83, recalled incidents, not context. Bosnia was a war "somewhere" fought by "stupid adults."

24. Adler et al., *Understanding Television*; Comstock, *Television and Human Behavior*; Fiske, *Television Culture*; Hank Whittemore, *CNN: The Inside Story* (Boston: Little, Brown, and Company, 1990).

25. Gans, *Deciding What's News*, 3, 31, 112; Bogart, *Press and Public*, 176–78; Lichter, *Media Elite*, 148. Like other media, TV provides the why, how, who, what, where, and when, but in a condensed, highly stylized form.

26. Zettl, "Aesthetics," 114–15; Robinson, "Reflections on the Nightly News," 331–37. TV's biases are "subtle, generally unpremeditated, and nonpartisan." They include a thematic tendency to tell simple, interesting short stories with negative themes and lots of conflict; a bias against facts and quantitative data in favor of anecdotal, image-based news that specializes in the sensational and bizarre; and a preference for discussing implications and interpretations over analyzing data; an artificial balance that strives to present "both" sides, regardless of reality; and a federal bias that focused attention on the D.C. area and the federal government.

27. Lichter, *Media Elite*, 152, 156–57, 161; Gans, *Deciding What's News*, 3. Robinson, "Reflections on the Nightly News," 334–35, noted that TV news sought a counterproductive artificial balance, owing to the FCC, which breaks reality into dichotomous relationships.

28. Paletz and Entman, *Media*, 9; Lee and Solomon, *Unreliable Sources*, 19–23. About 70 percent of weekday stories are duplicated on two of the three networks. The *Times*, the *Post*, and AP influence national and local media. AP serves 1,400 dailies and 6,000 TV and radio stations.

29. Tuchman, *Making News*, 12–15, 109–19; Fiske, *Television Culture*, 4–8, 105–7, 149; Berger, "Semiotics," 110. The six distances are intimate, close personal, far personal, close social, far social, and public. There are about fifty standard shots used to show "representational facticity," including the use of easily identifiable, symbolic locations, events to express activity, and people to represent other people (e.g., the White House press secretary to represent the president, or the State Department spokesperson to represent the Secretary of State or U.S. foreign policy).

30. Paletz and Entmann, *Media*, 23–24; Fiske, *Television Culture*, 236–39, 281–83, 284–85; Hal Himmelstein, "Television News and the TV Documentary," in Newcomb et al., *Television*, 261–71. Buckingham, *Moving Images*, 210, 301–16, would disagree. His kids saw the news as real, not fictional, and he criticizes Fiske for conflating the two genres.

31. Fiske, *Television Culture*, 283–85; Berger, "Semiotics," 92–107, as preparation for reading Fiske. See Gross et al., *Image Ethics*, 24–29, 238–47, for problems depicting marginal groups.

32. For a full discussion of this double standard, see Herman and Chomsky, *Manufacturing Consent*, passim.

33. Fiske, *Television Culture*, 286–88, follows Hartley (1982) in separating hard from soft news stories and seeing categories as "normalizing agents" that embed facts in a grid and make ideological choices appear to be natural.

34. Stjepan Meštrović, ed., *Genocide after Emotion: The Post-Emotional Balkan War* (London: Routledge, 1996), 12–22.

35. Fiske, *Television Culture,* 288–90. Clawback uses both material and symbolic space. The "news reader" iterates the objective discourse of "truth" within the central space of the studio, the reporter mediates reality and truth for the news reader, and the eyewitness, spokesman, or videotape of an event validates the reading and gives meaning to itself.

36. Fiske, *Television Culture,* 290–93, sees the news using metonymy (careful selection of people and incidents to represent more complex realities), metaphor, and cliché (convention in extremis). Such conventional metaphors as "time is money" can therefore be used to domesticate or repudiate inconvenient analysis or data.

37. Berger, "Semiotics," 105–6. Tacitly opposed to the negative images of irrational, chaotic, barbaric, primitive Balkan culture stood the positive ones of the rational, orderly, civilized, problem-solving West.

38. Fiske, *Television News,* 9–10, 292–302, for the essentially conservative nature of the narrative in TV news, its fictive qualities, its use of stereotypy to cast the actors within its stories, the idea that stories write journalists, not vice versa. On TV, white, male characters tended to survive in the early 1970s, others did not. Heroes are socially central types embodying dominant ideology, and villains and victims are drawn from subcultures and opposing ideologies. Morality is thus identified with social class.

39. Fiske, *Television Culture,* 303–7, for a fuller discussion of television texts and possible ways to read them.

40. Berger, "Semiotics," 99–105, for Propps's character functions, and Sharon Lynn Sperry, "Television News as Narrative," in Adler et al., *Understanding Television,* 297–306.

41. Sperry, "Television News as Narrative," 305–10; Meštrović, *Genocide,* 6–15; Buckingham, *Moving Images,* 182–85, 301–17.

42. Robinson, "Reflections on the Nightly News," 313–14, saw a steady ebb of public confidence in government and the onset of a malaise owing to the format of the shows and the increase in information they brought. The *Huntley-Brinkley Report* began in 1956, and the major networks went to half-hour nightly news programs in 1963.

43. Hachten, *World News Prism,* 51–53; and Whittemore, *CNN,* esp. 268–69. By the mid-1980s, CNN and Headline News were earning about $115 million annually, divided equally between advertising and subscriber fee revenues. Turner invested $80 million, while the three major networks were spending around $250 million each for their news shows.

44. Robert Cirino, "An Alternative American Communication System," in Lazere, *American Media,* 569. Lee and Solomon, *Unreliable Sources,* 84–89, for Robert MacNeil's comment that TV "does not enjoy rocking the boat, politically or commercially." Funded at a third the rate of Canadian public television, PBS was dependent on corporations to survive.

45. Lee and Solomon, *Unreliable Sources,* 75–82.

46. Radovan Tadić, "Sarajevo: The Living and the Dead," *Frontline,* PBS, 1 March 1994.

47. "Romeo and Juliet in Sarajevo," *Frontline,* 10 May 1994.

48. Postman, "The Teaching of the Media Curriculum," 426–28. Meštrović, *Genocide,* 17–18, noted Roger Cohen's remark in April 1995 that the world was weary of Sarajevo.

49. Tester, *Media Culture*, 117–30.

50. Paul Weaver, "TV News and Newspaper News," in Adler, ed., *Understanding Television*, 278–81; Bogart, *Press and Public*, 175, 212.

51. Weaver, "TV News and Newspaper News," 281–93; Bogart, *Press and Public*, 145–46, 208–10.

52. Bogart, *Press and Public*, 111–14, 147–48, 174–89, 262–63; Isaacs, *Untended Gates*, 217–18.

53. Bogart, *Press and Public*, 128–31, 168–70.

54. Gans, *Deciding What's News*, 146–81.

55. Lee and Solomon, *Unreliable Sources*, 19–23; Bogart, *Press and Public*, 152–53.

56. Gaunt, *Choosing the News*, 132, 136–37; Hachten, *World News Prism*, 45–53, 102. Of AP's 400 overseas staff, 100 were American in the early 1990s; the news service had 2,900 U.S. clients. Reuters maintained 115 bureaus with 1,200 reporters and editors to service 15,000 subscribers; UPI had only 450 employees with 3,000 subscribers.

57. Gans, *Deciding What's News*, 113–14, 163–71; Roy Gutman, *A Witness to Genocide* (New York: Macmillan, 1993), xiii–xvi, and his "Statement to CSCE Commission, US Congress," 4 April 1995, Bruna Saric, Croatian News.

58. Gans, *Deciding What's News*, 4 ff., 31, also notes a "gossip section" dividing the front and back.

59. Bogart, *Press and Public*, 150–52, 158–62.

60. Gaunt, *Choosing the News*, 63 65, 84–95, 103–6; Bogart, *Press and Public*, 142–43, 156–57, 160–62. Three-quarters of the dailies in the United States are owned by chains. As media groups diversified, the news was sacrificed to higher profits. News lost out to features, sports, and society pages.

61. Soley, *News Shapers*, 47–59. For example, AEI publishes *Public Opinion, AEI Economist, AEI Foreign Policy and Defense Review, Regulation*, and books, with the help of well-known experts like Jeane Kirkpatrick, Gerald Ford, David Gergen, and Philip Habibi.

62. Juan Señor preferred newsmakers to "armchair academic analysts," whereas CNN's Evans was more tolerant of academic types. Evidently, CNN dislikes having world leaders speak to each other via its broadcasts but can do little about it, and Evans believed that for someone like Karadžić, CNN was the easiest way to talk to world leaders. CNN has bureaus overseas and free lance staff in places like Zagreb to sort out "who's who, what's what, and who's believable." Telephone interviews, 16, 19, 20 July 1993; Bagdikian, *Media Monopoly*, 182–84.

63. Created in 1921 to shape foreign policy, the CFR (Council on Foreign Relations) has drawn half of its directors and two-fifths of its members from Ivy League schools (Harvard, Yale, Princeton, Columbia). Soley, *News Shapers*, 65–71.

4

Technique

FILTERS AND INFORMATION FLOWS

Gaye Tuchman defined the media as a social institution whose function is to distribute information and set the context for public debate by shaping and circulating knowledge, setting agendas, and forming the opinions of news consumers. Paletz and Entman believe that the media influence and insulate those in power from the public by shaping perceptions and setting priorities. Herman and Chomsky think the media do so by using filters to create a dichotomized view of reality made credible by a lack of alternate explanations, the use of authoritative sources, and a confident style.[1]

Their first filter is the cost of buying or creating a news outlet. Because only corporations or the wealthy can afford to do so, and because media are hierarchical, it is possible to set the media's agenda by appointing top management and controlling a relatively few major outlets. The second filter is advertising, which is essential to all types of media and serves as a subsidy for those that cater to audiences with significant buying power.[2]

This is especially true for television, which obtains all of its revenues from advertising, as opposed to three-quarters for newspapers and half for magazines. Like features, ads tend to squeeze out serious news, and they tend to undermine our sense of reality. They are open to interpretation, but they create realities with no context, inviting us to "strike a pose" and adopt the lifestyles associated with the products they urge us to consume.[3]

Cost limits coverage of foreign affairs. Because overseas bureaus are expensive, they are concentrated in hubs like London and Paris—or Sarajevo—and all media make extensive use of stringers overseas. As a result, perspective is distorted and most news is secondhand. Local media rely heavily on AP and UPI or on the larger dailies for foreign news. But wire services eschew analysis, so local media that use them get only the bare essentials and cannot give their audiences enough information to form an accurate picture of the world. With few full-time correspondents in eastern Europe in 1991, the media were poorly positioned to cover events.[4]

Sources are a third filter. News releases and official publications indirectly subsidize the media by reducing the costs of gathering the news, and beats circumscribe coverage. The fourth filter is "flak," or harassment of media that in some way offend elites. The fifth filter, anticommunism, no longer seems valid, but a combination of civic religion and ideological supposition limits what is reported. The result is a dichotomy in which two standards are applied, one for friends and clients of the United States, the other for enemies and aliens. The media thus distinguish worthy from unworthy victims, based on their political utility and cultural proximity.[5]

Isaacs also identified gatekeepers who limited information flows, and Gans discerned ten specific functions performed by the media in their management of the symbolic arena. They publicize events and actors; serve as intra- and intergovernment conduits; transmit values as moral guardians, prophets, priests, storytellers, and myth-makers; and act as economic, social, and political barometers.[6]

Fishman's description of beat reporting focuses on the constraints imposed by technique, while Gaunt deals with foreign news and the effect on its dissemination at the local level of managerial influences, professional and personal values, and intrinsic news characteristics. A major constraint is simply the space (newshole) available, determined in part by competition between editorial considerations and the need to run advertising. Technology tends to decrease staff, including foreign reporters, and to rush editing. Choice of news agency and syndicated copy is also crucial. Foreign editors have to fight for space, and local journalists tend to "pick and print," or "rip and read," wire service information.[7]

Because the media create leaders and use them to define movements, issues, and events, they can define, discredit, and rehabilitate groups by depicting their leaders in a certain way. Image thus becomes the ultimate filter the media use to define reality. To manipulate image is to manipulate the media. TV news programs simply ignore those whom the camera dislikes, because, contrary to common sense, cameras do lie, and quite regularly.[8]

Personalities, not ideas or issues, dominate the news. They serve as surrogates for other individuals, symbols for policies and events, and representatives of groups. Karadžić represented all Bosnian Serbs, their aspirations to self-determination, and their fear of Muslims and Croats; Tudjman became the symbol for Croatians and their history, including the most extreme examples of Croatian nationalism; and Izetbegović was the devout Muslim tainted by association with the mujahedeen. Their actions were generalized as Serbian, Croatian, or Bosnian, obviating the need to discuss the differences among members of the groups or analyze policies, events, or social processes.[9]

People and things familiar to the audience make up the bulk of the news. Those not readily identifiable tend to be dissidents or victims, so ordinary people, including those from the lower classes and minorities, do not find their way into the news.[10] There was no reason to expect in-depth reporting on Bosnians, who were victims, nor on the former Yugoslavia, because it was unknown to American audiences. After five years, only a few leaders are known in the West, and they are largely stereotypic creations.[11]

Because the media focus on action and disasters, coverage of Yugoslavia's breakup was intense. But the inability of most reporters to speak the language and get out of the major cities led to distorted, spotty coverage of a few locales and those who could speak English. Because the country, its languages, its history, its culture, and its politics were unfamiliar, reporters Americanized the crisis in Yugoslavia by applying themes and symbols used to cover domestic news. Even so, much of the war remained invisible because there were no domestic equivalents.[12]

The power structure, the social structure, and the political hierarchy of Yugoslavia were ignored in favor of easily manageable symbols like Ustaša (terrorists) and Chetniks (freedom fighters), a division that mirrored media conventions of good guys and bad guys. These were also World War II images and, if not familiar to the American public, they could be coupled with symbols like Nazis and the Allies—an old propaganda technique.

Coverage of villagers or the lower rungs of Yugoslav society was unlikely, because the U.S. media usually focus on the middle and upper classes. Assuming that reporters unconsciously applied domestic templates to foreign reporting, they would have distinguished public officials, such as Tudjman, Izetbegović, or Milošević, by their geographical provenance, ethnic background, and religious affiliations, not their economic position or social class. Anti-Catholic bias in the United States and Britain also may have shaped coverage, given theories linking the Vatican to Germany and Austria.[13]

The media conceive of the nation as an individual with its own will and feelings, so it was not surprising that they presented national groups in the former Yugoslavia less as actual or potential political entities than as individuals. Bosnia became a victim of its own poor judgment, Serbia a neurotic with admirable (freedom fighters against Nazism) and paranoid (fear of Croats and Muslims) characteristics. Because the media present the United States as "a conflicted nation and society," our view of Serbia was more sympathetic than that of Bosnia, which was torn by ethnic differences and not acceptable as an object for empathy; Serbia fit the image of a nation intending good but inadvertently doing bad. Croatia was simply a neofascist aberration.[14]

STENOGRAPHIC REPORTING AND PROPAGANDA

In real time actors cannot reflect on what they are doing or edit their actions, and in a real-time war, meaning varies by time, day, and source. Because events occur in real time, journalists cannot reflect and revise. Because they are not experts and because they seek to be objective, they risk becoming stenographers, uncritically describing events and repeating information supplied by their sources. In the Falkland Islands and Persian Gulf wars, the military sought to control access to information and the media sought to report directly from where the action was. Both journalists and the public were disappointed with the resulting coverage and criticized the use of pools and the CNN effect. But nobody resolved the problem created by reporting raw information or parroting sources whose information is carefully edited to make them look good.[15]

The media's regurgitation of raw and semidigested data hurt the Bosnians and Croatians. Most frames were supplied by American, UN, NATO, and EU officials. UN officials like Akashi and Owen were distinctly pro-Serbian, anti-Croatian, and anti-Muslim. Because Serbian sources dominated over Muslim and Croatian sources, their images and frames dominated as well.[16] The Serbians also tended to get their version of events out first and had access to major media through spokesmen like Milošević and Karadžić. Consequently, the language and frames employed by the media favored the Serbs, even if during election campaigns both parties used the Balkans as a club with which to beat the sitting president.

Merely by being professional, reporters legitimated official spokesmen and current policies in Yugoslavia. Their reporting was concise, detailed, and respectful. The use of titles and official language created illusions of authority for officials like Owen and analysts like Kissinger. Events seemed to be comprehensible if not predictable when explained by such authorities.[17] Interviews with U.S. and UN officials reassured the audience that everything was under control in the Balkans, and that the conflict was being contained.

The use of euphemisms like ethnic cleansing and techniques like clawback and inoculation to embed the outrageous and the radical in mainstream contexts tended to neutralize news at odds with the policies of the West and critical of the actions of Serbian leaders, and to damp down the horrors of war and make them acceptable nightly entertainment. But just as the media repeatedly explained the Serbs by bringing them back to the cultural center as the main actors, they cast the Croats and Muslims as deviant by making them peripheral actors, the victims and antagonists of Serb rebels and irregulars.[18] Limited sources, restricted information, and the indulgent attitude taken by Western elites toward Belgrade, Knin, and Pale tended to rationalize and validate Serbian policies and actions.

Reviewing propaganda techniques shows how reality was recast.[19] Name calling began almost immediately, with Croats as neofascist, insensitive, ultranationalists. Susan Woodward gave an example of how one associates glittering generalities with one side when she portrayed Milošević's concept of self-determination as democratic and Tudjman's as historicist. Reminders that the Serbs were our allies in World War II and pictures of Akashi with Karadžić were examples of transfer, the association of a group or individual with other groups or individuals. MacKenzie's remarks about the fighting qualities of the Serbs or the bad intentions of the Muslims were examples of testimonial; and Serbian leaders, like the hard-drinking, straight-talking Milošević, tried hard to parade as plain folks. Card stacking or slanting could be discerned in one-sided histories, selection of data, and discussions of the Croatian and Muslim, but not Serb, collaboration in World War II. And, of course, everyone was invited to jump on the bandwagon and approve a peace that ratified the gains of aggression and ethnic cleansing.

NEWS PEGS, FRAMES, AND STEREOTYPES

Because news does not keep and consumers are fickle, freshness is mandatory, but the boring, siegelike nature of the war in Yugoslavia often left the media indifferent. Interest peaked during peace missions, then rapidly fell off as they faltered. The quest for novelty reduced human sufferings to a clever story angle, film montage, and metaphor; the news often seemed supercilious precisely because reporters tried to craft clear and simple stories illustrated by dramatic film footage or photographs.[20]

Reporters use extremes because they are clear and dramatic, so they often present only two sides of a story. Balance eschews the moral implications and qualitative aspects of data, which are reported only if verifiable.[21] In November 1995, John Pomfret achieved a perfect, but misleading, balance that made Serbian aggression morally equivalent to Croatian reactions to it when he reported that the peace treaties signed at Dayton had ended the dreams of Milošević for a Greater Serbia *and* of Tudjman for a Greater Croatia.[22]

Reporting is stylized, not analytic. Narratives are coded, conventional, and embedded in a given culture and society. By accepting conventions as believable, the audience allows the media to manipulate reality and limit inquiry by presenting societal structures as mysterious and substituting concepts for reality. What needs explaining becomes fact, and inconvenient data are excluded. Routine supports the status quo, and ostensibly factual accounts reinforce one another to create a "web of facticity" that confers meaning, assures credibility, and makes the media arbiters of knowledge about the world.[23] Without an alternative source of information about Yugoslavia, the news, no matter how badly informed or biased, was the only reality the American public had.

That reality was dramatic, because drama sold, whether as death camps, rape, or the siege of Sarajevo. The actions of the powerful were serialized as soap opera, with Owen, Karadžić, and Clinton in the leads. Stories skimmed over the surface of social, political, diplomatic, economic, and military realities; threats to the West became dramatic markers with happy, or moral, endings, as Western statesmen brought the "warring parties" to heel.[24]

In short, reality was superficial and ahistorical.

When journalists translate reality for the rest of us, they hang their stories on news pegs—familiar facts and symbols. Linking new news to old (a.k.a., history) makes it comprehensible, whether the links are events, symbols, individuals, or story clusters. News pegs simplify the story, but give the illusion of complexity. They assure familiarity by using analogy to make the alien and the exotic comprehensible, and they guarantee an emotional response based on the pegs used. They can also determine a story.[25]

News pegs operate within news frames that organize and determine which data will be included and which excluded. Frames are cognitive patterns that interpret, select, emphasize, exclude, and organize data. John Pomfret used a very popular news frame in December 1995 (the role of the West in establishing and maintaining peace) and three familiar news pegs (World War II, America's occupation of Europe after 1945, and bilateral pacts) to explain deployment of U.S. forces in Bosnia.[26] Two wars explained a third in Graff's report on 105-year-old

Fatima Malokus. Caught in the Goražde pocket in 1993, she considered the war in Bosnia worse than either world war.[27]

One of the most common frames was that of a brutal tribal war not amenable to civilized resolution. A symptom of ignorance in 1991, this frame proved popular enough to survive through 1994, when it was expanded to include events in Rwanda. Unable to decide whether the conflict in Bosnia was "ethnic or tribal," Donatella Lorch concluded that "long-simmering ethnic divisions" had led to a "brutal result for their rivals and little but international ostracism for their own people." This was, of course, a variation on blaming the victim. To support her interpretation, she cited an expert, Fouad Ajami of Johns Hopkins, who warned that the "detour towards ethnicity is totally ruinous" and the "tribal consolation is a false consolation." That Ajami's field is the Middle East was irrelevant. He was an established expert, and that was what was needed.[28]

That detour went around another frame that saw the Serbs as the founders and "binding agent" of Yugoslavia. Using this frame, John Tagliabue could see the "collapse of the [Serbian] center" under "nationalist" pressure (both Serbian and non-Serbian) as precipitating Yugoslavia's disintegration. When juxtaposed with the stereotype of the fascist Croat, it rationalized the actions of rebel Serbs united to defend themselves from non-Serbs. Serbs in both Croatia and Bosnia-Herzegovina could not "forget that in 1941 when Croatia last obtained independence, as a Nazi puppet state, 500,000 Serbs were slaughtered."[29] In two sentences Tagliabue distilled pro-Serb and anti-Croat stereotypes into familiar news pegs and frames.

Tribal warfare and world war came together in the assertion that the Yugoslavs could not "get beyond World War II, when ethnic antagonisms between Serbs and Croats led to mass slaughter."[30] Like war, religion provided useful frames and news pegs. It became normal to refer to Sarajevo's government as "Muslim-led," but not to those in Zagreb and Pale as "Catholic-led" or "Orthodox-led." Of course, to present the war as a Christian-Muslim conflict was to solicit the sympathies of Christians and Jews.[31]

A. M. Rosenthal was one of the few who used the religious frame openly. In two pieces in mid-1995, he complained that whereas "Serbian Christian murders and ethnic cleansing were fully reported by the UN and foreign correspondents . . . Muslim murders received less attention than they deserved." He later alluded to "Bosnian Christians" and "Bosnian Serbian Muslims," implying that Muslims (and Croatians) were apostate Orthodox Serbs.[32]

George Moffett and Peter Grier framed the crisis as a complex and insoluble Balkan problem by quoting "a former U.S. diplomat" who believed that after the cold war "foreign problems" were so "unprecedented in complexity" that "no simple answers" existed. This was especially true of "internal conflicts" in places like Bosnia, Somalia, Rwanda, and Haiti. Charles Maynes used a West Coast news peg when he noted that we were "dealing with the equivalent of the Los Angeles riots" in the Third World. Because no one is in charge of a riot, we could either let them "burn out" or send in troops "to stop them"—both "daunting choices."[33]

Roger Cohen compared "Balkan politics" to an "endless hall of mirrors" and Colin Powell wrote off Bosnia, Haiti, North Korea, Rwanda, and Somalia as intractable problems. "We're not sure what to do about these places," he said. When "it was good vs. evil, East vs. West, democracy vs. communism, you had an answer. Now you don't."[34]

In July 1994, Sir Michael Rose worried that both sides (sic) would reject a peace plan, so he proposed a "third option between war and peace," and a very British one—"to muddle along and sort of stand still." Of course, muddling along was both the classic British response to reality and, as he noted, "really going backward." By mid-1994, Clinton was desperate to be rid of "intractable problems" like Bosnia and Haiti, which by then served as reciprocal news pegs.[35]

Clinton's trouble was partly the result of his failure to win over the media to his point of view, partly to the Bosnian refusal to surrender despite Western pressure to do so, and partly to the Serbian refusal to stop cleansing their areas of non-Serbs. Clinton's problems also had to do with the realization by many Americans that something was again seriously rotten in Europe. Yet most reporters were not critical, and officials framed discussion and set the agenda in the media, which usually presented the United States as the key to a peaceful resolution of the conflict.[36]

But events in Bosnia punctured the frame of a noble America bringing peace to the world and evoked less complimentary frames. An April 1993 *Los Angeles Times* editorial ridiculed Bush's New World Order as impotent and compared Vukovar to Warsaw and Srebrenica to Vukovar. Milošević and Karadžić had "fascist designs," yet Britain, saved from the Nazis by foreign arms, refused to let the Bosnians arm.[37] World War II was a key reference point. All that was missing were an allusion to the Holocaust, a comparison of Bush's New Order to Hitler's (or an aside on the hubris underlying both), and a nod to those Allied war aims that created the UN to end war, protect small nations, and guarantee self-determination for all peoples.

The editorial portrayed the EC as impotent, dismissed airdrops as "a feckless effort," and rejected the Vance-Owen plan as "a license for further Serb violence in Bosnia." Yet it let the Serbs off the hook by blaming the EC for not intervening in time "to guarantee the safety of Serb minorities in Croatia and Bosnia and to foil the neofascist designs of Yugoslavia's Slobodan Milošević and the Bosnian Serbs' Radovan Karadžić at the start."[38] The implication, of course, was that Serb actions resulted from justified fears of their neighbors and the influence of a few bad local leaders—hardly a clarion call to right the world's wrongs.

THE PASSIVE VOICE AND THE NATURAL ORDER

Complaints that the West failed to act ignored the arms embargo, which was a powerful form of intervention. The West acted, but its actions were cynical, calculated to contain the conflict and force peace on the victims of aggression rather than punish the aggressor. Its preference for diplomacy and the media's focus on effects, not causes, made Bosnia a victim without a victimizer. If there is a link between coverage of crime and racial bias, then the anti-Arab bias of the U.S. media would have made the Bosnian Muslims unworthy victims.[39]

Using passive and impersonal language, and attributing events to abstract or occult forces, conceals victimizers and implies that victims are to blame for their plight or that their condition is natural, not due to human actions. The media define events abroad differently than those at home. They portray the Third World as a place of famine, natural disaster, social revolution, and political corruption. So tribal, genocidal warfare is viewed as natural to places that lie on the edge of our world.[40] This was especially true for Yugoslavia, which was largely ignored before 1991.

Language creates, frames, and defines as it describes. If not apparent, facts are culturally determined by the media, which maintain their own culture within a larger one. Like historians and political scientists, reporters use analogy and abstract language, often ignoring human agents in favor of institutions and impersonal forces.[41] By doing so, they mislead; they do not explain.

Lenard Cohen, an academic, used an impersonal construction in which abstractions replaced human beings as actors when he wrote, "Political tension, interethnic conflicts, and the delegitimation of the federation intensified during spring 1991 as hope waned. . . . "[42] In mid-1994, the AP combined impersonal construction with euphemism and special labels, when it reported that "Bosnia's minority Serbs started the war" when they had "rebelled against the Muslim-Croat majority's decision to secede from Yugoslavia." It noted that about "200,000 people are dead or missing."[43]

In July 1991, Chuck Sudetic reported that fighting "broke out" in Slovenia, apparently on its own. In 1992, Marko Milivojević used impersonal language and analogy when he observed that "as the war has expanded and as Serbia and Croatia have tenaciously contested areas of dispute, casualties and property damage have mounted rapidly." Everybody was a loser in a conflict that was "very quickly turning into a nightmare of a Balkan Lebanon."[44] The AP used grammar to reverse cause and effect by implying that the Croats and Muslims had provoked the Serbs to rebel. Fighting, it noted, had begun in Bosnia "after Muslims and Croats voted to secede from Yugoslavia, sparking a rebellion by Bosnia's Serbs." It also reported that around "200,000 people have been reported killed or missing.[45]

The piece noted that Serbia had helped Bosnia's Serbs to seize most of Bosnia, but did not mention genocide nor who had killed whom. The "Muslim" Delić got some space, the Serb Karadžić more. The piece ignored the Croats, but made the Serbs into victims defending themselves against an aggressive Bosnian government by reporting that a cease-fire was "in tatters, *largely because* of a recent government offensive against Serbs" (emphasis added).[46]

The AP was more accurate in June when it reminded its readers that the war in both Croatia and Bosnia had begun "when Serbs [had] *claimed* they were threatened by Roman Catholic Croats and Bosnian Muslims aiming to destroy the Orthodox religion" (emphasis added).[47] Yet this was poor history, because it depicted the war as religious in character. If religion was a key to national identity, it did not cause hostilities. Ambitious politicians and arrogant generals, not religious fanatics, prepared and initiated the conflict. But the AP reported that *the war* had created 270,000 refugees in Croatia, where 10,000 had died during "Croatia's war of secession from Yugoslavia."[48] Passive voice and bad history combined to blame Croatian victims of Serbian and JNA attacks for their own suffering.

The AP chose to ignore individuals in these reports, but their preference for personalities led the media to censure Mladić for war crimes and Major for stupidity. Of course, focusing on individuals obviates analysis just as the use of unnamed forces and impersonal organizations by academics diffuses individual responsibility. The UN, NATO, the Serbian political system, nationalism, and ethnic rancor take the fall for real individuals. If journalists trivialize, academics use abstract analysis to diffuse responsibility. The media's high modality and the academy's institutional authority and taste for theory both helped to decriminalize the victimizer and scapegoat the victim.

The siege of Bosnia, atrocities, and UN peace plans become part of a natural order. Few questioned the West's moral authority to act as an international policeman, although Almond showed that everyone should have. Nor did many reassess the role of humanitarian aid, even after Guskind noted that it only fattened victims for the kill. Media that derived their information from the world's elites and their institutions could not easily question either, and our assumptions about the West and Bosnia precluded certain lines of questioning.[49]

Samantha Power used grammar to diminish horror in July 1995 when she wrote that Srebrenica had been "emptied" of 40,000 Muslims.[50] Of course, what had really occurred was that Mladić's forces had expelled or killed the town's inhabitants. Everyone knew this, but the passive voice made the event appear essentially causeless, totally impersonal, and almost normal.

Roger Cohen used an abstract causation and the passive voice by noting that the "sudden outbreak of a European war" had caught everyone unprepared, and Kurt Schork of Reuters exhibited dead-level abstraction in July 1994 when he wrote that "fighting has continued" in Bosnia.[51] John Pomfret used impersonal agents when he reported a UN official's remarks on ethnic cleansing. "Massacres, torture and appalling living conditions," the official said, had "quickly depleted the number of detainees." The actors were Serbs, but the sentence identified no human actors, only victims.[52]

Nor were many works with scholarly pretensions much better. Woodward repeatedly ignores human actors, beginning with her claim that the "real origin of the Yugoslav conflict" was "the disintegration of governmental authority and the breakdown of a political and civil order . . . over a prolonged period." That, of course, is like saying food rots if left unrefrigerated. It does not say who left the food out. But this is typical Woodward, who writes that, within six months of Yugoslavia's post-Communist elections, "the country was at war." There was some sort of cause and effect at work, but not necessarily human agents, because "barricades were being erected" in Mostar and the bridge at Bosanski Šama "was being blown up."[53]

Woodward extended her preference for vague forces to history. "Political instability plagued" Yugoslavia before the collapse of world economic markets created a royalist dictatorship in 1929. Sixty years later, "as civil order deteriorated, constitutional challenges escalated, and competing declarations of sovereignty made unclear where federal authority lay." Who prompted such deterioration, who posed the challenges, and who undermined federal authority is unclear. Instead, "hostilities simmering" between two parties suddenly "become an open war" that "claimed 300 lives" as "fighting in Croatia worsened dramatically" in the summer of 1991, and "the war in Bosnia and Herzegovina"—not ethnic cleansing carried out by the JNA and Serbian forces—"created the greatest refugee crisis" since 1945.[54]

In addition to such obvious obfuscation, the passive voice can combine with euphemism. For example, John Pomfret argued that ethnic cleansing (a euphemism for genocide) had been less brutal in Žepa than in Srebrenica because the UN had helped to evacuate those who would have "disappeared" (another euphemism). As a UNHCR spokesman said, when "you know they are going to do it [ethnic cleansing], it's much better" to have "some independent eyes watching." For balance, Pomfret quoted refugees who said that Mladić had told them that neither Allah nor the UN could help them. "I am your God," he said.[55]

Whatever the reporter's intention, the result was moral confusion for the reader, who must conclude that Mladić lied, but that an impotent UN acted morally by helping those slated for extinction escape the executioner. What the reader was not encouraged to think, and was not told until much later, was that UN and U.S. officials knew that Mladić's forces were killing Muslims en masse and the UN understood that by evacuating them it was an accomplice to genocide, defined in part as expelling a people from the territory on which they live.[56]

Of course, one can also make things appear beyond individual control by speaking of institutions as if they were autonomous actors. NATO thus proposes and the UN disposes, while the United States sits helplessly by.

VICTIMS WITHOUT VICTIMIZERS

During the Yugoslav crisis, the media employed myth, euphemism, and epithet to describe events that it characterized or dichotomized in ways that created what media critics call preferred readings. This was crucial to the inability of the audience to make sense of what was occurring in Yugoslavia. It also amounted to taking sides because political power is in part the ability to put one's language into wide circulation and assure that the terms used to describe and define reality are consonant with one's ideological agenda.[57] In other words, it is possible to become a POW of an opponent's language, and in Yugoslavia all sides sought to capture the media.

If obvious, it is worth repeating that despite satellite hookups and minicams, the conflict in Yugoslavia was not live, but mediated. The media had difficulty gaining access to Serbian areas, yet they talked to and reflected the views of Western officials and Serbian leaders. Consequently, they reported *and exaggerated* problems in Croatian and Muslim areas, reinforcing the idea of a "moral equivalence" among the ethnic groups.

As noted previously, the media often reported atrocities without attributing blame, making the victim both an object of voyeuristic curiosity and somehow guilty because the victimizer was absent and the crime was associated only with the victim. The media became Barthes's disembodied eye, reflecting nothing but pure images. The consumer of those images became a detached, invulnerable observer, fascinated by bad luck and safe at home, far from where the action was.[58] If the U.S. media are degraded carnival, then coverage of Bosnia was a "diversionary gratification" that reassured us regarding our own decaying society.[59]

But one need not be a postmodernist or a Marxist to see a disturbing tendency by the U.S. media to present victims without victimizers. By focusing on effects rather than causes, the media covered Bosnia as they do rape victims in the United States. The rape victim is often depicted as having asked for it, just as Croatian "nationalists" and Bosnian "Muslims" were depicted as having provoked Serbian "minorities," "frontiersmen," and "rebels" by not properly placating them or by improperly upsetting them. If the rape victim enjoys penetration and cooperates in the rape, Bosnian Muslims also embraced ethnic cleansing and made war on both Serbs and Croats.[60]

To the extent that we come to view all parties as equally guilty, we cannot identify victim or perpetrator; to the extent that we dismiss genocide as horrible but natural, or view its victims as having provoked aggression by behaving in unreasonable ways (e.g., by not allowing the Serbs to have their own states in Bosnia and Croatia), to that extent we rationalize genocide and excuse aggression. That Serb chauvinists felt "provoked" because Croatians and Muslims existed was a measure of their racism, not evidence of insensitivity on the part of their victims. Serbian leaders and ideologues argued that their followers were justified in exterminating Croats and Muslims merely because they existed in areas that Serbians wanted. Such arguments are rationales for racism and bigotry, and they led to war and genocide.

BALANCING ACTS

Examples of balanced reporting and equal treatment of the "warring parties" are easy to find, and can take on a polemical edge. Dana Priest juxtaposed "average American" voices opposed to the deployment of U.S. forces in Bosnia with officials and officers in favor of American policy, and Charles Boyd echoed A. M. Rosenthal by claiming that "ethnic cleansing evokes condemnation only when it is committed by Serbia, not against them."[61] Dan De Luce cited both Croatian and Serbian media in his reports on Bosnia, but the point of view was overwhelmingly Serbian.[62]

In May 1994, a UN officer labeled the Bosnian Serb announcement that they would pull back 1.9 miles from Goražde as "a stepping stone to further negotiations." When the Bosnians pointed out that the Serbs were to have pulled their guns back twelve miles in April and had built bunkers in the meantime, Sir Michael Rose noted that both sides had prevented civilians from leaving their sectors and encouraged the Bosnians to "do their part." But doing their part would have left Bosnians disarmed while Serb guns stayed within range of the city.[63] Ostensibly equal treatment disadvantaged the Bosnians, who were asked to place their faith in a UN commander whose sympathies appeared to lie with the Serbians and media that privileged the views of that commander.

In July 1995, Stephen Kinzer reported the massacres of Srebrenica's defenders, noting that "ethnic cleansing" was "a tactic of Serb forces and to a lesser extent of their Croatian enemies." In one sentence he used a euphemism for genocide, inculpated the Croats (and thereby lessened Serbian guilt), and implied that Muslims were only victims.[64] Chris Hedges implied that Muslims took hostages and that UN forces had been anti-Serb by reporting that the Bosnians suspected the Ukrainians of having switched sides and were threatening to use them as human shields.[65]

Evenhandedness and balance led to reports that established an equivalence between Serb and Croat actions and implied that the Balkans suffered cyclical violence. When Serbs fled the Croat advance in western Slavonia in 1995, the *New York Times* reminded its readers that the Croats had fled in 1991.[66] Yet the two events were distinct. In 1991, the JNA had seized a third of Croatia and Serbian forces had then "cleansed" it of Croats, whereas in 1995, Serbians fled approaching Croatian troops, who were occupying areas legally under Croatia's authority. Zagreb's use of military force was not part of a cycle of violence, but the result of the failure of diplomats and UNPROFOR to persuade the Serbs in Croatia to observe the terms of the cease-fire concluded in 1992.

Similarly, in June 1995, Stephen Kinzer announced that both Muslims and Serbs were "losing confidence in the UN peacekeepers to protect them."[67] This was not quite as bizarre as it sounded, because UN forces in Croatia and Bosnia had protected Serbian territorial conquests and allowed ethnic cleansing of both areas by Serbian forces. The evacuation of Žepa in 1995 was equivalent to the refusal of UNPROFOR to protect Croats wishing to return home after 1991.

Evenhandedness led the media to publish obvious Serbian propaganda, like the letter accusing Croatian forces of committing atrocities in the Krajina in August 1995. The writer claimed that bad information in the media had helped Croats and hurt Serbs. If Serbs committed atrocities, the media denounced them as war criminals, but, he complained, if Croat and Muslims did so, their actions were all but ignored.[68]

Given how many letters major newspapers receive and how few they publish, the decision to print this one betrayed a policy of evenhandedness tilted toward the Serbs. What Safire called the "immoral evenhand-edness" of the West justified such crimes of commission and omission by UN forces, NATO, and the media, and it rationalized maintaining an arms embargo on both victim and aggressor.[69] Yet Safire himself gave an example of inadvertently slanted balance when he wrote that peace would be possible only after the "Serbs, Croats and Muslims [struck] a balance of power that makes aggression too costly."[70] Although arguing to lift the arms embargo, he cast all sides as potential aggressors by using a balance-of-power argument.

A more conscious example was provided by Thomas Friedman, who reported that Croats had also "been blamed for killing civilians, most of them [sic!] elderly or infirm Serbs who remained in the Krajina after it returned to Croatian hands."[71] This was, to put it mildly, a wild exaggeration based on unsubstantiated reports from dubious sources.

HARD NEWS AND SOFT

Much of the reporting on the crisis was soft news—the sort that keeps until needed for a Sunday op-ed page or a late-night talk show. Typical was a June 1995 piece by Roger Cohen, who interviewed bankers, peasants, and others in Sarajevo. His article was almost antianalytic, because the impression conveyed was that the war was "madness," a "non-human" and violent event that made no sense.[72] Or perhaps it was simply postmodern.

In March 1993, as thousands died in Bosnia, ABC aired images. Peter Jennings closed his special on Bosnia by musing that "most of us [would] go on debating," so he would leave his viewers with "twelve months of images." Whatever their emotional impact, the images were presented as an artistic film montage, complete with negative frames, grainy stills, and other tricks of the video operator's art. In May, *This Week with David Brinkley* accompanied Tony Birtley's reports "with some outstanding pictures."[73]

Given the centrality of images and their failure to generate more than a distant clucking of tongues in the West, it seems that news reports on Bosnia were merely interesting essays in the depiction of mass murder.[74] Televised images could no more convince the cynical or outrage the neutral than photographs of the Yugoslav tragedy, even though TV is a cool medium that demands viewer participation and photographs are hot and keep the viewer at a distance.[75]

Perhaps no one really cared. I recall a conversation with local TV journalists in Hattiesburg, Mississippi, following the taping of a show on Bosnia. None could understand why increasing television coverage had not led to action on the part of America and its European allies. I was also bemused. I still am. Yet the remark of a colleague at the University of Southern Mississippi throws some light on why the nightly news did not move people.

When I mentioned that Americans might be uncomfortable with the tragedy in the former Yugoslavia because we also had ethnic problems, he became angry and hissed, "Well, if we were like *you people*, then we'd be killing each other too, wouldn't we? Thank God, we're not." What he was saying was that he did not want to be reminded of ethnic problems at home, and he avoided this by drawing a sharp distinction between "you people" (my roots are Croatian) and "his people," with all that the distinction implied. He believed that "those people" deserved what happened to them because they were "those people," not civilized, rational Westerners, not Americans, but "aliens" in the most basic sense of that word.

Even so, soft news often pulls at the heartstrings. This was the case with the message from Žepa's mayor in late June. "Help us. Help this suffering people," the mayor pleaded. "Do not let the Srebrenica tragedy happen again." But Hedges set this plea in an analysis that Bihać was of more strategic importance for the Serbs than Goražde, noting that Western leaders in London had discounted Žepa and were trying to save 23,000 UN peacekeepers.[76]

A week earlier, Stephen Kinzer had interviewed refugees from Srebrenica. They told him that the Serbs had taken the women and done "bad things to them, and killed men the way you slaughter cattle." Kinzer portrayed the Serbs as "sinners" who might still be redeemed after they "seemed to have gone crazy, killing people with knives," raping women, and behaving as in "past *episodes* of ethnic cleansing"— a Serbian tactic and "to a lesser extent" a Croatian one too.[77] By defining ethnic cleansing as spontaneous episodic behavior common to Serbs *and* Croats, he mitigated Serbian guilt and reduced genocide to the status of atrocity. But the premeditated slaughter of Muslims at Srebrenica was no more an episode than the systematic terrorizing and expulsion of Croatians and Muslims from Serbian areas.

The performance of some journalists and editors was as uninformed and biased as that of some diplomats and statesmen was cynical and self-serving. The result was the devastation of Croatia and Bosnia, the destruction of a people, and the evisceration of the spiritual core of the Balkans. As one old Muslim who had lost his sons told David Rieff in late 1992, Bosnia was "a dead country, at least for Muslims." It had become "Serbian," and all that was left for the survivors was emigration to the West, which was not anxious to have them.[78]

As José Mendiluce complained, no one heard UN relief workers who tried to make the international community grasp the seriousness of the crisis in 1992. By the end of the year a moral paralysis had set in, despite televised images of Serb concentration camps. Cynicism and simple fatigue had reduced the war to an entertainment in which tolerant, secular Muslims were viable only as victims.[79]

For the media, this was good news because the crisis became attractive only after it degenerated into conflict with identifiable victims and villains, sensational crimes, and a delectable tension generated by the nightly expectation of more horrors to follow. The media could tell human interest stories and describe carnage and destruction, thereby transforming reality into tragedy. *Nightline* focused almost exclusively on the dramatic and the personal, on sensational soft news. This may have increased the cues that enabled viewers to turn information about real events into fiction, and thereby reduce their sense of horror and responsibility by balancing distress with delight and turning information into entertainment.[80]

Certainly, using soft news items ensured the show politically safe programs that could be broadcast any time, because soft news is personal, not political. It combined the virtues of domestic soap opera and the hard edge of masculine news.[81] On 10 June 1992, *Nightline* visited Sarajevo under siege, interviewing Milošević, Karadžić, Bosnia's UN ambassador, and columnist Anthony Lewis. On 4 August, it assessed the effect of war on Bosnia's children (a variant on earlier reports on the Lebanese and Central American children) with Ilara Zorić, Radovan Karadžić, and Mike Nicholson.

On 6 August, and again on 10 and 11 November, *Nightline* reported on death camps, Bosnia's "Hidden Horrors." On 2 December, it interviewed Elie Wiesel, who denied that anything comparable to the "Holocaust" had occurred, as did such publications as *The Progressive*; and on 29 December the program focused on the plight of the refugees. The late-night show opened 1993 with reports on "Rape as a Weapon of War" (14 January) and "The Children of War," (3–4 February).

If treating Bosnia as soft news proved appealing to television, the print media also presented events in the Balkans as soft news. John Burns, a *New York Times* reporter, regularly focused on the human side of the story. In October 1992, he reported that in a week 67 had died and 456 had been wounded in Sarajevo, but he focused on lack of adequate medical care and the destruction of the city's last flour mill by Serb artillery. Careful to note that precise statistics did not exist, he reported the Bosnian government's estimate of 127,000 dead or missing, 16,000 confirmed dead, and 129,000 wounded.[82] In effect, he was bringing his readers up to date on the latest developments in the Balkans soaps.

David Rieff's pieces in *The New Yorker* portrayed Bosnia as a "frightening place" that became "terrifying" after dark as both "regulars and irregulars" got drunk and took to the streets with their weapons. Balkan nights had peculiar properties that made it easy to settle scores and made "tempers flare for no particular reason." Terror was simply "the norm." Rieff, Guskind, and Sikorski combined thoughtful analysis with the stuff of soft news and such programs as *Hard Copy*. Rieff reported a Serb irregular gone berserk in Banja Luka, and Guskind saw the war as a grim omen, "a nightmarish glimpse into the potentially violent post-Cold War future awaiting many countries."[83] Sudetic and Sikorski depicted the war as fantasy or lighthearted comedy—Disneyland or a Cary Grant flick—as Croats played at war in Mazdas, with cellular phones and tailored fatigues. It was, Sikorski observed, as "if the war had come to Scarsdale."[84]

Even when trying to be serious, the media often ended up being entertaining, not analytic, oriented toward personalities, not issues. Issues were usually dealt with in interviews with newsmakers or by expert commentators examining what British and American politicians had said. The database was therefore both narrow and presented in a manner that precluded thought.

Marshall McLuhan believed that criticizing the media for doing this is pointless, because to "deplore the frivolity of the press and its natural form of group exposure and communal cleansing" is to "ignore the nature of the medium and demand that it be a book," not "a free entertainment service paid for by advertisers who want to buy readers." The ads purvey good news, and news reports relate bad news, but in a "mosaic," not as serious analysis, with slang and snappy language, not with serious commentary (save in occasional editorials), with the aim of involving and exciting, not educating or informing. News is what is in the press, but the press relates "a world of actions and fictions." It is "a daily action and fiction or thing made," a reflection of the community, not of reality, and certainly not an academic exercise! The media always try to please the public, not inform it, because it is the medium that counts, not the message. Anyhow, people tend to read what they already know.[85]

In August 1992, ABC recast the conflict in familiar oral and visual clichés usually associated with the Middle East when it aired a report that the Bosnians had used their mortars to kill their own people to get sympathy from the media, then described the suffering of the Serbs with a clip of a Serbian family wailing over a single male supposedly killed in the fighting in Bosnia.[86] In March 1993, Susan Stamberg interviewed Tom Gjelton, a journalist, who told NPR's listeners that Bosnia was worse than Central America, that he felt guilty leaving his "friends" in Sarajevo, that his role was crucial because the State Department only reported what appeared in the press, and that—after two years covering the crisis—thanks to Ivo Andrić's novel, he realized that hundreds of years of commingling had ended in Bosnia. Impressed with his professionalism, Susan thanked him for being so "vital and courageous."[87]

Two days later NPR's Linda Wertheimer and the BBC's Justin Webb discussed the "lifeless eyes" of the women and young children in Srebrenica. Webb had seen "the most appalling scenes" and wondered about the ethics of transporting people from their homes because it helped the Serbs, but he concluded that doing so was better than letting them die. Able to imagine only two alternatives, he avoided blaming the Serbs or the UN who aided them in cleansing Srebrenica of its Muslims.[88]

Black markets are always good copy, and Bosnia was no exception, as Carol Williams showed when she contrasted a thriving black market to the "hell" experienced by those unable to shop there.[89] A 1994 AP piece on the loss of hope and dignity suffered by Bosnians after the Serbs cut utilities for eleven days complemented such reports.[90]

Moina Farrow tried to tie Bosnia to Canada, the United States, and the Third World by claiming that the media "barely" noticed the plight of poor children in Canada or the United States, or the tens of thousands who had been raped in Bosnia and thirty-two "savage ethnic wars" elsewhere.[91] The AP got some good copy in 1994 by quoting a senior associate at the Carnegie Endowment for International Peace, who mused, "If the Cold War was dominated by ideological conflict, the fear is widespread that the 1990s mark the beginning of a new era of ethnic violence."[92]

In the spring of 1994, Jane Lampmann suggested that the refugee problem was a pandemic because since 1989, between 40 and 50 million people had been uprooted, about 1 in 125; of the 4 million driven from their homes in 1993, 2.6 million were from Bosnia, Angola, Zaire, and Azerbaijan. According to Roger P. Winter, chair of the U.S. Committee for Refugees, the right of asylum guaranteed in the UN Declaration of Human Rights was threatened by "anti-foreign, anti-immigrant, anti-refugee" attitudes in the West. Those governments that had previously "set the standards" now preferred to create "safe areas" for Bosnians and Kurds rather than accept them as refugees. As usual, things were muddied owing to the disappearance of the cold war and its clearly delineated East-West dichotomies.[93]

One of the more questionable and tasteless bits of soft news to emerge from the war was an AP release that implied that following a Serb "pullback" and four months of peace between Croats and Muslims, *some* Bosnians were getting fat, owing to inequitable distribution of food. Only the careful reader would have noted that, at most, some Bosnians had regained three of the twenty-two pounds they had lost during the Serbian blockade.[94]

NOTES

1. As an integral part of the political structure, the media favor its survival. Tuchman, *Making News*, 2–4; Soley, *New Shapers*, 23–24; Paletz and Entman, *Media*, 240, 249; Herman and Chomsky, *Manufacturing Consent*, 3–34.

2. Isaacs, *Untended Gates*, 42, 183–203; Schiller, "Informatics," 16–27. S. I. New-house saw papers as vehicles for ads. By the mid-1980s twenty-four transnational corporations dominated international advertising.

3. Bagdikian, *Media Monopoly*, 85–87, 117–70; Kellner, *Media Culture*, 247–52, 257–59.

4. Hachten, *World News Prism*, 60, 134–43; Fishman, *Manufacturing the News*, 91; Cohen, *Media Diplomacy*, 37–38, 175–76; Stephen Cassidy, *CNN*, telephone interview, 20 July 1993. In 1982 the *New York Times* spent $8 million annually for thirty-two full-time and twenty-five part-time employees in twenty-three bureaus, down from forty-eight full-time employees in 1968. It currently has thirty-two correspondents in twenty-six bureaus, with three in eastern Europe (Budapest, Moscow, and Warsaw). *Time* had thirty-five full-time employees overseas, *Newsweek* twenty-one, *NBC* seventeen, *ABC* and *CBS* twenty-two each. *CNN* maintained eighteen bureaus, but relied on stringers. The *Financial Times* had twenty-six full-time correspondents abroad, including fifteen in western Europe, and one in eastern Europe. Reuters had 84 bureaus with 566 staff and 1,000 stringers. Satellite time is also expensive. In 1991, an hour of INTELSAT time from New York to London cost $2,637, but this was cheaper than maintaining bureaus. Combined with hub bureaus, it allowed news organizations to maintain the appearance of covering, not just gathering, news abroad.

5. Herman and Chomsky, *Manufacturing Consensus*, 3–34; Fishman, *Manufacturing the News*, 16–18, 49–52, 85–88, and 210 for "bureaucratic affinity," the "cooperative relationship" journalists establish with their sources.

6. Gans, *Deciding What's News*, 290, saw TV as a "secular religious institution." Mattelart and Piemme, "Twenty-three Guidelines," 211–23, noted a transformation of film and TV in the late 1960s and a major concentration and diversification of "cultural industries."

7. Gaunt, *Choosing the News*, 117–22; Fishman, *Manufacturing the News*, 27–84.

8. Gabe Pressman believed the camera was "the most faithful reporter we have" and that videotapes and film "don't lie," but provide "a very real insight into people as they really are." Pressman et al., "Ethics and Television Journalism," 242; Gitlin, *The Whole World*, 157, 160, 171–72.

9. For how media create, exploit, and discard leaders, and the effect on both the leaders and their movements, Gitlin, *The Whole World*, passim. Also Lichter et al., *Media Elite*, 297; Tuchman, *Making News*, 121–24, 134.

10. Gans, *Deciding What's News*, 9–13; Novak, "Why the Working Man Resents," 112. Incumbent presidents can get up to 23 percent of the news, which is dominated by federal, state, and local officials, who account for up to 65 percent of those known to the media.

11. Tudjman's image as a neofascist was a stereotype publicized by Western wire services. Bulgarian papers use both AP and Reuters, and *Standard* ran a Reuters piece with a picture of Tudjman, his right arm raised in an apparent fascist salute against a background including Croatia's coat of arms and military officials. The caption

read, "Serbians in the Krajina do not want to be under Franjo Tudjman's government and have left their birthplaces." Davor Hudžić, "Serbs in the Krajina Suffer Fear and Misery," *Standard*, 16 August 1996; also "Tudjman Declares War on Serbs in Croatia," *24 Chasa*, 16 January 1995.

12. Isaacs, *Untended Gates*, 180; and Gans, *Deciding What's News*, 16–20. Editors favor foreign news that involves the United States. To discuss unfamiliar symbolic complexes, the media nationalizes them. The urban crisis became manageable only after it was properly defined. Some, like class hierarchy, power structure, and social structure, are ignored to avoid admitting that the U.S. economy is actually "dominated by oligarchies." Something similar happened in Yugoslavia regarding U.S. diplomacy.

13. Gans, *Deciding What's News*, 22–26. The U.S. media present four strata of society: the poor underclass, the lower-middle working class, the middle professional and managerial class, and the wealthy. The white-collar lower-middle class is usually ignored, and the blue-collar working class is elevated to middle-class status. The U.S. media have little experience with villagers or peasants, save in places like Vietnam, and they appear to have depended heavily on middle-class commentators, like Slavenka Drakulić, and middle-class stringers, who would be expected to be similar to their American colleagues.

14. Gans, *Deciding What's News*, 20–22, for U.S. image.

15. McQuail, *Media Performance*, 185; Hachten, *World News Prism*, 79, 154–65; Cohen, *Media Diplomacy*, 35–55; and Kellner, *The Persian Gulf TV War*, passim. Matthews, *Newsmen and National Defense*, esp. the essays by John Waghelstein on El Salvador; Fred Hoffman on Panama; and Sam Sarkesian, Richard Halloran, and Bernard E. Trainor on relations between soldiers and journalists.

16. Silber and Little, *Death of Yugoslavia*, focus on the Serbs and their point of view. Of sixteen illustrations, nine depict Serbian leaders, one Tudjman (who shares the frame with Milošević), and one Izetbegović. Serbs are also depicted in five pictures in control of Bjeljina, Dubrovnik, Kosovo, Sarajevo, and Vukovar. In their "cast of characters," forty-two are Serbian, twenty-eight Croatian, and seventeen Muslim.

17. Paletz and Entman, *Media*, 151–57.

18. For clawback, inoculation, stenographic reporting, and the ways in which the media construct reality, see Fiske, *Television Culture*, 281–307; Tuchman, *Making News*, 12–15; McQuail, *Media Performance*, 185–88; Farrel Corcoran, "Television and Ideological Apparatus: The Power and the Pleasure," in Newcomb et al., *Television*, 533–49.

19. The model is from E. B. and A. M. Lee in *The Fine Art of Propaganda* (Institute for Propaganda Analysis, 1939), cited by Severin and Tankard, *Communications Theory*, 103–17. Also Jacques Ellul, *Propaganda: The Formation of Men's Attitudes* (New York: Vintage, 1973); Harold D. Lasswell and James Wechsler, *Propaganda Techniques in the World War* (New York: Knopf, 1927); James Morgan Read, *Atrocity Propaganda, 1914–1919* (New Haven: Yale University Press, 1941).

20. Gans, *Deciding What's News*, 167–74, and Lichter, *Media Elite*, 26–7, 55; McQuail, *Media Performance*, 213.

21. Gans, *Deciding What's News*, 167–74; McQuail, *Media Performance*, 186–88, sees technology as having underscored the importance of technique and format.

22. John Pomfret, "Plan Legitimizes Years of 'Ethnic Cleansing,'" *Washington Post,* 22 November 1995.

23. Tuchman, *Making News,* 12–16, 86, 106, 109, 179.

24. Bogart, *Press and Public,* 173. Paletz and Entman, *Media,* 16, 18, 21, concluded "journalists define events from a short-term, anti-historical perspective; see individual or group action, not structural or other impersonal forces, at the root of most occurrences; and simplify and reduce stories to conventional symbols for easy assimilation by audiences."

25. Lichter at al., *Media Elite,* 28–29, 135, 143, 145, for descriptors and composites; Paletz and Entmann, *Media,* 188.

26. John Pomfret, "Between War and Peace: Seeking Justice in the Balkans," *Washington Post,* 18 December 1995. Gitlin, *The Whole World,* 7, cites Erving Goffman, *Frame Analysis: An Essay on the Organization of Experience* (New York: Harper and Row, 1974).

27. James L. Graff, "The Road of White Death," *Time,* 15 March 1993.

28. Donatella Lorch, "Sowing Wind of Ethnic Hatred and Reaping the Whirlwind," *Ottawa Citizen,* 22 July 1994 (CDN).

29. John Tagliabue, *New York Times,* 3 July 1991.

30. "Yugoslavs, United or Not, Need to Talk," *New York Times,* editorial, 28 June 1991.

31. "Tensions Threaten Macedonia," *AP,* 29 June 1994, noted that the Orthodox were "uniting" against the Albanians in Macedonia and seeking Serbia's help "to deal" with the Albanians. The article also depicted the Bosnian war as a three-sided Orthodox, Catholic, and Muslim conflict.

32. A. M. Rosenthal, "Why Only Bosnia?" *New York Times,* 30 May 1995; also his 2 June 1995 column.

33. George Moffett and Peter Grier, "Search for a Foreign-Policy Fall Guy," *Christian Science Monitor,* 12 July 1994.

34. Roger Cohen, "Balkan Leaders Face an Hour for Painful Choices," *New York Times,* 1 November 1995, "Powell Shares Pride," *San Diego Union-Tribune,* 30 June 1994.

35. Kurt Schork, "Major Powers to Present Peace Map to Bosnian Serbs," *Reuters,* 3 July 1994; Ann Devroy, "Christopher's Job at State Is Said Safe until End of Year," *Washington Post,* 3 July 1994.

36. Lee and Solomon, *Unreliable Sources,* 298–99, see this sort of thing as typical.

37. "The New World Order of Indifference and Impotence," *Los Angeles Times,* 17 April 1993.

38. *Ibid.*

39. Herman and Chomsky, *Manufacturing Consent,* for worthy and unworthy victims. Lee and Solomon, *Unreliable Sources,* 233–50, 286–87, for Parenti's link and the U.S. media's tendency to blame victims or show them without victimizers. Of fifty-two *Nightline* shows on terrorism from 1985 to 1988, forty-eight reported Arab (a.k.a. Muslim) terrorism.

40. Fiske, *Television Culture,* 284–85. Paletz and Entmann, *Media,* 216, 220–21. A quarter of Latin American coverage concerned natural disasters, compared to 1 percent for western Europe, which got nine times the overall coverage.

41. For discussions of how language shapes perception and how perception is variously expressed through the languages of different cultures, see Barrington

Nevitt, *The Communication Ecology* (Toronto: Butterworths, 1982); Erich Fromm, D. T. Suzuki, and Richard De Martino, *Zen Buddhism and Psychoanalysis* (New York: Harper and Row, 1970), 1–10; Edward T. Hall, *The Hidden Dimension* (Garden City, NY: Doubleday, 1966), and *The Silent Language* (Garden City, NY: Doubleday, 1973).

42. Cohen, *Broken Bonds*, 200, 206, saw "mounting tension and military presence" in Serb areas as demonstrating "*how* the 'Serbian question' . . . had become a major impediment" to a compromise of any sort.

43. "Serbs Attack Government Forces," *AP*, 1 July 1994. Alison Smale, "War Appears Likely in Balkans," *AP*, 27 June 1994, concluded that after years of "fighting that has claimed more than 200,000 lives," peace seemed unlikely. "Bosnia Truce Growing Shaky," *AP*, 17 June 1994, identified no agent for the dead in Bosnia.

44. Chuck Sudetic, *New York Times*, 3 July 1991; Milivojević, "The Armed Forces of Yugoslavia," 79.

45. "Bosnian Serbs Test Russians," *AP*, 20 July 1994. Denitch, *Tragic Death*, 4, saw Croat "nationalists" as picking a fight with Serb "frontiersmen."

46. "Serbs Attack" *AP*, 1 July 1994, and "Many Ignore Bosnia Cease-Fire," *AP*, 24 June 1994, which reported that "Fighting surged in northern Bosnia Friday, further eroding a two-week-old cease-fire."

47. "Tensions Threaten Macedonia," *AP*, 29 June 1994.

48. "Tudjman Could Come Out Fighting," *AP*, 29 June 1994, quoted Ivo Banac, who was undoubtedly correct in seeing Tudjman's rhetoric, like his taking of the Maslenica bridge in 1993, to be a campaign tactic. The point is that the media did not report Milošević's bellicose rhetoric in a similar manner.

49. Lee and Solomon, *Unreliable Sources*, 184–95.

50. Samantha Power, "Bosnian Serbs Strike at Second Safe Area," *Washington Post*, 15 July 1995.

51. Like much reporting on the war, dead-level abstractions stick at one level. Severin and Tankard, *Communications Theories*, 58. Roger Cohen, "U.N. Mission in Bosnia: A Painful Lesson in Limits," *New York Times*, 20 December 1995; Schork, *Reuters*, 3 July 1994.

52. John Pomfret, *Washington Post*, 22 November, 18 December 1995.

53. Woodward, *Balkan Tragedy*, 15, 17–18.

54. Woodward, *Balkan Tragedy*, 23, 139–40, 146–47, 173. Stokes et al., "Instant History," 144–47, praise Woodward and Lenard Cohen.

55. John Pomfret, "Serbs Drive Thousands from Žepa Enclave," *Washington Post*, 27 July 1995.

56. BIF Bulletins # 044 and 045, Elizabeth Neuffer, 19 May 1996.

57. Robert Stam, "Mikhail Bakhtin and Left Cultural Critique," in E. Ann Kaplan, ed., *Postmodernism and Its Discontents: Theories, Practices* (New York: Verso, 1988), 116–28. Journalists help officials shape language by narrating it to a "stammering infantilized populace."

58. Arthur Kroker and David Cook, *The Postmodern Scene: Excremental Culture and Hyper-Aesthetics* (New York: St. Martin's, 1988), 73, 278–84; Goffman, *Interaction Ritual*, passim. If, as audience, we are merely voyeurs, then we all were guilty, and everyone in Bosnia must have been guilty too.

59. Stam, "Mikhail Bakhtin," 134–38.

60. Lee and Solomon, *Unreliable Sources*, esp. 248–50. For rape in Bosnia, Amnesty International, *Rape and Sexual Abuse*, and Stiglmayer et al., *Mass Rape*, passim.

Meštrović, *Genocide*, 22–23, saw events in 1993–94 as a prison riot encouraged by the West.

61. Dana Priest, "Fear of Casualties Drives Bosnia Debate," *Washington Post*, 2 December 1995; Charles G. Boyd, "America Prolongs the War in Bosnia," *New York Times*, 9 August 1995; also Rosenthal, *New York Times*, 6 June 1995.

62. Dan De Luce, "Bosnian Foes Fight On, Diplomats Press for Peace," and "Signs Emerge of Progress toward Bosnian Peace," *Reuters*, 15, 16 May 1994. The United States joined Russia, Germany, France, Britain, Belgium, Greece, and the Netherlands to press for peace.

63. Dan De Luce, "Serbs Back Down on Gorazde Agreement," *Reuters*, 23 May 1994; "Serbs Make New Bosnia Pledge," *AP*, 24 May 1994.

64. Stephen Kinzer, "Muslims Tell of Atrocities as Safe Town Fell," *New York Times*, 14 July 1995.

65. Chris Hedges, "Second 'Safe Area' in Eastern Bosnia Overrun by Serbs," *New York Times*, 20 July 1995.

66. *New York Times*, 25 May 1995.

67. Stephen Kinzer, "Bosnian Muslim Troops Evade U.N. Force to Raid Serb Village," *New York Times*, 27 June 1995.

68. Miki Prific Knezevic, "What Makes a Serb a Villain and a Croat a Hero?" *New York Times*, 16 September 1995.

69. Safire, *New York Times*, 15 June 1995.

70. William Safire, "Balance the Power," *New York Times*, 9 October 1995.

71. Thomas Friedman, "Proceed with Caution," *New York Times*, 11 October 1995.

72. Roger Cohen, "As Lull in the War Ends, Sarajevo Is Shellshocked," *New York Times*, 28 June 1995.

73. Jennings, "Bosnia: Land of the Demons," and "This Week with David Brinkley," *ABC*, 9 May 1993.

74. Kroker and Cook, *The Postmodern Scene*, 10–15, 272–76. If the real is only interesting to the extent it contains an "imaginary catastrophe," like Bosnia, reality is nothing more than a simulacrum, a "virtual technology mediated with designer bodies processed through computerized imaging-systems." It's all virtual.

75. Elizabeth Kastor, "Indelible Images? Do the Pictures of Tragedy Inspire Compassion or Complacency?" *Washington Post*, 6 October 1994, for an exhibition at the Corcoran Gallery of Art, entitled "Farewell to Bosnia."

76. Chris Hedges, "Bosnian Serbs Surround 'Safe Area' but Defenders Are Defiant," *New York Times*, 21 July 1995.

77. Kinzer, *New York Times*, 14 July 1995.

78. Rieff, "Letter from Bosnia," 88, 90, 95.

79. *Ibid*.

80. Buckingham, *Moving Images*, esp. 249–50, for the use of horror films to delight and entertain.

81. For the distinctions, Fiske, *Television Culture*, esp. 179–222.

82. John F. Burns, *New York Times*, 12 October, 18 October, 19 October 1992.

83. Rieff, "Letter from Bosnia," 83, 93; Robert Guskind, "Ethnic Time Bombs," *National Journal*, 18 January 1992.

84. Radek Sikorski, "Déjà Vu/War in Europe Again," *National Review*, 16 December 1991, 40–42; Chuck Sudetic, *New York Times*, 28 June 1991.

85. McLuhan, *Understanding Media*, 182–93; and Powers, *The Newscasters*, passim.

86. "ABC Nightly News," 31 August 1992, echoed the Serbian version of events. Thompson, *Forging War*, 102–10.

87. "All Things Considered," *NPR*, 27 March 1993. Ali and Lifschultz, *Why Bosnia?*, 163–64, for Banac's criticism of Andrić.

88. "All Things Considered," *NPR*, 29 March 1993.

89. Carol J. Williams, "A Hell for Have-Nots in Sarajevo," *Los Angeles Times*, 16 September 1994.

90. "Bad Old Days Back in Sarajevo," *AP*, 25 September 1994.

91. Moina Farrow, "Health of World's Children Steadily Improving," *Montreal Gazette* (CDNB), June 1994; Dave Pommer, "City Group Investigates Mass Rape," *Calgary Herald* (CDNB), 8 June 1994, who reported that Kathleen Mahoney, a University of Calgary law professor, was gathering evidence to argue at the World Court that rape had served a genocidal purpose in Bosnia.

92. "Migration Rising around the World," *AP*, 13 June 1994.

93. Jane A. Lampmann, "Caring for the Uprooted: Do New Refugee Policies Threaten Rights?" *Christian Science Monitor*, 27 May 1994; "Report: 1.5 Million Flee Rwanda," *AP*, 24 May 1994. Bosnia, Iraq, and Liberia each had a million "internal" refugees.

94. "Peace a Mixed Bag for Bosnians," *AP*, 9 June 1994.

5

Performance

THE QUANTITY AND QUALITY
OF EARLY COVERAGE[1]

One gauge of media coverage of Yugoslavia was a general failure to report the genocide perpetrated by Serbian forces in Croatia in 1991 and Bosnia in 1992. It is not clear why the media ignored reports of massacres carried out by Serbian forces or rationalized ethnic cleansing by inculpating all sides, but Helsinki Watch also was cautious in reporting human rights abuses in 1991 and gave the impression that there was a moral equivalence between the actions of Croatian and Serbian forces. This confused matters, because it was clear that the JNA was acting to secure areas that Serbian irregulars then cleansed and resettled, and that the scale and quality of atrocities committed by Serbian forces was much worse than anything attributed to Croatian forces.

There were reports of massacres and mass expulsions in Croatia in late 1991, but the U.S. media largely ignored them. However, in April 1992, Spain's *ABC* reported that Serbian forces were burning Muslim houses and forcing Muslims to flee Bosnia, "just as" the JNA had done in Croatia. Two weeks later, as *Panorama* reported Bosnia's Muslims feared a repetition of Serbian atrocities that had filled the Drina with corpses during World War II, the *New York Times* ran pieces on how reasonable the Serbs had become and how pained they were by their bad image abroad.[2]

Croatians had difficulty getting their point of view into the media, particularly into America's newspaper of record, but the *New York Times* printed Alex Dragnich's letter defending Serbia's policies, and John

Burns implied that all sides were to blame for the deaths and expulsions in Bosnia. *The Nation* paid scant attention to the crisis, with articles by Borden in April, August, and October; a surreal piece by Slavenka Drakulić in June; and two essays by Hitchens, both anti-Croatian, in September, two more by Neier, and one by Cockburn.[3]

Even assuming a desire to cover all aspects of a story and to analyze it in depth, the formats of shows like the *MacNeil-Lehrer Newshour* precluded critical analysis. CNN had the luxury of continuously adjusting its coverage and correcting errors, but it could not undo what had been broadcast, nor could viewers follow every update. Like CNN, *MacNeil-Lehrer* and *Nightline* reacted to events, and they could not sustain coverage of the Yugoslav crisis in part because in early 1991 the Gulf War captured headlines and monopolized talk shows.

Nightline was particularly slow to react, airing only one show on the subject in July 1991, and a second on the religious shrine at Medjugorje in December.[4] CNN's only special report was a two-minute interruption of a Pentagon briefing on the Persian Gulf War to report the resignation of Yugoslavia's president, Borislav Jović, on 15 March 1991. But it was not clear that Jović's resignation was merely a symptom of Milošević's manipulation of the Yugoslav presidency. Before the onset of hostilities, the *MacNeil-Lehrer Newshour* discussed the crisis only twice, then twice more in July after the JNA had attacked Slovenia, and eight more times by the end of the year as fighting spread to Croatia and the JNA targeted cultural monuments, including the city of Dubrovnik.[5] (See Table 5.1.)

Table 5.1

Coverage by the *MacNeil/Lehrer Newshour* of the Yugoslav Crisis, 1991–92

Month	Number	Month	Number
1991		1992	
January	0	January	1
February	0	February	0
March	1	March	0
April	0	April	5
May	0	May	2
June	1	June	3
July	2	July	5
August	1	August	6
September	2	September	1
October	0	October	3
November	4	November	2
December	1	December	8
1991	12	1992	36

After UNPROFOR was deployed in early 1992, the *MacNeil-Lehrer Newshour* lost interest, airing only one discussion on Yugoslavia from January through March. The JNA's attack on Bosnia prompted the *Newshour* to discuss the crisis ten times in April, May, and June. As news of the death camps and ethnic cleansing finally permeated the filters of the U.S. media in July and August, the show devoted eleven shows to the crisis. The siege of Sarajevo and the peace efforts led to fourteen more discussions in 1992 and several programs in 1993. Coverage then rose and fell in 1994 and 1995, usually reflecting U.S. involvement.

Typical of the balanced coverage provided by this show was its 8 February 1993 segment that featured the Croatian prime minister of Bosnia-Herzegovina, Mile Akmadžić, who reluctantly supported the Vance-Owen plan; Radovan Karadžić, who was already accused of war crimes; and David Owen, who blamed the Serbs *and* the Muslims for failing to "compromise" and claimed that the Croats were "irritated" with the Muslims. Silajdžić, the only Muslim invited, had refused to appear, probably because the show seemed designed to promote the Vance-Owen plan. No experts with different points of view were invited, only players. The show's guest list implied that neither Serbia nor Croatia was involved in the conflict, whereas it was common knowledge that Belgrade stood behind Pale and Zagreb had forces operating in Bosnia.

MacNeil-Lehrer also promoted the Vance-Owen plan on 25 March 1993 when the show televised a long interview with "Lord Owen," who repeated the familiar refrain that the conflict was "fundamentally a civil war" with "a confessional aspect," that the Serbs were "testing the mettle of the international community," that the Croats were getting enough arms despite the embargo, and that lifting the embargo would be a "disincentive to the Muslims" to negotiate seriously. "Those people," Owen insisted, "have to live together," and although it was "agonizing" to watch the killing, a military solution was impossible since it would only "tilt the balance."

Washington Week in Review also ignored the crisis in Yugoslavia until the fighting started in mid-1991, then betrayed its domestic bias by mentioning the crisis only twice that year and twice in the first half of 1992, but eight times in the second half as the election campaigns took note of ethnic cleansing (see Table 5.2). *Firing Line* discussed the crisis once in 1991, and *American Interests* not until May and June 1992. In two years, the crisis was mentioned or discussed on a total of thirty-six PBS programs, once every two weeks on average. Like network news, PBS programs reacted to dramatic events.

The nightly newscasts of the three major networks provided the most superficial coverage. Whereas CNN devoted up to 1:30 minutes to regular news items and six minutes to an interview, network spots

Table 5.2
Coverage by *Washington Week in Review* of the Yugoslav Crisis in 1991–92

Month	Number	Month	Number
1991		1992	
January	0	January	0
February	0	February	0
March	0	March	0
April	0	April	0
May	0	May	1
June	0	June	1
July	1	July	2
August	1	August	2
September	0	September	0
October	0	October	0
November	0	November	1
December	0	December	3
1991	2	1992	10

varied from 20 seconds to 2:00 minutes. The crisis was mentioned in 173 newscasts during 1991, but any given report could be as little as twenty seconds (see Table 5.3). Before June, fourteen newscasts mentioned the crisis, an average of 2.8 per month, or less than one per network per month. The networks reported fighting in Slovenia and skirmishes in

Table 5.3
Coverage by the Three Major Networks of the Crisis in Yugoslavia in 1991

Month	Nightly News	Specials	Totals
January	2	0	2
February	0	0	0
March	10	1	11
April	0	0	0
May	2	0	2
June	21	0	21
July	39	1	40
August	20	0	20
September	26	0	26
October	13	0	13
November	24	0	24
December	15	1	16
Totals	172	3	175

Croatia on sixty-one shows in July and August, or ten per network per month.[6]

The Serb-Croat war got relatively less coverage, about five newscasts monthly per network from October through December. The war quickly became old hat, and coverage declined steadily after the first two months, from 30.5 newscasts per month, to 23.0 in August and September, to 18.5 in October and November, to 15 in December. On average, in 1991, 14.4 network newscasts per month mentioned the war, but stories often ran on the same days in the same time slots, so coverage really averaged five days monthly.

How uniform network slotting of stories could be is shown in Table 5.4. All nightly news programs covered the crisis in Yugoslavia from 1 through 8 July, when fighting in Slovenia was both intense and novel; then again on July 14, when Serb forces attacked Croatian police stations in the Krajina for the first time. With the cease-fire, coverage became sporadic, and if the networks did not coordinate their coverage of Yugoslavia, it seems that instinctive feelings about what was newsworthy were so deeply ingrained that they effectively worked as a

Table 5.4
Nightly Network News Coverage of the Crisis in Yugoslavia in July 1991
(NC=No Coverage)

July	ABC	CBS	NBC
1	5:44:00	5:48:30	5:49:40
2	5:30:00	5:30:20	5:30:10
3	5:30:00	5:30:20	5:30:10
4	5:30:10	5:30:20	5:36:50
5	5:35:40	5:32:20	5:49:10
6	5:32:20	5:32:30	5:30:10
7	5:33:00	5:30:20	5:30:20
8	5:44:40	5:41:20	5:45:50
9	NC	5:43:00	NC
10	5:44:20	5:43:30	NC
13	NC	5:43:40	NC
14	5:40:10	5:44:50	5:52:10
15	NC	NC	5:50:30
18	NC	5:47:20	NC
20	5:50:30	NC	NC
22	NC	5:46:40	5:50:20
28	NC	NC	5:41:20
29	NC	5:45:20	NC
30	5:40:50	NC	NC

single unit and did not so much cover the news in real time as define what exists in real time on any given day.[7] But if death, destruction, political crises, and human interest stories caught the medium's attention, they could not hold it. Episodic and focused on novelty and action, network news could not describe, much less explain and analyze, the forces that had emerged in the region.

Coverage in major newspapers paralleled that of the major networks, but it was more comprehensive and consistent. Three major papers (the *New York Times*, the *Los Angeles Times*, and the *Washington Post*) ran front-page articles on the crisis in Yugoslavia. Of the ninety-three coverage days in July (thirty-one days × the three papers), they ran front-page articles twenty-one times (23 percent of the month). The networks made the crisis their lead story on only fourteen days, or 15 percent of those available to the three of them. The newspapers continued to run stories on the crisis, albeit on pages A10 or A16, missing only twenty-four of ninety-three days (26 percent), but the networks did not mention the crisis on fifty-six days (60 percent). A comparison of network transcripts would yield an even greater disparity, since a newscast is less than a page of newsprint.

In 1991, the *Washington Post* and the *Los Angeles Times* each published an average of twelve articles monthly on the crisis, the *Washington Post* printing seventy-three articles in fifty-nine issues and the *Los Angeles Times* seventy-two in fifty-seven issues. The *New York Times* seems to have done better, publishing 109 items in 75 issues, but several items were photographs, and the average monthly count was still only sixteen.[8] In July coverage rose, and even with a drop-off in reporting later in the year, the *New York Times* published 236 items over 167 days, an average of thirty-nine items over twenty-eight days monthly. The *Washington Post* printed 214 articles in 145 days (averages of thirty-six and twenty-four, respectively), and the *Los Angeles Times* 136 pieces in 102 days (twenty-three and seventeen respectively). (See Table 5.5.)

Coverage then declined in early 1992, but less dramatically than in television or periodicals. The *Los Angeles Times* published only 103 articles over 74 days, but the *Washington Post* printed 187 pieces in 121 days, for averages of seventeen articles over twelve days monthly and thirty-one over twenty, respectively. The discovery of camps and the focus on ethnic cleansing stimulated coverage in the second half of the year, as the *Washington Post*'s coverage doubled to 371 articles over 167 days, and the *Los Angeles Times* published 185 articles over 120 days.

Coverage of the crisis by periodicals followed a similar pattern, climbing from 1 article in June to 17 in July, falling to 10.0/month through the rest of the year and 5.0/month in January and February 1992, then rising to 8.5 in April and May, jumping to 19 in June and 25 in July, and maintaining an average of 25.0/month during the second

Table 5.5
The Appearance of Newspaper Articles on the Crisis in Yugoslavia

Period	Washington Post	LA Times	NY Times
January–June 1991			
Total days	59	57	75
Total items	73	72	109
Days per month	9	9	12
Items per month	12	12	16
July–December 1991			
Total days	145	102	167
Total items	214	136	236
Days per month	24	17	28
Items per month	36	23	39
January–June 1992			
Total days	121	74	150
Total items	187	103	315
Days per month	12	20	25
Items per month	17	31	53
July–December 1992			
Total days	167	120	183
Total items	371	185	584
Days per month	28	20	31
Items per month	62	31	97

half of 1992. Major weeklies and periodicals carried pieces on the crisis in Yugoslavia in only fifty-five issues in 1991 (including thirty-one in three weeklies) and 109 in 1992 (sixty-five in the three weeklies). (See Table 5.6.)

Periodical coverage was highest in the summer and fall (seventy-two of ninety-two in 1991 and 153 of 204 in 1992). It also responded to the dramatic. In 1991, seventy-two of ninety-two articles appeared after the JNA had attacked Slovenia and Croatia; of 204 published in 1992, 128 followed reports of death camps and mass murder in Bosnia. Had periodicals been engaged in a systematic and sustained analysis of the crisis, there should have been a more even distribution of articles, including a response to ethnic cleansing by Serb forces in Croatia. But in the first five months of 1991, only nineteen publications contained pieces on the crisis, and in early 1992, despite the arrival of UN forces

Table 5.6

Major U.S. Periodicals Carrying Articles on the Crisis in Yugoslavia

Publication	1991	1992
The Atlantic	0	1
Esquire	0	1
Forbes	2	1
Foreign Affairs	1	1
Foreign Policy	1	0
Jet	0	1
Life	0	1
Ms.	1	0
Nation	4	8
National Review	3	5
New Republic	5	11
New York Review of Books	2	4
New York Times Magazine	1	2
New Yorker	1	4
Newsweek	8	23
Progressive	0	2
Psychology Today	0	1
Reader's Digest	1	0
Sports Illustrated	2	1
Time	10	26
U.S. News and World Report	13	16
Totals	55	109

in Croatia and the Serbian attack on Bosnia, only thirty-two issues had pieces on Yugoslavia. Like television, periodicals seem to have responded more readily to political crises, diplomatic offensives, warfare, and atrocities than to policy issues, diplomacy, and the domestic politics of foreign countries. (See Table 5.7.)

Coverage of the crisis in Yugoslavia was too often sporadic, misinformed, superficial, and biased. It focused on the sensational, not the substantive; concentrated on personalities, not issues; and defined an essentially Balkan affair in terms of U.S. policy or of international organizations like the EC, NATO, and the UN.

A wide variety of opinions found a venue in various media, but most tried to balance their coverage. Thus the *National Review* published both the staunchly pro-Serbian Nora Beloff and Ivo Banac, a Croatian scholar critical of Serbian and Croatian nationalists. Oddly, hard news was harder to balance and keep unbiased, owing to the effect of location on

Table 5.7
The Appearance of Periodical Articles on the Crisis in Yugoslavia

Month	1991	1992
January	2	7
February	1	3
March	9	4
April	5	8
May	2	9
June	1	19
July	17	25
August	6	29
September	14	23
October	10	19
November	10	28
December	11	20
Trimesters		
I	12	14
II	8	37
III	40	85
IV	32	68
Totals	92	204
Major U.S. Weeklies	31	65
All others	61	139

reporters, who tended to repeat, not question, sources. Hard news was rushed, contained errors, and employed simplistic explanations and stereotypes to frame complex issues and events. Given the episodic, superficial, and fragmentary nature of coverage, only by living in front of the TV with a Sony Walkman plugged in one ear and newspapers and periodicals at the ready for commercial breaks could one have gathered enough information to make sense of events in the Balkans. Even then, the average reader would not found it easy to assess which sources and arguments reflected Yugoslav realities, because most media repeated misconceptions, cloaked their biases, and related everything to American interests.

PLACING COVERAGE: WHERE THE ACTION WAS

According to Goffman, to seek action is to split the world in two—safe and boring on one hand, perilous and adventurous on the other. The media did just this with Yugoslavia. Where the action was in the '90s also had to be fictional in a basic sense, because if the audience had perceived events as real, they would have had to act. Instead, we distanced ourselves psychologically from the action like people about to leave friends and family, to preserve our emotional equilibrium and our sense of integrity. But we achieved only psychic stasis, because we belonged neither in Bosnia nor in policy-making circles. By definition we were eavesdroppers and voyeurs. We were also embarrassed by what we saw.[9]

In December 1994, Roger Cohen complained that because journalists could not get to where the action was, the war in Bosnia was becoming "increasingly invisible," enveloped in a "fog of second-hand reporting." He noted that there were few reliable casualty figures, local witnesses were no more trustworthy than photographs, and television crews sought out "bang-bang" pictures. Indeed, a journalist's "access to information [stood] in inverse proportion to the volume of sophisticated gear they [carried] around to communicate what they know." Both "Muslims and Serbs" tried to manage and manipulate the press, but the Serbs and the UN were particularly responsible for "the war's increasing disappearance from view." Cohen singled out Sir Michael Rose, who berated Sarajevo for risking World War III by inflating "Muslim casualties" but refused to allow reporters into Goražde because it might make the Serbs "angry." He also accused the UN of hypocrisy, because it claimed to "facilitate the work of the media," but actually restricted access. Journalists still found ways to cover the war, and 46 died doing so in Bosnia—more than had perished in Vietnam— largely because Serbs targeted them.[10] So getting to the action in Bosnia was difficult, and being there could be deadly.

As early as July 1992, Roy Gutman was unable to get to the action at Serb concentration camps. He was finally allowed to visit Manjača, just fifteen miles from Banja Luka, but he was not allowed to tour the camp and could talk to only eight prisoners as the camp doctor, guards, and a JNA film crew stood watch. He did not manage to reach Omarska or Keretem while they were operating, and the residents of Croatia's Slavonski Šamac could only listen to the screams coming from Bosanski Šamac, just across the Sava River in Serb-controlled territory. Reporters did not visit bordellos and were not present during rapes. Nor were they allowed access to trains used to expel non-Serbs or the mountain paths used by fleeing refugees. In fact, most of the war crimes and genocide occurred without any media present, allowing Eagleburger to deny that death camps existed and Frits Kalshoven, who was appointed to the UN war crimes panel in early 1992, to delay investigating allegations of war crimes and genocide. On the other hand, Lewis MacKenzie benefited financially

Table 5.8
Location of *New York Times* Reporters, January–June 1991

From:	Belgrade	Zagreb	Ljubljana	Sarajevo	Other
Binder	7	—	—	—	8
Bohlen	3	2	1	—	—
Engelberg	10	—	1	—	7
Friedman	1	—	—	—	—
Kinzer	—	—	—	—	2
Lewis	—	1	—	—	—
Riding	—	—	—	—	2
Sudetic	8	5	9	—	2
Tagliabue	2	—	—	—	—
Totals	31	8	11	—	21

from having been where the action was, even for a brief period in early 1992.[11]

Whatever editorial decisions media made, reports were likely to reflect a Serbian bias, owing to where reporters were. Discounting op-ed pieces by those who were not reporters by profession, thirty-one of seventy-one pieces appearing in the *New York Times* came from Belgrade in 1991. Subtracting reports filed by David Binder from Washington, D.C. (eight), Alan Riding from Paris (two) and Luxembourg (two), and Stephen Kinzer from Bonn (one) leaves fifty-eight reports from Yugoslavia. So 54 percent of the reports came from the Serbian capital. Adding reports from Serb-controlled areas by Engelberg (Pakrac, Knin, Borovo Selo, Civljanje) and Sudetic, thirty-six of fifty-eight, or 62%, of the reports came from Serbian sources. (See Table 5.8.)

It is instructive how few reports came from Croatia, given that most reporters made biting remarks and easy generalizations about its fascist past, its nationalist present, and its treatment of its Serbian minority. Only eight reports emanated from Zagreb, or 14 percent, and eleven from Ljubljana. Sarajevo was simply off the media's map before July 1991. Not a single report came from the Olympic city, even though tensions there were extremely high.

It is therefore no surprise that reports by reporters who used the Serbian press agency, Tanjug, and relied on RTV and *Politika*, both controlled by Milošević, tended to reflect Serbian points of view. For example, Engelberg reported that Croatian police and the JNA were working together in Pakrac, despite knowing that the army had turned the town over to "local" Serbs. Both Engelberg and Binder saw the Croats as neofascists, implied that Serbs in Croatia had reason to feel threatened, and saw the JNA as keeping the peace. However, Bohlen, who was based in Zagreb, tended to see Croatia's Serbs as under Belgrade's thumb, and blamed them for clashes with Croatian authorities. No one got their chronologies or histories straight.[12]

Several journalists made quick tours to become instant experts. Flora Lewis visited Zagreb, Thomas Friedman stopped in Belgrade, John Tagliabue filed two reports from Belgrade, and Stephen Kinzer one from Sintilj on the Austro-Slavonian border. Engelberg was peripatetic, filing eighteen reports, ten from Belgrade, most of the rest from Serb-controlled areas. Alan Riding did not go to Yugoslavia at all, and David Binder filed half his reports from Washington. Of course, Washington was also where the acton was, and a partial survey of guests on *MacNeil-Lehrer*, which draws heavily on D.C.'s elites, is instructive.

Of twenty-six guests, almost half (43 percent) were from the government, over a quarter (27 percent) from journalism. Adding the four UN representatives, Western officials accounted for over half the guests (58 percent). Only one Croat appeared and only one Serb, but tapes of Karadžić and Milošević were featured. Bianca Jagger got as much time as the Croatian government and more than the Bosnian government. Whether this showed American TV to be in full postmodern decline, it did indicate that media history is not history and media politics are not politics; both are essentially caricatures of politics and history presented by a small group who talk to one other, not the public.[13] (See Table 5.9.)

The distribution of guests on *Nightline* over the same period was similar. Kissinger and Kirkpatrick, both influential news shapers, were also former government officials, as was Schultz. So U.S. government and UN officials (David Owen) accounted for nine of twenty-five guests, or about one-third. Journalists accounted for nine more. Four appearances were by pro-Serbians—Lewis MacKenzie, whose speaking tour had been sponsored by a Serbian organization; Henry Kissinger, whose associates lobbied for Belgrade; and Radovan Karadžić, who headed Pale's government. One Croat, but no Bosnian, appeared. Such guest lists suggest that it was hard for Croatian or Bosnian spokesmen to get a hearing on major American talk shows. They also showed a certain parochialism, bounded by Washington's Beltway. *Nightline* used more reporters (36 percent) than *MacNeil-Lehrer* (27 percent), but fewer officials (36 percent to 59 percent). If Kissinger, Kirkpatrick, and MacKenzie are included in the first three groups, approximately half (48 percent) of Koppel's guests could be classified as officials. (See Table 5.10.)

The answer to the question, Where was the action in 1991? was—in Belgrade and Washington. Yet the action, like reporters, moved a good deal. By 1993, it was in Sarajevo, which everyone, including Sam

Table 5.9
Provenance of Guests on *MacNeil-Lehrer*, February–May 1993

Date	USG	UN	NATO	J	S	C	B	Other
8 Feb		1			1	1		
25 March		1						
30 March				1				1*
2 April		1		1				
5 April	1							
6 April	1(1)				(2)			
22 April								1**
28 April	4			1				
3 May	2			1				
6 May	4			3				
24 May	1	1						
Totals	13(1)	4	0	7	1(2)	1	0	2

Key: USG(overnment), J(ournalist), S(erbian), C(roatian), B(osnian)
*Bianca Jagger
**Vaclav Havel
Parentheses indicate person appeared on tape.

Table 5.10
Provenance of Guests on *Nightline*, January–May 1993

Date	USG	UN	NATO	J	S	C	B	Other
14 Jan	1							
8 Feb		1			1	1		
25 March		1						
6 April				1				
9 April				1				
18 April	2							
22 April								2*
26 April	1							
29 April	2			1				2**
5 May				4				
6 May		1		1	1			
14 May				1				
Totals	6	3	0	9	2	1	0	4

*Henry Kissinger and Leon Wiseltier
**Lewis MacKenzie and Jeanne Kirkpatrick

Donaldson, paid at least one visit. But the action could move with people, as reporters followed U.S. and UN officials around Europe. By late 1995, the action had moved to Dayton, the site of the peace conference. What occurred every time that the action—or the major players and their journalistic entourage—moved was that the rest of the territory where the tragedy that was Yugoslavia was played out simply disappeared from sight. It was not just the media that mediated; the guests the media hosted and the locales from which the media reported also shaped perceptions.

There were five places from which reports emanated: official sites (Belgrade, Washington, European capitals, UN offices, and NATO headquarters); Serbian strongholds (Knin, Pale); Bosnian enclaves (Sarajevo, Tuzla, Goražde, Žepa, Srebrenica); Croatian towns (Dubrovnik, Vukovar); mixed areas (Mostar); no-man's-land (northern Bosnia, Brčko, Prijedor, Omarska). Zagreb got little play, less than some villages. Access was uneven, with most reports filed from capitals and official sites.

Reports from the Krajina tended to present the Serbians there as heroic and beleaguered—"an enclave of fiercely proud Serbs," to use Engelberg's description. Binder gave the impression that the area was compact and linked to Serbia proper. Some areas became Serbian by reporting their position relative to Serbia. Borovo Selo, where one of the first clashes occurred, was reported by the media as eighty miles from Belgrade; one dispatch reported that a helicopter carrying the Croatian vice-president had been attacked 210 miles west of the Serbian capital.[14]

Vukovar was inaccessible to the media once the siege had begun. Only after the city fell ninety days later were reporters allowed into the town. Then they were carefully shepherded by Serbian authorities and treated to a series of crude propaganda tableaux.[15] However, reporters were in Dubrovnik when Serbian artillery shelled the old city; this caused considerable embarrassment for Belgrade and led to one of the few appearances by a Croat on *MacNeil-Lehrer*. It also led to some specious analyses, including Woodward's claim that the Croats had planted sharpshooters on the walls to provoke the Serbian gunners.[16] Sarajevo created similar problems for propagandists and caused figures like MacKenzie to make untenable claims that seemed calculated to show one side in a bad light.[17]

Access was therefore crucial, but most sites were in a sort of no-man's-land. Reporters knew of them, but rarely could reach them. Generally these were the places where ethnic cleansing occurred. They included all of northern Bosnia, with camps at Omarska, Brčko, and over ninety other places; parts of Mostar; and villages occupied by the JNA, like Dvor and Struga. Numerous other sites of massacre, genocide, and war crimes were also invisible to the media. A notable exception was the village of Kijevo in Croatia, razed on 28 August 1991 by Milan Martić and his Serbian irregulars in front of a BBC film crew.[18]

LATER COVERAGE

If early coverage tended to focus on violent or dramatic events, later coverage was similar, except that there was a lot more of it.[19] Flurries of diplomatic activity, reports of ethnic cleansing, and military operations were covered in detail. Even so, aside from sporadic human interest stories or op-ed pieces, there was little effort to follow up events and less to gain any real understanding of why they had occurred. Nor did many attempt to find out who the players were *inside* the successor states of the former Yugoslavia, or how people within those states viewed the whole process. Rieff, Malcolm, Gutman, and a few others were exceptions. Others, like Glenny and Woodward, appeared to be exceptions, but delivered biased, superficial analysis.

The summer of 1995 was a particularly busy period, as Serbian forces overran Srebrenica and Žepa, and Croatian and Bosnian forces occupied Bosnian towns and the Krajina. *The Washington Post* published seventy-seven articles on Yugoslavia in July, but only nine of them before the Serbian attack on Srebrenica. Coverage was intense through early August, owing to the unexpected success of Croatian-Bosnian military operations, but dropped off after the middle of August, only to pick up again with NATO air strikes against Serb targets in September, followed by the peace initiative.

As usual, the views presented over the summer were mostly derived from official sources. The *Washington Post* cited sixty sources in June and July. Only seven (11.3 percent) were not official, and two of these were reporters. Most were UN officials, military officers, or western European or American officials and leaders. Karadžić was cited, as were a Croatian and two Bosnian officials. One article sampled the views of Serbian "refugees," four others the views of ordinary people, including those from Srebrenica and Sarajevo. Bob Dole was also cited, reflecting concern that U.S. troops would be deployed in Bosnia.

News coverage increased whenever Americans were involved. The *New York Times* ran thirteen articles regarding a downed American pilot, including two full-page spreads and a follow-up after he returned to the States. The articles depicted him as a real person, even reporting that at a lunch with Clinton, he preferred to skip the salad. In June, the *Times* ran seventy-two articles on Bosnia, about the same as the *Post* and a third more than it had published in May, when forty-two pieces on Bosnia appeared. July coverage in the *Times* increased to eighty-three articles as the Serbs overran and cleansed Srebrenica, which made the front page on July 11. Coverage remained intense in August (sixty-nine) and September (seventy-four). Croatia's offensive got the most coverage, but on 31 August four articles spread over two pages discussed NATO bombing.

In October, the number of articles on Yugoslavia dropped to sixty, then increased to seventy-five in November, largely owing to the peace conference. Coverage remained high in December (seventy-five) as Congress debated the wisdom of sending troops to Bosnia, but it was overwhelmed by the Russian elections and the murder of Yitzak Rabin. The Middle East and great-power politics therefore continued to enjoy precedence over events in peripheral areas like the Balkans, a gauge of news values. In all areas dramatic and violent events continued to make the news.

Coverage had picked up in 1992 with the war in Bosnia, then followed an uneven course through the early summer of 1995, when it hit a trough. The reasons were various. The discovery of Serbian death camps in 1992 and repeated exposés in 1993 kept interest alive. Clinton's election in 1992 and his rhetoric in early 1993 led the media to expect a story that never materialized. The failure of diplomacy was news in 1993, and the increased involvement of Islamic states and the United States made news in 1994. Interest was piqued in 1993, when the war became a truly three-sided affair as Croats and Muslims, unable to contest the more heavily armed Serbian forces, turned on each other and began to emulate the Serbs in desperate attempts to salvage some territory before the West imposed its terms for peace.

The publication of books also had an impact after 1991, beginning with Djilas's 1991 anti-Croatian and pro-Serbian history of the Communist Party of Yugoslavia (KPJ), which was partially corrected by Irving's book on the Croatian question two years later. (See Table 5.11.) During 1992, Dragnich provided a pro-Serbian apology, Glenny a more nuanced reading of the conflict, Thompson a witty and well-informed travelogue from the left, Ramet a critical look at the crisis, and Helsinki Watch an ambivalent series of anecdotes.

The following year brought works on war crimes by Gutman and Amnesty International, Kaplan's superficial but influential travel book, Cohen's political history, Magaš's collection of articles from 1990 to 1991, Meštrović's analysis of South Slavic cultural values, Stokes's survey of change in eastern Europe, and the motley collection of articles in Ali and Lifshultz. Crnobrnja's pro-Serbian work was balanced in 1994 by Stiglmayer's collection on rape and the carefully done studies by Almond and Malcolm. Thompson's study of the media and the history of Bosnia by Donia and Fine filled out some background.

In 1995 a variety of works appeared, ranging from the frankly pro-Serbian apologies of Woodward and O'Ballance to the clinical analysis

Table 5.11
Publication Dates of Major Works on Yugoslavia in English after 1991

Year	Author	Title
1991:	Aleksa Djilas	*The Contested Country*
1992:	A. Borden et al.	*Breakdown*
	Alex Dragnich	*Serbs and Croats*
	Misha Glenny	*The Fall of Yugoslavia*
	James Gow	*Legitimacy and the Military*
	Helsinki Watch	*War Crimes in Bosnia*
	Jill Irving	*The Croat Question*
	Sabrina Ramet	*Balkan Babel*
	Mark Thompson	*A Paper House*
	John Zametica	*The Yugoslav Conflict*
1993:	Ali and Lifschultz	*Why Bosnia?*
	Amnesty Internat.	*Rape and Sexual Abuse*
	Lenard J. Cohen	*Broken Bonds*
	Zlatko Dizdarević	*Sarajevo: A War Journal*
	Slavenka Drakulić	*The Balkan Express*
	Roy Gutman	*A Witness to Genocide*
	Helsinki Watch	*War Crimes in Bosnia*
	William T. Johnsen	*Deciphering the Balkan Enigma*
	Robert J. Kaplan	*Balkan Ghosts*
	Branka Magaš	*The Destruction of Yugoslavia*
	Stjepan Meštrović	*Habits of the Balkan Heart*
	Laslo Sekelj	*Yugoslavia*
	Gale Stokes	*The Walls Came Tumbling Down*
	Bob Stewart	*Broken Lives*
1994:	Mark Almond	*Europe's Backyard War*
	Mihailo Crnobrnja	*The Yugoslav Drama*
	R. Donia and J. Fine	*Bosnia and Herzegovina*
	Brian Hall	*The Impossible Country*
	Noel Malcolm	*Bosnia*
	A. Stiglmayer et al.	*Mass Rape*
	Mark Thompson	*Forging War*
	Ed Vuilliamy	*Seasons in Hell*
1995:	Christopher Bennett	*Yugoslavia's Bloody Collapse*
	Norman Cigar	*Genocide in Bosnia*
	David Rieff	*Slaughterhouse*
	Edgar O'Ballance	*Civil War in Bosnia*
	Ramet and Adamovich	*Beyond Yugoslavia*
	Susan L. Woodward	*Balkan Tragedy*

of genocide by Cigar, the passionate reportage of Rieff, and the ambivalent collection of papers by Ramet and Adamovich. Continued resistance by the Bosnians, the conclusion of a Croatian-Bosnian federation in the spring of 1994, and the emergence of viable Croatian and Bosnian military forces kept the story alive and gave it an unexpected twist in the late summer and early fall of 1995 as the action returned to Croatian territory and the Bosnian and Croatian armies drove deep into Serbian areas.

NOTES

1. Tables in this chapter, which also appeared in Stjepan Meštrović, ed., *Genocide after Emotion: The Post-Emotional Balkan War* (London: Routledge, 1996), were compiled from *Reader's Guide*, the first refuge of college students doing term papers; *Television News Index and Abstracts* (Nashville, TN: Vanderbilt TV News Archives, 1991), which has short summaries and times of news broadcasts for the major networks; and the hard-copy indexes of the *New York Times*, *Los Angeles Times*, and *Washington Post*. I talked to those willing to talk to me at NPR, PBS, and the major networks (including CNN). In addition to books and hard-copy texts of newspapers and periodicals, I have used data from *CD Newsbank*, transcripts from *Journal Graphics*, and my own notes from radio and television broadcasts. I did not tabulate the length of stories or the quality of coverage, which varied considerably. There are thus some lacunae and undoubtedly some will lament my failure to include more publications in my samples. My only answer to those who do so is that time and money simply were not available.

2. *ABC* (Spain), 12 April 1992; *New York Times*, 29 April, 1 May 1992; *Panorama*, 26 April 1992.

3. France's *L'Express* ignored the war, but on 20 and 27 April, Germany's *Der Spiegel* recalled Serb atrocities during World War II, and reported that Genscher had warned Serbia's foreign minister that the Serbs would be held responsible for the fighting in Bosnia.

4. The first show featured Slovene Foreign Minister Dimitrij Rupel, "Yugoslavia's" UN ambassador, Darko Silović, and Mark C. Wheeler, the author of *Britain and the War for Yugoslavia, 1940–1943* (Boulder: East European Monographs, 1980). The second show was just silly.

5. The media ignored events in the Balkans because they were focused on the Gulf War and the coup attempt in the USSR. The 23 November 1991 issue of *National Review* was devoted to the Soviet coup and the USSR, even though by that time the coup had failed and dramatic events were unfolding in Yugoslavia. The media preferred to focus on large powers and strategically sensitive regions, not small powers and areas of marginal interest.

6. *Television News Index and Abstracts* (Nashville, TN: Vanderbilt TV News Archives, 1991), passim.

7. Paletz and Entman, *Media*, 9. Of weekday news stories on two of the three major networks, 70 percent are the same.

8. Photographs, of course, can have more of an impact than printed columns, for example, the picture of a Serbian family mourning a member killed in the fighting probably has as much, if not more, impact than a column noting that Serbian forces had devastated a number of Muslim villages and, if published in juxtaposition with the column, would tend to cancel its message.

9. Goffman, *Interaction Ritual*, esp. the sections on face-to-face contact, where the action is, and situational embarrassment. Whether audiences can act is another question. For the audience as individual voyeuristic and parasitic blips with life-styles living vicariously through broadcast disaster, see Kroker and Cook, *The Postmodern Scene*, 270–85. If "in postmodern America even true confessions are lies," then we are all guilty, and everyone in Yugoslavia must be as well.

10. Roger Cohen, *New York Times*, 25 December 1994. Cohen also saw the Bosnians as guilty of muzzling and harassing the press, and he compared the difficulties of journalists in Bosnia to those they encountered in Algeria, where twenty-four had been killed in 1993 and 1994.

11. Gutman, *Witness to Genocide*, 28–30, 34–35, 44–46, 53, 92, 120–22, 150–56, 168–73. The UN Security Council demanded that the Red Cross be admitted to the camps, *New York Times*, 5 August 1992.

12. For Tagliabue, Engelberg, and Bohlen, *New York Times*, 3, 4, 10, 11, 12, 13, 14, 16, 17, 18 March, 7, 8, 9, 10, 11, 16 May, and 30 June 1991; also compare Cohen, *Broken Bonds*, 201, 208–9, to Cigar, "Serbo-Croat War," 307–8.

13. Kroker and Cook, *Excremental Culture*, 274–76, for the concept that in an information society the simulacrum replaces historical contexts and deterritorializes and dehistoricizes reality.

14. Pieces in the *New York Times* by Engelberg, 24, 26, 28 March, 1991, 4 May 1995; Binder, 18 March 1991; Sudetic, 1, 2 April 1991; also AP, 3 May 1991.

15. Igor Primorac, "The War against Croatia: Salient Traits," 93–96; and Vesna Bosanac, "Vukovar's Destruction," *Journal of Croatian Studies* (1991–92), 217–25, got her eye-witness report into a specialized journal well after it would have made an impact; Almond, *Europe's Backyard War*, 220–27; and Cigar, "The Serbo-Croatian War," 112–15.

16. Almond, *Europe's Backyard War*, 228; Woodward, *Balkan Tragedy*, 182; Vesna Herman, "Destruction of Art and Architecture in Croatia," *Journal of Croatian Studies* (1991–92), 231–32; Primorac, "War against Croatia," 103–10; 24 Часа, 3, 4 Oct. 1991; and *MacNeil-Lehrer*, 1991.

17. Gutman, *Witness to Genocide*, 168–73, for MacKenzie.

18. Magaš, *Destruction of Yugoslavia*, 320–22, 344; Helsinki Watch, *Yugoslavia: Human Rights Abuses in the Croatian Conflict* (Washington, DC, September 1991), 6–10.

19. For example, in 1994, *CD NewsBank* compiled 1,291 items for Bosnia, 656 for Croatia, 750 for Serbia, and 37 for Slovenia. Although most of these are duplicate sources, the amount of information available had increased dramatically.

6

Stereotypes:
Croats and Muslims

VICIOUS TRIBES AND ENDLESS CIVIL WAR

Among the misconceptions popularized by the media was the belief that ethnic groups within Yugoslavia had been at each other's throats for centuries, and its corollary, that all sides were irrational and vengeful. "Many analysts," Stephen Engelberg noted, believed that "in a nation where longstanding enmity is commonplace," the split between Croat and Serb had undone Yugoslavia.[1] In short, all sides were responsible for the mess following Yugoslavia's collapse, because everyone was consumed by passions as powerful and enduring as those that drove the Hatfields and McCoys to slaughter one another.

Rather than modern nations comprising civilized peoples, South Slavs were "atavistic tribes" whose psyches thirsted for blood. Lenard Cohen perceived "a pattern of ethnoreligious violence and atrocities against innocent civilians that was all too familiar in the region." He thought its roots lay in "intergenerational socialization of negative stereotypes regarding the history and behavior of other groups."[2] The argument that atavistic urges on all sides were responsible for the crimes and atrocities attendant on the conflict was seductive because it seemed an evenhanded, fair approach and reflected pop psychology.

Alfred Meyer echoed the theme of "they're a mess, but we're all right, Jack" when he concluded that the Serbian "program of what they've termed 'ethnic cleansing' . . . was a clear case of regression, of atavism— a desperate resort to behaviors and strategies pertinent in the past but now obsolete." Serbs have evidently not been properly domesticated, and there is a lesson there for Americans. Bosnia had showed "where the deprivation of ritual can lead," so Meyer urged us to be content with our imperfect political system, because it is only "the rituals of our politics—like them or not—that keeps us from expressing our differences in more aggressive ways."[3]

Meyer was not alone in viewing Balkan nationalisms as anachronistic atavisms and the region as a peculiarly primitive place. Craig Whitney characterized Bosnia-Herzegovina as "a vast and perilous ethnic morass that innocent outsiders enter at their peril."[4] Gale Stokes picked up the mantra of tribalism when he intoned, "Ethnic emotions run deep throughout Eastern Europe, but nowhere did they reach the level of bestiality they did in Yugoslavia."[5] More accurately, Sabrina Ramet noted that after four years of "officially sponsored hate propaganda, the Serbs felt fully justified in perpetrating utterly ghoulish atrocities" in Croatia.[6]

Atavistic nationalism was the liberal historian's Schumpeterian equivalent of a lack of ritual coping mechanisms, and even Noel Malcolm concluded, "Old-fashioned atavistic nationalism [had] not disappeared from Slovenia or Croatia (especially not from Croatia), though it no longer dresse[d] up in peasant costumes."[7] Yet the neonationalisms that overwhelmed Yugoslavia were distinct in their use of sophisticated psychological techniques and their grounding in a post-Communist mentality.

Even so, Lance Morrow mused that mass rape of Muslims by Serbs and similar, unspecified actions by Croats and Muslims suggested that "atavistic nationalisms, or tribalisms, [lay] just beneath the civil veneer" in Bosnia. Yet Amnesty International concluded that Serb forces raped systematically and everywhere, and Morrow noted that the "elite" Serbian White Eagles saw it as a gesture of group solidarity. It would seem that the Serbs consciously used rape to terrorize Muslims, but an "anonymous" EC source claimed that non-Serbs had committed "some mass rapes" at some unspecified date in some unnamed location.[8] Morrow's balance was forced at best. Calling the White Eagles, a murderous paramilitary group, "elite" was as odd as the conclusion that raping women was a way that guys show their affection for each other.

The media routinely labeled the conflict a "civil war," and in early 1993, Malcolm Rifkind, Britain's defense secretary, officially declared the conflict "a civil war."[9] But, as Chuck Sudetic noted, Muslims and Croatians did not fight one another until fourteen months after the war had begun, and it gradually became clear that the fiction of civil war was necessary to absolve the West of complicity in genocide.[10]

Even so, most media failed to distinguish aggression and genocide from civil war and ethnic cleansing. Their failure echoed earlier coverage of Central America, an area of "mindless, increasing violence" and "civil war." In both regions some media ignored the perpetrators and discounted the suffering of the victims by placing them in a context in which violence was a natural by-product of civil war, all sides were equally guilty, and murder was a political tool, not a moral question.[11] With murder an impersonal political question, the great powers could preside as disinterested referees and the public could consider the carnage as disinterested observers.

Robert Guskind was typical in his objectivity, balance, and outrage. Like others, he blamed "centuries-old enmities" for the slaughter, and he evenhandedly condemned Tudjman and Milošević for unleashing "ethnic hatred" while chiding both sides for breaking cease-fires. A breakdown in the JNA's internal discipline had left Croatian Ustashe and Serbian Chetnik irregulars free to commit heinous acts like the downing of an EC helicopter. With the JNA prepared to "methodically inflict any level of punishment to win," the Serbs to "commit collective suicide," and the Croats to fight to the bitter end, Guskind foresaw only "disaster." All sides were guilty, unreasonable, intractable; to resist aggression rather than surrender made the victims their own victimizers.[12]

By depicting all South Slavs as troublesome tribesmen and the war as a Serbian rebellion, the media defined the conflict. By portraying Serbs defending their homes against Muslim fundamentalists and Croatian fascists, they blurred the distinction between victim and aggressor. The *New Yorker* reduced the war to mere technique by reporting Milan Vasić's analysis, which saw fomenting war and mass murder as "very easy," a matter of distributing guns in villages after using television to set people against one another. This, of course, was the stuff of American melodrama, and not a few academic treatises. It also complemented explanations that without Communism to keep the lid on social problems, people "terrified" of democracy and the free market had been easy prey for nationalists. Nationalism became a continuation of the old Communist, not the bright new capitalist, order; the magazine applauded Yugoslav liberals, "marginalized by the war parties," who continued to try to create "secular, democratic, multiethnic political systems."[13]

More realistic was Ramet's list of causes for the crisis that ensued after 1989, among them Serbia's boycott of Slovenia; the disintegration of the Croatian, Slovene, and Yugoslav Communist parties; the collapse of a federal budget in 1990 after the republics stopped contributing; and the JNA's transformation into a political force geared for repression. Cohen and Magaš list many of the same factors, with particular stress on the role played by the JNA, whose repression of Kosovo in the 1980s changed its nature and delegitimized the federal government, and whose 1990 maneuvers cast Croatia and Slovenia as the enemy.[14]

What the media consistently lacked was a sense of history and chronology. Economic problems in the 1980s coincided with Tito's death, and various tensions predated the introduction of economic and political forms usually associated with the free market. Serbian nationalism was already on the rise in the early 1980s, and its spread was aided by Serbian intellectuals and the Serbian media. IMF requirements exacerbated Yugoslavia's economic crisis as the collapse of the nonaligned bloc and the end of the cold war left Yugoslavia adrift diplomatically and politically. Milošević's control of Serbia after 1987 and his alliance with a politicized JNA were crucial.[15]

The crisis became critical not because someone created fear, distrust, and panic, but because state-controlled media in Serbia and Serbian intellectuals spent the 1980s instructing Serbs to hate non-Serbs. It was not civilians with machine guns distributed in villages, but JNA regular troops who overran Croatia and Bosnia. It was not the fear of the free market, but the unilateral revision of the Serbian constitution and an aggressive Serbian nationalism that tore Yugoslavia apart.

All this can be traced, but has nothing to do with vicious tribes, romantic rebellions, or civil wars. Among the themes of Serbian propaganda were the ideas that Serbs and Serbdom were endangered, that Serbians outside Serbia had a right to live in a Serbian or Serbian-dominated state, and that non-Serbs had no rights. The Serbian media and intellectual community fanned the embers of hatred against Croats, Muslims, and Albanians, so when the JNA began to arm Serbs in Croatia and Bosnia, it seemed as natural as the creation of various krajinas in 1990. Propaganda made it seem proper for the JNA to disarm and absorb the Territorial Defense units, to purge unreliable officers, and to reorganize its military regions and add new corps in places like Knin.

Both aggression and genocide need an ideology, and the SANU (Serbian Academy of Arts and Sciences) provided it in a 1986 memorandum. Its anti-Albanian racism was congruent with Serbia's anti-Turkish tradition and was then transferred to Bosnian Muslims. Intellectuals like Rašković and Cosić paved the way for aggression and genocide, and because Serbian institutional voices were mute, protests from those associated with *Vreme* were ineffectual.[16]

The same was true in the United States once the media and intellectuals like Dragnich and Beloff had spread the ideas that the Balkans were a backward area where vicious tribes lived uneasily with one another, romantic rebellion was common, conspiracy normal, civil wars cyclic events, and murdering one's neighbor nothing special. Typical was Guskind's observation that the "single bloody reality" was that Serbia and Croatia, whose leaders "either unwilling or unable to compromise," were "stuck in a vicious circle of escalating violence and revenge."[17]

Croatia was singled out for being insensitive to its Serbian minority and for closing its borders to Bosnian refugees in September 1992. Yet it was the world's fourth-largest receiver of refugees, accepting 500,000 Bosnians in eighteen months—an influx comparable to the arrival of 25 million people in the United States. The strain on its economy, already badly damaged by Serbian attacks, had been severe, but the West had done much less. Germany had taken 220,000 refugees, the United States a thousand.[18]

Croatia was sheltering, not cleansing, Muslims, and its own Serb minority's rights were constitutionally guaranteed. Yet the media repeatedly tarred all sides with the same brush. An AP release evenhandedly implied that all sides had broken a cease-fire in 1994, even though most incoming shells were Serbian.[19]

To not take sides was to eschew accuracy. In June 1994, Alison Smale reported the "diplomats and UN officials [were] deeply skeptical that any side want[ed] peace."[20] This was a gross oversimplification, but a common one. AP announced, "Many Ignore Bosnia Cease-Fire," and *Reuters* that "U.N. Reports Major Truce Violations in Bosnia," and "Heavy Fighting Further Damages Bosnian Truce." Someone skimming headlines would have concluded, as AP did, "Bosnia Truce Growing Shaky."[21]

Confusion regarding the crisis in Yugoslavia was exacerbated by organizations like Helsinki Watch, whose evenhanded approach reinforced the concept of moral equivalence. The implication of this approach was evident in its letters to Tudjman and to Milošević and Adžić in January and February 1992. Both ended with pleas to end human rights abuses, making it seem that the Croatian government was as guilty as the Yugoslav army, Serbian irregulars, and the Serbian government. Format was partly to blame, but the letters left an impression that all parties had committed "serious human rights abuses."[22] Helsinki Watch abandoned this position, but diplomats like David Owen did not, and the media did so only slowly.

Even Noel Malcolm, who later was instrumental in exposing aggression and atrocities by the Bosnian Serbs and Croats, initially chided the Slovenes for indulging in "half-measures" and having "done curiously little to make a clean break with the rest of Yugoslavia." He was not sure whether they lacked "a genuine willingness to negotiate" or were simply inept.[23] When leveled against Zagreb and Sarajevo, such criticism inadvertently helped to excuse Serbian aggression.

By focusing on Croatian gunmen and war criminals, John Pomfret made it seem that all sides were similarly guilty. Yet of forty people then indicted for war crimes, thirty-three were Serbian, seven Croatian. Pomfret also played down Milošević's role in the war and announced "Tudjman's record on justice ruined" by his promotion of an accused war criminal. He also quoted a "Bosnian army officer" who expected "all sides" to rearm, leaving the impression that everyone was intent on vendetta.[24] Croatian units did engage in ethnic cleansing, but not on the same scale as Serbian units.

Finally, it is worth looking at *Nightline*, which exercises considerable influence on public opinion. In January 1993, Dave Marash reported that UN sources said that if Muslim women accounted for "the vast majority" of victims, "all sides" in "the brutal war" were raping women. On a later program Koppel concluded that children were being taught to hate their neighbors because they belonged to a different ethnic group. The impression was that hatred made everyone guilty, leading a "confused" William Styron to long for the Nazi era, when things had been "clear-cut."[25]

DEMONIZING THE VICTIM: THE CASE OF CROATIA

Several myths about the Serbs helped to demonize their victims: that Serbs were the only victims of genocide in Yugoslavia during World War II, that they had supported the Allies while Croats and Muslims collaborated with the Axis, that they were the core of the country, and that they were invincible guerrilla fighters. But Yugoslavia collapsed in 1941 for military reasons, no group had a monopoly on resistance or collaboration, and Yugoslavism was a Croatian, not a Serbian, invention.[26] Because Serbian versions of history dominated in the 1990s, it seemed plausible that Croatian nationalists were neofascists and Muslims a latent threat to Serbians in Bosnia. Such myths were used to rationalize Serbian aggression and genocide, confuse world public opinion, and paralyze the West. As Aryeh Neier noted in early 1993, by attributing "collective guilt" to their victims, the Serbs could claim that they were merely avenging crimes that had occurred from 50 to 500 years ago.[27]

Typical was a piece in late 1991 that mentioned only Croatian atrocities during World War II and labeled Serb terrorism in Croatia an "uprising," even if it was not clear why Vukovar had to undergo an eighty-six–day siege.[28] John Tagliabue had earlier introduced the JNA's chief of staff, Blagoje Hadžić [sic=Adžić], by noting that as a youth the Serb had watched as family members were "slaughtered by pro-Nazi Croatian guerrillas." According to Tagliabue, Serbs could not "forget that in 1941 when Croatia last obtained its independence as a Nazi puppet state, 500,000 Serbs were slaughtered."[29] No one introduced Tudjman, Izetbegović, or any Croat or Muslim by noting that Serbs had killed their families, but they could have, given the mass murder perpetrated by Serbian forces in Bosnia and by Serbs and partisans in Croatia.

Of course, doing so would have reinforced the myths that all sides were vicious and that the Balkans were seething with hatred and ethnic animosities. Such myths distorted forecasts and paralyzed policy makers by making everyone a potential enemy.[30] Even after the creation of the Croat-Bosnian federation and abundant proof that Serb units had committed the vast majority of war crimes, the *Washington Post* ran an article implying that both Bosnian and Bosnian Serb forces would attack exiting UN troops and seize their equipment.[31]

So strong was the myth of a fascist Croatia and a pro-Allied Serbia that Guskind believed Croatia had "sided with the Nazis, Serbia with the Western Allies." He noted a "gruesome Ustashe World War II record" that supposedly included the murder of 500,000 to 750,000 Serbs, Jews, and Gypsies, and he reported anti-Serbian and anti-Semitic remarks attributed to Tudjman. But he did not discuss Nedić's collaboration with the Nazis, nor the genocide carried out by Serbian Chetniks in the 1940s. Clearly, what journalists omitted, as well as what they included, lent credibility to Milošević's claim that he was "simply fighting for the unity of Serbia."[32]

Interestingly, nobody actually discussed the Nezavisna Država Hrvatska (NDH), although everyone condemned it. The state was proclaimed on 10 April 1941 by Slavko Kvaternik, a former member of the Austro-Hungarian general staff and a Croatian nationalist active in the Ustaša movement from its inception in 1929. His son, Eugen Dido Kvaternik, had helped to organize the assassination of Alexander at Marseilles in 1934 and took over the police in the NDH. The younger Kvaternik had spent several years languishing in Italy, where the Italians had confined the Ustaša in a few cities, in inaccessible regions of southern Italy, or on islands off Sicily. Imprisoned by Italy from 1934 to 1941, the Ustaša quickly turned on their former patrons once they were in power.[33]

Because it was recognized by twelve states, the NDH was a nominally legitimate, if unfortunate, political entity, but Croatians are just now fitting it into their history.[34] This has not been easy, because the NDH followed a fascist model and promulgated laws that discriminated against non-Croats, and the Ustaša committed genocide. A citizen was defined as "a national of Aryan origin" who had not opposed "the liberation efforts of the Croatian people" and who was "ready and willing to serve faithfully the Croatian nation and the Independent State of Croatia." This definition allowed everyone but Jews to hope for full citizenship, even in a state that protected "Croatianism" and punished disloyalty by death. But not even creating a Croatian Orthodox Church reassured the Serbs, whom the Ustaša considered the source of all Croatian misfortunes and had slaughtered in large numbers after taking power.[35]

Because the Ustaše lacked the cadre to staff the new state, they appealed to as many Croatians and Serbians as ideology would allow. They strove to identify themselves with the Peasant Party, to appropriate national icons like Stjepan Radić and Ante Starčević, and to make Croats persecuted by the Yugoslav regime into national heroes and martyrs. They saw the NDH as the culmination of a thousand-year struggle by the Croatian people, but with 3.3 million Croatians, 1.9 million Serbs, 700,000 Muslims, and 40,000 Jews, the state was not ethnically homogeneous. If the Ustaše considered Bosnia-Herzegovina as "our body and our heart," the Muslims did not feel this way.[36]

Slavko Kvaternik attempted to build a credible military, with discrete Ustaša and Domobran (Home Defense) units. By 1943, there were 260,000 men under arms, and during 1944 the Ustaša units began to absorb the Domobran. As the Germans retreated, some Ustaša leaders found their way to Latin America as hard-pressed NDH military units retreated into Austria and surrendered to the British. The British then turned over those Croats who had sought shelter with them to the partisans, who slaughtered between 40,000 and 100,000.[37] The rank and file thus paid for the genocide directed by their leaders, but the massacre of Domobran units was invisible during the 1990s, because the media had latched onto a Serbian version of history that exaggerated Serbian suffering during the war and minimized the suffering of other nationalities.

Typical was Alexander Cockburn's claim that from 750,000 to 1.2 million Serbs had perished "in the pogroms organized by the Nazi puppet state of Croatia." Cockburn inflated the numbers (about a million Yugoslavs had been killed during the war), and he ignored both Serb collaboration with the Axis and Serbian massacres of Croats, Muslims—and Serbs. Instead, he insisted that if Bosnia's Serbs deserved some of the "hammering" they were taking in the media, they felt threatened and "the rhetoric of Western commentators" had gotten "entirely out of hand." Anthony Borden even chided Izetbegović for not having done more "to address Serb concerns."[38]

More accurate statistics on the number killed during World War II were available, and it is not clear why Cockburn and others did not refer to them. Bogoljub Kočović published a study in 1985 that estimated wartime losses at 487,000 Serbians, 207,000 Croats, and 75,000 Muslims. As many as 334,000 Serbians died in the NDH, an enormous figure, but far short of a million. Kazimir Katalinić revised Kočović's estimates downward, to 330,000 Serbians, 276,000 Croats, and 96,000 Muslims, with 235,00 Serbs killed in the NDH. These are still depressing figures, but somewhat qualified. Whereas 133,000 perished in Ustaša camps,

79,000 died in Serbian camps and 446,000 in some form of combat. The Serbs suffered the most deaths, but in proportion to population, the Muslims led, losing 8.1 percent. The Serbs lost 7.3 percent, the Croats 5.0 percent.[39]

Most of those reporting and commenting on the war ignored these studies and continued to rely on outdated and partisan sources like Rebecca West and Alex Dragnich, a Serb royalist. One could dismiss Katalinić because he was Croatian, but Kočović was a Serb, and his reconstruction made it clear that thousands of Serbs died in Serbia at the hands of Germans and Serbian collaborators. Cohen's recent work on Serbian collaboration notes the work by Vladimir Žerjavić, who put the total number killed at 947,000, including 131,000 Serbs and 106,000 Croats killed in Croatia proper, and 164,000 Serbs, 64,000 Croats, and 75,000 Muslims in Bosnia-Herzegovina, where Ustaše, Chetniks, partisans, and the Axis had armed units. Of 320,000 Serbs killed in the NDH, 48,000 died in the concentration camp at Jasenovac, 82,000 fighting with the partisans, and 50,000 because they were pro-Axis. Of 142,000 Serbs who died in Serbia proper, 23,000 were collaborators, 39,000 partisans. The Axis killed 81,000 Serbs, the Ustaša 76,000, and both collaborators and partisans killed tens of thousands from their own ethnic groups.[40]

Many scholars and popular authors have criticized the Ustaša and the NDH. Gale Stokes claimed that neither Serbs nor Croats ever had an opportunity to "atone" for crimes committed during the war. Openly sympathetic to Slovene nationalism, he hinted that Milošević had been elected democratically, but denounced Tudjman and the Hrvatska Demokratska Zajednica (HDZ) (Croatian Democratic Union) for being destructively and dangerously xenophobic, and for "praising ... the degenerate fascist state of World War II" as an expression of Croatian "historical aspirations." Following Rusinow, he labeled the Croatian "spring" of 1971 "fascist."[41]

Such distorted history, partisan commentary, and superficial analysis encouraged people to see the victims as no better than their tormentors and allowed the Serbs to argue that condemnation of their actions was unfair because Croats and Bosnians were potential aggressors.[42] Not everyone who demonized Croatia as a resurgent fascist state or depicted Muslims as latent fanatics did so unconsciously. Darko Tanasković, who teaches "oriental studies" in Belgrade, depicted Izetbegović as a proponent of "radical Islamization"; Nora Beloff excused Serbian actions as a reaction to Ustaša atrocities in the 1940s; a UN report claimed that Serbs in Croatia would never accept Croatian sovereignty; and John Hoey blamed the United States, not the Serbs, for the fighting in Bosnia.[43]

In late 1993, NPR's "All Things Considered" carried Silvia Faggioli's report that Croatia's Jewish community was worried over the "quiet rehabilitation" of the NDH. She noted that streets [sic] and a school in Zagreb had been named after the Ustaša leader, Mile Budak, and that a square dedicated to the victims of fascism was renamed the Square of Croatian Geniuses. She reported that "some people" worried that the government was trying to "rehabilitate the NDH." After repeating the usual refrains about genocide in Croatia, she noted that Jewish leaders had written an "unprecedented" letter protesting the new *kuna* (marten) monetary unit. She also claimed that Tudjman had minimized the number killed at Jasenovac, had not "openly" disavowed the Ustaša and NDH, and was "said to be beholden" to Ustaša emigrants. She concluded that Croatians were the worst offenders when it came to rewriting history.[44] Although some Croats were rehabilitating the NDH, Croatians were hardly the worst offenders in revising history to serve political ends.

Of course, they were rewriting Communist history, and it was clear that Faggioli, who was based in Italy, was not familiar with Yugoslav history. Her exposé echoed an earlier NPR story on anti-Semitism in Nicaragua that was also misleading. There had been protests over the use of the *kuna*, but there had also been protests over the Croatian coat of arms, which the Ustaša had appropriated. Mile Budak had been an Ustaša and an NDH minister, but was also an important Croatian literary figure. But Faggioli seemed unaware of this, and her one-sided report seemed designed to make Croatians look bad.[45]

Mark Heinrich used the first papal visit to Croatia to smear both the Vatican and Croatia. He reported that while Tudjman's "right-wing nationalist government" had "billed the trip as an endorsement of independent Croatia," Serb "rebels" had "urged the pope to condemn Croatian fascist persecution of Serbs in World War II and alleged Catholic church complicity in it." Cardinal Kuharić invited clergy of all denominations to attend the ceremonies, but Heinrich equated Catholicism with Croatian "national pride" and ended his piece by again noting that the church had played a "controversial" role in World War II when "a number of clergy collaborated with Ustasha fascists who murdered many thousands of Serbs and Jews."[46] He thus echoed Kaplan, who made Stepinac a clerical symbol for Croatia and left the impression that the Croats were clerical neofascists.[47]

Heinrich's use of emotional images to associate fascism and genocide with the Vatican and Croatia echoed Serbian propaganda that claimed the "Khomeini-Ustasha conspiracy" was a new version of the Vatican-Comintern plot against the Serbs.[48] But he failed to remind his readers that Karadžić had threatened the pope's life; that Serbs had murdered their Croat neighbors during World War II, that the Serbian Orthodox Church had collaborated with the Nazis, or that Serbian nationalists saw all non-Serbs as racial enemies.[49] At best, his article failed the ethical test of completeness.

In April 1993, as the West seemed about to undertake military action against the Serbs, *Newsweek* carried Charles Lane's article on Belgrade's Genocide Museum, dedicated to the victims of both "the Hitlerite Croat Ustasha" and "recent fighting in Croatia." By blaming Milošević, not the Serbian people, for the fighting, and by citing Vuk Drašković, who claimed that Serbs were merely fighting for their survival, Lane could conclude that "Serbian protestations of innocence in Bosnia cannot be dismissed as empty posturing" and urged "western policy-makers" to "pay a visit" to the museum. It had certainly had the desired effect on Lane, who did not mention that Drašković was an ultranationalist who wanted all Serbs in Serbia, and did not question linking victims of genocide in the 1940s to those killed while committing genocide in the 1990s.[50]

Pomfret demonstrated both a lack of balance and an obsession with Croatian misdeeds by focusing on Ivica Rajić, a Croatian accused of war crimes and acquitted by a local court of the murder of five Croats who had refused to fight the Muslims. Such actions are war crimes, but by focusing on Rajić, who had indeed been indicted, when most other indicted war criminals were Serbian, Pomfret reinforced the image of Croats as genocidal fascists.[51]

But this was normal. Photographs of Tudjman and Croatian soldiers were cropped so they appeared to be giving fascist salutes. Tudjman was portrayed as a bellicose and duplicitous figure, who might "come out fighting" just to win Croatia's parliamentary elections and had "once favored allying with the Serbs in Bosnia at the expense of the Muslims." Only Western "pressure" had made him agree to a "loose confederation" with Bosnia, which Croatia's parliament had resisted.[52]

Lenard Cohen repeated a plethora of anti-Croatian motifs, from the assertion that Croatians were not ready for democracy, to claims that Tudjman had threatened the privileged position of Croatia's Serbs, that all Croatian "schemes" were "highly inflammatory" to Serbs who recalled Croatian genocide during World War II, that the 1990 elections were "a clear shift to the right" and put an "assertive Croatian nationalism" into power, that the Croatian constitution made the Serbs "nervous" because they feared being ruled by Croatians, that Tudjman had upset the Serbs by suggesting Bosnia-Herzegovina be restructured, that the Croatian government failed to "cooperate" with the JNA in the Špegelj affair, that Slovene and Croat proposals for a confederation upset Yugoslavia's "Serbian majority," that Slovene and Croat military units were "illegal," that the Serbs feared Mesić might not let the JNA protect Serbs in Croatia, that Croatia and Slovenia had undercut peace plans, that Croatia had triggered attacks by the JNA by declaring its independence, that Vukovar was a "Serb Golgotha," and that Zagreb was largely to blame for the war in Bosnia.[53]

In short, everything was Croatia's fault.

DEVOUT, INCOMPETENT AND OBSTREPEROUS MUSLIMS

If Croatia was a resurgent fascist state, and Serbia the last bastion of Communism, Bosnia was a potential Muslim beachhead in Europe; if Croats were dangerous and Serbs united, Muslims were divided, thanks to the split between Izetbegović and Fikret Abdić, former head of Agrokomerc, a company that had collapsed after issuing $500 million in false promissory notes.[54] Based in Velika Kladuša, his forces joined Serb attacks on Bihać for much of the war, leading the *New York Times* to run such clever, and confusing, headlines as "Conflict in the Balkans . . . Muslims vs. Muslim vs. Serb."[55]

Throughout the conflict, the media identified the Bosnian government as "Muslim-led." Because the phrase became second-nature, pro-Serbian writers could present the struggle as religious and appeal to Western Christians to support the Serbs against a nebulous Islamic threat.[56] Roger Cohen combined anti-Islamic and anti-Croatian threats by noting that while Bosnia was producing many of its own small arms, it obtained heavier weapons from Iran, Turkey, and Malaysia. Croatia took a large share of arms shipments to Bosnia as they went through its territory, but enough had reached Bosnia to make its army a credible force—and a considerable improvement on the early "ragtag collection of thugs, kids, and patriots."[57]

If MacKenzie, Owen, and Vance convinced many that Serbian military gains were irreversible, it followed that Muslim efforts to win back territory obstructed the peace. "Muslim-led government troops" upent the war "chipping away at the 70 percent of Bosnian territory the Serbs had cleansed in 26 months of war in which more than 200,000 people are dead or missing."[58] In May 1994, AP implicitly linked a Bosnian attack to the arrival of a "Turkish reconnaissance team" that was preparing the way for 2,700 Turkish peacekeepers. The Serbs, who referred to the Bosnians as "Turks," were "especially angry" over the arrival of the Anatolian Turks, "because of historic animosity between Slavs and Turks." This was one way to describe the arrival of UN peacekeepers, and unique. No one noted Muslim resentment when French and British units arrived in Bosnia, owing to the historic animosity between Muslim and Christian. AP seemed biased. In one piece it reported that the Saudis had paid for a trip to Mecca by Izetbegović and 300 "Slavic Muslims," and in another speculated that "Bosnia's Muslim-led government" might emulate the Turkish model for a "secular Islamic state."[59]

By mid-1994, Muslims and Croats were seen as uneasy allies, owing to the creation of an American-sponsored Bosnian-Croatian confederation on March 18, 1994. A new "federation" cabinet led by Haris Silajdžić was to contain fourteen Muslims, thirteen Croats, and one Serb.[60] If Silajdžić thought Bosnia might serve as "an example to the West" of a "multicultural and multinational" state, AP noted that Bosnia lacked "one basic prerequisite, territory."[61]

While Silajdžić was quoted, others often spoke for the Muslims. In June 1994, "U.S. officials" announced that the new peace plan, which gave 49 percent of Bosnia-Herzegovina to Sarajevo "reflect[ed] largely what Muslims wanted." If so, Christopher and Kozyrev did not have to threaten to lift sanctions on the Serbs should the "Muslims" reject the plan, and to lift the embargo should the Serbs do so. In fact, the "Muslims" were passive players; what counted were the opinions of the G-7, who were expected to approve the plan.[62]

In July, AP saw the Bosnians as accommodating, but not quite happy with the peace plan put forward by the Contact Group. While the plan allowed "the Serbs to keep territory from which they had forcibly driven tens of thousands of Muslims during the war," Izetbegović had accepted it as "less favorable to them than it is to us." AP reported Karadžić's denunciation of the plan as "an absolute American dictate" and of the embargo as a farce that allowed "the Muslims" to "receive regular, large-scale shipments of arms via Croatia." This, of course, tarred two birds with one brush.[63]

It was in any case, unlikely, as the AP noted, that the Muslims would recover any Serbian-controlled areas, even though they were "mainly populated by Muslims before the war." What was important was that Warren Christopher and Andrei Kozyrev agreed on the plan.[64]

The Muslims were both spectators and pawns, and one of the more interesting stories of the war was the existence of Fikret Abdić's Serb-supported ministate near Bihać. Characterized as the leader of the "breakaway Muslim forces," Abdić's "revolt" against Sarajevo's "Muslim-led" government undercut Sarajevo's legitimacy and showed Serbs to be tolerant of "good" Muslims.[65] When Bosnia's V Corps took Velika Kladuša and ended Abdić's "eleven–month revolt" in August 1994, an AP release reported the action as the biggest victory in twenty-eight months for the Bosnian Muslims.[66]

Since 1992, the Bihać pocket had been a focal point for hostilities, involving Bosnian Serbs, Bosnians loyal to Sarajevo, Croatians, and Croatian Serbs. Consequently, when Vance and Owen floated their plan in 1993, the opinions of the V Corps, which was defending Bihać, and local Muslim leaders were crucial.

Time's Bruce Nelan reported that both rejected the peace plan as conceding victory to the Serbs. They put their faith in Clinton and their own ability to win a military victory. Bosnians seemed determined to fight on until they had liberated Bosnia and Herzegovina, but their hopes seemed misplaced after Clinton refused to act unilaterally and the Pentagon expressed doubts about committing troops. The Serbs, who had continued to cleanse their areas under the watchful eye of UNPROFOR, had no use for a plan that forced them to "give back" land to the "Muslims."[67]

In 1993 and 1994 the media implied that both Muslims and Serbs opposed peace. In July 1994, Reuters reported that the "warring parties" in Bosnia were all equally intransigent, because "neither the Serbs nor the Muslims [had] given any real indication that they [were] ready to compromise in the interests of peace."[68] Yet in 1994, Sarajevo began to try those accused of having committed atrocities, and that was more than the Serbs had done.[69]

It was, in some ways, a question of how one defined peace.

MILITARY PROWESS AND
UNDESERVING VICTORS

Although the Croatian military offensive in August 1995 was the most unexpected and stunning event of the conflict, it had been foreshadowed. That the West failed to see the weaknesses of the Serbian armed forces owed something to faulty or misleading analyses by experts, particularly those associated with British think tanks, who consistently denigrated Muslim and Croatian forces. However, by mid-1994, the Muslims were beginning to press the Serbs, thanks to support from the Croats, help from the Islamic states, and their own efforts to create a competent officer corps, a solid rank and file, and an embryonic armaments industry.

In January 1993, when Croatian forces advanced on the Peruca dam above Sinj, the UN and Moscow condemned the action, and the Serbs appealed to the UN for protection. This was bizarre, given UN reports that the Serbs were driving 7,000 Muslims from Trebinje and cleansing the Krajina of the region's last Croatian inhabitants—as UNPROFOR troops looked on. When the Croats took the Maslenica bridge over the inlet leading to Zadar, the Serbians blew the dam, prompting Russia's Boris Yeltsin to urge sanctions against the Croatians, while Vance and Owen urged sanctions against anyone who refused to sign their peace plan. Unable to impose sanctions, Owen threatened Zagreb and Sarajevo by announcing that there would be no military intervention, and

Colin Powell urged that the embargo be maintained on all warring parties.[70]

Croatia's display of military competence was clearly unwelcome, as were Tudjman's threats to expel UNPROFOR because it had failed to enforce the terms of the 1992 cease-fire. The media were very concerned over Croatian attacks on Muslims and Croatian successes against Serb troops. In May 1993, the *New York Times* ran an editorial by an "anonymous" U.S. official who reminded the paper's readers that both Croatia and Serbia had to "be brought to heel if there is to be progress toward peace."[71]

A year later, as Serbs lost ground near Mount Ozren and Bosnians took the communications tower on Mount Majevica, severing Bosnian Serb links to Serbia proper, the military balance seemed to be shifting. Bosnian successes near Travnik and Vitež only led UN officials to accuse them of seizing areas while the world's attention was focused on Goražde. Nor were Bosnian successes evidence of much. According to Paul Beaver, editor of Jane's *Balkan Sentinel,* they could only "challenge" the BSA (Bosnian Serb Army) "in limited fighting."[72]

Of course, that was exactly the sort of fighting that had characterized the war, and the Serbs were so uneasy that they demanded a cease-fire at Brčko, the choke point linking their forces in Croatia and western Bosnia to those in eastern Bosnia and Serbia. The Bosnian commander was optimistic, because Brčko was "the key to the war in Bosnia-Herzegovina." The French Foreign Minister hurried to support the Serb request and urged that the city be put under UN protection.[73]

Following an exchange of mortar and artillery rounds between Serbian and Croatian forces in late 1994, Roger Cohen reported that Gojko Sušak, Croatia's Minister of Defense, had warned that Zagreb would not led Bihać fall. This prompted Cohen to comment that Croatia had "used bluster repeatedly without taking action," but Serbia had recently "appeared committed to seeking resolution of the region's problems through negotiations."[74] In May 1995, both the UN and the media condemned Croatia's seizure of western Slavonia. In short, while the Croats rattled their swords, the Serbs sought peace.

Some shows of military prowess were obviously more acceptable than others. After Croatian troops seized Grahovo and Glamoč in July 1995, UN military analysts described Croatia's concentration of armor, artillery, and troops as "a very worrisome military buildup."[75] They "feared" a "Croatian drive on Serb zones," because by isolating Zagreb, U.S. policy was forcing Croatia to attack. But Pomfret prepared his readers for a poor Serbian performance by speculating that Milošević would defend only the eastern areas, which had oil, timber, and other resources.[76] Of course, Mladić and Martić were supposed to defend themselves; Milošević was legally neutral.

When the Croatians mounted Operation Storm in August, UN offi-cials and much of the media reacted negatively. The *Washington Post* quoted Carl Bildt, who found it "difficult to see any difference" between attacks on Zagreb by the Serbs in the Krajina and the Croatian shelling of Knin, for which he held Tudjman responsible. William Perry was relieved that the Croats had helped the Bosnians lift the Serbian siege of Bihać, precluding the need to use U.S. airpower there, but UN, French, and British officials condemned the offensive.[77]

When Croatian and Bosnian forces seemed about to defeat the Bos-nian Serbs decisively, Western diplomats denounced them for tilting the balance of power. Western analysts announced that Croatian successes were really American because Washington had surreptitiously armed, trained, and encouraged the Croats to create a "counterweight" to Serbia. Analysts at the Royal United Services Institute, London's Inter-national Institute of Strategic Studies, and Brookings were especially unhappy. Supposedly, the Americans had managed all this by using a DIA-CIA front, Military Professional Resources, Inc. (MPRI). Croatia had done its bit by spending a billion dollars on its military in a single year, or perhaps three, "evading" the embargo, and "projecting" its power beyond its borders.[78] In other words, both Croats and Americans were sneaky and aggressive.

At least this seemed to be Roger Cohen's point in late 1995. He claimed that Clinton had decided that Croatia would be its "pivotal Balkan ally" and then used MPRI to create a military counterweight to Serbia. Washington had given Croatia a "green light" by issuing "half-hearted" "admonitions" to Zagreb, then Croatian "aggression" had got out of control and had to be "contained." Cohen also noted the illicit flow of arms into Croatia, but he ignored the breaking of the arms embargo and sanctions by Serbia's neighbors, something the Bulgarian press covered in detail. He also ignored Croatian-Muslim military co-operation and seemed unaware that the Croatian offensive had ended an attack on Bihać by Bosnian and Croatian Serbs. Instead, he depicted Croatia as a rogue state threatening Bosnia.[79]

Charles Boyd, a former deputy commander with the U.S. European Command, accused Washington of prolonging the war in Bosnia by sup-porting Croatia. Boyd saw Washington's pro-Muslim bias as making it unreasonably anti-Serbian. He complained that the Croats had "cleansed" 90 percent of the Serbs in western Slavonia, but only Serbian cleansing in Žepa had received any attention. He also implied that the Muslims were not victims and condemned the Croatians for chasing the Serbs from the Krajina, "their" home for over 300 years.[80] Obviously, his grasp of history was no firmer than his understanding of current events.

Mike O'Connor struck an interesting theme in September 1995 when he reported the arrival of Željko Ražnjatović, a.k.a. "Arkan," a "swaggering Serbian warlord," who arrived in Prijedor like a Balkan "Zorro." Arkan had the "biggest gun" and the "biggest knife" of his immediate retinue, and he ridiculed the Krajina Serb army for being "too stupid to stop an attack by Boy Scouts." The message was subtle, but unmistakable: real Serbs like Arkan could have easily dealt with the Croatians.[81]

Whether O'Connor was serious is another question.

NOTES

1. Stephen Engelberg, "Warily, Croats Move toward Slovene Side," *New York Times*, 3 July 1991.

2. Cohen, *Broken Bonds*, 239; Denitch, *Tragic Death*, 7, 11, 29, 55, 62, 83.

3. Alfred Meyer, "Dog Eats Dog," *Psychology Today* (November–December 1992), 95.

4. Craig R. Whitney, "Peacemaking's Limit," *New York Times*, 21 May 1993.

5. Stokes, *The Walls Came Tumbling Down*, 218.

6. Ramet, *Social Currents*, 406.

7. Noel Malcolm, "On the Scene," *National Review*, 29 July 1991, 18.

8. Lance Morrow, "Unspeakable," *Time*, 22 February 1993.

9. Whitney, *New York Times*, 21 May 1993.

10. Chuck Sudetic, "Muslim-Croat Clashes," *New York Times*, 21 May 1993. For the West's complicity, Jean Baudrillard in Thomas Cushman and Stjepan G. Meštrović, *This Time We Knew: Western Responses to Genocide in Bosnia* (New York University Press, 1996). These were originally published in *Libération*, 7 January 1993, and 3, 17 July 1995.

11. Herman and Chomsky, *Manufacturing Consent*, 38, 51–53, 76.

12. Robert Guskind, "Letter from Croatia: Mostly They Sob" and "Ethnic Time Bombs," *National Journal*, 4, 18 January 1992.

13. "Quiet Voices from the Balkans," *New Yorker*, 15 March 1992.

14. Ramet, *Social Currents*, 403–4; Magaš, *Destruction of Yugoslavia*, 232, 266–73; Cohen, *Broken Bonds*, 183.

15. Magaš, *Destruction of Yugoslavia*, 333, 353–54.

16. Cigar, *Genocide in Bosnia*, 4, 16–17, 22–37, 44–49, 102–3. Genocide is "a rational policy, the direct and planned consequence of conscious policy decisions taken by the Serbian establishment," including Drašković, Rašković, Jevtić, Ćosić, and Tanasković. Also Patricia Forestier, "The Use of Social Sciences to Stir Up Ethnic Conflict," *International Conference on Bosnia-Herzegovina*, Ankara, April 1995.

17. Guskind, "Ethnic Time Bombs."

18. Rieff, "Letter from Bosnia," 88, and *Slaughterhouse: Bosnia and the Failure of the West* (Simon & Schuster, 1995), for a condemnation of Western policy in Bosnia; Gutman, *Witness*, 102–8, for refugees. Anthony Lewis reviewed the book sympathetically in "War Crimes," *The New Republic* (March 1995), and "Bosnia's Fall, Our Failure," *Harper's* (Feb. 1995); but in *New York Review of Books*, 23 March 1995, Misha Glenny, whose bias is usually carefully veiled, panned Rieff's book and argued that the absence of a "viable Bosnian state" precluded Serbian "aggression."

19. *AP,* 24 June 1994. Serb mortars had shelled Croat positions and Bihać, as Bosnians attacked Abdić's Muslim forces.

20. Smale, *AP,* 27 June 1994; and "Bosnians Select Government," *AP,* 23 June 1994; "Muslims, Serbs Argue on Truce," *AP,* 6 June 1994, whose lead sentence began, "Bosnia's warring factions argued Monday over the length of a proposed cease-fire."

21. *AP,* 24 June 1994; "U.N. Reports Major Truce Violations in Bosnia," *Reuters,* 20 June 1994. Serbian sources left the impression that they were reacting to Bosnian violations; Kurt Schork, "Heavy Fighting Further Damages Bosnian Truce," *Reuters,* 18 June 1994, sympathized with the Serbs; *AP,* 17 June 1994, implied "both" sides had broken the cease-fire.

22. Helsinki Watch, *Letter to F. Tudjman,* 13 February 1992, and *Letter to S. Milošević and B. Adžić,* 21 January 1992.

23. Malcolm, "On the Scene," 18.

24. John Pomfret, "Success of Bosnia Pact Hangs on Timing, Tests," and "Plan Legitimizes," and "Between War and Peace," *Washington Post,* 18, 20 December, 22 November 1995, 18 December 1995, noted that in 1993 "Croatian gunmen in Bosnia" had followed suit and were "rounding up Muslims . . . and subjecting them to similar treatment."

25. "Nightline," 14 January, 3 February, 28 December 1993.

26. Denitch, *Tragic Death,* 37, 56, saw Serbs as "tolerant" of demanding Croats. For the "first" Yugoslavia, see Ivo Banac, *The National Question in Yugoslavia: Origins, History, Politics* (Ithaca, NY: Cornell University Press, 1984), and Alfredo Breccia, *Jugoslavia, 1939–1941: Diplomazia della neutralità* (Varese: Giuffrè, 1978), passim.

27. Aryeh Neier, "Watching Rights," *The Nation,* 18 January 1993.

28. *New York Times,* 23 December 1991 and 27 December 1991, for reports that Croats had "seized" six villages.

29. John Tagliabue, *New York Times,* 1, 3 July 1991.

30. As Banac noted, in Ali and Lifschultz, *Why Bosnia?,* 163–64, Ivo Andrić and Robert Kaplan had spread such "banal half-truths" very widely. Louis Adamić, *My Native Land* (New York: Harper and Brothers, 1943), 406–16, noted that one editor complained in the early 1940s that those "crazy Yugoslavs" were "always fighting among themselves."

31. Dana Priest, "U.S. Planners Fear Heavy Pullout Costs," *Washington Post,* 14 July 1995.

32. Guskind, "Ethnic Time Bombs," thought the conflict's "roots" went back 600 years.

33. Sadkovich, *Italian Support,* 250–302; Fikreta Jelić-Butić, *Ustaše i Nezavisna Država Hrvatska, 1941–1945* (Zagreb: Liber, 1977), 71; Jill Irving, *The Croat Question: Partisan Politics in the Formation of the Yugoslav Socialist State* (Boulder, CO: Westview Press, 1993), 90–95; K. Meneghello-Dinčić, "L'État Outacha de Croatie (1941–1945)," *Revue d'histoire de la deuxième guerre mondiale* (1969).

34. Jelić-Butić, *Ustaše,* 96, did *not* see the NDH as a viable state, but Hrvoje Matković, *NDH* (Zagreb, 1995), treats it as a historical reality. Angelo Piero Sereni, "The Status of Croatia under International Law," *American Political Science Review* (1941); Milan Blazekovich, "El status internacional del estado independiente de Croacia del 1941 al 1945," *Studia Croatica* (1966).

35. Jelić-Butić, *Ustaše*, 75–135; Raphael Lemkin, *Axis Rule in Occupied Europe: Laws of Occupation, Analysis of Government, Proposals for Redress* (Washington, DC: Carnegie Endowment for International Peace, 1944), 606–26.

36. Jelić-Butić, *Ustaše*, passim; Ivan M. Tomić, *Čija je Bosna i Hercegovina?* (London: Almanah HSS, 1994), 18, 30.

37. Ivan Košutić, *Hrvatsko domobranstvo u drugom svjetskom ratu* (Zagreb: Matica Hrvatske, 1992), passim; Ivo Babić, in Francis Eterovich and Christopher Spalatin, eds., *Croatia: Land, People, Culture* (Toronto: University of Toronto Press, 1964), 155–66; "La Tragedia de Bleiburg," Special edition, *Studia Croatica* (1963); and Stanko Guldescu and John Prcela, eds., *Operation Slaughterhouse: Eyewitness Accounts of Postwar Massacres in Yugoslavia* (Philadelphia: Dorrance & Co., 1970). Tomašević, "Yugoslavia during the Second World War," in Wayne Vucinich, ed., *Contemporary Yugoslavia: Twenty Years of Socialist Experiment* (Berkeley, CA: University of California Press, 1969), 113, estimated "several scores of thousands" had perished.

38. *The Nation*, 31 August–7 September 1992; Hitchens in *Why Bosnia?*, 7–9.

39. Bogoljub Kočović, *Žrtve Drugog svetskog rata u Jugoslaviji* (London: Naše delo, 1985), passim, and Kazimir Katalinić, "Hrvatske i srpske žrtve 1941–1945," *Republika Hrvatska* (April 1988), 15–63; Vladimir Žerjavić, *Opsesije i megalomanije oko Jasenovca i Bleiburga* (Zagreb: Globus, 1992); Magaš, *Destruction of Yugoslavia*, 314–315, for a summary.

40. Cohen, *Serbia's Secret War*, 106–12; Žerjavić, *Opsesije i megalomanije*, passim, esp. 75–79, 105–278. Of the 83,000 who died at Jasenovac, 48,000 were Serbian, 12,000 Croatian, 13,000 Jewish, 10,000 gypsy.

41. Stokes, *Walls*, 222–23, 227, 242. Mladen Colić, *Takozvana Nezavisna Država Hrvatska, 1941* (Belgrade: Delta-Press, 1973); Jelić-Butić, *Ustaše*; Bogdan Krizman, *Ante Pavelić i Ustaše* (Zagreb: Globus, 1978) and *NDH izmedju Hitlera i Mussolinija* (Zagreb: Globus, 1983); Milan Basta, *Agonija i slom Nezavisne Države Hrvatske* (Belgrade: Rad, 1971); Viktor Novak, *Magnum Crimen: Pola vijeka klerikalizma u Hrvatskoj* (Zagreb: Nakladni Zavod Hrvatske, 1948).

42. Roger Cohen, *New York Times*, 18 October 1992.

43. Darko Tanasković, "Religion and Human Rights"; Nora Beloff, "Eastern Approaches," *National Review*, 13 April 1992; Craig R. Whitney, *New York Times*, 21 May 1993; John Hoey, "The U.S. 'Great Game' in Bosnia," *The Nation*, 30 January 1995.

44. Silvia Faggioli, "All Things Considered," *NPR*, 8 April 1993.

45. NPR's reporting could be shoddy, for example, "All Things Considered," *NPR*, 7 May 1994, made it seem as if the United States had tried to save Haiti when it occupied the island in the early 1900s. NPR noted that 3,000 Haitians had died, but only fourteen U.S. Marines; it did no detailed historical analysis.

46. Mark Heinrich, "Pope Makes First Trip to Ex-Yugoslavia," *Reuters*, 10 September 1994.

47. Hungarian and Polish prelates are seen as anticommunists, Stepinac as a fascist. Richard Pattee, *The Case of Cardinal Aloysius Stepinac* (Milwaukee: Bruce Publishing, 1953), defended the archbishop, but Kaplan, *Balkan Ghosts*, 10–28, implied that Croatians need to apologize for the Holocaust and saw the Roman Catholic Church as the "greatest stimulus to anti-Serb feeling in Croatia."

48. Cohen, *Broken Bonds*, 144; Magaš, *Destruction of Yugoslavia*, 263; and Ramet, *Social Currents*, 407. Croatian support of Muslim victims of Serbian aggression became a Catholic-Islamic conspiracy.

49. Kurt Schork, "Pope Insists He Want to Visit Sarajevo" and "Sarajevans Bitter at U.N. over Pope's Cancellation," *Reuters*, 4, 7 September 1994. The Serbian leader had told the papal nuncio that "he feared Muslims might attack the pope and blame the Serbs." Because the UN would not guarantee the Pope's safety, he canceled his visit to Bosnia.

50. Charles Lane, "The Ghosts of Serbia," *Newsweek*, 19 April 1993; Cohen, *Broken Bonds*, 151–53; Elie Wiesel visited the museum in 1992. Dave Marash reported that it "focuses on Croatian atrocities during World War II and during last year's Serbo-Croatian war." *Nightline*, 2 December 1992.

51. John Pomfret, "Wanted Man Tests NATO's Mission," *Washington Post*, 14 December 1995. As this book goes to press, over 70 have been indicted, the vast majority Serbs.

52. *AP*, 29 June 1994, cited Ivo Banac, who saw Tudjman's rhetoric, like his taking of the Maslenica bridge in 1993, as campaign tactics. At the same time, the media depicted Milošević as someone with whom Eagleburger and Vance could work.

53. Cohen, *Broken Bonds*, 94–99, 130–31, 140–41, 191–97, 204, 211–14, 225–26, 236–37.

54. Magaš, *Destruction of Yugoslavia*, 111–12.

55. Roger Cohen, "Conflict in the Balkans . . . Muslim vs. Muslim vs. Serb," *New York Times*, 4 December 1994.

56. For example, Jonathan Landay, "Contact Group Muddle Through on Bosnia," *Christian Science Monitor*, 1 August 1994.

57. Roger Cohen, "Bosnia's Army Emerges as a Formidable Enemy," *New York Times*, 15 June 1995.

58. *AP*, 24 June 1994; Cigar, *Genocide*, 118.

59. "Bosnian Fighting Intensifies," *AP*, 20 May 1994; "Muslims Press Bosnia Offensive," *AP*, 17 May 1994.

60. Cigar, *Genocide*, 135–37. Izetbegović had proposed a union in August 1993, and Tudjman ousted Boban in February 1994, but not until HVO losses made a deal with the Muslims attractive did Tudjman finally approve one.

61. *AP*, 23 June 1994.

62. Carol Giacomo, "G7 Expected to Endorse Peace Plan Dividing Bosnia," *Reuters*, 22 June 1994.

63. "Bosnian Leaders OK Peace Plan," *AP*, 7 July 1994; "Peace Plan under Fire by Serbs," *AP*, 6 July 1994.

64. "Bosnia Issued Peace Ultimatum," *AP*, 5 July 1994. The headline was extremely misleading.

65. Kurt Schork, *Reuters*, 3 July 1994.

66. Mark Heinrich, "Bosnian Government Ends Bihać Revolt," *Reuters*, 21 August 1994; "Bosnia Airlift Resumes," *AP*, 9 August 1994.

67. Bruce Nelan, "The Balkans: Getting with the Program," *Time*, 22 February 1993.

68. Kurt Schork, *Reuters*, 3 July 1994.

69. Cigar, *Genocide*, 137–38.

70. *New York Times*, 29, 30, 31 January 1993, and 22 December 1992, for Russian support of the Serbs.

71. *New York Times*, 4 January, 20 May 1993.

72. *AP*, 17 May 1994; "Bosnian Troops Push Back Serbs," *AP*, 19 May 1994; David Hujić (Davor Hudžić), "Muslims Seized Land While World Watched Gorazde," *Reuters*, 6 May 1994.

73. "Bosnian Government: No Peace Talks," *AP*, 3 May 1994, and "Bosnian Serbs Block U.N. Group," *AP*, 3 May 1994.

74. Roger Cohen, "Conflict in the Balkans: In Croatia," *New York Times*, 2 December 1994.

75. James Rupert, "Croats' Forces Cut Serb Lines inside Bosnia. Drive Could Push War across Border," *Washington Post*, 29 July 1995.

76. John Pomfret, "Croatian Drive on Serb Zones Feared by UN Officials," *Washington Post*, 7 July 1995.

77. Dana Priest, "U.S. Cautiously Supports Offensive against Serbs," *Washington Post*, 5 August 1995.

78. James Rupert, "Croatia, Evading UN Arms Embargo, Projects Its Military Power in Balkans," *Washington Post*, 2 August 1995. For an example of the partisan scholarship published by those associated with these organizations, see Edgar O'Ballance, *Civil War in Bosnia 1992–94* (London: St. Martin's Press, 1995).

79. Roger Cohen, "U.S. Cooling Ties to Croatia after Winking at Its Buildup," *New York Times*, 28 October 1995; Maria Spirova, "Razpaddaneto na iugoslavia v bulgarskata presa (1991–1995)," *Balkaniistichen Forum* (1996), 202–211. The issue involved Bulgaria's diplomatic relations and its economic health. A Gallup poll reported 30 percent of their sample wanted strict enforcement of sanctions, 30 percent compensation from the West; and 16 percent thought sanctions should not be enforced. Many urged Sofia to follow Bucharest and Athens and play up to Belgrade, since Milošević could do as he pleased with the West.

80. Boyd, *New York Times*, 9 August 1995.

81. Mike O'Connor, "Arrival of Serb Warlord Raises Faltering Spirits," *New York Times*, 20 September 1995.

7

Stereotypes: Serbs

THE USES OF HISTORY IN REAL TIME

Even historians like to debunk their discipline as esoteric and useless, and too much history is specialized, ideological, partisan, or faddish. But history played a crucial and tragic role in Yugoslavia's dissolution because a lot of bad history was easily available when careful analysis was needed to correct the real time of the media, inform public opinion polls, and expand time scales compressed by those who insisted that Balkan types experience World War II as a contemporary event.

During the 1980s, Serbian intellectual and political leaders resurrected and publicized atrocities committed against Serbs during World War II, but were silent regarding similar actions by Serbian forces. The combination of propaganda and silence prepared the ground for genocide, and in the 1990s, the media argued that outrages committed fifty years ago justified contemporary war crimes.

Because English-language histories of the Balkans were skewed toward Serbian or Yugoslav points of view, media summaries were too. Ostensibly presenting "both" Muslim and Serbian sides, by reporting that Ozren had "historical significance only for the Serbs as a stronghold of resistance to the occupation during World War II," Bradley Graham repeated the myth that only Serbs had fought the Axis during the war. Using only Serbian sources, Lenard Cohen concluded that Serbs found "any schemes advanced by Croatian nationalists . . . highly inflammatory," because during the war "thousands of their brethren under Croatian rule had perished as a result of ethnic genocide."[1]

The inaccurate, often apologetic history repeated by journalists rationalized Serb actions and inculpated Croats and Muslims by blaming past actions for current atrocities. History was not trivial or irrelevant antiquarianism. Even David Rieff's history could be incomplete and inaccurate. He reported that the "Germans and their Croat allies" had practiced "ethnic cleansing" and a Serb's remark that mujahedeen were worse than the *handžar* (an SS formation of Bosnian Muslims), but he did not mention Serbian collaboration or atrocities, or note that "ethnic cleansing" was a Serbian phrase. If ubiquitous, Serbian history was also one-sided.[2]

A pandemic of bad history meant that no one was prepared to analyze the war, and its ending remains clouded. But it is clear that the precarious end-state left the Serbs winners, the Bosnians losers, and the Croats qualified victors. Yet the habits of the previous years led to articles that depicted Serbs as bitter and disgruntled because they saw themselves, again, as victims of a peace imposed by outside powers who robbed them of their conquests.[3] Perhaps, but had peace *not* been imposed, Croatian and Bosnian forces might have rolled over Pale and into Belgrade, consolidated a viable Croatian-Bosnian federation, and forced Serbia to fight or to admit defeat. Such accounts were bad history in the making.

Raymond Bonner's sources used history to argue that both the Croatian government and Serbian "rebels" had "legitimate grievances and claims" in "Krajina," depending on how far back one went to establish a claim. He noted that in World War II Croatian Ustaše had "supported the Nazis" and killed "thousands of Serbs," and he implied that in 1995 "Croatian solders" had killed civilians while "Serbian fighters" had mutilated innocent Croats. He tarred all sides, and by citing Glenny, he indicated where his bad history had originated.[4]

Bad history usually disadvantaged Croats and Muslims, not Serbs. In 1993, an "anonymous U.S. official" argued in the *New York Times* that recent fighting in Mostar had "reminded the world that Croatia as well as Serbia must be brought to heel if there is to be progress toward peace." The piece urged a policy of "safe havens" and endorsed the Vance-Owen plan, a diplomatic solution opposed by the Bosnians. It smeared Croatia with a genocidal brush by calling for sanctions against Zagreb unless it stopped "ethnic cleansing," a Serbian concept carried out in Croatia and Bosnia by Serbian forces.[5] But bad history had convinced public and experts that Croats had been profascist butchers and Serbs anti-Nazi partisans.

Nora Beloff demonstrated the uses of history when she tried to discredit Croat demands for independence. Although the Croats had a medieval state and maintained their identity under Hungarian and Habsburg rule, Beloff asserted that no "historic Croatia" had existed before 1941, when Hitler created the NDH, which was ruled by the Ustaša, "the Croatian equivalent of the Nazis." Even though Serb cliques had dominated Yugoslavia from 1918 to 1991, she insisted that the current "resistance of Serbs to Croat domination" [sic!] could not "be fully appreciated" without taking into account the Serb desire to avenge previous Croatian genocide against Serbs.[6]

Her focus on a single event in a single period was as disingenuous as her claims that Croats provoked fighting when they "tried to take over contested regions [of historic Croatia] and were shot by Serbs" in 1990; that Croatia discriminated against Serbs by taxing their properties, failing to protect Serbian and "mixed families from arson and assault," and allowing a street and a school to be named after Mile Budak, an Ustaša leader; and that Tudjman had "presided over a revival of the Ustashi's 'Croatia for the Croats' racialism." Tudjman's record may have been dismal, but Beloff failed to mention that most Serbs elected to stay in Croatia and that Budak was both a member of the Ustaša and one of Croatia's leading literary figures. Following her logic, one might have to excise Ezra Pound from English literature, even though he merely broadcast pro-Axis propaganda while Budak served as an NDH minister.[7]

Beloff also neglected to mention that Croatian nationalists reacted to aggressive acts by Serbians both inside *and* outside of Croatia. If the slide to a one-party state in the 1990s was lamentable, it was recent and understandable. During the "Croatian spring" of 1970–71, Croatian nationalism, and Tudjman, had been liberal and progressive. Croatia's Serbs were not monolithic, and as Ante Čuvalo noted, Croatia represented the rare instance of a majority trying to gain equality with a privileged (Serbian) minority.[8]

In autumn 1992, Max Primorac reported that the Serbs were "deliberately terrorizing non-Serbian populations" and waging a "Nazi-like campaign" with "death camps, summary executions, and the creation of millions of refugees."[9] Yet the media carried Serb claims that they were simply practicing a form of self-defense and self-determination by striking at the Croats and Muslims before they became the victims of oppression and genocide. At worst, they seemed to be acting on reasonable fears that a Croatian state would repeat the Ustaša atrocities of fifty years earlier and that a Muslim state in Bosnia would impose another 500 years of Muslim rule on the Serbs.

Serb atrocities thus became preventive retaliation for past and possible Muslim and Croatian actions, and the issue became Croat and Muslim insensitivity to Serb feelings, not Serbian aggression against Croatians and Muslims. In short, the media was "Serbocentric." Rieff noted that this line was so effective *within* Bosnia that "Serb fighters" justified their actions as retaliation for Muslim atrocities and most Serbs denied ethnic cleansing, even though Serbs were colonizing Bosnia and Croatia.[10]

Bad history had an impact everywhere, leading the media to depict Croats as aggressive and genocidal, and excuse Serbs as reacting to perceived and real threats. The reverse was true, historically and recently, but Paul Lewis worried that the Croats might occupy the Serbian "enclave" in Krajina, a reasonable assumption given that it was formally part of Croatia. The logical comparison would have been with Kosovo, but Serbian repression there was largely ignored. Croat and Muslim atrocities seemed to confirm that deadly threats to the Serbs existed, and that the conflict was not a unilateral Serbian assault on their neighbors, but a fratricidal civil war in which all sides committed atrocities.[11]

THE INVINCIBLE SERB AND THE VIETNAM SYNDROME

The high modality of the news, which presents events as facts and opinion as truth, needs historical analysis and context to correct the false certainties generated by the seeming transparency of TV news and to question the assumption of expertise surrounding the news shapers who validate and legitimate elite models and policies. Accurate history could have corrected accounts of World War II, Western intervention, and collective guilt. But reliable history was precisely what the media lacked.

So the media persisted in viewing everyone in Bosnia as guilty and were skeptical regarding proposals to intervene militarily, owing to the risk of provoking a guerrilla war by Serbian forces. Such assumptions justified inaction by pleading Vietnam syndrome, or its 1990s equivalent, Somalia syndrome, both diseases of the will exacerbated by a misreading of history. Such syndromes and misreadings were complemented and augmented by the British Ulster syndrome and the French Vietnam-Algeria syndrome. Any of these could paralyze action and distort analysis, and so contagious were they that Boutros-Ghali warned that the "rich man's war" in Bosnia would end up as "a kind of Vietnam for the UN."[12]

Rick Atkinson and Charles Krauthammer presented two textbook cases of Vietnam syndrome in 1995. Atkinson reported concerns among policy makers that deploying U.S. troops to Bosnia was another sign of "the West's deepening involvement in the Bosnian quagmire," and he noted Karadžić's threat that the more soldiers NATO deployed, "the more violence" they would encounter. Krauthammer urged the evacuation of all Western forces in Bosnia, arguing that the effort to establish "safe areas" was reminiscent of the "enclave [strategic hamlet] strategy in Vietnam" that had ended so badly. By 1996, Krauthammer was railing against U.S. involvement in Bosnia, "our new beachhead in the Balkans, a miasma of ethnic strife with a net strategic value . . . less than zero."[13]

As the possibility that U.S. troops would be deployed increased, so did worries that they would become involved in "a war with no foreseeable end."[14] But if Vietnam had ended badly and nineteenth-century theorists were leery of irregular or revolutionary warfare, contemporary theorists have constructed elaborate models of small conventional wars, and military organizations have compiled detailed studies on the efficacy and technique of military coercion and psychological suasion based on successful operations.[15]

The vulnerable supply lines and the dispersed deployment of Serbian forces almost guaranteed that airpower would be effective in Bosnia, especially if combined with well-armed ground forces. Rather than basing policy on the flawed lessons of Vietnam and the myths of World War II, we should have been examining successful examples of the use of military force in Libya and Ethiopia by the Italians, or in Aden and Malaya by the British.[16]

Few did so. Instead, most echoed Walter Russell Mead, who used the mythic Serbian fighter to rationalize Western inaction and legitimate Serbian conquests. In a *Los Angeles Times* column, he argued that since the Serbs had "won" the war and given Clinton and the Democrats a "course in humiliation," it was time to run up the "white flag," let the Bosnian Serbs "rejoin" "Yugoslavia" [sic], and promote reconstruction and reconciliation. Two weeks later, on *This Week with David Brinkley* Senator Dole noted that if regrettable, it was clear that the Serbs had "won," and a year and a half later, William Perry favored "reconciliation" when he appeared on the *MacNeil-Lehrer Newshour*.[17] Like accurate history, reality did not affect the opinions of policy makers, politicians, and commentators.

This was particularly true of discussions regarding military intervention and the arms embargo. Stephen Stedman argued that with nineteen Serb groups in Bosnia, there seemed to be no "unified command," and that an attack on Serbia would only make sense "to deter aggression against Kosovo and Macedonia, to prevent escalation to interstate war, and to weaken Serbia's capability to carry out further attacks." Even then, he warned that to commit ground forces would lead to "a protracted guerrilla war."[18]

An ABC special in the spring of 1993 conveyed a similar message. George Kenney claimed that to "directly confront Serbian aggression" would require a minimum of 50,000 troops; Peter Jennings concluded that 400,000 troops would be needed to contain "the hatred of three peoples for one another"; and a Serbian general threatened to defeat the West, should it act against the Serbs.[19]

By popularizing the image of the invincible Serb guerrilla fighter, the media provided a clinching argument for those determined not to intervene in the former Yugoslavia and justified the futile "internationalist shuttling" of "superannuated diplomats."[20] In 1992, John Newhouse reported that the "buzz words" at the Pentagon were "quagmire" and "Dien Bien Phu," and that London feared Bosnia would become another Northern Ireland. In 1993, Newsweek reported that Colin Powell had expressed similar fears. Although John Barry ridiculed Powell's doctrine of "overwhelming force" as "a pretext for overwhelming reluctance" to get involved in the Balkans, David Hackworth warned that the United States would only get "stuck in a bottomless swamp." "The bottom line," he wrote, "is: we don't have the right stuff to do the job; and if we did it, it wouldn't work against a guerrilla fighting in favorable terrain."[21]

But was that the case?

WORLD WAR II REALITIES

The media portrayed the Serbian Chetniks as guerrillas and the Croatian Ustaša as collaborators, although both collaborated with the Axis, and some Chetniks cooperated with the Ustaša. Neither Axis partner trusted them, and an Italian general dismissed the Chetnik formations as corrupt and useless in combat.[22] During the war, Louis Adamić, Stojan Pribićević, and Nikola Tesla tried to correct propaganda issued by Yugoslav officials, Serbian-American organizations, and the Anglican Church, but even though Chetniks were slaughtering Croats by 1942, Adamić had difficulty publishing pieces critical of Draa Mihailović.[23]

Whether today's Chetniks are premodern, with hajduk roots, or contemporary skinheads, Chetniks have never been freedom fighters. They were nationalist formations whose members "pacified" areas conquered during the Balkan Wars, and then terrorized the Yugoslav opposition after 1918.[24] In 1928, a Chetnik murdered Croat deputies in parliament. During the war a Chetnik manual proposed "cleansing" "Serbian" areas of 800,000 Croats, and Kosta Pećanac's men collaborated with Milan Nedić's State Guard and Dimitrije Ljotić's fascist Serbian Volunteers. Chetnik ideology was anti-Croat, anti-Muslim, and anti-Yugoslav. Stevan Moljević called for a "homogeneous Serbia" to avoid "the great sufferings which the Serbs' neighbors inflict upon them whenever they have the opportunity to do so."[25]

MacKenzie's claims that Chetniks held thirty-seven German divisions at bay during the war were as specious as wartime assertions that a million Serbs had been killed by 1943. There were never thirty-seven Axis divisions in the Balkans; most Serbs collaborated with the Axis powers and the Nedić regime; and the much-maligned Italians had little trouble containing Serb and Montenegrin rebels.[26]

During operations against guerrillas in the fall of 1941, the Germans used only two divisions (704th garrison and 342nd infantry) and two regiments (125th infantry and 202nd Panzer Jäger), supported by the 714th and 717th garrisons and the 113th infantry division. Although weak, these forces pacified northern Serbia. The Chetniks cooperated with Milan Nedić, who presided over a pro-Nazi Serb state, or withdrew into remote areas of Serbia and Bosnia, where they were contained and harried by Bulgarian troops and Serbs loyal to Nedić.[27]

The 718th was in Bosnia, reinforced by Croatian units, the 704th near Valjevo, the 714th at Topola, and elements of the 717th at Bor. The 342nd division reached Serbia in September as the 125th regiment was transferred to Crete and elements of the 202nd Panzer Jäger battalion were withdrawn. When the 113th division moved to Russia and the 342nd to Bosnia, Bulgarian units relieved the 717th, which took over for the 113th. The Germans blamed the Italians for the failure of disjointed antipartisan operations to eradicate the insurgents in Bosnia, but the main obstacle to suppressing unrest in the NDH was Axis policy vis-à-vis the Chetniks and the Ustaša, not rugged terrain or the quality of irregular units.[28]

The Axis mounted their first large-scale operations against insurgent forces in early 1942. The Germans had three divisions in Serbia and one in the NDH. Italy had seventeen, spread from Istria and Slovenia to Montenegro and Bosnia. Three Bulgarian divisions were deployed around Niš, leaving six Domobran divisions and some Ustaša units to support Axis operations in Bosnia. Only one German and three Italian divisions, supported by eight to ten Croatian battalions, were deployed—hardly an imposing array.[29]

In late 1943, the Axis had twenty-seven divisions scattered throughout the Balkans. The Italians had eight in Dalmatia, seven in Montenegro, four in Slovenia, and one in Karlovac. The Germans had two in Bosnia and four in Serbia. The only Italian motorized division was stationed in Karlovac, far from Serbia. None had to fight the Chetniks, who were collaborating with the Axis.[30]

By 1943, the British, who had seen the Chetniks as a bulwark against "anarchy and communist chaos after the war," concluded that only the partisans were fighting the Axis. An SOE major dismissed Mihailović as "a quisling like Nedić," the only difference being that one worked with the Germans, the other with the Italians. Mark Wheeler, whose study reinforces those by Milazzo and Tomašević, concluded that it was "difficult to understand how the British could have taken Mihailović so seriously for so long."[31]

In early 1943, antipartisan operations lasted from January to April, but the Axis deployed only three Italian, three German, and two Croatian divisions, units from two other divisions, and an armored battalion. The partisans had nineteen brigades, equivalent to six divisions. While the Italians fought the partisans, the Germans negotiated with them and disarmed the Chetniks. The partisans fought through the Chetniks, but the effort exhausted them. By then, the Chetniks were losing both Axis and Allied support, and rapidly became marginal. A postwar U.S. Army analysis concluded they "could not act effectively without considerable support from the Italians." When confronted by partisan formations reinforced with Italian deserters and arms following Italy's surrender, the Chetniks fled Bosnia.[32]

Until then, Axis operations against partisan forces had been sporadic, limited in their aims, confined to relatively small areas, and badly coordinated. Only small numbers of troops were used, with most assigned defensive tasks. During the fifth antipartisan offensive most of the 86,000 troops committed were used as blocking forces. With 90,000 troops, the partisans had a rough parity with Axis forces and enough for local superiority against troops deployed in static, defensive positions.

Neither Chetniks nor partisans were very effective. Well-planned, properly coordinated, and determined Axis antiguerrilla operations usually succeeded. In 1941, the Italians suppressed a Chetnik revolt, and two years later, four Italian divisions pushed the partisans out of Montenegro. Until September 1943, Italian units controlled urban areas from Ljubljana in Slovenia to Podgorica in Montenegro, forcing the partisans into thinly inhabited areas far from major centers. The Germans gave priority to protecting their lines of communication, sources of raw materials, and industrial areas, not destroying ineffectual irregular forces. Rugged terrain hampered Axis efforts to contain or destroy the partisans, but it made it hard for the partisans to avoid being trapped and annihilated, and they occupied large areas only after the Axis had evacuated them.[33]

Before 1943, German divisions were poorly armed and comprised largely untrained and overage men. Even after Germany took over antipartisan operations, it deployed only fourteen badly equipped, poorly trained, overage divisions, scattered from Slovenia to Serbia. During 1943, it moved twenty divisions to the Balkans, including six in Greece, to replace and to fight Italian units, which held out through October as thousands of Italian veterans joined the partisans in Greece and Yugoslavia and the Chetniks joined the Germans.[34]

In Istria, Italians gave up their arms and headed home or joined the partisan battalions. *Bergamo* division held *Prinz Eugen* division for nineteen days, and the *Marche* division fought the Germans and were massacred after surrendering in Dubrovnik. Tito got all the arms from the *Cacciatori delle alpi, Macerata,* and *Celere* divisions, and some arms from *Ferrara, Messina,* and *Zara.* Elements of *Firenze, Pinerolo, Bergamo,* and *Arezzo* divisions formed the *Garibaldi, Gramsci,* and *Matteotti* battalions, and *Venezia* joined *Taurinese* division to form the *Garibaldi* division. As many as 150,000 Italians may have joined the partisans in their struggle against the Germans.[35]

It was therefore not military acumen or toughness that accounted for Tito's change of fortune in late 1943 and early 1944. It was the British decision to back the partisans, the Italian surrender, and an influx of Italian veterans into partisan ranks, which swelled to 390,000 by mid-1944—more than double the 169,000 personnel in the JNA in 1991. Because Germany could not control the Balkans alone, liberated territory in Bosnia expanded from 50,000 to 130,000 sq. km. Yet the partisans were unable to do more than survive, and by late 1943, the Germans disarmed most Chetnik units. It is unlikely that the Bosnian Serbs would have proven more formidable.[36]

By 1993, Serbian forces were deployed in an arc from Osijek to Knin to Sarajevo to the Neretva, making them easy to contain, isolate, and destroy—thanks to the nature of the terrain and the choke points along their supply routes. Neither Serbian regulars nor irregulars proved formidable during World War II, and those who claimed that military intervention would be ill-advised and costly because it ran the risk of being opposed by massive Serbian irregular forces depended on a myth to sustain their argument. World War II suggested that few Serbs would resist and most, along with their leaders and institutions, would collaborate with an occupying force.[37]

Moreover, NATO forces would have been in a very different situation from that of the Axis in 1943. They are well-equipped frontline units; they would not have pursued a brutal, racist occupation policy; and they could have counted on the support of most of the population within Bosnia where Serbs were a minority.[38]

There would still have been problems, but not of such a magnitude as to preclude an occupation. Defining political objectives would have been facilitated by the readiness of the Croats and Muslims to cooperate with the West. Nor would fixing a timetable and assessing the relative usefulness of air and ground forces have been difficult. The identification of military objectives would have been a technical problem contingent on the political goals being pursued.[39]

Strategic surprise would have been precluded, but tactical surprise would have been guaranteed because technology would have given the

West a monopoly of intelligence and control of the air. Irregular forces would have been of marginal importance because most of the heavy fighting was been done by JNA units and Bosnian Serb regular forces. Irregulars were usually used to cleanse areas already occupied by regular troops using conventional tactics. Without tanks and heavy artillery, Bosnian Serb troops did not perform well. Even with them, in August 1995, Serb forces in the Krajina broke and ran under Croat pressure, and Bosnian Serbs yielded to Croatian and Bosnian attacks.

AGGRESSORS AS VICTIMS: THE SERBS

A number of commentators have portrayed the Serbs as the real victims of the tragic events in Yugoslavia. Even Branka Magaš saw the war as a tragedy for the Serbs, and Ramet detailed its devastating effect on the Serbian economy. Of course, Magaš also blamed the Serbs for the war, and Ramet considered Milošević's Serbia the "last bastion of total-itarianism in Eastern Europe."[40] The Serbs themselves rediscovered their victimhood in the 1980s, with the publication of works by the Serbian Academy and others; Milošević used self-pity and paranoia to mobilize mass support. The Serbs seem to have projected their dark side onto Albanians, Muslims, and Croats to justify their aggression. Whether this was a case of a nation splitting and projecting its person-ality or evidence of "narcissistic rage," it was deadly.[41]

If Serbs suffered from low self-esteem, they still considered them-selves warriors and any setback smarted. Milošević had insisted that if they could do nothing else, Serbs excelled at war, and as the Slovenes forced the JNA back to its barracks in 1991, Vuk Drašković "fumed" that amateurs had defeated "one of the best equipped armies in Europe." "The Serbian soldier," he lamented, "has been humiliated." John Tagliabue, who reported the remarks, insisted that the army was not "a Serbian tool," even if its officers were mostly Serb.[42]

Yet by the late 1980s the Croats, Slovenes, and Albanians saw the JNA as a repressive tool of the central government, which was manipulated by Jović and Milošević. By March 1991 Magaš had concluded that Serbian military and nationalist circles were collaborating, and the JNA's arming of Serbs in Croatia in mid-1990 left few doubts regarding the army's sympathies and intentions.[43]

Both pundits and scholars have excused Serb aggression and atroci-ties as understandable, if unfortunate. As victims of similar outrages by their neighbors in the past, Serbs were merely retaliating; fearful that their neighbors might attack them, they engaged in the victim's equiv-alent of preventive war. In either case, they could not escape their victimhood, because even when they killed their neighbors and destroyed their property, they remained the real victims. Depicting an aggressor as victim, Lenard Cohen introduced the JNA Chief of Staff, Blagoje Adžić, as "a Serb whose family had been killed by Croatian fascists during World War II."[44]

The assumption of Serbian victimhood was a corollary to Serbocentric coverage of Yugoslavia's dissolution and led politicians, journalists, and analysts to exaggerate the effects of sanctions on Serbia, to present history from a Serbian point of view, and to blame the victims of Serbian aggression for their plight. The assumptions of Serbian victimhood diverted discussion from Serb actions to Serbian feelings, and justified atrocities and criminal actions by individual Serbians and Serbian institutions based on Serbian perceptions, Serbian beliefs, and Serbian history. Susan Woodward excused Serb murders of Croats and their refusal to cooperate with Zagreb by stressing their belief in "German and fascist revanchisme, foreign victimization of Serbs," and their "need to protect each other."[45] But this is not analysis, it is paranoia.

Influential academics in organizations like the American Association for the Advancement of Slavic Studies (AAASS) and Brookings Institute helped the Serbs get attention and sympathy, as did Yugoslav diplomats and Serbian-American groups. The media had easy access to Serbian and pro-Serbian sources. The large number of Serbian businesses in the United States may also have helped by maintaining contacts and funneling money and information to consultants, lobbyists, and U.S. officials.[46]

If the Serbs were the real victims of their aggression, their military prowess and support for the Yugoslav idea also made them uniquely admirable among South Slavs. John Tagliabue speculated that Milošević might be the "main victim" of events because "it was his uncompromising policies that set in motion the developments leading to the present crisis"; John Newhouse cited a German diplomat who mused that if Serbia was "a nation gone mad," in the end theirs would be "the greatest tragedy." Apparently some Serbs suffered as much as Croats or Bosnians because they had bad leaders, given Daniel Plesch's remark that Serbs bought the opposition newspaper *Vreme* so they could "feel that they are sane, because they are surrounded by a truly psychotic culture."[47]

The claim that only Serbs espouse the Yugoslav idea and have a right to areas inhabited by Yugoslavs and those occupied by Serbs was picked up by the media from analysts like Nora Beloff and from White House, UN, and EC officials, who reinforced the image of well-intentioned Serbs trying to preserve a Yugoslav state against recalcitrant Croats, Slovenes, and Muslims.[48]

In his analysis of Yugoslavia's breakup, Gale Stokes noted that granting equal rights to Vojvodina and Kosovo had been "particularly repugnant to some Serbs"; that any restructuring would be unfair to Serbs living outside Serbia; and that "the sovereign national state of the Croatian nation" was a phrase that would be "offensive to the 600,000 Serbs living in Croatia."[49] He did not make the same argument for the Croats and Albanians living in Kosovo and Vojvodina, which Serbia had recently annexed.

As the JNA seized chunks of Croatia and gave them to Serb irregulars in 1991, the *New York Times* implied that Serbs were only reclaiming what they had lost fifty years earlier. It downplayed or ignored the genocide being carried out by Serbs in Croatia, and mentioned only Croatian atrocities and collaboration with the Axis during World War II. The newspaper of record left the impression that a popular Serb uprising had begun in 1990, whereas in reality the JNA had incited, armed, trained, and protected Croatia's Serbs.[50]

In January 1993, Dobriša Cosić reacted to the Vance-Owen plan by appearing on Serbian TV to denounce the West for demanding "national capitulation" by the Serbs and subordinating "the Serbian people to Muslim hegemony." Bruce Nelan quoted Miloš Vasić, the ubiquitous editor of *Vreme,* who noted that the Serbs had a "siege mentality" because they saw themselves as defiant heroes fending off a hostile world. A symbol of the Serbian opposition to Milošević and an expert on things Serbian, Vasić provided easy-to-digest rationalizations for Serbian behavior, and always burdened a few individuals with responsibility for Serbian actions. But he did not disavow Serbian claims or question a mentality that pretended to be a victim while committing atrocities against defenseless civilians.[51]

The Western media could be as partisan. AP ran a blatantly pro-Serbian piece in May 1994 that reported "a pregnant woman and two children" killed in the shelling of Brčko by Bosnian forces, and quoted Karadžić's threat that such "criminal behavior by Muslims and Croats" would make the Serbs "much more reserved in ceding territory." There was no mention of the 3,000 Croats and Muslims slaughtered in Brčko by Serbs, nor of the thousands who had died and the tens of thousands who had been mutilated by Serb shelling of Muslim and Croat areas.[52]

In the spring of 1993, NPR gave a Serbian couple from Mostar a national platform to denounce Croatians and elicit sympathy for Serbs. Purportedly refugees from Mostar, the husband, Mladen, had been serving in the army and fled in the fall of 1991, taking his wife with him. According to Mladen, only 300 of 35,000 [sic] Serbs were left in the city, where his father had disappeared after his arrest by "Ustaša." He admitted that Serbs had done "most" of the ethnic cleansing, but he insisted that they were victims too. Prompted by the reporter, he complained that the "one-sided" anti-Serbian reporting in the United States made him "sick to [his] stomach."[53] Because no effort was made to check information or set it in context, the interview effectively elicited sympathy for the Serbs and presented all sides as guilty.

In July 1994, Kurt Schork reported that Bosnia's Serbs disliked recent peace proposals because they required them "to surrender about one-third of their war gains" and would divide Bosnia "roughly evenly between the two [sic!] sides."[54] In other words, the Serbs had a legitimate claim to territory because they had won it, and a minority of 32 percent deserved more than 50 percent of Bosnia.

Similarly, AP published Karadžić's complaint that the Serbs would have to give up thirteen towns to get peace, and it depicted the Posavina corridor as linking "Serb holdings in Croatia."[55] Even when the Serbs stalled peace talks by refusing to leave the safe area around Goražde, the perspective remained Serbian. The safe area had—as the AP was careful to note—"strategic importance" for the Serbs.[56] Evidently, it had none for the Bosnians.

Whether the Serbs deserved their gains, it was easy to forget that they had not won the areas they controlled in a fair fight, because the media did not remind the audience of their advantage in heavy weapons, enhanced by the West's embargo. In May 1994, National Security Adviser Brent Scowcroft implied that the Serbs deserved to win because they had fought long and hard, and in July, AP implied the same by reporting that "after 27 months of fighting, the Serbs control 70 percent of the former Yugoslav republic."[57]

Julijana Mojsilović, who had been covering "her native Yugoslavia" for AP during the war, portrayed Serbs as victims in her analysis of the Contact Group's peace plan in 1994. Claiming that the Serbs would "have to give up the most" and see their "holdings" dwindle from 70 percent to 49 percent of Bosnia, she warned that the plan would "face tough opposition among soldiers and politicians" and that it had "glaring problems" for "all Bosnian Serbs." By analyzing the plan from a Serbian perspective, stressing such factors as strategic location and prewar "Serb pluralities" as implicit justifications for revising the plan in favor of the Serbs, she made Silajdžić appear to be a poor sport for complaining that the Serbs would retain some areas that they had "conquered and cleared of non-Serbs."[58]

In August 1994, as Serbs plundered UN weapons-storage compounds and Muslims shelled Serb positions, Mark Heinrich discerned a "relapse towards war," an odd phrase given that fighting in Bosnia had been continuous, if low grade, since 1992. The Serbs were violating agreements with the UN, but he excused their behavior by noting their "fury at being pressed by the world to cede territory for peace," another odd phrase, given that they had seized that territory from their defenseless neighbors. Heinrich depicted the Bosnians as finally wearing down "a foe now faltering on the battlefield after two years of dominance"—

like the Chicago Bulls battling the Phoenix Suns in a double overtime in the seventh game of the playoffs.[59]

In August 1994, Pale conducted yet another referendum to "buy time," instead of signing the latest peace plan, which Serb leaders saw as an effort to get Serbs "to sign their own death warrant." According to AP, Serbs were being asked to "give up" territory, not to return it, and "Bosnia's Serbs" were cast as rebels "forced" to act "against a Muslim-Croat vote to secede from Yugoslavia." AP noted that there had been 700 cease-fire violations in Sarajevo and that 200,000 people had "been killed" in Bosnia, but it laid no blame.[60] It seemed that the Serbs were being bullied by the West to give up land that they had held against an aggressive Muslim-Croat alliance.

In December 1994, as Bosnian Serbs held UN troops hostage, Roger Cohen filed a story from Croatia that portrayed Serbs in a sympathetic manner and reminded his readers—again—of Croatia's fascist past. Reporting from Knin, "a bleak place," he noted that the "Krajina" Serbs had "seceded" from Croatia owing to "memories of genocide" by Croats against Serbs in World War II. Both the UN and NATO had accommodated the Serbs by refusing to use force "to thwart them," and thus encouraged Milošević, Karadžić, and the "gang of nationalists" who had begun the war and were "sustained" by it. But if a gang of Serbian nationalists "thrive[d] on intimidation, propaganda and the fog of war," the average Serb in Bosnia had suffered and the average Serb in the Krajina was unemployed and disenchanted. "Only the politicians are guilty," one told Cohen, adding that being Serbian was "not important."[61]

The success of Croatian and Bosnian offensives in August and September 1995 again allowed the Serbs to claim victim status. Some reports put Serbian refugees at 250,000, others at 40,000, but the theme was that the "fourth [Croatian] Blitzkrieg" had proven "tragic" for the Serbs, who appealed to "Orthodox and Slavic countries for military aid."[62] If the Serbs wanted the world to pity them, their actions argued for a different emotion. While they accused Croats of atrocities in the Krajina, they continued to cleanse their areas of non-Serbs, and in October they tortured and murdered scores of Muslims who had purportedly balked at being cleansed.[63]

Misha Glenny was one of the most persistent purveyors of the image of the victimized Serbs.[74] In September 1995, he diverted attention from the actions of Serbian forces and argued that sanctions on Serbia be lifted because "ordinary Serbs" had suffered for three years, Serbians had been treated as "pariahs," and Serbian refugees were "shattered" people. Of course, sanctions were supposed to hurt, but Serbia could count on its neighbors to violate them.[65]

Nonetheless, Glenny argued that Serbia, which had supported aggression and ethnic cleansing against its neighbors but sustained no wartime damage itself, had lost the war, while Croatia, which had suffered $20 billion dollars in damage from Serbian attacks and reclaimed territory lost to Serbian aggression, had emerged as the real "winner." In a similar vein, R. H. Silk accused the United States of encouraging Croatia's "brutal blitz against the Serbs," insisted Banja Luka be declared "a protected enclave," and condemned the U.S. Navy for using hundreds of jets in thousands of sorties to pave the way for the Croatian "blitz."[66]

Both men echoed the line take by Milošević in late 1995, that there are no "winners" in a "civil war," that everyone loses and "peace is the only victory."[67] Yet what happened in Yugoslavia was not a civil war, and it was Milošević who armed, financed, and dispatched forces to Croatia in 1991 and Bosnia in 1992 in an effort to conquer a Greater Serbia militarily. Thanks to Western actions, he was largely successful in doing so.

Unfortunately, accurate history and careful analysis seldom found their way into reporting on Yugoslavia. In a dispatch from the Serbian town of Dubica, where eight people had died following an artillery attack by Croatian "fascists," Mike O'Connor reported that local Serbians were comparing the Croatian action to the "'43 horror" in which Croats had killed 17,000 of the town's 27,000 residents. He reported that two of the dead, including an elderly woman, "had had her eyes taken out, although there was no way to determine when this had been done." He might have added, "nor by whom," since artillery shells rarely take out a victim's eyes. But he did not. Nor did he report whether the town had been held by Serbian armed forces, or why the Croats had shelled it, or the ethnic identity of the victims. But, then, corpses are not articulate. Instead, he used the attack to let the Serbs rehash their fears of Croatian fascists, dredge up one-sided memories of World War II, and proclaim their satisfaction that their former Croatian and Muslim neighbors were gone, "killed or expelled in earlier ethnic purges."[68]

In late 1995, Chris Hedges reported that a Serbian attack on a Muslim refugee camp near Tuzla had killed six and wounded thirty—the worst attack on civilians since the Serbian mortar round had struck Sarajevo on 28 August, killing thirty-seven people.[69] The Serbs were also busy cleansing the last Croats and Muslims from Banja Luka in October 1995.[70] Nonetheless, in October Thomas Friedman depicted a beleaguered Serbia by reporting that "it was Germany's desire to dismember Yugoslavia"—apparently a function of "the love affair between Germany and Croatia"—"that helped to start the war in the first place."[71]

Susan Woodward also saw the Serbs as victims of an international conspiracy. She blamed Germany for forcing Yugoslavia's dissolution, in collusion with Austria, Hungary, Italy, the Vatican, Denmark, . . . and the U.S. Congress. This seems an unlikely coalition, but Woodward insisted that Vienna and the Vatican "had pursued a strategy to increase their sphere of influence in central and eastern Europe, respectively," and she speculated that Austrian support for self-determination was "the continuation of Austria's century-old [sic] enmity toward Serbia."[72] Evidently, Woodward did not know that Belgrade had sheltered Austrian Nazis after their abortive putsch in 1934.

Whether the Serbs will continue to feel that they were the real victims of the conflict is hard to say, but it seems appropriate to give T. D. Allman the last word here. The Serbs, he concluded after a bizarre trip through Serbian-occupied territory, need to "find some way to confront not what 'the world' has done to them, but what they have done to themselves."[73] Instead, they are now the key to peace in the region, a bizarre ending to a bizarre conflict.

NOTES

1. Bradley Graham, "A Bosnian Hot Spot Awaits GIs," *Washington Post*, 15 December 1995; Cohen, *Broken Bonds*, 98. Vladimir Dedijer was his source. In effect, both failed the test of ethical completeness.

2. David Rieff, "Letter from Bosnia, Original Virtue, Original Sin," *New Yorker*, 23 November 1992, 83, 84, 87, 93.

3. Chris Hedges, "Serbs Near Sarajevo Pack and Curse Peace," *New York Times*, 15 December 1995.

4. Raymond Bonner, "A 'Frontier' Land of Ancient Rivalry," *New York Times*, 3 August 1995.

5. Anonymous, "End the War in Bosnia Peacefully," *New York Times*, 20 May 1993. Cigar, *Genocide*, esp. 123–27, for "spin-off" war crimes by Croatian and Muslim forces, who followed the Serbian lead and began to cleanse their areas in 1993.

6. Beloff, "Eastern Approaches," passim.

7. *Ibid.* For Budak and the Ustaša, Sadkovich, *Italian Support*, esp. chapters 4–8.

8. Ramet, *Social Currents*, 427–28; Ante Čuvalo, "Croatian Nationalism and the Croatian National Movement (1966–1972) in Anglo-American Publications: A Critical Assessment," *Journal of Croatian Studies* (1989), 74–82, 84. Čuvalo's discussion of efforts by Rusinow, Denitch, and others to discredit Croatian nationalism is useful.

9. Max Primorac, "Serbia's War," 46.

10. Rieff, "Letter from Bosnia," 84. Ramet, *Social Currents*, 418–20, speculates that their low level of education made many Serbs vulnerable to the propaganda carried by *Politika*, RTV, and other Serbian media.

11. Paul Lewis, *New York Times*, 21 October 1992, and ABC's *Day 1/one*, 9 May 1993, for an atrocity committed by Croatians and the theme of civil war. There was no effort to balance the report or put it in context.

12. For Somalia and the "Mogadishu line," William Drozdiak, "France, Britain Push to Form Quick-Reaction Force," *Washington Post*, 2 June 1995; Cohen, *Broken*

Bonds, 242; Peter Jennings, "While America Watched: The Bosnia Tragedy," *ABC*, 17 March 1994.

13. Charles Krauthammer, "And the 'Enclave Strategy,'" *Washington Post*, 2 June 1995, and "Who Would Want Bosnia? Surely Not the U.S.," *International Herald Tribune*, 6–7 January 1996; Rick Atkinson, "Strategy to Make War, Not Peace," *Washington Post*, 1 June 1995. The Bulgarian daily, *24 Chasa*, 27 November 1994, noted that Karadžić had threatened the United States with a new Vietnam should it intervene.

14. Dana Priest, *Washington Post*, 14 July 1995.

15. Peter Paret, ed., *Makers of Modern Strategy from Machiavelli to the Nuclear Age* (Princeton, NJ: Princeton University Press, 1986), 123–85, 735–62; Robert C. North, *War, Peace, Survival: Global Political and Conceptual Synthesis* (Boulder, CO: Westview Press, 1990); and Robert Gilpin, *War and Change in World Politics* (New York: Cambridge University Press, 1981, 1991).

16. Claudio Segrè, *Fourth Shore: The Italian Colonization of Libya* (Chicago: Chicago University Press, 1974); George W. Baer, *The Coming of the Italian-Ethiopian War* (Cambridge, MA: Harvard University Press, 1967); Thomas R. Mockaitis, *British Counterinsurgency, 1919–60* (New York: St. Martin's, 1990).

17. Walter Russell Mead, "Looking at Bosnia, Clinton Sees Only Ugly, Bad Choices," *Los Angeles Times*, 19 April 1993; *This Week with David Brinkley*, 2 May 1993; *MacNeil-Lehrer Newshour*, 6 October 1994.

18. Stephen John Stedman, "The New Interventionists," *Foreign Affairs* (1992–93).

19. Jennings, *ABC*, 18 March 1993.

20. Michael Lind, "Serbicide," *New Republic*, 22 June 1992.

21. Newhouse, "Diplomatic Round," 60; *Newsweek*, 26 April, 3, 10, and 17 May 1993.

22. Stefano Bianchini and Francesco Privitera, *6 Aprile 1941: L'attacco italiano alla Jugoslavia* (Milan: Marzorati, 1993), 75–76, 95. Matteo J. Milazzo, *The Chetnik Movement and the Yugoslav Resistance* (Baltimore: Johns Hopkins University Press, 1975), 90–112. Irving, *The Croat Question*, 93–95, distinguishes a pro Allied Chetnik movement under Mihailović from a pro-Axis one under Kosta Pećanac. In reality, the former was an Italian ally, the latter a German accomplice. For pro-Chetnik views, Michael Leon, *The Rape of Serbia: The British Role in Tito's Grab for Power 1943–1944* (New York: Harcourt, Brace, Jovanovich, 1990); David Martin, *The Web of Disinformation: Churchill's Yugoslav Blunder* (New York: Harcourt, Brace, Jovanovich, 1990), and *Ally Betrayed: The Uncensored Story of Tito and Mihailovich* (New York: Prentice-Hall, 1946).

23. Adamić, *My Native Land*, 81–87, 399–406. For pro Chetnik works, see Kirk Ford, *OSS and the Yugoslav Resistance, 1943–1945* (College Station: Texas A & M Press, 1992), and Konstantin Fotić, *The War We Lost: Yugoslavia's Tragedy and the Failure of the West* (New York: Viking Press, 1948).

24. Adamić, *Native Land*, 399–405. Ali and Lifschultz, *Why Bosnia?*, 157, 288.

25. Jožo Tomašević, *War and Revolution in Yugoslavia, 1941–1945: The Chetniks* (Stanford, CA: Stanford University Press, 1975), 108–19, 167–78, 256–61; Cohen, *Serbia's Secret War*, 28–62; and Nusret Šehić, *Četništvo u Bosni i Hercegovini (1918–1941)* (Sarajevo: ANU/BiH, 1971). The Guard's 17,000 men, Ljotić's 4,000 Volunteers, and Pećanac's 9,000 Chetniks attacked *all* ethnic groups.

26. Mark F. Canciar, "The Wehrmacht in Yugoslavia: Lessons of the Past?" *Parameters* (Autumn 1993), esp. 75; William T. Johnsen, *Deciphering the Balkan*

Enigma: Using History to Inform Policy (Strategic Studies Institute, March 1993), passim; Cohen, *Serbia's Secret War*, 28–62.

27. Paul N. Hehn, *The German Struggle against Yugoslav Guerrillas in World War II: German Counter-Insurgency in Yugoslavia, 1941–1943* (New York: East European Quarterly, 1979), 32–69. Milazzo, *The Chetnik Movement*, 32–60.

28. Hehn, *German Struggle*, 82–97.

29. Hehn, *German Struggle*, 104–5, 110–11, 142–44; Milazzo, *Chetnik Movement*, 60.

30. Stato Maggiore dell'Esercito, Ufficio Storico (SME/US), *Le operazioni delle unità italiane in Jugoslavia (1941–1943)* (Rome, 1978), 194 and passim, and *Le operazioni delle unità italiane nel settembre-ottobre* (Rome, 1975), 321–436.

31. Wheeler, *Britain and the War for Yugoslavia*, 163–97, 234–44. Lucien Karchmar defends Mihailović in *Draža Mihailović and the Rise of the Četnik Movement, 1941–1942* (New York: Garland, 1987), 2 vols.

32. United States, Department of the Army, *German Antiguerrilla Operations in the Balkans (1941–1944)* (August, 1954), 36–37; SME/U.S., *Le operazioni . . . in Jugoslavia,* 212–19; Vladimir Dedijer et al., *History of Yugoslavia* (New York: McGraw-Hill, 1974), 632–38; Milazzo, *Chetnik Movement*, 113–39, 162–81; Jože Tomašević in Vucinich et al., *Contemporary Yugoslavia*, 101.

33. SME/US, *Le operazioni . . . in Jugoslavia,* 242, 249–60; Dedijer, *History,* 595–7; Bianchini and Privitera, *6 Aprile 1941,* 61–62. Also Giulio Bedeschi, ed., *Fronte jugoslavo-balcanico: c'ero anch'io* (Milan: Mursia, 1986); Giacomo Scotti, *Ventimila caduti, gli italiani in Jugoslavia dal 1943 al 1945* (Milan: Mursia, 1970).

34. SME/US, *Le operazioni . . . settembre–ottobre*, 17–21, 321–436, 634–44.

35. Mario Pacor, *Italia e Balcani dal Risorgimento alla resistenza* (Milan: Feltrinelli, 1968), 280; Bianchini and Privitera, *6 Aprile 1941,* 83–96; Giovanni Padovan, *Abbiamo lottato insieme: partigiani italiani e sloveni al confine orientale* (Udine: Del Bianco, 1965).

36. *German Antiguerrilla Operations*, 26, 44–49; Norman Cigar, "How Wars End: War Termination and Serbian Decisionmaking in the Case of Bosnia," *South East European Monitor* (Vienna, 1996) and "The Serbo-Croatian War"; Dedijer, *History,* 653–55.

37. Cohen, *Serbia's Secret War*, passim. Compare Mark Canciar's analysis to Johnsen's cautious conclusions. How well Croatian and Bosnian forces did during World War II is a matter of opinion. For that of a former *Domobran* officer, Babić, Eterovich et al., *Croatia,* 148–66. Also Košutić, *Hrvatsko domobranstvo*, passim. By 1944, the NDH had 258,000 men under arms, including 50,000 Ustaša.

38. Canciar, "Wehrmacht," 82–83.

39. Johnsen, *Deciphering,* 75 ff., and the remarks of Gen. J. H. Binford Peay III, U.S. Central Command, to Bryant Gumbel on NBC's *Today,* 13 October 1994.

40. Magaš, *Destruction of Yugoslavia,* 354; Ramet, *Social Currents,* 413–15, 418–21. Not everyone saw Serbia as suffering, for example, Barbara Demick, "Seeming to Thrive, Despite Sanctions, Belgrade Rife with Talk of Economic Miracle and Dark Conspiracy," *Philadelphia Inquirer,* 9 September 1994. Sympathy for Serbia was strong among Bulgarians, for example, Albena Shkodrova, *Standard,* 10 January 1995; *24 Chasa,* 27 September 1994; Iulia Radeva, "The Policy of Bulgaria toward the Embryo-States on the Territory of Ex-Yugoslavia," *Mezhdunarodni Otnoshenija* (1994).

41. Almond, *Europe's Backyard War,* 179, 197; C. G. Schoenfeld, "Psychoanalytic Dimensions of the West's Involvement in the Third Balkan War," in Meštrović et al., *Genocide after Emotion,* esp. 159–61.

42. Tagliabue, *New York Times*, 1 July 1991.

43. Cohen, *Broken Bonds*, 183; Magaš, *Destruction of Yugoslavia*, 276; and Ramet, *Social Currents*, 404.

44. Cohen, *Broken Bonds*, 203.

45. Woodward, *Balkan Tragedy*, 221.

46. Brad K. Blitz, "Serbia's War Lobby: Diaspora Groups and Western Elites," in Cushman and Meštrović, *This Time We Knew*; Michael R. Gordon, "U.S. Companies Helping Serbs Defy U.N.," *New York Times*, 21 May 1993, counted 165 Serbian "fronts" in the United States. Dragnich was tied to Hoover, Woodward to Brookings, Zametica to London's International Institute for Strategic Studies. Sources clearly influenced Francisco Veiga, *La trampa balánica: Una crisis europea de fin de siglo* (Barcelona: Grijalbo Mondadori, 1995).

47. Tagliabue, *New York Times*, 3 July 1991; Newhouse, "Diplomatic Round," 70; "Quiet Voices from the Balkans," *New Yorker*.

48. For the White House, see Lind, "Serbicide," 16–18.

49. Stokes, *Walls*, 221, 225–26, 301, considered Alexander a well-intentioned dictator. For a corrective, Sadkovich, "Il regime di Alessandro," passim.

50. *New York Times*, 23 December 1991.

51. Bruce Nelan, "Serbia's Spite," *Time*, 25 January 1993.

52. "Serbs: Cease-Fire before Talks," *AP*, 11 May 1994. The details were repeated in a later AP release.

53. "All Things Considered," *NPR*, spring 1993, interview with Mladen and "Suzanne" Bozović.

54. Kurt Schork, "World Pressure on Bosnians Could Put UN at Risk," *Reuters*, 14 July 1994.

55. "Shelling Shatters Bosnia Truce," *AP*, 14 July 1994; *AP*, 6 July 1994. Only Karadžić was cited.

56. "Serbs Pull Out, Talks to Begin," *AP*, 4 June 1994, and Kurt Schork, "Peace Talks at Impasse as Serbs Remain in Gorazde," *Reuters*, 3 June 1994. The Serbs were to have left the area six weeks earlier.

57. *AP*, 20 July 1994; *This Week with David Brinkley*, 9 May 1993.

58. Julijana Mojsilovic, "Bosnian Maps Ask a Lot: An AP News Analysis," *AP*, 7 July 1994, noted the threat to the "northern corridor" endangered "Serb strongholds" like "Knin in Croatia and Banja Luka in Bosnia," and that Modrica, Doboj, and Derventa, which had "Serb pluralities" before the war and were "strategically located," might be lost.

59. Mark Heinrich, "Serbs, Muslims Play Deadly Games with U.N. Weapons Ban," *Reuters*, 14 August 1994.

60. "Bosnian Serbs Snub Peace Plan," *AP*, 3 August 1994.

61. Roger Cohen, "The World: The Serbs Dream, But Dare Not Wake," *New York Times*, 4 December 1994. *24 Chasa* published a long article by Ventsislav Nachev, "Serbs in the Krajina Do Not Want the West to Teach Them How to Live." Illustrated with a picture of Serbs ethnically cleansed by Croats, the article called for Bulgaria to lift the embargo on the Serbs, who were well armed for defense and ready to defend their right to be a *nezavisan narod* (independent people).

62. John Pomfret, "Serbs Threaten to Pull Out of Cease-fire," *Washington Post*, 14 October 1995. The appeal appeared in *Standard*, "Russians to Help Slavic Brothers," 24 January 1993.

63. *Washington Post,* "UN Reports Massacre of Bosnian Muslims in Expulsions," 19 October 1995.

64. See Banac's remarks on Glenny in Ali et al., *Why Bosnia?*, 153.

65. Greece violated sanctions first, and Viktor Radulov, *24 Chasa,* 4 August 1994, complained that as Bulgaria sought compensation for economic damages resulting to its economy as a result of enforcing sanctions against Serbia, Hungary, Romania, and others had made millions circumventing them.

66. Misha Glenny, "And the Winner Is . . . Croatia," *New York Times,* 26 September 1995; R. H. Silk, "Talk of Bosnia Peace Only Abets Carnage," *New York Times,* 5 October 1995. Ramet, *Social Currents,* 416, noted that by the end of the war, Serbian forces had caused $21.6 billion in damages in Croatia, and destroyed 14 hospitals, 250 schools, 50,000 houses, 210,000 apartments, and 40 percent of the country's industrial capacity, leaving a million unemployed.

67. Roger Cohen, "An Imperfect Peace," *New York Times,* 22 November 1995.

68. Mike O'Connor, "For Serbs, a Flashback to '43 Horror," *New York Times,* 21 September 1995.

69. Chris Hedges, "Bosnian Serbs Hit a Refugee Camp, Killing Six Civilians," *New York Times,* 9 October 1995.

70. *New York Times,* 11 October 1995.

71. Friedman, *New York Times,* 11 October 1995.

72. Woodward, *Balkan Tragedy,* 148–49, 159–60, 164.

73. T. D. Allman in Ali et al., *Why Bosnia?*, 65.

8

Legal and Moral Issues

SELF-DETERMINATION

Self-determination is both a political concept and a legal principle that sets individual against collective rights. It therefore undermines the doctrine of state sovereignty and threatens the territorial integrity of existing states. As a legal principle it is so poorly defined, and as a political concept so corrupt, that some scholars believe it is only useful as a political tool.[1]

Self-determination's lack of jurisprudence testifies to its thorny nature. It is hard to distinguish a people from a minority and determine when it has a right to secede, so application begins with the legal and political task of deciding when a minority is a people.[2]

Self-determination posed a direct threat to multiethnic empires before 1914, and it continues to pose threats to the integrity of contemporary states. Both nationalists and leaders of new states have appreciated and exploited its revolutionary, seditious, and imperial potential. Politicians found it useful to forge national identities, legitimate demands for independence, and validate expansion.

During the Great War, all belligerents employed the principle against their enemies, and wartime propaganda led "oppressed" peoples in Europe and those in the overseas empires of the victorious powers, like the Irish and the Indians, to expect to be able to choose the state to which they would belong or form new states after the war. This expectation, support for the principle, and its inclusion in the war aims of the belligerents laid the moral foundation for an era of expanding human rights. The League Covenant, the UN Charter, and other treaties and conventions have since built its legal framework.[3]

Because self-determination undermined old multiethnic empires and could be manipulated by new nation-states, it has appeared exquisitely political. During the 1950s, it came to be identified with colonial wars of liberation and the right of secession, and the Covenant on Civil and Political Rights conceded a broadly defined self-determination to everyone. But not everyone can claim the right to exercise it. A group must belong to a state comprising different national groups of comparable dimensions, not one with a majority and one or more identifiable minority groups; it must be recognized constitutionally and have a distinct legal status.[4]

Self-determination does not automatically entail secession, and a minority's failure to secede does not justify intervention by a third party. Self-determination implies secession only if independence is a necessary condition for the realization of the principle, but self-determination without independence is possible, and at times preferable.[5] In Yugoslavia, allowing everyone to exercise the right would have led to chaos. Only Slovenia would have come close to a homogeneous population. All other areas would have been fragmented among noncontiguous minorities.

Minorities have the right under Article 27 of the Covenant on Human Rights "to enjoy their own culture, to profess and practice their own religion, or to use their own language." They cannot be forced to assimilate, but individuals may do so. Governments are not obliged to finance a minority's institutions or assist it through legislative or administrative action.[6]

These points have implications for Yugoslavia, where the definition of a state determined who was a minority. Albanians in Albania are a people, but Albanians in Macedonia are a minority because they live in a state made up of noncomparable ethnic groups of which they are one of the smaller. Albanians in Kosovo were a minority only because they were part of a Serbian state. Had they been a republic rather than an administrative unit, they would have been a people with a right to secede. That their autonomous status was illegally destroyed by Belgrade raises serious questions regarding their current status.

Because their community is compact and contiguous with Albania, they can secede if Serbia abridges or denies their right to self-determination. The 1970 Declaration on Friendly Relations stipulates that states have "the duty to refrain from any forcible action which deprives people of [their] right to self-determination and freedom and independence," and other states would have a moral, if not a legal, right to intervene to protect them.[7]

However, Serbs in Croatia and Bosnia-Herzegovina were minorities because both republics had the status of states in the 1974 Yugoslav constitution and both had historic claims to statehood. Unlike the Albanians in Kosovo, the Serbs did not live in a single compact group in a defined area that was contiguous with Serbia. Nor were their rights abridged and denied—they were guaranteed.

Once Yugoslavia ceased to exist, Serbs living outside Serbia became minorities who could justify secession from Yugoslavia's republics only if their rights were being denied or abridged, because these republics were states, not administrative units. Serbia's unilateral abrogation of the 1974 constitution did not lessen the minority status of Serbs in other republics; it reinforced it. Because Croatia and Bosnia were states before EC recognition and guaranteed the rights of their Serbian minorities, the latter had no grounds to secede.[8]

Ethnic minorities in federated states and those living under colonial rule or racist regimes have a much stronger claim to self-determination and independence. During the 1960s, international consensus that colonial, dependent, and less-developed peoples have a right to political and economic self-determination transformed the principle into "a preemptory norm of international law."[9]

Like others, Lenard Cohen treated self-determination as a political question. By focusing on Serbian points of view, he made it seem that they were oppressed and that Milošević was trying to salvage Yugoslavia, not using the JNA to expand Serbia's borders. Stipe Mesić's remark regarding the Serbs therefore applies to some analysts as well. "These people," he complained, "think that everything in Yugoslavia should be measured with criteria that suit the Serbs." One of the few who escaped this trap was Sabrina Ramet, who believed Croats and Slovenes had reason not to trust Belgrade, given their "memories of Serbian hegemony in the interwar period."[10]

Cohen made Serbs appear more concentrated than they were by lumping together the eighteen communes in Bosnia and Croatia where they were 63 percent of the inhabitants. His maps inflate and conflate Serb populations, by showing no others and by combining areas where they were 20 percent of the population with those where they were 40 percent. His maps leave the impression that Croatia and Bosnia were largely populated by Serbs, and his use of phrases like "absolute majority" and "relative majorities" to describe Serb majorities and pluralities is misleading.[11]

Woodward denied that Yugoslavia's constitution gave anyone the right to secede, but she repeated Karadžić's claim that Serbs "owned" 64 percent of Bosnia. She did not follow up her comparison of Albanians in Kosovo to Serbs in Croatia and Bosnia; she claimed Yugoslavs had no clear word for "people"; and she depicted Croat claims to self-determination as "historicist" and Serb claims as "democratic."[12]

Serbia's use of self-determination should not be confused with its use by Croatia, Slovenia, or Bosnia. The Helsinki Declaration can be interpreted to mean that a people can secede if that is the "only means available to implement their right to self-determination." But the Serbs tried to exploit the principle to enlarge Serbia, whereas Yugoslavia's other ethnic groups sought to establish states based on existing borders.[13]

The Helsinki Declaration has achieved the status of customary law and become binding on all signatories because most signatories have honored its principles. Because self-determination can encourage separatism and secession, the Declaration limits the right to secede. In effect, as the right to self-determination has been extended and strengthened, the right to secede has been circumscribed. Moreover, the UN gives priority to the sovereignty and territorial integrity of established states; practice favors existing states, discounts the ideals embedded in the concept of self-determination, and shows a disinclination to apply inconvenient treaties.[14]

Caution regarding secession and custom regarding internal conflict predisposed the international community to try to maintain a unified Yugoslav state, even at the cost of giving the JNA free rein and ignoring Belgrade's denial of basic civil and human rights to both Serbs and non-Serbs. By posing as the old Yugoslavia, the new Serbian-Montenegrin state could ignore the human rights conditions that the successor states had to meet. Most states initially refused to recognize Croatia, Slovenia, and Bosnia, but tacitly accepted Serbia's revision of the 1974 constitution and its arming of separatists in Croatia and Bosnia both before and after they were recognized as sovereign entities. But international law circumscribes interference in struggles for independence, and forbids arming and inciting people to rebellion.[15]

Like many writers, Nora Beloff inflated the number of Serbs in Croatia and Serb property holdings in Bosnia. She argued that because Yugoslavia's "hodge-podge of nationalities" made self-determination "a delusion" and 17 percent of Croatia's population was non-Croatian, Serbs and "Yugoslavs" of mixed parentage should take a third of the country.[16] Beloff's argument would have given non-Serbs, who were 30 percent of Serbia's population, over half of Serbia. But if Hungarians, Croats, and Albanians were concentrated in Vojvodina, Kosovo, and Sandžak, Serbs were scattered throughout Croatia; in Dalmatia and Slavonia, both areas claimed by Serbs, Croats were a majority. In 1991, Dalmatia had 944,026 inhabitants—774,934 Croats (82 percent) and 113,438 Serbs (12.0 percent). (See Table 8.1.)

Table 8.1
The Ethnic Composition of Dalmatia, 1991

	CROATS		SERBS	
County	Total	Percent	Total	Percent
Benkovac	13,430	40.6	18,987	57.4
Biograd	16,113	92.0	648	3.7
Brač	12,854	93.9	177	1.3
Drniš	18,552	76.8	5,145	21.3
Dubrovnik	58,304	82.5	4,735	6.7
Hvar	10,450	91.8	204	1.8
Imotski	37,976	95.5	111	2.9
Kaštela	28,856	92.4	937	3.0
Knin	3,641	8.6	37,511	88.6
Korčula	18,043	92.0	215	1.1
Lastovo	923	76.6	61	5.1
Makarska	18,523	88.5	418	2.0
Metković	21,339	93.7	705	3.1
Obrovac	3,684	32.2	7,540	65.9
Omiš	24,987	97.3	102	0.4
Ploče	11,161	85.1	550	4.2
Sinj	55,724	92.6	2,708	4.5
Solin	25,422	94.1	567	2.1
Split	180,372	87.3	8,677	4.2
Šibenik	71,009	84.1	8,865	10.5
Trogir	20,173	92.5	283	1.3
Viš	3,741	86.8	116	2.7
Vrgorac	7,169	96.8	14	0.2
Zadar	112,490	83.4	14,162	10.5
Totals	774,934	82.0	113,438	12.0

Source: I. Crkvencic and M. Klemencic, "Southern Croatia and Dalmatia, Borders and Population," unpublished paper, 1992.

Most of the Serbs in Dalmatia, 86,202 (76 percent), were concentrated in five unconnected urban areas—Benkovac, Knin, Split, Šibenik, and Zadar. They could not be easily disentangled from the Croatian population, and they had majorities in only three counties: Benkovac, Knin, and Obrovac. Their attacks on Split, Dubrovnik, and other Croatian areas could not be justified on the basis of self-determination. Nor were they acts of defense, because the Serb minority in Dalmatia was not threatened. The attacks were war crimes, because they were unprovoked and they targeted civilian areas.

Table 8.2
Eleven "Krajina" Counties with Serbian Majorities

County	Total	Croats	Percent	Serbs	Percent
Benkovac	33,549	13,450	40	17,781	53
Donji Lapac	8,447	—	—	7,695	92
Dvor	16,307	1,533	9	13,192	81
Glina	25,079	8,950	35	14,220	56
Obrovac	12,362	4,178	33	7,430	60
Gračac	11,863	2,147	18	8,577	72
Knin	43,731	4,154	9	34,504	79
Kostajnica	15,548	4,291	28	8,629	56
Korenica	12,261	2,305	19	8,485	69
Vojnić	8,908	—	—	7,892	89
Vrginmost	18,841	4,126	22	13,452	71
Totals	206,896	45,139	22	141,857	68

Source: John Kraljic, *Belgrade's Strategic Designs on Croatia*, Washington, DC, 1991.

Three-quarters of eastern and western Slavonia was Croatian, no more than a quarter Serbian. Only 17.5 percent of Croatia's Serbs lived in this region, another 26.7 percent in the thirteen counties of the "Krajina." Both areas accounted for less than half—44.2 percent—of Croatia's Serbs. Yet the JNA occupied both regions on the basis of self-determination.[17] (See Tables 8.2, 8.3.)

Most Serbs in Croatia lived in large urban areas with Croatian majorities. They had majorities in eleven counties, pluralities in two— Daruvar (9,512 of 31,424) and Pakrac (10,715 of 27,903). "Krajina's" capital, Knin, had fewer Serbs than Zagreb. Pakrac was the first county taken by the Serbs in 1991, although they outnumbered the Croats only by 2,232. With 30 percent of Croatia's Serbs, "Krajina" had about 5 percent of its total population.[18]

Serbian majorities varied widely, and to use "absolute majority," suggesting two-thirds or more, is as misleading as to use "relative majority" to refer to a plurality. In Croatia, Serbs comprised 53 percent to 60 percent in four counties (53%, 56%, 56%, 60%), 69 percent to 79 percent in four others (69%, 71%, 72%, 79%), and over 80 percent in three (81%, 89%, 92%). The "Krajina" had a population of 206,896—69 percent Serbian, 22 percent Croatian. But the counties had no border with Serbia, and were not even contiguous with one another. Moreover, historically they were part of Croatia, not Serbia, and to grant them independent status would have dismembered Croatia.[19]

Table 8.3
Population Distribution in Croatian Areas Occupied by Serbs

Region	Total	Non-Serb	Percent	Serbs	Percent
"Krajina" (12 counties)					
N. Dalmatia	87,000	23,000	26.6	64,000	73.4
Western Lika	30,000	6,000	19.7	24,000	80.3
Banija i Kordun	113,000	43,000	38.1	70,000	61.9
Subtotals	230,000	72,000	31.4	138,000	60.0
Slavonia (12 counties)					
Western	250,000	183,000	73.1	67,000	26.9
Eastern	401,000	310,000	77.4	91,000	22.6
Subtotals	651,000	493,000	75.7	158,000	24.3
Totals	881,000	565,000	64.0	316,000	36.0

Source: Dušan Bilandžić et al., *La Croazia tra la guerra e l'indipendenza* (Zagreb: Zagreb University, 1991), 55–59.

Belgrade was obviously not trying to bring all of Croatia's Serbs into a Greater Serbia, only the half who lived in those areas seized by the JNA. Had Serbian propaganda been true, the JNA's actions should have provoked a brutal repression against those Serbs trapped in Croatia. But neither oppression nor flight occurred until August 1995, when Serbs in areas which they had conquered and cleansed of Croats in 1991–92 fled *before* an approaching Croatian army.

Belgrade was most interested in securing areas with economic and strategic importance, especially eastern Slavonia, which bordered Vojvodina, annexed by Serbia in 1989 when it unilaterally abrogated the 1974 constitution. The JNA attacked both Vukovar and Osijek, even though of Osijek's 158,790 inhabitants, 90,828 were Croatian and only 28,582 Serb. Vukovar, whose citizens Serb units expelled and massacred following their seizure of the area, had 81,203 inhabitants—30,126 Croats, 26,173 Serbs, and 17,215 Yugoslavs. The JNA also seized Beli Monastir, where Serbs made up only 12,872 of its 53,409 inhabitants.

Possession of Slavonia gave Serbia both banks of the Danube; Vukovar, Croatia's second largest river port; and some of the most productive agricultural areas and largest food processing plants in Croatia. "Krajina" lacks arable land and industry, but rails and roads pass through Knin, Gračac, and Benkovac, connecting Croatia's interior to the coast. Serb forces targeted areas with Croat majorities, like Sisak, a rail center with oil refineries and heavy industry. The JNA cut Croatia into fragments, took its farmlands, blocked its riverine trade, and destroyed its tourist trade.

Although strategic and economic considerations seemed more important to Serbian leaders than ethnic solidarity, Serbian propaganda and obfuscating diplomats, politicians, and pundits sought to justify Serbia's role in fomenting violence in Croatia and Bosnia by depicting the new states as racist or inviable. Ironically, third parties could have supported minorities only within Serbian-controlled areas in Bosnia and Krajina, because both were racist entities engaged in genocide against non-Serbs on their territories, and colonies of Serbia, whose support was crucial to their creation and survival.[20]

The shift toward giving priority to preserving states, no matter how corrupt, and discouraging secession, no matter how justified, was gradual and subtle. The end of the cold war and the Helsinki Declarations seemed to indicate progress toward codifying human rights in international legal instruments and respecting them in practice, and protests have been raised whenever rights have been violated. But the shift has occurred. The CSCE (now OSCE) and the Security Council were impotent unless the major powers agreed to act to protect human rights and support secession by groups denied self-determination.

Even if the prerogatives of existing states have priority over the rights of peoples, the Serbian state had no right to speak for all Serbs within Yugoslavia. Nor did the SDS (Serbian Democratic Party) in Croatia and Bosnia represent all of Croatia's Serbs. One measure of the lack of support for the SDS was its poor showing in the 1990 elections for the Sociopolitical Chamber of the Croatian parliament. (See Table 8.4.) Whereas Tudjman's HDZ obtained strong support and the reformed communists and socialists (SKH/SDP) did well, the SDS polled only 1.6 percent of the vote (46,000) in the first round and 2.0 percent (35,000) in the second, as turnout declined from 84.5 percent to 74.8 percent. Given

Table 8.4
1990 Elections for Croatia's Sociopolitical Chamber (000s)

Round/ % of vote	HDZ	SDP	SDS	Total	Turnout
First	1,201	994	46	2,875	84.5%
- %	41.8%	34.5%	1.6%	100%	
Second	708	627	35	1,678	74.8%
- %	42.2%	37.3%	2.0%	100%	
Seats	54	19	1	80	

Source: L. Cohen, *Broken Bonds: The Disintegration of Yugoslavia* (Boulder, CO: Westview, 1993), Table 3.1.

a Serbian population of 532,000, it seems that Croatia's Serbs had little use for the ultranationalist politics of Rašković and the SDS.[21]

Tudjman's HDZ had done better than Milošević's SPS, which took more of the vote in Serbia (46 percent), but with a lower turnout (71.5 percent and 48.3 percent). Even in Slovenia, DEMOS managed only 55 percent of the vote and Kučan 44 percent.[22] In other words, the margins of victory for Kučan, Tudjman, and Milošević were similar, but the latter got a lower percentage of votes than his two counterparts. It would seem that even most Serbians *within* Serbia did not support Milošević's project for a greater Serbia.

In Bosnia-Herzegovina election results were more ambivalent. The number of seats won by the SDS reflected the Serbian proportion of the population, 72 of 250, with Izetbegović's SDA obtaining 86, and the HDZ 49. Although the Serbs claimed to own two-thirds of the state, in 1991, of 109 municipalities in Bosnia-Herzegovina, Muslims had a majority in thirty-five, Serbs in thirty-two, Croats in seven. Muslims had a plurality in fifteen municipalities, Croats in seven, Serbs in five. Two-fifths (1.7 million) of all Bosnians lived in areas with no clear pluralities.[23]

When the EC invited a referendum in Bosnia, it was obvious that most voters wanted an independent, multiethnic state. As they had done in Croatia, the Serbs staged their own referendum, which excluded non-Serbs. They then set up several "krajinas," most not contiguous with Serbia.[24] They clearly were seeking to preclude the formation of a viable Bosnian state, not on the basis of self-determination, but on the basis of their wish to join Serbia. Whether the referendum was representative is in many ways irrelevant, because the Serbs outside Serbia were no higher a percentage of the population than non-Serbs inside Serbia—and not nearly as oppressed as non-Serbs within Serbia.

As Magaš noted, *only* the Serbs sought to include all of their nationals in their state. Serbia's core had a population that was mostly Serbian, but after annexing Vojvodina and Kosovo in 1989–90, Serbia had fewer Serbs as a percentage of its population than Croatia did Croats—69 percent compared to 78 percent. Croatians could have argued that the 254,000 Croats in the new Serbian Yugoslavia be included in a Croatian state, and Albanians and Hungarians both had strong arguments that they should be included in Albania and Hungary—if the logic of Serbian claims is accepted.[25]

The Croatian state is more ethnically homogeneous than Serbia or the new Yugoslavia, and in 1992, Bosnia had as many Serbs (32 percent) as Serbia did non-Serbs (31 percent). Arguments about self-determination for Serbians simply missed the point. Had everyone set up a "krajina," Yugoslavia would have degenerated into a contemporary equivalent of the Holy Roman Empire, with scores of sovereign entities. The only way

Table 8.5
Relative Populations in Yugoslavia (1981 Census, in 000s)

	Serbs*	(%)	Croats	(%)	Muslim**	(%)	Total
Old Yugo	8,136	38	4,428	20	3,731	17	21,590
Croat/BiH	1,852	22	4,212	49	1,665	21	8,517
-BiH	1,320	32	758	19	1,635	40	4,057
-Croatia	532	12	3,454	78	30	1	4,460
New Yugo	6,597	69	254	3	1,683	18	9,508
- Mont.	419	73	8	1	115	20	577
- Serbia	6,178	69	148	2	1,568	18	8,931
(- Serb.	4,861	87	31	-	223	4	5,505
(- Vojv.	1,107	60	109	6	9	1	1,845
(- Kos.	210	13	8	-	1,336	85	1,581

* *Serbs* includes Montenegrins in New Yugo and Montenegro.
Muslim includes Albanians in all areas where they live.
Source: Branka Magaš, *The Destruction of Yugoslavia: Tracking the Break-up 1980–92*. New York: Verso, 1993, 14.

to divide the state without violence and without crippling the successor states was to do what advocates of sovereignty proposed—temper the concept of self-determination with guarantees for existing borders (in this case, republican) and define minorities according to their situation within a particular state. But the media and the West bought Serb arguments that Belgrade had the right to look after all Serbs, everywhere. The result was an expansionist war waged by the JNA and Belgrade's proxies, 200,000 deaths, and the end of an era in Europe.

CUSTOMARY LAW AND CIVILIZED BEHAVIOR

For four years, the media reported sieges of civilian areas by Serb forces and the massacre of their inhabitants after they had surrendered. Siege and massacre are war crimes, genocide a crime against humanity; those who commit them void their claims to self-determination. It was morally necessary, if not legally obligatory, to defeat them militarily and punish them publicly, because those guilty of aggression unleash the horrors of war; by bringing those guilty of genocide to justice, the sacrifice of their victims is remembered and the civilized nature of the international community is affirmed.[26]

But the major powers only sent mediators to press the victims of aggression and genocide to accept settlements that rewarded aggression and consolidated genocide. They also maintained an embargo on the legitimate governments of Croatia and Bosnia and they covered up genocide. The flouting of the norms of war by Serbia and its clients and the international community's indifference seemed to show that international law had given way to the theories and practice of a brutal realpolitik with no moral ends.[27]

Both the public and the media dismissed international law as toothless and confused genocide with the Holocaust. Poor reporting, propaganda, misrepresentation, and superficial commentary reinforced such misconceptions. Rather than explain how international law applied, the media reported efforts to resolve the crisis diplomatically and debated the wisdom of military intervention by the West. But laws need not be enforceable to be binding; and as *jus cogens*, genocide conventions bind both individuals and states.[28]

Paul Sieghart thought history necessary to understand the evolution of international law, because it is based on instruments like the UN Charter, the Universal Declaration of Human Rights, and the Helsinki Accords. States create the international system, but it exists in its own right and has precedence over individual states.[29] If not everyone understood this, Senator Moynihan did, and he expressed his dismay that Clinton's policy on Bosnia was "shredding the entire legal order" that the United States had helped "put into place at the end of World War II."[30]

International law and diplomatic practice are elusive concepts, and states define both to suit policy. But some practices historically have been considered outside the pale. International law exists as a complex weave of implicit values, custom, and ethical norms shared by most nations, enunciated in specific decisions by international tribunals, and described in treaties and conventions.[31]

Much international law is normative or customary. The former sets standards, the latter is the extensive and uniform adherence to concepts expressed in treaties over time. Some authors deny the existence of customary law, arguing it is merely a cover for new policy, but others insist that certain customs exist and have the force of law. Among these is the prerogative of third parties to intervene to stop cruel treatment of their own nationals by a state, as the United States did in Grenada in 1983 and Panama in 1989. This concept is important to any discussion of the conflicts in Croatia and Bosnia, especially if there is no intrinsic or absolute meaning to domestic jurisdiction, because it is defined by international relations.[32]

All laws reflect the essential features of their societies, and international law is no exception. States make up "a society without a government," with its own morality and its own institutions of international law, diplomacy, and balance of power. Even if the Helsinki Accords are soft law and quasi-obligatory, they bind all states aspiring to membership in today's international community, which demands its members observe certain minimum standards that prevent them from determining the scope of their own obligations and thereby gutting human rights and international law.[33]

Because international law is created by the states who are its subjects and must be enforced by either individual or collective coercive measures, it rests on consent and remains primitive in form. Consent is usually explicitly established via treaty, but can be inferred from customary law, which is binding on everyone, and principles of humane conduct in war need not be written down, because to respect them is "a prerequisite for membership [in] the community of states." To be civilized, a state must honor both international conventions and customary law.[34] The 1903 Hague Conventions are as relevant as the Dayton peace accords, because both are guides to good behavior.

If those who control the Security Council wanted the UN to be seen as a civilized organization with enforceable principles, they would at least have conceded the Bosnian and Croatian states the right to self-defense under the UN Charter. Human rights law also allows intervention to protect people from persecutory states, but the Security Council rejected military action. Instead, it dispatched mediators, deployed peacekeepers, and decreed a war crimes tribunal. Such actions and omissions were a sad comment on the international community's refusal to protect human rights. Yet effective action was needed because any aggression challenges the whole international system.[35]

Amnesty International and Helsinki Watch detailed the war crimes in Croatia and Bosnia, and enough prima facie evidence existed to convince even the dullest mind that Serbian forces had been guilty of aggression, genocide, and the bulk of the war crimes committed. Serbian leaders announced the goals of ethnic cleansing, and only the deliberately obtuse could fail to understand them.[36]

It was therefore disappointing to find Telford Taylor, the American prosecutor at Nuremberg, adopt a realist posture and urge those who wanted to help to "work for a truce that will stop the killing." He gave peace priority. But peace is easily gained by surrender to the aggressor. The trick is to realize a peace that protects and guarantees the vital interests and basic concepts of international morality. Taylor's advice derived from the belief that only military victory could ensure the prosecution of war criminals. Indeed, coercion has moral force if used to assure the observance of international norms, and international society proves itself by assuring justice to those who cannot protect themselves from stronger states.[37]

By stressing the need for military victory, Taylor unintentionally argued for the use of force, because only by defeating the aggressor and aligning the victims with the victors could those who unleashed war and perpetrated genocide be brought to justice. But Western intervention to end the war in the fall of 1995 precluded this outcome. A grand alliance was needed, and NATO seemed ideal for the role, but it would not act unilaterally. Consequently, accused war criminals continued to influence politics and be hailed as heroes; only moral suasion and international pressure could be used to convince Zagreb, Belgrade, and Sarajevo to turn over those accused of war crimes.[38]

Many public officials and pundits argued that Serbian aggression against Bosnia and Croatia was not worth contesting with force. Boutros Boutros-Ghali should have taken the moral high ground as Secretary General of the UN, but instead dismissed the carnage in Bosnia as not comparable to genocide in the Third World, and Ted Koppel juggled statistics to make massacres in African states appear similar to the slaughter in Bosnia. Journalists interviewed those responsible for ethnic cleansing as if they were run-of-the-mill politicians.[39]

Charles Maynes thought ethnic cleansing useful in places like Poland; Brent Scowcroft argued that we should accept Serbian gains in Croatia and Bosnia, because the Irish also practice ethnic cleansing, the Serbs had "fought long and hard" to realize a Greater Serbia, and the United States "cannot do everything everywhere" or restore peace where "people don't want to keep the peace themselves."[40]

Because the victims of aggression were depicted as potential killers themselves, their deaths became their own fault, but Serbs were the only minority in Yugoslavia who were not threatened before 1990 and who have not been ethnically cleansed in reprisal for what occurred in Serb-controlled areas. Serb propagandists used fantasy to justify aggression and genocide. The reality was that no one protected non-Serb minorities in Serbian areas.[41] UN forces helped to consolidate Serbian gains, not protect human rights. They prevented the victims of Serbian aggression from rearming, and they accelerated the process of ethnic cleansing by evacuating Muslim areas under attack by Serb forces as peacekeepers protected gains by the aggressor and became accomplices to genocide.[42]

At best, the new realism pays lip service to human rights and international law. Although Congressman David Bonior condemned the United States for "licensing torture" by not using "economic leverage to force China to end human rights abuses," China would not accept U.S. "dictates" on the treatment of its citizens, and Clinton separated human rights and trade by conceding Beijing most-favored-nation status.[43]

Commerce obviously took priority over human rights, and in the spring of 1994, Clinton rejected suggestions to lift the embargo on Bosnia because doing so would "kill the peace process" and hurt relations with U.S. allies in Europe. Mitterand agreed, and Sir Michael Rose,

UN commander in Bosnia, "told the Muslims bluntly they had no hope of achieving a decisive victory" for years. This was a cynical and a disingenuous position, because as Rose pooh-poohed Bosnian military capability, a "Croatian-Muslim" offensive was pushing back Serb lines in Bosnia.[44] In effect, realpolitik and professional military analysis merely rationalized iniquitous Western policies.

Hard-nosed realism and soft-brained conflict resolution are the fashion in the closing decade of the century, with pundits and academics echoing politicians and military leaders, prompting Ortega y Gasset's chorus to join in the mantra that unless a state's strategic or commercial interests are at stake, enforcing international agreements, assuring human rights, and siding with the victim are luxuries no government can afford. The documents of the Nuremberg era have become irrelevant scraps of paper; only the narrow interests of states count. So the UN pressed to end apartheid in South Africa, but imposed it in Yugoslavia, and Washington condemned Moscow for using force against the Baltic states, but soft-pedaled Belgrade's actions in Bosnia.[45]

It was not that international law was lacking, or that the international community was unaware of what was occurring. It was simply, to paraphrase Wells, that we lacked the will to enforce the law, and by not doing so, as Bull implied, we allowed might to triumph over right.[46]

WAR CRIMES

If there is no consensus, many of those who have studied human rights and international law agree that past conventions and treaties technically no longer in force still retain moral authority and legal standing because their role in the evolution of international law makes them moral guides to the behavior of states and individuals.[47] The laws of war, like international law, are a reality, no matter how compromised by the actual behavior of governments and individuals. Their force depends on the perceptions and actions of those applying them, and they are moral and ethical as well as legal injunctions.[48]

Among the important guides are the Covenant of the League of Nations, the 1928 Pact of Paris, the UN Charter, and the Nuremberg Principles—all of which mandate the use of pacific means to resolve disputes. The 1907 Hague and 1949 Geneva conventions define treatment of combatants and noncombatants. Also of interest are the U.S. Army's *Law of Land Warfare* and the Yamashita decision, the trials of American soldiers for atrocities in Vietnam, and those of the U.S. government at Stockholm and Denmark in 1967.[49]

The use of coercive force has always been problematic, and laws of war rest on a shared interest by belligerents in realizing economies of force. McDougal and Feliciano saw a trend to inclusive systems of "minimum destruction," and Michael Howard thought absolute war impossible in the real world. In fact, considerations of military necessity and humanity do limit the levels of destruction in war.[50]

However, the doctrine of military necessity and the concept of superior orders qualify war crimes, and the increased destructive power of modern weapons has led us to tolerate higher levels of destruction and brutality. The problem is to set permissible levels and decide degrees of guilt associated with strategic, operational, and tactical levels of responsibility. The Nuremberg principles specify the responsibility of diplomats and government officials and those at all levels of command, but application of legal principles has been inconsistent. The United States condemned Yamashita for crimes committed by his subordinates in the Philippines, but it exculpated Calley's superiors and did not even entertain the idea that Westmoreland and others might be guilty of war crimes committed by U.S. troops in Vietnam.[51]

But matters are not quite that ambiguous. A given act is a war crime if it is criminal, or its quantity or intensity constitutes a crime. It is not just a matter of who is killed, how they are killed, and how many are killed, but of how enemy nationals and property are treated. Commanders also have an obligation to inform their subordinates of the laws of war and act to avoid violations. Armies understandably prefer to use maximum firepower, so the atom bomb was the logical extension of this preference embodied in the doctrine of strategic bombing. Not surprisingly, proponents of strategic bombing fought efforts to circumscribe it after 1945. Airpower and nuclear weapons seemed to obliterate the distinction between combatant and noncombatant and transform the wholesale slaughter of civilians and indiscriminate destruction of property into military norms.[52]

Because military considerations have tended to influence political aims, the distinction between war and peace has been blurred. But the 1977 Protocols reaffirmed and expanded the Geneva Conventions, and Geoffrey Best considered progress made in guaranteeing human rights and protecting noncombatants after 1945 a "revolution in international law and organization." If not all noncombatants everywhere are protected, they enjoy specific protection under a number of conventions.[53]

The doctrine of superior orders has often been used as a defense, because soldiers are trained to obey without question. However, Nuremberg seems to have established a doctrine of strict liability, and the 1993 Statute of the Yugoslav War Crimes Tribunal makes superiors liable for crimes by subordinates if they knew of them and did not act to prevent them. However, the laws of war are undermined by appeals to military necessity, the right to retaliate, and claims by states to absolute sovereignty.[54]

Nonetheless, there are rules to war, and most states in most wars seek to honor them. McDougal and Feliciano suggested that peoples do not do so only if they view their opponent as an "absolute enemy . . . belonging to a different mankind whose gods are utterly false." This attitude and the actions of specific individuals, not impersonal forces, or the sort of banalities purveyed by some writers, caused the havoc and death in Slovenia, Croatia, and Bosnia.[55]

If under the sway of the nationalist propaganda, most who carried out the slaughter were probably as normal as Adolf Eichmann. Individuals operating in organizations tend to obey, not debate, superior orders, and it is precisely because it is ordinary people who commit atrocities that the rules of war exist and those who break them are punished. As Hannah Arendt noted, evil is banal, at least at the strategic and operational levels, and it was under the goad of Western peace plans rewarding aggression and genocide that Croats and Muslims followed the Serb example and took up ethnic cleansing.[56]

The most basic war crime is to provoke war. As the Nuremberg Tribunal observed, "War is essentially an evil thing" and to "initiate a war of aggression . . . is the supreme international crime differing only from war crimes in that it contains within itself the accumulated evil of the whole."[57] Because aggression is difficult to define, the UN Charter charges the Security Council with deciding whether it has occurred.[58] The trials of German and Japanese leaders somewhat muddied the legal water, and a great deal of disingenuous language has been used to lay blame to all sides, but there is no doubt that Serbia and the Serbian-controlled JNA initiated hostilities in Croatia and Bosnia to create a Greater Serbia.

Nor is there any doubt that the victims of Serbian aggression had a right to defend themselves. In a 1986 decision against the United States, the ICJ decided that states had the right to defend themselves if another state attacked them, sent irregulars to attack them, or supported rebels acting against them.[59] In Croatia and Bosnia, all three criteria obtained. The JNA, acting for the Yugoslav government, attacked directly; both Belgrade and the JNA sent irregulars into other republics; and both armed, trained, and incited rebel forces on their territories.

In 1993, the ICJ ruled that Yugoslavia's failure to comply with injunctions to stop aiding the Bosnian Serbs made it an accomplice of genocide. Judge Lauterpacht noted that the JNA was a Serb force and that territory could not be lawfully acquired by aggression. He censured Yugoslavia for supporting genocide by Bosnian Serbs against the Muslims, but he dismissed Serb complaints of genocide against them because Serb atrocities committed against the Muslims far exceeded any wrong done Bosnia's Serbs. Because the embargo operated unequally on both sides, he hinted that the West was an accomplice to war crimes and concluded that the embargo was not valid.[60]

The JNA was a Serbian force, and it acted without the authorization of a federal presidency that was deadlocked because Milošević controlled four of its eight delegates. The JNA prepared Serb rebellions in Croatia and Bosnia, then used the rebellions as excuses to intervene in both republics. Once Croatia and Bosnia were recognized as states, actions by the JNA and Belgrade to aid Serbian forces in either republic constituted aggression, not civil war.[61]

Even if one accepted the fiction useful to both the Serbs and the international community, that the conflict was a civil war, the rules of war applied, particularly after the war became internationalized. Lauterpacht's opinion on the embargo seemed morally and legally well founded, and states can intervene to protect the victims of internal wars.[62]

Some saw Belgrade as using the JNA to create "an atavistic 'Greater Serbia,'" but others insisted that it lacked "adequate control" of Serb forces in Bosnia and was merely "assisting" them, a crucial distinction, and one that increased individual responsibility for war crimes. Even if true, the distinction was irrelevant to the extent that a state cannot use its territory to supply subversive or terrorist activities. By doing so, Belgrade committed aggression against Croatia and Bosnia.[63]

Third states can support wars of liberation, but once Serbia intervened to support Knin and Pale, it made the conflicts international, just as Serbian threats to target nuclear facilities in western Europe internationalized the conflict by threatening third states.[64] One wonders if the West's response would have been less ambivalent had the JNA targeted a nuclear reactor in Italy or used poison gas rather than artillery shells and fragmentation bombs on civilians in Bosnia, Croatia, and Slovenia.[65]

Clearly, there is a hierarchy of horrors, and perhaps the conventional nature of the shells and bombs dumped by Serbian aircraft and artillery on Vukovar, Sarajevo, and other Croatian and Bosnian cities, towns, and villages worked to reduce the horrible emotional charge that they should have borne. Nonetheless, fragmentation (cluster) bombs are horrible enough—and closer kin to unclean killing devices like the dumdum bullet than they are to the standard artillery round. They have no effect on military facilities. Their 360-degree killing radius is designed solely to kill human beings. So when Krajina's leaders dropped cluster bombs in Zagreb, they intended to murder civilians, and international conventions forbid attacks on civilian areas with any weapon unless one is trying to hit legitimate military targets.[66]

Under international law, both combatants and noncombatants have the right to be humanely treated and to have their property spared the ravages of war. The Geneva Conventions and the 1977 Protocols protect both POWS and civilians from unnecessary confinement and guarantee them humane treatment regardless of race, color, religion, sex, birth, or wealth. They also protect undefended areas, monuments, hospitals, and buildings. That Serbian forces systematically murdered civilians and POWs and destroyed buildings and monuments is well documented. Such behavior constituted both war and civil crimes, and disbarred governments tolerating it from the comity of nations.[67]

War crimes are not confined to murder, rape, and destruction of property. They include propaganda inciting to war and the "advocacy of national, racial, or religious hatred." The use of ethnopsychology to whip up ethnic hatred in Serbia was both prelude and precondition for aggression and genocide by Serbian forces, and a crime. There is enough evidence in the public domain to indict Croatian, Bosnian, and Serbian leaders for war crimes.[68] That the UN did so reluctantly and belatedly and that no sustained effort has been made to force the extradition of accused war criminals indicate that we have yet to learn the moral lessons of Yugoslavia's tragedy.

HUMAN RIGHTS AND GENOCIDE

Although some were pessimistic regarding progress on human rights, Geoffrey Best and Paul Sieghart saw World War II as a turning point in human affairs, because since then the manner in which sovereign states treat their citizens has became "the legitimate concern of all mankind." International conventions, declarations, resolutions, and accords have created shared standards of legally binding rules that together form international human rights law against which a state's behavior may be measured and judged.[69]

McDougal and Leighton saw the codification of human rights in the UN charter as part of a "fundamental democratization of society" essential to the "fundamental dignity of the individual." Its signatories, including Yugoslavia, pledged themselves to respect and observe "human rights and fundamental freedoms for all without distinction as to race, sex, language, or religion." They also promised to act jointly or separately to guarantee respect for human rights. So the Charter could be read as exhorting its members to intervene in Yugoslavia, and in practice, collective action and intervention is obviously sometimes needed to halt "continuous, notorious, grave and shocking" violations of human rights.[70]

Human rights were formulated and elaborated in the 1600s by theorists of natural law, then codified in the documents of the American and French revolutions. However, there was no consensus regarding basic freedoms, post–World War I treaties protecting minorities lacked teeth, and slavery was only banned in 1926. But a little over twenty years later, in 1948, the Universal Declaration on Human Rights made a state's treatment of its citizens everyone's concern by setting an international standard that displaced natural law and stood above the constitutions of individual states.[71]

Since 1945, human rights law has obtained binding force through seven basic instruments: the UN Charter (1945), the Universal Declaration of Human Rights (1948), the International Covenant on Civil and Political Rights (1966, 1976), the International Covenant on Economic, Social, and Cultural Rights (1966, 1976), the European Convention on Human Rights (1953), the European Social Charter (1965), and the Helsinki Accords (1975).[72]

Human rights are unique in that they cannot be transferred, disposed of, or extinguished. They adhere to all human beings and are inalienable. Everyone has the right to be treated equally (not suffer discrimination), live under a rule of law and be judged by an impartial tribunal (not be subject to arbitrary judgments), and have recourse to remedies if their rights are violated.[73]

Basic to all rights is the right to life, defined as the right not to be murdered or killed arbitrarily. The Helsinki Accords oblige states to ensure—not just respect—this right by seeking to prevent individuals from killing others. The laws of war prohibit execution without trial of military commandos and guerrillas.[74] International law also prohibits torture, cruel, inhuman, or degrading treatment and punishment. It expressly forbids "any act that lowers a person in rank, position, reputation, or character." States must assure their citizens freedom of movement and may not exile or expel them. Nor may they arbitrarily arrest, detain, expel, or exile aliens.[75]

The prohibitions against degrading treatment and the use of torture and terror were particularly relevant to the conflict in Yugoslavia. These prohibitions appear to have acquired the status of customary international law, and may even be preemptory norms of general international law (*jus cogens*). Torture differs in intensity from cruel, inhuman or degrading treatment and punishment. It can take the form of treatment or punishment and may be physical or mental. The motivation of the torturer is immaterial, and even during war, summary executions, torture, and slavery are outlawed. Sadly, although human rights law and the laws of war exist and are legally binding, the will to enforce them is often lacking.[76]

Of some interest for the Yugoslav conflict are the linked concepts of equality and nondiscrimination. The only distinctions allowed under international law concern aspects of character and conduct controlled by the individual (e.g., laziness) or inherited and relevant to the social order (e.g., talent). Discrimination implies unequal and unfavorable treatment by bestowing favors or imposing burdens for whatever reasons based on natural or social categories and bearing no relation to individual capacities, merits, or behaviors.[77]

In Serbian-controlled areas, non-Serbs were systematically subjected to discrimination and unequal treatment; Serbian authorities in Krajina, Bosnia, Kosovo, and Vojvodina failed to protect both individuals and groups from adverse distinctions and undue preference. Indeed, they encouraged discriminatory behavior. In contrast, the Croatian and Bosnian constitutions guarantee human rights to their citizens; in both states, there was institutional opposition to ethnic cleansing. That social discrimination exists everywhere is a sad, but trivial, observation. The key is whether it is systematic and promoted or condoned by state institutions.[78]

In 1991 Radek Sikorski doubted that Serb authorities would allow Croatian refugees from "disputed" areas to return, but would resettle the areas with "ethnically sounder [Serbian] elements." However, the genocidal nature of such ethnic cleansing by Serbs in Croatia escaped most commentators and statesmen, perhaps because they had not read the genocide conventions and associated the term only with efforts to exterminate a people.[79]

In 1992, as Roy Gutman documented the existence of death camps, David Rieff described the mechanics of ethnic cleansing. He reported that the Serbs would divide the Muslims into groups, then usually kill the professionals, local notables, and able-bodied young men. Those in "intelligence camps" were killed or held for later release. The most fortunate were housed in "open centers" accessible to relief organizations.[80]

Others filed similar reports, but few saw ethnic cleansing as genocide. Rather it was viewed as a peculiarly Balkan, and therefore particularly brutal, form of population transfer. Unlike the Holocaust, defined as "a systematic effort to eradicate a whole people from the face of the Earth," ethnic cleansing was seen as an effort by "ethnic groups to control the territory they live in." Elie Wiesel's confusion helped disorient the media and reinforced the misinformation peddled by lobbyists, politicians, and UN officials. Lack of clarity led to unfortunate attacks on those who defined ethnic cleansing as genocide by those who resented what they saw as efforts to denigrate the Holocaust by making it equivalent to ethnic cleansing.[81]

Such arguments ignore the legal definition of genocide, and by making the Holocaust a unique event, they make it irrelevant for non-Jews. The Holocaust, or Shoah, has a unique and sacred meaning for many Jews, but because something lacks the scale and efficiency of the genocides carried out by the Nazis against Jews, Gypsies, and Slavs does not mean that it is not genocide. Rather, the Shoah and other genocides should be studied so that we can understand and avoid repetitions. Resentful denunciations of those who correctly labeled ethnic cleansing as genocide confused our thinking about genocide in general and discounted and cheapened the suffering of those who perished during World War II. Ironically, the same attitudes that distorted the media's reporting on ethnic cleansing had earlier hindered their reporting on genocide and population expulsions during World War II.

Deborah Lipstadt's 1985 study of American reactions to the Shoah is instructive. "Sophisticated" people believed "self-serving" parties manufactured reports of atrocities in Germany; reporters could neither find "reliable" sources nor gain access to German-occupied territory; many were cautious owing to memories of World War I propaganda; and few saw "expulsion" as "extermination." Once the story got out, it was greeted with skepticism and quickly became "old news." Lipstadt concluded that our tendency to ignore reports of persecution and mass murder far from home "almost guarantees that the cycle of horror which was initiated by the Holocaust will continue."[82]

In Bosnia, access to Serb-controlled areas was also difficult, sources were unreliable, propagandists confused and misled, and ethnic cleansing quickly became old hat. By defining genocide as the Shoah, we failed to recognize ethnic cleansing for what it was, and we denatured and neutralized the moral and practical usefulness of the Shoah and the Nuremberg principles. The Shoah was a unique case of genocide, but it helps us understand the stages of a genocidal policy. In addition to sympathy for the victim of violence, for non-Jews it carries meaning as a case-study and a warning. Those who perished are not insulted if suffering and death cease to belong to a particular ethnic group and are not moral commodities to be compared and discounted. Comparison is futile. Hell is hell, whether in Germany, Bosnia, or Croatia.

Understanding what constitutes genocide and being clear about who committed it is particularly important given the rationalizing apologies of Western governments and the myths of privileged suffering that abound in the Balkans, where each group has its own ethos of martyrdom and victimization, and where history is conveniently rewritten to reflect national interests. The Serbs saw themselves as uniquely victimized by their neighbors and justified their own aggressive behavior as defensive responses to the latent threat of neighboring ethnic groups.[83]

But all ethnic groups are both potential victims and perpetrators of genocide; Croats and Bosnians who condoned or partook in ethnic cleansing were no less guilty than Serbs who did so. The eradication of ethnic groups from a particular territory in Indonesia, Cambodia, Croatia, Bosnia, or Serbia are genocides, and they must be taken as seriously as the Shoah. Genocide is racist, but it is ethnically neutral—

any group can practice it, and too many have done so. Adopting clear definitions is simply a practical way to focus moral energy and mobilize effective coercive force to stop such gruesome practices and punish those who implement such antihuman policies.[84]

Serbian forces systematically maltreated POWs and civilians, and they denied international organizations access to their areas. They razed whole towns and systematically destroyed evidence of Croatian and Muslim culture in areas that they occupied. By August 1992, thousands had already died in Serb camps, but the Red Cross was able to visit only ten of ninety-four camps in Serb-controlled areas. The UN later estimated that 50,000 people had been tortured and killed in 700 camps.[85]

By March 1992, Serbian forces had damaged 235 Catholic churches and monasteries, 162 civil buildings, sixteen libraries, and seven archaeological sites. They also destroyed some 200 mosques between April and July 1992. Radovan Ivancević, a professor of art history, believed that Serbian attacks "were intended to destroy the memory of [the Croatian] people." They were clearly intended to eradicate evidence of Muslim culture.[86]

During its siege of Vukovar, the JNA fired up to 15,000 rounds daily into the city. Croats believed that it was out "to destroy the very roots of Croatia," whose economy it had devastated and whose population it had decimated and expelled. As Serb "refugees" were settled in Croatian towns and villages, JNA spokesmen insisted that it sought only "to protect Serbians from the threat of genocide" and to prevent "the outbreak of bloody interethnic conflict and a repetition of the genocide committed in Croatia during World War II."[87]

In effect, the JNA argued that it could commit genocide to prevent genocide. Yet the media generally followed the lead of UN, U.S., and NATO officials who insisted on maintaining the fiction of a civil war in which all sides were committing atrocities or provoking the other to do so. Some even implied that nothing that bad had actually occurred. One of the more interesting exercises during the war was to draw comparisons with Rwanda to imply that the slaughter in Bosnia was not so horrendous after all. During an interview with the U.S. ambassador to Rwanda, Katie Couric noted that 200,000 had been killed in Rwanda "in less than a month," whereas it had taken "over two years" to reach that number in the Balkans.[88]

If a case of victor's justice, the Nuremberg trials still set a precedent, and if not legally binding, the Nuremberg principles retain moral significance. Genocide is a crime against humanity, and thus basic. It is both criminal and extraditable, and it cannot be excused by the defenses of military necessity, superior orders, act of state, or right of reprisal. The argument that Serbian actions were justified owing to their fear of their enemies was never a viable defense. Nor can the law of double effect be invoked in a siege in which targets are visible, or after hostilities are over, because it assumes that precise targeting is impossible and collateral casualties are the result of military operations.[89]

Echoing official spokesmen and self-styled experts, the U.S. media have repeatedly obfuscated the question of what genocide is, whether it occurred, and who was responsible for it. Despite the existence of a war crimes tribunal in the Hague, by making Milošević its agent and Serbia its base for peace in the Balkans, the West has precluded any serious effort to identify and bring to justice those who were ultimately guilty of the mass slaughter in Croatia and Bosnia. In effect, Western diplomacy has short-circuited international law, already rendered null and void by governments that act as if the sovereign nature of independent states puts them above all laws but their own.[90]

NOTES

1. Werner Levi, *Contemporary International Law: A Concise Introduction* (Boulder, CO: Westview, 1979, 1991), 185–88.

2. Paul Sieghart, *The International Law of Human Rights* (Oxford: Clarendon Press, 1983), 368–70; Louis B. Sohn, "The Rights of Minorities," in Louis Henkin et al., *The International Bill of Rights: The Covenant on Civil and Political Rights* (New York: Columbia University Press, 1981), 276–78.

3. Victor S. Mamatey, *The United States and East Central Europe, 1914–1918: A Study in Wilsonian Diplomacy and Propaganda* (Princeton, NJ: Princeton UP, 1957); Loyd Gardner's study of Wilsonian and Leninist propaganda; James J. Sadkovich, "The Former Yugoslavia, the End of the Nuremberg Era and the New Barbarism," in Meštrović and Cushman, eds., *This Time We Knew*, passim.

4. Antonio Cassese, "The Self-Determination of Peoples," in Henkin et al., *The International Bill of Rights*, 92–96.

5. Cassese, "Self-Determination," 96–113, and "The Helsinki Declaration and Self-Determination," in Thomas Buergenthal and Judith R. Hall, *Human Rights, International Law and the Helsinki Accord* (New York: Allanhead, Osmun, and Co., 1977), 90; Michael Walzer, *Just and Unjust Wars: A Moral Argument with Historical Illustrations* (New York: Basic Books, 1977), 90–91.

6. Sohn, "Rights of Minorities," 270–87. Minorities are "non-dominant groups . . . which possess and wish to preserve ethnic, religious, or linguistic traditions or characteristics markedly different from those of the rest of the population."

7. Walzer, *Just and Unjust Wars*, 55, 86–108; Hilaire McCoubrey and Nigel D. White, *International Organizations and Civil Wars* (Brookfield, NH: Dartmouth, 1995), 8–14.

8. Magaš, *The Destruction of Yugoslavia*, 310–316, 349; Tomislav Z. Kuzmanović, "Croatia's Constitution: A Blueprint for Democracy in Croatia," *Journal of Croatian Studies* (1991–92), 164–72.

9. Cassese, "Self-determination," 92–113, and "Helsinki Declaration," 90–93, 100.

10. Ramet, *Social Currents*, 405; Cohen, *Broken Bonds*, 135, 191, 207–8. Denitch, *Tragic Death*, 49, dismissed constitutional guarantees as meaningless. Mesić made the remark after Knin's referendum excluded Croats in "Krajina," but included Serbs living outside the area. Even though a KOS film showing Martin Špegelj plotting to assassinate JNA leaders was "half genuine, half fake," Cohen believed the Croats should have helped the JNA apprehend Špegelj.

11. Cohen, *Broken Bonds*, 141, 129.

12. Woodward, *Balkan Tragedy*, 209–18, objected to the wording of the Bosnian referendum, which asked whether people wished to belong to "a state of equal citizens," and dismissed Bosnia's referendum, which 99.7 percent of the voters had approved (in a 63% turnout).

13. Cassese, "Helsinki Declaration," 92–93, 99–105.

14. Cassese, "Helsinki Declaration," 95–98, 105–7; Levi, *Contemporary International Law*, 34. Customary law derives from treaties and extensive, uniform practice over time.

15. For internal disturbances, McCoubrey and White, *International Organizations*, passim, esp. 61–75; W. Raymond Duncan, "Yugoslavia's Break-up," in W. R. Duncan and G. Paul Holman, Jr., *Ethnic Nationalism and Regional Conflict: The Former Soviet Union and Yugoslavia* (Boulder, CO: Westview, 1994), 19–21, saw all sides as guilty of "fratricidal mayhem" and "ethnic wars."

16. Beloff, "Eastern Approaches."

17. Magaš, *The Destruction of Yugoslavia*, 312–13.

18. Kraljic, *Belgrade's Strategic Designs*, Appendix B. 162,000 lived in the Krajina, 181,959 Serbs in thirteen cities. Knin had 34,504, Zagreb 41,923.

19. Cohen, *Broken Bonds*, 128–31, thought Serbs made up "a significant portion" of "Krajina's" Yugoslavs. For Croatia's borders, see Ljubo Boban, *Hrvatske granice, od 1918. do 1993. godine* (Zagreb: HAZU, 1993), 62–65, and Magaš, *The Destruction of Yugoslavia*, 313–14.

20. Cassese, "Helsinki Declaration," 92.

21. Denitch, *Tragic Death*, 42–48, glosses over the elections; Cohen, *Broken Bonds*, 98–101, 128–31, put the best face possible on Serbian results, noting that Serbs voted "heavily against" Tudjman's HDZ. Perhaps, but they did not vote *for* the SDS.

22. Cohen, *Broken Bonds*, 155–59, and Magaš, *The Destruction of Yugoslavia*, 254–55, for Croatian and Slovenia.

23. Magaš, *The Destruction of Yugoslavia*, xv, xvii–xviii; Cohen, *Broken Bonds*, 146.

24. Magaš, *The Destruction of Yugoslavia*, xv, 313, 349.

25. Magaš, *The Destruction of Yugoslavia*, 316. The Serb majority in Vojvodina was 53 percent to 60 percent, the result of Serb colonization after expelling 500,000 Germans in 1945. Wayne S. Vucinich, "Nationalism and Communism," in Vucinich et al., *Contemporary Yugoslavia*, 252–57.

26. Walzer, *Just and Unjust Wars*, 51–64, 101, 106, 121, 162–75; James Podgers, "The World Cries for Justice," *ABA Journal* (April 1996), 53; Hersch Lauterpacht's remarks in International Court of Justice, *Reports of Judgements, Advisory Opinions and Orders: Case Concerning Application of the Convention on the Prevention and Punishment of Genocide (Bosnia-Herzegovina vs. Serbia-Montenegro)* (The Hague, 13 September 1993), 408–48.

27. Walzer, *Just and Unjust Wars*, 96–102. North, *War, Peace, Survival*, 5–9. Gilpin, *War and Change*, 1–15, 206–9, believed "hegemonic war" routinely changes systems,

peace has a low priority, and peaceful change occurs only when it does not threaten the system undergoing change.

28. ICJ, *Reports of Judgements*, 374, 390, 440. *Jus cogens* are crimes against humanity, so basic and universal that their force is automatic.

29. Gilpin, *War and Change*, 25–26; Sieghart, *The International Law of Human Rights*, xix, 3–32. Martin Wight, "Western Values in International Relations," in Herbert Butterfield and Martin Wight, eds., *Diplomatic Investigations: Essays in the Theory of International Politics* (Cambridge, MA: Harvard University Press, 1966), 96, believed international society should be described "in historical and sociological depth" as "the habitual intercourse of independent communities" through space and over time.

30. Karen Tumulty, "The Lost Faith of Daniel Patrick Moynihan," *Los Angeles Times*, 19 June 1994.

31. Geoffrey Best, *War and Law since 1945* (Oxford: Clarendon Press, 1994), 3–41. Wight, "Western Values," 90–95, 120, 128–29, cited Reinhold Niebuhr, who thought ideals have meaning in national life and institutions, and in individuals who defy them for moral reasons.

32. Levi, *Contemporary International Law*, 34, 172; Sieghart, *International Law*, 14; Myres S. McDougal and Florentino P. Feliciano, "International Coercion and World Public Order: The General Principles of the Law of War," and Myres S. McDougal and Gertrude C. K. Leighton, "The Rights of Man in the World Community: Constitutional Illusions versus Rational Action," in Myres S. McDougal and Associates, *Studies in World Public Order* (New Haven, CT: New Haven Press, 1987), 287–88, 360, 365.

33. Hedley Bull, "Society and Anarchy in International Relations," in Butterfield and Wight, *Diplomatic Investigations*, 48; Yoram Dinstein, "The Right to Life, Physical Integrity, and Liberty," in Henkin et al., *The International Bill of Rights*, 131.

34. Sieghart, *International Law*, 10–11; McDougal et al., *Studies*, 291–92.

35. McCoubrey and White, 157, 268–77; Walzer, *Just and Unjust Wars*, 59–66. Wight, "Western Values," 102–11, 120, derived "a certain satisfaction" that the UN had "accidentally developed into the first international organization that has been able to subject the Great Powers to systematic nagging."

36. Helsinki Watch, *War Crimes in Bosnia-Hercegovina*, esp. vol. II, 394–409; Norman Cigar and Paul Williams, *War Crimes and Individual Responsibility: A Prima Facie Case for the Indictment of Slobodan Milosevic* (Washington, DC: The Balkan Institute, 1996), 9–28; Walzer, *Just and Unjust Wars*, 287–327.

37. Marc D. Charney, "Conversation with Telford Taylor: The Laws of War Are Many, but Self-interest Is the Only Enforcer," *New York Times*, 25 December 1994; Wight, "Western Values," 108; Bull, "Society and Anarchy," 43.

38. Charney, "Conversation with Telford Taylor," op. cit.; Wight, "Western Values," 108, for the concept of the grand alliance to assure collective action against those who transgress the international order.

39. *Nightline*, 6 May 1993; *MacNeil-Lehrer*, 8 February, 6 April 1993; *This Week with David Brinkley*, 25 April 1993; *New York Times*, 24 July, 3 August 1992 for Boutros-Ghali's complaint that Bosnia was getting too much attention.

40. Charles William Maynes, "Containing Ethnic Conflict," *Foreign Policy* (Winter 1992–93), 11; *This Week with David Brinkley*, 9 May 1993, for Scowcroft. On *MacNeil-Lehrer*, 18 April 1994, Congresswoman Furse suggested that we ignore

Bosnia, but prepare for "future Bosnias." Judging by her remarks, conflict resolution is a euphemism for redlining war in the Third World and doing nothing to stop mass slaughter.

41. Sieghart, *International Law*, 35 ff., 72 ff., 174, 370–76. For the rights of minorities, see Sohn, "The Rights of Minorities," and B. G. Ramacharan, "Equality and Nondiscrimination," in Henkin et al., *The International Bill of Rights*, esp. 259, 262–64, 282. States must assure freedom of thought, conscience, religion, equality and nondiscrimination, and minorities can preserve and develop their ethnic, religious, and linguistic characteristics, rights denied non-Serbs in Serb-controlled areas, but enjoyed by Serbs in Croatia and Bosnia.

42. UNPROFOR's role was not a happy one. The first units arrived in Croatia in late 1991, but failed to disarm Serbian forces there and did not resettle those expelled from their homes by the JNA and Serb irregulars. Bruna Saric, 21 April 1995, "UNPROFOR in Croatia."

43. *MacNeil-Lehrer, PBS*, 26 May 1994.

44. Dan De Luce, "Muslims, Croats Fight Serbs as Peace Talks Open," *Reuters*, 26 May 1994.

45. *New York Times*, "U.S. on Secession, Maybe," 28 June 1991.

46. Donald A. Wells, *War Crimes and Laws of War* (Washington, DC: University of America Press, 1984), 116; Bull, "Society and Anarchy," passim.

47. Basic are Buergenthal and Hall, *Human Rights, op. cit.*; Levi, *Contemporary International Law, op. cit.*; Sieghart, *The International Law of Human Rights, op. cit.*; Best, *War and Law since 1945, op. cit.*; McDougal et al., *Studies in World Public Order, op. cit.*; Wells, *War Crimes, op. cit.*; Richard A. Falk et al., *Crimes of War: A Legal, Political-Documentary, and Psychological Inquiry into the Responsibility of Leaders, Citizens, and Soldiers for Criminal Acts in Wars* (New York: Random House, 1971); Marshall Cohen, Thomas Nagel, and Thomas Scanlon, eds., *War and Moral Responsibility* (New Brunswick, NJ: Princeton University Press, 1974); Herbert W. Briggs, *The Law of Nations* (New York: Appleton-Century-Crofts, 1952); Ian Brownlie, *Basic Documents in International Law* (Oxford: Clarendon Press, 1983).

48. Fallows, "Why Americans Hate the Media," for the failure of the journalists Peter Jennings and Mike Wallace to reach the moral level of a Marine Corps colonel. The colonel's moral certainty contrasted with a lack of moral rectitude by all the civilians on the show, who tended to take expedient, not moral, positions. Perhaps the colonel was less ambiguous because for soldiers the laws of war are questions of life and death, not subjects for debate on PBS by clever lawyers and superannuated statesmen.

49. McDougal et al., *Studies*, 277–79; Wells, *Law of War*, 104–5; Richard A. Falk et al., *Crimes of War*, passim.

50. McDougal et al., *Studies*, 290, 296–97, 309–17; Michael Howard, "War as an Instrument of Policy," in Butterfield and Wight, *Diplomatic Investigations*, 195.

51. Wells, *War Crimes*, 81–82, 95, 104; Falk, *Crimes of War*, 141–61; and Richard L. Lael, *The Yamashita Precedent: War Crimes and Command Responsibility* (Wilmington, DE: Scholarly Resources, 1982), passim.

52. Lael, *Yamashita*, 123–34; Wells, *War Crimes*, 83–87; Falk, *Crimes of War*, 395–96; Pick, *War Machine*, passim; Best, *War and Law*, 112–14; Claudio G. Segrè, "Giulio Douhet: Strategist, Theorist, Prophet?" *Journal of Strategic Studies* (1992), 362–64.

53. Howard, "War," 196–200; Best, *War and Law*, 45–114.

54. Wells, *War Crimes*, 85–99; McCoubrey and White, *International Organizations*, 277–78.

55. McDougal et al., *Studies*, 258–59. Woodward, *Balkan Tragedy*, 13–15, thought the war's "real origin" lay "in the disintegration of governmental authority and the breakdown of a political and civil order" "over a prolonged period." That, of course, is like saying someone died of old age because he was old.

56. Wells, *War Crimes*, 109–10. Because evil is institutional, normal people can commit heinous crimes as easily as they close a business deal. Gregory Bateson made a similar argument in *Steps to an Ecology of Mind* (New York: Ballantine, 1972) with regard to goal-oriented, amoral, unipurposeful behavior, which we all risk when we park our humanity at the door of our workplace. War is just another job. For behavior in battle, J. Glenn Gray, *The Warriors: Reflections on Men in Battle* (New York: Harper, 1986), and Richard Holmes, *Acts of War: The Behavior of Men in Battle* (New York, 1986).

57. Cited by McDougal and Feliciano, *Studies*, 298; Walzer, *Just and Unjust Wars*, 21–33.

58. Levi, *Contemporary International Law*, 302; Wells, *War Crimes*, 81–2.

59. Levi, *International Law*, 303–4.

60. ICJ, *Reports of Judgements*, 408–48.

61. Internal war is a useless catch-all category. See McCoubrey and White, *International Organizations*, passim, and the excerpt from Harry Eckstein in Bruce Mazlish, Arthur D. Kaledin, and David B. Ralston, eds., *Revolution: A Reader* (New York: Macmillan, 1971), 18–44.

62. Levi, *International Law*, 307–12; McCoubrey and White, *International Organizations*, 23, 62–75, 114–31.

63. Sieghart, *International Law*, 370–72. As with self-determination and propaganda inciting to war, there is no jurisprudence. Primorac, "Serbia's War/Out of the Rubble," 46; Maynes, "Containing Ethnic Conflict," 9–10.

64. "Se Mosca non vuole," *Panorama*, 10 January 1993, for threats of "total war" by Gen. Momir Talić, including targeting nuclear power plants; Levi, *Contemporary International Law*, 275–76, 315–17.

65. Serbia's manufacture of Sarin nerve gas should have been particularly disquieting. My thanks to Brad Blitz for information on the gas.

66. Wells, *Laws of War*, 107.

67. Falk, *Crimes of War*, 33–40, 50–51; Best, *War and Law*, passim; Wells, *War Crimes*, 99; Helsinki Watch, *War Crimes in Bosnia-Herzegovina*, vols. I and II, passim.

68. Sieghart, *International Law*, 370–72; Cigar, *Genocide in Bosnia*, 22–37; Forestier, "The Use of Social Sciences to Stir Up Ethnic Conflict," concluded that the genocide in Bosnia was planned and that Rašković, Jovan Striković, Radovan Karadžić, and Cosič were responsible and should be treated as war criminals. For evidence, Cigar and Williams, *War Crimes and Individual Responsibility*; Helsinki Watch, *War Crimes in Bosnia-Hercegovina*, vols. I and II.

69. Levi, *International Law*, 163–65; Best, *War and Law*, 62–64; Sieghart, *Human Rights*, xix–xxi. Dinstein, "Right to Life," 111–15.

70. McDougal et al., *Studies*, 335–46, 368–69.

71. Carl Joachim Friedrich, *The Philosophy of Law in Historical Perspective* (Chicago: University of Chicago Press, 1958, 1963), 178–88; Sieghart, *Human Rights*, 8–15.

72. Sieghart, *International Law*, 24–32.

73. Sieghart, *International Law*, 17–23.

74. McDougal et al., *Studies*, 322–23; Dinstein, "The Right to Life," 115–19; Sieghart, *International Law*, 128 ff.; Best, *War and Law*, 126–33.

75. Sieghart, *International Law*, 135–74; Dinstein, "Right to Life," 128; Levi, *Contemporary International Law*, 170. States must "observe a certain standard of decent treatment" of aliens on their territory.

76. McDougal et al., *Studies*, 317; Dinstein, "Right to Life," 122–36; and Levi, *International Law*, 184.

77. Ramacharan, "Equality and Nondiscrimination," 252–69.

78. *Ibid.*, and Cigar, *Genocide*, 101–3, 127–32. Denitch, *Tragic Death,* 49, appears to equate violations of constitutional guarantees with ethnic cleansing.

79. Sikorski, "Déjà Vu/War in Europe Again," 40–42. His use of the passive voice made the Croats victims without victimizers.

80. Rieff, "Letter from Bosnia," 83–84, 87, 93; Gutman, *Witness,* passim. Also Ed Vuilliamy, *Seasons in Hell: Understanding Bosnia's War* (New York: St. Martin's, 1994), and Stokes et al., "Instant History," 140–43, for their negative judgment on accounts by journalists and their extremely cynical approach to international relations.

82. Erwin Knoll, "The Uses of the Holocaust," *The Progressive* (July 1993), 16, condemned "such invocation of the Holocaust as inappropriate and even offensive." By doing so, he erased the difference between victim and victimizer. George Schultz and Leon Wieseltier found such distinctions specious, because genocide is not civil war and the Shoah should have taught us to recognize, and intervene to end, genocide. *Nightline,* 22 April 1993 for Wieseltier and 26 April for Schultz.

82. Deborah Lipstadt, *Beyond Belief: The American Press and the Coming of the Holocaust* (New York: The Free Press, 1985), esp. 137–84, 240–78. For propaganda, see Read, *Atrocity Propaganda, 1914–1919,* passim; Lasswell and Wechsler, *Propaganda Techniques,* passim; and Spencer C. Tucker, ed., *The European Powers in the First World War: An Encyclopedia* (New York: Garland, 1996).

83. Cohen, *Serbia's Secret War*, 136; Cigar, *Genocide,* passim.

84. Kuper, *Genocide,* passim, esp. his discussion of the debate over the genocide convention.

85. *Panorama,* 23 August 1992; Gutman, *Witness,* 46, 141. The Red Cross still lacked access in early 1993.

86. Roy Gutman, "War in Bosnia Leaving Muslim Heritage in Ruins," *Newsday,* 3 September 1992; *Archaeology* (March–April 1992), 20–21.

87. Paul Lewis, *New York Times,* 21 October 1992; Guskind, "Letter from Croatia," and "Ethnic Time Bombs."

88. *Today, NBC,* interview with James Rawson, 3 May 1994.

89. Wells, *Laws of War*, 98, 101–2; Nagel, "War and Massacre," and Wassertrom, "Relevance of Nuremberg," passim.

90. For a defense of Western policy, James Gow, "Nervous Bunnies: The International Community and the Yugoslav War Dissolution," in Lawrence Freedman, ed., *Military Intervention in European Conflicts* (Oxford: Blackwell, 1994). For a condemnation, Almond, *Europe's Backyard War*, passim. For an argument to limit the UN's role, see Viscount Maugham, *U.N.O. and War Crimes* (Westport, CT: Greenwood, 1951/1975).

9

A Truly
International Conflict

THE GOOD OLD DAYS OF IMPERIAL RULE

As Yugoslavia unraveled, officials gave peace priority, urged compromise, blamed all sides equally, and justified inaction by insisting that vital Western interests were not involved. Some saw "a period of volatile transition" marked by "xenophobic brands of ethnic nationalism" and Western confusion after the cold war ended, but others had a sense of nostalgia, of old blocs reemerging, rather than a new order being born, as Germany, Austria, and Italy backed Slovenia and Croatia, and Russia, France, and Britain supported Serbia.[1]

Many saw the conflict as an opportunity to create a neoimperialist system. Arguing that new "ministates" would never be "productive enough on a large enough scale to make a modern state function," David Andersen suggested the United States, an international organization, or a consortium of Western states "manage or at least control" Yugoslavia's dissolution. William Pfaff thought an EC core might assimilate eastern European states, because western Europe was the source for "modern civilizations."[2]

The chaos on the world's periphery led Gerald Helman and Steven Ratner to urge the creation of guardianships, with "failed" states like Bosnia delegating governmental functions to the UN. Paul Johnson wanted a new imperial order to guarantee stability and peace, and Boutros-Ghali lobbied for more resources for peacekeeping, one of the decade's "growth industries."[3] Leftists also saw small states as not viable. Anthony Borden suggested placing Bosnia under "UN trusteeship"; Alexander Cockburn seemed to argue for a Greater Serbia by excusing Serb conquests as redressing borders drawn to "punish" them; and Aryeh Neier asserted a dubious moral equivalency while letting Milošević off the hook on a technicality.[4]

Because many thought secession had provoked the war, human rights without secession appealed to leaders of states with fissiparous polities. George Will mocked the West as a more impotent Holy Roman Empire, but many longed for a Holy Alliance to assure international order by containing internal dissent. Joseph Nye argued that since less than a tenth of the world's states are ethnically homogeneous, self-determination is a chimera; Robert Cullen suggested that Washington preclude "the disastrous potential of the assertion of collective rights in the postcommunist era" by rejecting secession and promoting individual and minority rights within existing states.[5]

Hard-liners like Stephen John Stedman ridiculed "the new interventionists" who wanted "to end civil wars [sic!] and stop governments from abusing the rights of their peoples." Unlike those who believed that war on civilians justified intervention, Stedman dismissed "humanitarian concerns" as insufficient to justify using force. He warned that it would be hard to tell civilians from soldiers in Bosnia's "civil war," so he advised letting the "warring parties" end the war themselves.[6]

But in Bosnia all sides wore uniforms, and military operations were conventional. The embargo and the Serbian monopoly of heavy weapons seriously handicapped Bosnians and Croats; but in 1995, Stedman's position was echoed in both radical and conservative publications, which urged the West to forgo bombing, seek out democratic forces, and treat everyone alike, especially since the Serbs were just trying to avoid Muslim domination.[7]

In a civil war no one could be trusted, and as Ronald Steel warned, should the West defeat the Serbs, something not even the Germans could do, "the Croats would rush in to take their share, and the Muslims to exact retribution," because that "is the history of the Balkans." And yet, as Åge Eknes noted, by maintaining the embargo, the UN and the West became accomplices to genocide.[8]

Among those in favor of drawing the imperial wagons together to fend off the Balkan Indians was Foreign Policy's editor, Charles Maynes, who warned that attacking Serbia could shatter a fragile great-power consensus and undo the new world order. Among those who thought the United States and the EC caricatures of the gutless lion and the brainless scarecrow in the Wizard of Oz was Michael Clark of the Center for Defence Studies at King's College.[9]

As it turned out, the new world order was a sham and Hegel's philosophy worked no better for capitalism than for Communism. Still, at the time, Fukuyama's "good news" that history had ended with the triumph of capitalism was widely touted as the ultimate wisdom. But even a quick glance at the newspapers should have sobered up the more ingenuous pundits, and Maynes was certainly not wearing rose-colored glasses when he argued that after the Serbs had rejected power sharing, and the Croats and Muslims repression, only ethnic cleansing remained as a solution to Yugoslavia's crisis, a solution he thought had worked well in Poland, Greece, Turkey, and Czechoslovakia.[10]

Advocating a hard-nosed solution for the Yugoslav crisis rationalized Western policies and peace plans that favored the Serbs. Brent Scowcroft put it bluntly on several occasions, at one point noting that if nobody was ready to pay the cost of intervention, the West should "just wink at the Serbs and let them take what they want." While some commentators wallowed in pseudo-realpolitik, a few grasped what a pragmatic politic was all about.[11]

A realist with a Serbian bias, Misha Glenny argued that in the real world "nobody should expect" peace "to be evenhanded or fair." In March 1995, he advised lifting sanctions on Serbia to encourage it to recognize Croatia. In September, he announced that the Croats had "hit the jackpot," while the Muslims had fulfilled their "destiny" by losing, and the Serbs had been inadequately compensated in Bosnia for their losses in Croatia.[12]

Thomas Friedman combined bad chronology with anti-German sentiment to give a neoisolationist spin to the realist approach, arguing that U.S. troops should stay home and Germany should pay the costs of peacekeeping because its support of Croatia had triggered war. George Kenney jettisoned morality altogether in favor of moral equivalency by dismissing simplistic concepts like good and evil, and defining fairness as giving equal weight to everyone's claims.[13]

While Anthony Lewis and Roger Cohen reminded readers that the West's policy had favored Serbian fanatics, William Safire restated a cold war theorem when he warned that a viable peace would come only once all sides were sufficiently armed to make war too costly. A "workable interventionist strategy" would therefore have included use of NATO airpower to police Bosnia's skies, manipulation of economic sanctions and incentives to convince Belgrade and Zagreb to cooperate with "what's left of Bosnia," lifting the arms embargo, and NATO and U.S. training of Bosnia's armed forces.[14]

APPROPRIATING YUGOSLAVIA'S WAR

For most of the crisis, Serbians were antagonists, Muslims victims, Croats accomplices or allies, and the great powers and their agencies, the UN and NATO, the real protagonists. By adopting the perspectives of Western diplomats, the media made it seem that the crisis was the property of the great powers, and that the only way to end it was for them to impose peace on the belligerents. In effect, the media appropriated the crisis for the statesmen and publics of the West. This sleight of hand made it harder to get the cooperation of Croats, Muslims, and Serbs, who were only allowed to vote up or down on Western proposals. How cynical and callous the process could be became clear when David Owen insisted that lifting the arms embargo would be a "disincentive to the Muslims" to negotiate seriously.[15]

Because the West appropriated the crisis, even hints that it might act decisively provoked a flurry of media coverage that quickly dissipated. There were flurries in 1993, when Clinton seemed about to act, and Vance and Owen pressed their new peace plan; in 1994, when the Contact Group took over the peace process and Washington brokered a Croat-Bosnian federation; and in 1995, when the United States made peace and deployed troops to Bosnia.

By containing the crisis within Western frames, the media avoided grappling with the internal politics of the belligerents and made idealism seem helpless and morality hopelessly ingenuous against the stubborn realities of ancient Balkan feuds, an impotent UN, and an indifferent American public. Reporters uncritically repeated claims that the United States had no vital interest in the Balkans, that there was little domestic support for intervention, and that there was no reasonable chance of success should outside military forces be sent to Bosnia.[16]

When discussing the rape of Bosnian women by Serbian forces, Ted Koppel asked Robert Dole if Americans were ready to pay the "high cost" of getting "involved." His question suggested that moral issues are subject to cost-benefit analysis and measured rape against the domestic costs of U.S. foreign policy. The women became factors in an equation whose solution was known because the variables on our side were obvious. For Slavenka Drakulić, systematic rape was genocide, but like *The Nation*, she seemed more upset by rape than mass murder, a moral selectivity apparently based on feminist ideology.[17]

In the early 1990s, both journalists and diplomats mixed cynicism, idealism, and self-conscious naivete. They saw UN peacekeepers as the best hope for shoring up a shaky international order, yet viewed both international organizations and conventional military forces as ineffectual and impotent in nations like Somalia and Bosnia. Many were morally confused. Unable to see ethnic cleansing as genocide, they retreated to East-West/North-South news frames in which tribes commit massacres in the South and East and ethnic groups confront one another in the North and West. Bosnia was not LA; it was Rwanda.[18]

It was disheartening to see the *Progressive*, a pillar of the American Left, ignore the crisis in 1991 and 1992, then in July 1993 criticize comparisons between Bosnia and the Holocaust as "inappropriate and even offensive."[19] Or to see the *New Republic* condemn failed policies, but print the sort of scabrous anti-Croatian articles found in *The Nation*.[20] Moral confusion resulted because objectivity ended in moral equivalence, and, as Susan Sontag noted, Western intellectuals simply failed. In December 1992, Elie Wiesel still saw no parallels with the Holocaust; three years later, *The Nation* could compare mass murder in Srebrenica to the flight of refugees from Croatia and equate accusations that Croats had "torched" towns and Bosnian troops had seized UN equipment to reports of upset Serbs. Others were less confused. In April 1993, Leon Wiseltier condemned the "realist analysis" as "spectacularly inadequate," insisting that the genocide occurring in Bosnia was not the same as a civil war.[21]

Because the West sought only to contain the crisis, the Serbs could do as they pleased. In 1991, George Bush ignored genocide, and in 1995, Kenneth Roth, executive director of Human Rights Watch, complained that the lack of a strong Western response to the seizure of Srebrenica and Žepa had confirmed "an assumption of impunity" among Serb leaders. Haris Silajdžić had earlier castigated the UN for failing to protect Bosnian "enclaves" (a.k.a. safe areas) from Serbian attack, because Serbian leaders threatened the UN as their forces cleansed Muslims.[22]

Reflecting on her situation after Serbs had driven her from her home, a woman from Srebrenica concluded, "We're just pawns in everybody's games." Another Bosnian complained to John Pomfret that the hoopla over the rescue of a U.S. pilot had "reinforce[d] the impression here that the people of Bosnia have become bystanders in their own country." As Slaven Letica noted, the West not only managed the crisis, it defined it.[23]

The West strove to make it clear that none of our guys was going to die in a conflict in Yugoslavia, that Berlin's recognition of Croatia and Slovenia would not result in military aid, and that UN forces would withdraw should they be attacked. When Alija Izetbegović asked for UN forces to be deployed in Bosnia to prevent violence, a former U.S. ambassador to Yugoslavia advocated a policy of allowing the Yugoslavs to "exhaust" themselves even though it was clear that only Croats and Muslims besieged by the Serbs were being exhausted.[24]

In other words, after appropriating the crisis and containing the violence, the West let the Yugoslavs rot.

THE UN AND NATO

By early 1992, events in Yugoslavia had involved the West, but to act consensus was needed, and there seemed to be none. By late 1994, it was clear that the UN and NATO had both failed. Misha Glenny was touting Milošević, the man who had started the conflict, as the only hope for peace, and the West continued to press the Muslims to be reasonable. James Gow concluded that "the undeniable bottom line" was that neither the UN nor NATO had been "adequate to the challenge." Gow thought that bad timing, inconsistency, lack of coordination, and the Yugoslavs had undone the two organizations, but Barnett saw bureaucratic priorities as overwhelming good intentions.[25]

Early on, it was obvious that diplomacy and economic pressure would not curb Serbian expansion, but no one responded to the specter of Munich or took up Radek Sikorski's suggestion that the West deliver an "old-fashioned ultimatum" to Serbia to get out of Croatia or see Europe support Zagreb's armed forces. Failing that, Sikorski predicated "a long war" and warned that should the Croats lose, they would bide their time, then reclaim their losses.[26]

They eventually did just that, but in 1992 the media trumpeted the deployment of UN troops in Croatia as a victory for peace. Although the *New York Times* applauded the deployment of peacekeepers (UN-PROFOR), their arrival helped the Serbs, who had been pressing for them as a way to consolidate their gains in Croatia, where they were already "resettling thousands of refugees."[27]

Gow later concluded that if UNPROFOR was "successful in stabilizing the cessation of open hostilities," the EC "increasingly found itself bullying the Serbs." But the UN did not guarantee the safety of Croats in Serb-held areas, and so allowed the Serbs to consolidate their gains. As Serb forces cleansed Bosnia, the UN and NATO delivered "humanitarian aid" and Boutros-Ghali boasted of the size of the peacekeeping effort in Yugoslavia; and as Colin Powell warned that U.S. armed forces would undertake peacekeeping and humanitarian missions only if objectives were "clear and unambiguous," Vance and Owen tried to do to Bosnia what Vance and Carrington had done to Croatia.[28]

The UN and NATO were key players in Croatia and Bosnia, but they neither enforced nor kept the peace, safe areas were not safe, and peace plans condoned genocide. Their failure to stop aggression and genocide eroded their credibility for all but a few true believers. As Clinton put it, "We should not say things that we do not intend to do." But within months, Clinton himself had been dubbed "Mrs. Dontfire," and it was clear that the UN had effectively intervened "on the side of the aggressor."[29]

Although Bosnia received twenty-five times more coverage than Rwanda, both got enough publicity to make them test cases. But the UN lacked the funds and the institutional autonomy to act on its own, and its most powerful members were ambivalent about enforcing peace on the periphery of their world.[30] Containment and compromise became familiar words as the West used the UN to manage the crises, and both adopted policies reflecting their interests, not those of Bosnians, Serbs, or Croats. A recurring worry was that pressing Pale might put peace-keepers "at risk," and in return for the release of UN troops, the UN envoy, Yasushi Akashi, turned a blind eye when the Serbs redeployed their armor around Sarajevo. By 1995, UNPROFOR's chief task seemed to be to provide hostages for the Bosnian Serbs.[31]

Edward Luck, president of the American UN Association, saw the UN as impotent and worried peacekeeping might become "a form of sub-contracting" because the major powers favored "low-risk, low-cost, minimalist" foreign policies. Although Boutros-Ghali exhorted the great powers "to enforce peace," he suggested withdrawing UN troops, and his assistant announced that the UN could not use force. Unimpressed, Silajdžić criticized the Secretary General for pressing the contact group rather than the Serbs.[32]

Even though UNPROFOR could do whatever was necessary to protect the safe areas, in late 1994, NATO and the UN yielded to the Bosnian Serbs, who held 400 peacekeepers hostage. While Juppe and Hurd presented yet another peace plan to Milošević for his approval, a U.S. diplomat, Charles Redman, trekked to Pale. The media blamed the humiliating episode and the world's cowardice on the "war" and other impersonal forces. "Talk of firmness in dealing with the Bosnian Serbs," Craig Whitney reported, "has now given way to expressions of impotence to deal with a conflict that has shaken both NATO and the United Nations to their roots." Bosnia had become a "sorry affair," a "tragedy," a "dreadful conflict" for "NATO diplomats."[33]

By blaming "the conflict," the media attained levels of abstract causation that would have challenged even S. I. Hayakawa. But Warren Christopher and Douglas Hurd were equal to the task. Bosnia was not a test of anyone or anything. "It is not," the Secretary of State insisted, "about NATO," which, his British colleague added, was not "born to solve the Bosnia problem." Still, NATO's new Belgian Secretary General, Willy Claes, declared NATO's mission in Bosnia successful. If NATO lacked the "will" to stop the fighting there, "even Hitler's 42 divisions" (up five from MacKenzie's thirty-seven) had been unable to "impose a solution on what was then Yugoslavia." NATO could only "organize a debate" on the war's history and "look very carefully to the conditions, and to the rules of the game before saying yes" to future peacekeeping. Whether NATO forces and Nazi legions were comparable, Claes clearly suffered from "Colin Powell Syndrome," a need to be assured of quick and bloodless victory before undertaking any operation.[34]

The Bosnians discerned a certain egoism in efforts to protect UN troops rather than the civilians who were being terrorized, besieged, and killed, and the media speculated that the UN might withdraw after Srebrenica's fall had put its troops at risk and cost it credibility with Pale and Sarajevo. Lacking "the political will" to deal forcefully with the Serbs, it could neither protect its troops, held hostage by the Serbs, nor succor the refugees generated by Serb offensives in June and July.[35]

After Srebrenica's fall, many assumed NATO would take over from a discredited UN. Yet NATO's credibility needed the rescue of a downed American pilot to redeem it. Evidently, the Americans had not given NATO the leadership needed to convince its members to impose their political will in Bosnia. Or perhaps it was the West that suffered from ancient hatreds. Noting NATO's disarray, Michael Dobbs chided Bush for having left Yugoslavia to the Europeans. France and Britain favored the Serbs, Germany helped the Croats, and the United States supported the Bosnians. As the *New Republic* put it, the early 1990s had not been a good time for the West.[36]

Nor was tomorrow better. As NATO stared at its Balkan navel, searching for a meaning to life, Clinton found himself under pressure to act. At odds with the French and British, who threatened to withdraw if the embargo was lifted, he was under attack from his domestic constituencies for standing by as the Serbs committed genocide.[37]

But then, yesterday had not gone well either. William Perry had urged NATO to use "compelling force" in Bosnia "to make it clear that there is a heavy price to pay for violating the rules that NATO [had] established." But Akashi and Rose, who held the keys to NATO airpower, spurned compelling force. When Serbs took a Bangladesh battalion hostage, Akashi only protested. Rose, who had led the SAS team that stormed Iran's London embassy, publicly argued that hostages held by Serbs in the open were not comparable to those held by terrorists in a building, and he secretly sabotaged air strikes against Serb positions.[38]

Neither the UN nor NATO reacted to what one journalist labeled Serbian blackmail. When twenty-one French soldiers joined 300 hostages already held by the Serbs, Roger Cohen concluded that air strikes "intended to cow the Serbs" had "had the reverse effect," and UN troops under order neither to fire nor to surrender had been placed in a dilemma. In fact, the troops surrendered, and Dutch and Ukrainian units stepped aside later that summer to let the Serbs take Srebrenica and Žepa. There were few air strikes, their targets were absurdly marginal, and the no-fly zone had already been breached 465 times by early 1993.[39]

As UN officials studied the Geneva Convention, four American A-10s, four Dutch F-16s, four French Mirages, and four British Jaguars hit a Serb self-propelled gun. If the amount of force used seemed excessive, the operation showed that NATO could cooperate, and an upbeat Warren Christopher pronounced the strike "a good step forward."[40]

NATO again "punished" the Serbs in September when two Jaguars and an A-10 demolished an unmanned T-55 tank following a Serb attack on a UN vehicle, and after Akashi had vetoed a request to hit a Serbian ammo dump.[41]

When the Serbs took 400 peacekeepers hostage, NATO promptly suspended its flights over Bosnia, and the U.S. Secretary of State announced that force would not be used because Washington wanted "peace, not the reign of terror that would come from carpet bombing."[42] No one had said anything about carpet bombing, which would have served no purpose in Bosnia. But perhaps the United States had used up its smart bombs in 1991, and grounded its AWACs and tactical aircraft. It was not airpower that failed. It was never used. Rather, appeasement had failed, and by 1995 some Americans were urging a policy of "Lift and Strike"—lifting the embargo on the Bosnians as NATO mounted air strikes against the Serbs.

Newt Gingrich found Clinton's failure to use airpower to retaliate against the Bosnian Serbs to be a lovely club with which to beat the Democratic incumbent. Rebutting claims that airpower could settle the war in three to five days, Christopher won the prize for the use of conditionals by a diplomat when he warned that bombing *might* fail and that the Bosnians *might not* be able to defend themselves *should* the Serbs attack in force, but using airpower *might* force the United States to commit "hundred of thousands" of troops to Bosnia.[43]

With its members divided, NATO could not define its role. When it finally bombed a Serbian ammunition dump near Pale in May 1995, Bosnian Serbs responded by raiding UN weapons depots and shelling five of the six safe areas, leaving 71 dead and 150 wounded in Tuzla. Mr. Juppe acknowledged that diplomacy was "useless" unless "backed by force," but NATO's retaliation was muted because the Serbs used UN peacekeepers as human shields.[44]

So farce was the logical outcome of four years of dithering. The UN had played an ignoble role in Croatia and displayed a supine impotence in Bosnia. NATO proved to be a neurotic pussycat. When the U.S. Congress unilaterally lifted the embargo on Bosnia's "Muslim-led" government in early August 1995, their action was rightly interpreted as a slap in the face to both NATO and the UN for their "seeming indifference to Bosnian Serb aggression."[45]

It was less than they deserved.

THE UNITED STATES, THE UN, AND NATO

It is difficult to disentangle U.S. policy from those of NATO and the UN, because the United States was not an isolated actor. Yet Washington pursued its own interests. Its debates over policy in Yugoslavia and Bosnia often involved domestic, not foreign policy, issues, and the media's interest was greatest when Americans were involved. Because Bosnia became a domestic political issue, the establishment of an American embassy in Sarajevo was news, and Carol Giacomo viewed Clinton as a "velcro president" because he could not shake off the Bosnian "blot" on his record.[46]

Bosnia was a persistent foreign policy headache for an ambivalent Clinton administration, which talked tough and did next to nothing. In May 1993, Warren Christopher told CNN that it was necessary to deal "quite resolutely with the Serbs." However, this was unlikely given Christopher's pledge to find "common ground" with the British, who opposed lifting the arms embargo on "the Bosnian Muslims" and vetoed the use of force against the "Bosnian Serbs." His tour of European capitals in 1993 to drum up support for joint action ended in embarrassed rationalizations and criticism in the press.[47]

Until it brokered the Croat-Bosnian federation in March 1994, the United States seemed to have no policy at all, and in May, Samuel R. Berger, Deputy NSA, told *Meet the Press* that Bosnia had been "probably the most difficult situation we have inherited." But he declared that by linking NATO's power to diplomacy, Clinton had achieved "peace [sic] in Sarajevo and many of the cities in Bosnia." If things were still "very, very difficult," "American leadership" had "produced whatever progress" there had been.[48]

Perhaps, but CNN's Christiane Amanpour pressed Clinton to explain whether he felt that his "constant flip-flops" on Bosnia might "lead people such as Kim Il-Sung or other strong people to take [him] less seriously than [he] would like to be taken." Irritated and confused, Clinton could do little more than lose his temper, to the delight of the right-wing talk shows that replayed the confrontation.[49]

As British and U.S. policies began to diverge in 1994, the "special bond" that tied the two states to each other began to fray, so William Crowe, U.S. Ambassador to Great Britain, appeared on NBC's "Today" to assure Katie Couric that the "frank" relationship was holding. But Carl Rowan doubted that Clinton enjoyed support for his foreign policy from either the "West" or "the American people," who were too "realistic" to "rush into Bosnia." Charles Krauthammer argued that if appeasement had led to World War II and "every once in a while there's a dictator who's got to be stopped," Bosnia and Haiti were not such cases and U.S. intervention would be inappropriate.[50]

By mid-1994, Bosnia was an embarrassment for the White House. Following a spate of articles questioning U.S. resolve and leadership, Anthony Lake, Clinton's NSA chief and "quiet adviser," attacked the media for creating problems. He had no more patience with Pale, when it rejected a peace plan. "We did not," he declared, "enter into this diplomatic process to preside over the creation of a Greater Serbia."[51] It just seemed that way.

Even Washington's bureaucrats turned on the administration. Stanley Sloan, a Library of Congress researcher, warned that failure to commit could lead to "an increasingly chaotic international situation in which countries have little or no faith in the will of the United States to honor its international commitments." The United States had become "increasingly gun-shy," content to pursue "stringent conditionality." This encouraged the Republicans, who, like the media, were looking for a "foreign-policy fall guy," preferably an incumbent Democrat.[52]

If the Balkans remained murky, there were signs that the mood in America was changing, influenced by journalists like Gutman and Rieff, columnists like Lewis and Safire, and the sheer accumulated weight of reporting on the region. Although a majority of Americans still did not see Bosnia as "our" problem, two-thirds began to see a moral obligation and half perceived some U.S. interests.[53]

In June 1994, the House voted 244 to 178 to lift the embargo on Bosnia, despite warnings by the Pentagon and the administration that doing so would endanger NATO and anger Moscow. Both Lee Hamilton, chair of the Foreign Relations Committee, and Ronald Dellums, chair of the Armed Services Committee, had "invoked the specter of Vietnam," but David Bonior, the majority whip, chastised the West for appeasing "fascism." After two years of looking the Serbs in the eye and warning that if they went one step further we would take "definitive action," the West had done nothing, and Stuey Hoyer warned that "an old, old historical lesson" taught that "tyrants never respond to weakness."[54]

Tyrants, of course, respond well, if not positively, to weakness, and Serb leaders ignored Clinton's confused rhetoric in 1994. At the Naval Academy, Clinton saw a "clear U.S. national interest" in stopping the fighting in Bosnia and the "slaughter of innocents," but mused that it might take decades, and lots of patience, to resolve such "bloody ethnic and religious conflicts." So Americans had to "be willing to pay the price of time," which was, of course, a lot cheaper in dollars and less traumatic than a blood-tax on America's military aristocracy. Tom Raum thought such "aggressive statements" and "words of retreat" just confused U.S. allies.[55] They would also have confused Democratic icons like Truman and Roosevelt.

In July, Bosnia had become an afterthought linked to Haiti, Korea, and U.S. foreign policy in general—and an albatross around Warren Christopher's neck. Michael Mandelbaum, from the Johns Hopkins School of Advanced International Studies, thought it would be hard to sell intervention to the public without the "rationale" of defending against the USSR, especially since Clinton had "set the standard for intervention rather high" in Bosnia, perhaps in an effort to avoid having to intervene there.[56]

By autumn 1994, the media and Republicans were touting Bosnia and Haiti as tests of Clinton's foreign policy and urging him to "stand up somewhere." Happily for the beleaguered president, the media saw him as a good guy compared to the Serbs, and treated both issues as unimportant compared to major domestic questions like the Whitewater scandal unraveling around the White House.[57]

The problem nearer home, Haiti, took precedence. It was more politically correct, easier, and cheaper. It was also morally incumbent on us to do something, since the mess there was largely our doing. Joshua Epstein, "a senior military analyst" at Brookings Institute, thought the United States could bring peace to Bosnia as well, but only at great cost.[58]

Brookings was also home to Susan Woodward, who seemed obsessed with what she called "undefined borders" when she appeared on *Nightline* with Newt Gingrich. Gingrich—not yet in campaigning mode—simply proclaimed Bosnia "a mess" and doubted U.S. forces could do much because everybody was killing everybody else. Woodward's sage advice was that as a superpower the United States should work with others, not go it alone. She also noted that losing a quarter of its territory to Serb forces in 1991 had been a "political and propaganda victory" for Croatia and a defeat for the Serbs.[59]

This may seem a bizarre assertion, but no more so than David Binder's claim, which echoed Serb propaganda, that Bosnians killed their own and blamed the Serbs to provoke air strikes. Given similar claims by the French and UN officials, it is tempting to see some Western splitting and projection here, but then we would be left with the uncomfortable suspicion that we do such things. It was more reassuring to assign bad motives to others and dismiss them as "clerical fascists" or Muslim fanatics whose dead do not need sympathy.[60]

For most Americans, Bosnia was the main event in Yugoslavia's dissolution, and we quickly learned to talk for the Bosnians. In September 1994, Senators John F. Kerry and John S. McCain argued about whether the Bosnians wanted the embargo lifted immediately or after six months so they could get through the winter safely. The distinction would have surprised the Bosnians, who had repeatedly asked that the embargo be lifted, and it was moot in any case, once the Senate had voted to lift the arms embargo.[61]

But Congress did not make policy. The Secretary of State, Warren Christopher, the head of the JCS, John M. Shalikashvili, and Clinton's National Security Advisor, Anthony Lake, made policy. Their priority was holding NATO together—and the British and French were clearly hostile to Sarajevo. Their foreign ministers, Douglas Hurd and Alain

Juppe, labeled the Bosnians "aggressors" for attacking out of the Bihać pocket, but did not condemn Serbian attacks on the enclave, nor Belgrade's support of Pale and Knin. Rose defended the Serbs, Lapresle ordered NATO not to anger them by enforcing the no-fly zone, and William Perry announced that air strikes would not work and Serb territorial gains were irreversible.[62]

As early as June 1991, Bruce Lambert helped to domesticate the crisis in a piece on Chicago's South Slavs. He focused on Croats and Slovenes frustrated at Washington's refusal to recognize what the director of a Slovenian radio program called "two young democracies." "Our people," she explained, "are very, very upset—I would use the word appalled or ashamed—that the U.S. Government is supporting the Yugoslavian Communist government." Lambert parried this neo–cold war ploy by noting that Yugoslav-American organizations tended to mirror "the divisions of the old country." So the crisis was ethnic, not ideological.[63]

Because ethnic divisions are part of American culture, Bosnia became a persistent subtext to domestic policy as well as an embarrassing comment on the morality of foreign policy. Even so, unless elections are in the offing, hyphenated Americans have a marginal impact on domestic politics. People readily sympathized with the victims of violence, but they were not sure who was to blame. The whole business was confusing, and became boring.

Then, in June 1995, the Serbs shot down an American pilot named O'Grady and gave the media a nice adventure story with a happy ending involving a real American. The death of Robert Frasure in a road accident also provided good, if somber, copy for the media. Frasure's death was embedded in a larger diplomatic context, and O'Grady's saga confirmed the limits of airpower. Both were human interest stories that could be retold, one with a happy ending, the other with a sad one; both were also breaking news that could be updated daily.

The treatment of the Americans was personal compared to that given the victims of ethnic cleansing. The media detailed O'Grady's rescue and reception at the White House, and the "whole country was elated" when he was rescued. But the affair did not raise the spirits of Sarajevo's citizens. One Bosnian wondered how Americans could "celebrate so much when hundreds of thousands of people remain locked in a cage." Another concluded that the rescue showed that the Bosnians had indeed "become bystanders in their own country."[64]

When Sara Rimer visited "a small midwestern town," she found its residents were horrified, saddened, and outraged that "Serbs [were] raping Muslim women and kidnapping their sons," that "atrocities" were being committed, and that children were homeless. Nazis and Jews sprang to mind, as did Nuremberg in a debate at Boston College, but the Balkans in the 1990s lacked the clarity of Germany in the 1940s. One resident found the war too "confusing" to understand, and, like A. M. Rosenthal, too reminiscent of Vietnam to risk involvement. Another was wary of the United States acting as "the world's policeman." That, after all, was what the UN was for.[65]

Gary Garneau, a Connecticut machinist running for the Senate, dismissed Bosnia as "a Western European problem," and wondered why we should be nervous, if nobody in Europe was. Yet some Americans were nervous, because they saw Bosnia as a model for what went wrong when community collapsed and only ethnic animosity remained. Amitai Etzioni worried that we were "on the road to Bosnia" because Americans had no shared values. "If you have to negotiate everything," he warned, "there are no rules around which the moral voice of the community congeals."[66]

In his keynote address to the Urban League's annual conference in July 1994, Hugh Price urged his listeners to "get on with making our gloriously multicultural society work." Acknowledging that racism was still a problem in the States, he warned against "wallow[ing] forever in real or perceived grievances lest we become Bosnia someday." Like Rwanda, Bosnia had become a symbol for genocide and a news peg for our racial problems.[67]

Bosnian policy was heatedly debated because it came to be viewed as our problem. In early June, the CIA director summarized policy choices. We could let the UN and NATO "muddle through," try massive intervention, or withdraw. He thought muddling through best, in the hope that the fighting would stop, a remarkably naive or predictably disingenuous conclusion for someone in his position.[68]

The fall of Srebrenica in July 1995 led to sharp criticism of Clinton and the UN. Yet if Charles Gati advocated action, Boutros Boutros-Ghali warned that UN forces could not defend the other safe areas and Pomfret reported that NATO aircraft had missed their targets. Lest anyone miss the message, a picture showed the Serb commander, Mladić, toasting the Dutch commander of the UN forces that had supposedly been protecting Srebrenica. Diplomacy, a.k.a. muddling through, was clearly the West's preferred course of action.[69]

Time put Mladić on its cover, a formal portrait of a serious military man against a background of refugees. The headline read "At the Helm of Horror" and asked whether by taking "personal charge of ruthless ethnic cleansing," the Serb leader would force the UN to leave Bosnia. Inside, the magazine ran a picture of the Serb "Conqueror" toasting the Dutch UN commander. Although it included a piece highly critical of the UN and the West by Zlatko Dizdarević, the impression was of a supervillain overseeing a natural disaster that no one could stop.[70] This was the stuff of comics and action films, but the 1990s found the Fantastic Four retired and the X-Men simply neurotic.

This was not muddling through, this was rank capitulation to evil, and Holly Burkhalter of Human Rights Watch was outraged that the UN stood by as Serbs seized and cleansed safe areas. She wanted the other enclaves protected, and she chided Congress for worrying that American lives might be lost in Bosnia to stop genocide but being indifferent to the loss of life in operations against Grenada, Panama, and Iraq. The *Washington Post* took a more moderate position, suggesting that since Americans would not countenance "a major assault with full American participation," we could obviate the need for U.S. troops by arming Muslim and strengthening NATO forces.[71]

Anthony Lewis urged the United States to guide the "feckless" Europeans and save Bosnia because such Western values as tolerance were being tested there. He warned that giving Bosnian territory to Serbia would reward genocide and validate the creation of "ethnically pure" states antithetical to the "civilized," multiethnic West. Upset that Pale was getting a better deal than Vance and Owen had proposed, Lewis still commended Richard Holbrooke for single-handedly securing a peace made possible by Croatia's battlefield successes.[72]

If American policy appeared inconsistent, inept, improvised, bizarre, or immoral, it was because it reflected the interests, assumptions, and illusions of domestic American elites, their counterparts in Europe, and a few powerful people at the UN. When Bosnia became an "American" concern in late 1995, a chorus of Cassandras warned of imminent disaster. Among them was a former Reagan-administration official who calculated that intervention in an area where the United States had no vital interests would reach $5 billion.[73]

If the bookkeepers in Ljubljana had opened the crisis by appealing to principles, it seemed that the economists in the United States had discovered a dollar value for principles, and then concluded that morality was a luxury item, like Chivas Regal and designer jeans.

EMBARGO OR INTERVENTION?

By contrasting military intervention to diplomacy, the media failed to see that the arms embargo was a crucial form of intervention, as were Baker's declarations in favor of a unitary Yugoslav state. In retrospect, this is obvious, but it escaped the notice of most commentators and journalists, who viewed the embargo as the best way to contain the slaughter, and intervention as the ultimate tar baby.

Military analysts adopted a cautious attitude toward military intervention or dismissed it as dangerous and futile. David Hackworth saw

the Balkans as "a bottomless swamp" where not even the "right stuff"—
which we did not have—would work "against a guerrilla fighting in
favorable terrain."[74] Mark Canciar reached similar conclusions in *Parameters*, as did William Johnsen in a study for the Strategic Studies
Institute. The military was clearly loath to get involved in Bosnia or
Croatia.[75]

Their determination not to fight was reinforced by Lewis MacKenzie,
whose warning that the West would become bogged down in an endless
guerrilla war against a Serbian enemy who had held thirty-seven German divisions at bay during World War II became conventional wisdom. When William Perry called for "effective air action" delivered
with "compelling force," Rose insisted that the West could not "bomb
[its] way to peace" and the use of force was "not a solution at the
moment."[76]

This argument did not apply to the Serbs, who seized large chunks
of Croatia and Bosnia by using force and who were indifferent to moral
suasion and diplomatic pressure. Bosnian leaders believed that more
weaponry and NATO air strikes would have tipped the balance in their
favor. Jovan Divjak, Bosnia's deputy chief of staff, saw the Serb advantage in heavy weapons and aircraft as crucial. The no-fly zone was mute
testimony to the West's belief in the efficacy of airpower, and constant
witness to its hypocrisy. Like the Bosnians, Jonathan Landay and a
majority of the U.S. Congress understood the importance of Serbian
aircraft, AFVs, and artillery.[77]

On May 12, 1994, the Senate followed the House by the barest of
majorities (50–49) in calling on Clinton to seek to end the embargo.
Robert Dole declared this "a big, giant step toward lifting the embargo"
and "a very strong signal" to U.S. allies that Congress would not
indefinitely be quiet "on the right to self-defense." John Warner fretted
that Bosnians might try to "regain what they have lost," a not unreasonable expectation. Daniel Moynihan struck a more principled pose
when he castigated the Security Council for abridging Bosnia's right to
defend itself under the UN Charter by imposing the embargo.[78]

In fact, the arguments against intervention and for the embargo were
mutually reinforcing. The official line was that arming "the outgunned
Muslim side" would delay peace and increase casualties on both sides,
and Misha Glenny warned that "large-scale military support" of Bosnia
would "trigger a ferocious response from Belgrade, bringing the unbri-
dled might of the Serbian and Bosnian armies into play." More powerful
and determined than the UN, the Serbs even threatened to use SAM
missiles to bring down NATO aircraft.[79]

So rather than defend the victims in Bosnia, the West policed them,
transforming Yugoslavia into the world's largest prison yard. In May,
as NATO welcomed eastern Europe into the fold, the EU created a

"Eurocorps" of French, German, Spanish, and Belgian forces, and sent 400 police to patrol Mostar. Within a month, London, Paris, and Ottawa threatened to pull their forces out of Bosnia. Whether they did so to force the "warring sides" to make peace or, as Rose claimed, because "some peacekeeping nations" thought they might get "a better return for their peacekeeping efforts elsewhere" was not clear. But Canada's prime minister, Jean Chretien, wanted peace imposed on all sides, and he warned that lifting the embargo would only "increase the possibilities of war," an odd but common belief.[80]

The Bosnians certainly wanted the embargo lifted. They repeatedly declared that they preferred arms to peacekeepers—a position also adopted by the Croatians in 1994.[81] But the embargo continued, while regular shipments of weapons seeped through the porous border dividing Serbia from Bosnia. In September, Bosnia's chief of staff, Rasim Delić, urged the West to lift the embargo and mount air strikes, because sanctions against the Serbs were "a farce, a show" for "TV coverage to give the international community an excuse to do nothing."[82]

If the West was indifferent, the fifty-one Muslim states of the OIC (Organization of Islamic Conference) urged individual and collective action to aid Sarajevo after Bosnia's Haris Siladžić and Pakistan's Benazir Bhutto appealed for opposition to aggression.[83] Yasushi Akashi condemned Serbian expulsions of Muslims and Croats, and Peter Kessler and Nicholas Morris of the UNHCR labeled such actions "state terrorism," but no one acted to stop them. Some UN officials even characterized them as a Serbian gesture of defiance, noting that the Serbs were not willing "to give up land won militarily."[84]

The British were especially opposed to lifting the embargo, but their claim that the Bosnians were not ready for sophisticated weaponry seemed rather disingenuous given the assumption that Balkan "tribes" shared similar levels of development. The Serbs had shown how useful heavy weapons could be against lightly armed Muslim forces, and Izetbegović and Jovan Divjak saw them as the keys both to Serbian successes and Bosnian failures.[85]

Some argued that the inequitable nature of the embargo was offset because Croats and Bosnians evaded it. AP noted that it guaranteed "the weapons superiority of the Serb-dominated military," but then cited Paul Beaver of Jane's Information Group, who implied that only Croats and Muslims benefited from lax enforcement. If Bosnia got $162 million worth of weapons, to $476 million each for Croatia and Serbia from April 1992 to April 1994, the Serbs should have maintained their edge. But AP focused on arms arriving by sea for Croatia and Bosnia, not those coming overland or by the Danube for the Serbs.[86]

No one took the leaders in Zagreb and Sarajevo very seriously, and journalists continued to speculate on how and when the Croat-Muslim federation would fall apart. Jasmina Kuzmanović reported that the Croatian and Bosnian chiefs of staff were cooperating and the "Croat-Muslim" offensive on the Kupreš plateau linking Sarajevo to the Adriatic was gaining ground. But she mused that "Muslim-Croat differences" and memories of the previous conflicts might "undo the new military alliance," and Roger Cohen implied that Croatian nationalists would wreck the federation.[87]

In late 1994, as Republicans pressed for air strikes, the *New York Times* rejected "punitive bombing" as "reckless" and applauded Clinton for being "sensible" in seeking a diplomatic solution. David Hackworth warned that lifting the embargo would bring disaster, yet noted that Serb tanks outnumbered Muslim 300 to 2 near Sarajevo, and that anti-tank weapons had earlier shifted the balance between Croat and Serb forces. This was an argument for lifting the embargo, but Hackworth insisted that only intervention would work, and he urged the UN to find the resolve it had mustered when Iraq invaded Kuwait.[88]

Despite the embargo, Bosnia and Croatia managed to build up viable military forces, and Bosnia's conclusion of a military alliance with Croatia in the spring of 1995 reinforced the July 1994 Muslim-Croatian confederation. The pact also removed an argument against intervention and put Belgrade in a difficult position, as Croatian-Muslim military cooperation put pressure on Pale and Knin. So the media warned that a "new" war might be imminent, evidently unaware that fighting in Bosnia and Croatia had continued through all the peace plans and no-fly zones.[89]

Many still saw Croatia and Bosnia as potential, if not actual, enemies, but public opinion and official policy in Croatia and Bosnia seemed to be running on parallel tracks. In March 1995, Zagreb's *Globus* reported that most Bosnians and Croatians favored closer ties between their states. At the same time, the Bosnian army was emerging as a highly motivated, well-trained, and decently equipped force; in May, the Croats easily overran Serb forces in western Slavonia.[90]

If the combat efficiency of Croatian and Bosnian forces disconcerted a media used to denigrating them, Muslim countries continued to press to have the arms embargo lifted. At its Casablanca conference, the OIC promised to help Bosnia obtain the "means for self-defense." Turkey's foreign minister condemned the embargo as having encouraged Serb aggression against UN safe areas and warned that peace would be a chimera until Bosnian Muslims were allowed to defend themselves.[91]

But the embargo stayed in place. NATO and the UN were quiescent, as Owen and Stoltenberg offered peace plans no belligerent would accept. The safe areas were safe only for UN troops, and not until the Serbs gave a dramatic illustration of this at Srebrenica was the way open to a military solution. The embargo continued to handicap Zagreb and

Sarajevo, but both built up their armed forces to the point at which they could resolve the conflict.

Roger Cohen later implied that the embargo had been marginal, because arms had "flowed into Croatia . . . in flagrant defiance of the embargo," Washington had "systematically ignored" violations, and some of America's "top retired generals" had been "allowed to advise the Croatian Army on modernizing." The implication that the Croats needed the advice of retired American generals to perform well was patronizing. It also left the impression that the Croatians had a large arsenal and were unique in flagrantly violating the arms embargo. But Bosnia had also profited from breaches of the embargo; Greece, Albania, Romania, Bulgaria, and Iraq had flouted both sanctions and embargo to supply Serbia and its puppets. By ignoring other violations and using the language he did, Cohen made Croatia seem uniquely guilty.[92]

If force ultimately proved to be the way to resolve the conflict, two questions remained: whether intervention was ever feasible, given the legendary military prowess of the Serbs, and whether it was necessary, given efforts to depict the Bosnians as too primitive to use modern weapons and too savage to be allowed to have them.

The answers to be found in the media were ambiguous. To a media hooked on official sources, intervention seemed the only alternative to continued war, but a risky one. Still, officials should have known—and the media should have guessed—that Serb military prowess was a fiction. Pale had serious problems recruiting men as early as 1993, and Karadžić called on the UN for protection following Bosnian success in April 1995, because so many young Bosnian Serbs had fled conscription. Cigar's analyses of the JNA did not appear until 1995, but earlier discussions by Canciar and Johnsen suggested that most bogeys raised against intervention were legendary or illusory.[93]

Worries that Bosnians might retaliate were cynical given Serbian atrocities, and concerns regarding technical aptitude were specious Rasim Delić, Bosnia's chief of staff, found British allegations that Bosnians were not ready for sophisticated weaponry absurd. "We just want to use the weapons," he said, "not build them." Yet the West refused weapons to the victims of aggression and never seemed to consider military intervention a serious option. Rather, it practiced containment, advised amnesty, and counseled reconciliation, which William Perry saw as preferable to retribution for war crimes.[94]

If the embargo was disguised intervention, overt military intervention was an illusory option used to validate diplomatic intervention. Just as the concept of moral equivalence justified the arms embargo, the bogey of the invincible Serb rationalized the West's failure to intervene and justified inequitable peace plans. A. M. Rosenthal, a staunch opponent of intervention, argued as late as May 30, 1995, that if the United

States intervened, it would have to commit 100,000 troops over a fifty-year period.[95]

But the United States did not have to do so, because Croatia overran western Slavonia and showed the Serbs to be less formidable than their public relations suggested. Obfuscation was about to give way to action in Bosnia and Croatia. Perhaps that was why Rosenthal wrote his editorial.

NOTES

1. Joseph Joffe, "The New Europe: Yesterday's Ghosts," Foreign Affairs (Winter 1992–93), 31–32; Duncan, "Yugoslavia's Break-up," 34–35, 41–42.

2. David Andersen, "A Diplomat Explains Yugoslavia," Wall Street Journal, 21 February 1992, and William Pfaff, "Reflections (The Absence of Empire)," New Yorker, 10 August 1992.

3. Gerald B. Helman and Steven R. Ratner, "Saving Failed States," Foreign Policy (Winter 1992–93), 12–16, and David A. Kay's letter in the Spring 1993 issue, 169–70; Paul Johnson, "Wanted: A New Imperialism," National Review, 14 December 1992, 28–34; Boutros Boutros-Ghali, "Empowering the United Nations," Foreign Affairs (Winter 1992–93), 89–90.

4. The Nation, 31 August–7 September 1992, and Aryeh Neier, "Watching Rights," 20 March, 3 July 1995, doubted Milošević had effective control of Bosnia's Serbs; Alex Dragnich, Serbs and Croats: The Struggle in Yugoslavia (New York: Harcourt, Brace, Jovanovich, 1992), 121.

5. George Will, "A Dog in the Fight?" Newsweek, 12 June 1995; Joseph Nye, "What New World Order?" Foreign Affairs (Spring 1992); Robert Cullen, "Human Rights Quandary," Foreign Affairs (Winter 1992–93), 81, 84–86; and Åge Eknes, "The United Nations' Predicament in the Former Yugoslavia," in Thomas G. Weiss, ed., The United Nations and Civil Wars (Boulder, CO: Lynne Rienner, 1995), 110.

6. Stedman, "The New Interventionists," 3, 7–8, 14–16; Margaret O'Brian Steinfels, "The Virtues of Sarajevo: Reflections of a City Dweller," Commonweal, 18 June 1993.

7. George Kenney, "Snowed in Bosnia," The Nation, 14–21 August 1995, Michael H. Shuman, "Force for Peace," The Nation, 17–24 July 1995, and editorial, "Gunning for Peace," The Nation, 2 October 1995; Charles Boyd, "Making Peace with the Guilty," Foreign Affairs (Sept./Oct. 1995), and the responses by Noel Malcolm, Norman Cigar, David Rieff, and William E. Odom, and Boyd's rebuttal, Foreign Affairs, (Nov./Dec. 1995).

8. Ronald Steel, "Let Them Sink," New Republic, 2 November 1992, 15–16; Eknes, "United Nations' Predicament," 123–24; and "A Debt Repaid: Rescuing the Future," Commonweal, 23 September 1994.

9. Maynes, "Containing Ethnic Conflict," 7–11; Tom Post and John Barry, "Bluff or Action?", Newsweek, 30 July 1995.

10. Ibid.; Fukuyama, The End of History, xii and passim.

11. Ljubomir Čučić, *U.S. Foreign Policy and Croatia* (Zagreb: European Movement, 1995), 46; John Garvey, "Would Bombing Work? First a Few Questions," *Commonweal*, 11 March 1994.

12. Misha Glenny, "A Fragile Hope in Croatia?" *New York Times*, 16 March and 26 September 1995.

13. Thomas L. Friedman, *New York Times*, 11 October 1995; George Kenney, "Snowed in Bosnia."

14. *New York Times*, William Safire, 9 October 1995; Anthony Lewis, "Fanatical and Ruthless," 10 March 1995; Roger Cohen, "The Serb in Western Eyes" and "President of Serbia," 3 February, 8 March 1995.

15. R. C. Longworth, "Peace vs. Justice," *Chicago Tribune*, 2 September 1994; *MacNeil-Lehrer Newshour*, 25 March 1993. Cheriff Bassiouni, who led the investigation of war crimes, accused Owen and Boutros-Ghali of obstructing the investigation to placate the Serbs.

16. David H. Hackworth, "Learning about War the Hard Way," *Newsweek*, 4 December 1995; "Between Dracula and Bovary: Yugoslavia's Romantic Nationalism," *Commonweal*, 21 May 1993.

17. Slavenka Drakulić, "Rape after Rape after Rape," *New York Times*, 13 December 1992; Joffe, "The New Europe," 33; Maynes, "Containing Ethnic Conflict," 3–5, 7, 10–11; *Nightline*, 14 January 1993.

18. Garvey, "Would Bombing Work?" draws parallels with Burundi and Afghanistan.

19. Knoll, "The Uses of the Holocaust."

20. *The Nation*, Martin Peretz, "Nationalism and Before," 7 August 1995, and Samantha Power, "Guns and Pigs," 22 March 1995; Christopher Hitchens, "Minority Report," 20 November 1995.

21. *Nightline*, 2 December 1992 and April 1993; *The Nation*, Susan Sontag, "A Lament for Bosnia," 25 December 1995; Christopher Hitchens, "Minority Reports," 20 November, 18 December 1995; "Bosnia's Trials," 4 December 1995; and "Bosnia's Rescue," 25 December 1995.

22. Dana Priest, "Coalition Calls for Action in Bosnia," *Washington Post*, 1 August 1995; Roger Cohen, "Tribunal Charges Genocide by Serbs," *New York Times*, 14 February 1995; Giles Elwood, "U.N. under Serb Pressure to Pull Out," and "Muslims Bemoan World Inaction on Sarajevo Blockade," *Reuters*, 12, 17 October 1994.

23. John Pomfret, "We Count for Nothing," and "Bosnians Are Bystanders in Own Country," *Washington Post*, 19 July, 9 June 1995; Slaven Letica, "The West Side Story of the Collapse of Yugoslavia and the Wars in Slovenia, Croatia, and Bosnia-Herzegovina," in Meštrović and Cushman, *This Time We Knew*, 163–65.

24. Andersen, "A Diplomat Explains Yugoslavia," and *New York Times*, 24 December 1991; *Newsweek*, Rod Nordland, "The Never-Ending Story," "Mission What's-the-Use," and "Let's Get out of Here," 26 December 1994, 26 June, 10 July 1995.

25. Gregory F. Treverton, "The New Europe," *Foreign Affairs* (Spring 1992); "The Abdication, Again," *New Republic*, 19 June 1995; Misha Glenny, "Council of Despair," *New York Times*, 6 December 1994; Michael N. Barnett, "The Politics of Indifference at the United Nations and Genocide in Rwanda and Bosnia," in *This Time We Knew*, 150–51.

26. Radek Sikorski, "Déjà Vu/War in Europe Again."

27. Guskind, "Ethnic Time Bombs"; *New York Times,* 1 January 1992, noted *how many* refugees had left Croatia, not their nationality. Most refugees were Croats.

28. Boutros–Ghali, "Empowering the United Nations," 89–90; Colin L. Powell, "U.S. Forces: Challenges Ahead," *Foreign Affairs* (Winter 1992–93), 36–37; Gow, "Nervous Bunnies," 16–23.

29. Nicholas Doughty, "One Year after Threat, NATO Sapped by Bosnia," *Reuters,* 2 August 1994; Eknes, "The United Nations," 122–24; *Newsweek,* 5, 26 December 1994, "A Fight among Friends" and Clinton as Dontfire; and Shuman, "Force for Peace."

30. "Traumatized Relief Workers Struggle with Horrors of Rwanda Crisis," *New York Newsday,* 3 August 1994; "USA Now Timid on Force," *AP,* 29 July 1994; Garth Myers, Thomas Klak, and Timothy Koehl, "The Inscription of Difference: News Coverage of the Conflicts in Rwanda and Bosnia," *Political Geography* (1996), esp. 30–43.

31. Kurt Schork, *Reuters,* 14 July 1994; Robert Wright, "Who Lost Bosnia?" *New Republic,* 29 May 1995; "Bosnia Wants U.N. Head Out," *AP,* 5 May 1994; Neely Tucker, "U.N.'s Man in Bosnia Is Making Enemies on all Sides," *Detroit Free Press,* 5 May 1994. Susan Woodward advised Akashi.

32. Warren Strobel, "Boutros-Ghali Wearies of Burden, Urges Big Nations to Enforce Peace," *Washington Times,* 29 July 1994, and Evelyn Leopold, "Trend in U.N. toward Farming Out Dangerous Missions," *Reuters,* 26 July 1994.

33. Craig R. Whitney, "NATO Turns from Force to Diplomacy in Bosnia," and Chuck Sudetic, "Allies Agree to Suspend Flights of NATO Planes over Bosnia," *New York Times,* 3 December 1994; Eknes, "The United Nations," 118; Charles Lane, "Call to Arms," *New Republic,* 17, 24 July 1995; "Bad to Worse in Bosnia," *The Nation,* 19 June 1995.

34. Elaine Sciolino, "Dispute on Bosnia War Is Resolved," *New York Times,* 2 December 1994; Charles Lane, "The Legend of Colin Powell," *New Republic,* 17 April 1995, 25, 32. Vietnam and the Persian Gulf had taught Powell the need for clear goals, quick victories, and a tightly managed media.

35. *Washington Post,* 7 June 1995; Christine Spolar, "Bosnian Serbs Say World 'Has Started to Respect Us,'" *Washington Post,* 8 June 1995; Samantha Power, "Bosnian Serbs Seize 'Safe Area,'" *Washington Post,* 12 July 1995; Michael Dobbs, "Serbs May Have Dealt Death Blow to UN Peacekeeping," *Washington Post,* 12 July 1995; Dana Priest, *Washington Post,* 14 July 1995; John Pomfret, *Washington Post,* 19 July 1995; and "Accomplices to Genocide," *New Republic,* 7 August 1995.

36. Michael Dobbs, "Post–Cold War Challenges Put NATO's Credibility on the Line," *Washington Post,* 3 June 1995; John Pomfret, *Washington Post,* 27 July 1995; *New Republic,* 31 July, 7 August 1995.

37. *Washington Post,* 2, 3 June 1995, 12, 14, 22, 28 July 1995, and 3 August 1995; *Newsweek,* Scott Sullivan, "Dwindling Options," and Michael Elliott, "Held Hostage by Hypocrisy," 12 June 1995.

38. Charles Aldinger, "U.S. Presses for Tougher Bosnia Action," *Reuters,* 29 September 1994; "Rebel Serbs Trick U.N. on Captives," *New York Times,* 7 December 1994; Ed Vuilliamy, "How the CIA Intercepted SAS Signals," *The Guardian,* 29 January 1996.

39. Roger Cohen, "How NATO Air Strikes Put UN Troops in Harm's Way," *New York Times,* 30 May 1995; Almond, *Europe's Backyard War,* 288; "NATO Planes Strike in Bosnia," *AP,* 5 August 1994.

40. "U.S. Lauds Bosnia Air Strikes," *AP*, 5 August 1994.

41. Davor Huic, "NATO Jets Bomb Bosnian Serb Tank Near Sarajevo," *Reuters*, 23 September 1994.

42. Whitney and Sudetic, *New York Times*, 3 December 1994.

43. Steven Greenhouse, "Gingrich Is Urging a Tougher Policy on Bosnia's Serbs," *New York Times*, 5 December 1994.

44. Roger Cohen, "NATO Jets Bomb Arms Depot at Bosnian Serb Headquarters," and "After a Second Strike from NATO, Serbs Detain UN Forces," *New York Times*, 26, 27 May 1995.

45. *Washington Post*, editorial, 3 August 1995.

46. Carol Giacomo, "Is Clinton the Velcro President?" *Reuters*, 24 October 1994; "Embassy Entrenched in Sarajevo," *AP*, 8 August 1994. Victor Jackovich, the new ambassador, was married to a "Sarajevan."

47. Čučić, *U.S. Foreign Policy*, 70–75; *Daybreak*, CNN, 3 May 1993; "The International Hour," CNN, 3 May 1993; and "Common Decency," *Commonweal*, 4 June 1993.

48. "Meet the Press," *NBC*, 8 May 1994, interview with Samuel R. Berger, Deputy National Security Adviser; J. Bryan Hehir, "Clinton's Foreign Policy," and "The Age of Restraint," *Commonweal*, 19, 24 November 1993.

49. "John McLaughlin's 'One on One,' " with Mike Chinoy (CNN) and Josette Shiner (*Washington Times*), 8 May 1994.

50. *Today*, NBC, 17 June 1994; "Inside Washington," *Federal News Service*, 4 June 1994.

51. George Moffett, "U.S. Foreign Policy: No Easy Answers," *Christian Science Monitor*, 1 August 1994; "Tony Lake: A Quiet Adviser," *AP*, 22 June 1994; *AP*, 20 July 1994.

52. *AP*, 29 July 1994; George Moffett and Peter Grier, *Christian Science Monitor*, 12 July 1994. A "high-level" official at State saw a gap between its "political echelon and its career foreign service professionals."

53. Čučić, *U.S. Foreign Policy*, 99; Russell Watson, "A No-Win War," *Newsweek*, 12 June 1995; Myers et al., "Rwanda and Bosnia," 27, counted 2,000 articles in six U.S. newspapers for April and May 1993, and over 1,400 for February and March of 1994.

54. "House Defies Clinton on Bosnia," *AP*, 9 June 1994; Brad K. Blitz, "Serbia's War Lobby: Diaspora Groups and Western Elites," in *This Time We Knew*, 214–23. William Perry, John Shalikashvili, and a Deputy Secretary of State lobbied Congress; Hamilton took Serb campaign donations.

55. Tom Raum, "Clinton Targets Foreign Image," *AP*, 1 June 1994.

56. *Meet the Press*, NBC, 10 July 1994; Doyle McManus, "Indecisiveness Is Crux of U.S. Policy on Haiti," *Los Angeles Times*, 8 July 1994.

57. Peter Grier, "Clinton's Showdown Diplomacy Has Limits," *Christian Science Monitor*, 20 September 1994; Steven Greenhouse, "Gingrich Urging a Tougher Policy," and Chuck Sudetic, "Clinton Writes to Reassure Bosnian Government," *New York Times*, 5 December 1994; Nina Totenberg et al., "Inside Washington," Federal News Service, 7 August 1994 broadcast.

58. Juan Williams (*Washington Post*), "America's Talking," *NBC*, Interview with Senator John McCain, Representative Donald Payne; Peter Grier, "Next Haiti Test," *Christian Science Monitor*, 28 September 1994. The United States left Haiti amid accusations against the USMC of genocide. See Hans Schmidt, *The United States Occupation of Haiti, 1915–1934* (New Brunswick, NJ: Rutgers University Press, 1971).

59. *Nightline,* 12 July 1993; Woodward, *Balkan Tragedy,* 221.

60. David Binder, "Bosnia's Bombers," *The Nation,* 2 October 1995; Aryeh Neier, "Watching Rights," *The Nation,* 9–16 January 1995; and Martin Peretz, *New Republic,* 7 August 1995.

61. Jim Adams, "Congress Approves Bosnian Policy," *Reuters,* 13 September 1994; "John McLaughlin's 'One on One'," and Williams "America's Talking."

62. Michael R. Gordon, Douglas Jehl, Elaine Sciolino, "Conflict in the Balkans: The Policy," *New York Times,* 5 December 1994.

63. Bruce Lambert, "For Yugoslav-Americans, Parties and Emotions and Worries over the Bloodshed," *New York Times,* 30 June 1991. Chicago has 150,000 Croatians and Slovenes, some of whom had raised money and rallied at Daley Plaza.

64. John Pomfret, *Washington Post,* 3, 9 June 1995, and *Newsweek,* 12, 19 June, 28 August, 4 September 1995.

65. The town was *both* blue-collar *and* Republican. Sara Rimer, "Bosnian War Bewilders a Midwestern Town," Anthony Lewis, "Never Again," and A. M. Rosenthal, "Dole in Bosnia," *New York Times,* 3, 18 April 24 July 1995.

66. Matthew Daly, *The Hartford Courant,* 2 August 1994; Susan Cohen, "Missing Links: We Know We Want It, But Does Anyone Know What 'Community' Means?" 31 July 1994, CD Newsbank.

67. "Urban League Talk on Children," *AP,* 24 July 1994; Donatella Lorch, *Ottowa Citizen,* 22 July 1994. Myers et al., "Rwanda and Bosnia," 32–40, for some suggestive framing.

68. *Washington Post,* 3 June 1995.

69. Charles Gati, "Tell It to Srebrenica," and John Pomfret, "Serbs Start Expelling Muslim Civilians from Seized UN Enclave," *Washington Post,* 13 July 1995; *New Republic,* 31 July, 7 August 1995; *Newsweek,* 10, 24, 31 July 1995.

70. Zlatko Dizdarevič, "Why Are You Shocked?" *Time,* 24 July 1995.

71. Holly Burkhalter, "What We Can Do to Stop This Genocide"; editorial; Ann Devroy and Michael Dobbs, "US: Unity Must Precede Balkan Action," *Washington Post,* 18, 20 July 1995.

72. Anthony Lewis, "How Serious Are We?" and "What Weakness Brings," *New York Times,* 8, 11 August 1995.

73. Dov S. Zakheim, "Adding Up the Taxpayer's Tab for Bosnia," *New York Times,* 2 October 1995.

74. *Newsweek,* 17 May 1993.

75. Canciar, "The Wehrmacht in Yugoslavia," 75–86; Johnsen, *Deciphering the Balkan Enigma,* passim.

76. Charles Aldinger, *Reuters,* 29 September 1994.

77. Jonathan Landay, "British, UN Question Effect of Lifting Arms Embargo," *Christian Science Monitor,* 9 September 1994.

78. "Senate Lifts Bosnia Embargo," *AP,* 12 May 1994.

79. Misha Glenny, *New York Times,* 6 December 1994; "Bosnians Say They Got Weapons," *AP,* 13 May 1994.

80. Nicholas Doughty, "WEU Defense Group Takes Eastern Europe into Fold," *Reuters,* 8 May 1994; Allan Thompson, "PM Threatens to Pull Troops from Bosnia," *Toronto Star,* 10 June 1994; Almond, *Europe's Backyard War,* 308–9.

81. Evelyn Leopold, "Bosnia Chooses End of Arms Embargo over Peacekeepers," *Reuters,* 3 November 1994; Giles Elwood, *Reuters,* 17 October 1994.

82. Robert Marquand, "Bosnian Army Chief Presses Case for Lifting Arms Embargo," *Christian Science Monitor*, 20 September 1994.

83. Farhan Bokhari, "Islamic Nations Urge UN to Exempt Bosnia from Arms Embargo," *Christian Science Monitor*, 12 September 1994; Kyodo News International, "Bhutto Calls for Joint Islamic Action," September 1994, CD Newsbank.

84. Jonathan Landay, "Bosnian Serbs Expel Non-Serbs from the North," *Christian Science Monitor*, 7 September 1994; Kurt Schork, "Serbs Gain Grip on Land by New Ethnic Expulsions," *Reuters*, 1 September 1994.

85. Jonathan Landay, *Christian Science Monitor*, 9 September 1994.

86. "Bosnia Arms Embargo Has Holes," *AP*, 30 July 1994.

87. Jasmina Kuzmanović, "Alliance Could Turn around War," *AP*, 3 November 1994; Roger Cohen, "Croatian-Muslim Link Is as Flimsy as a Bridge of Rope," *New York Times*, 13 February 1995.

88. David Hackworth, *Newsweek*, 12 October 1992; Chuck Sudetic, "Serbs Step Up Bombardment of Besieged Muslim Enclave," Greenhouse, "Gingrich Is Urging a Tougher Policy," and "Mr. Clinton's Future and the G.O.P.," *New York Times*, 5, 6 December 1994.

89. "U.S. Effort Fails to Calm Bosnia-Croatia Pact Concern," *International Herald Tribune*, 8 March 1995.

90. "Most Citizens of Sarajevo Want the Croatian Army to Intervene in Bosnia-Herzegovina" ("Većina gradjana Sarajeva traži intervenciju Hrvatske Vojske u BiH"), *Globus* (Zagreb), 10 March 1995; Tony Baker, *Independent*, 25 March 1995 (Bruna Sarić, 28 March 1995); and James L. Graff, "A Compulsion for War," Alexandra Stiglmayer, "We Can't Give Up," *Time*, 10 April 1995.

91. "World News Briefs," *New York Times*, 16 December 1994; *International Intelligence Report*, 2 May 1994, "Çetin Asks UN to Lift Bosnian Arms Embargo," originally transmitted on Ankara TV, 28 April 1994.

92. Roger Cohen, *New York Times*, 28 October 1995.

93. FPBZG (Foreign Press Bulletin, Zagreb), 28 March and 10 April 1995; Canciar, "The Wehrmacht in Yugoslavia"; Johnsen, *Deciphering the Balkan Enigma*; Norman Cigar's articles, "The Right to Defence: Thoughts on the Bosnian Arms Embargo," *Institute for European Defence and Strategic Studies* (1995), "The Serbo-Croatian War," "How Wars End," and "War Termination and Croatia's War of Independence."

94. Landay, and Marquand, *Christian Science Monitor*, 9, 20 September 1994, Johnsen, *Deciphering*, 75; *MacNeil-Lehrer Newshour*, 6 October 1994.

95. Rosenthal, *New York Times*, 30 May 1995.

10

End Games

REALIZING ETHNIC PURITY:
SREBRENICA, ŽEPA, AND KRAJINA

In late 1994, the American diplomat, Charles Redman, carried what was in effect a proposal to Pale for trading the safe areas of Goražde, Srebrenica, and Žepa for Serb-controlled areas around Sarajevo. He told the Serbs that they were no longer ostracized for rejecting the most recent peace plan and that the West was interested in redrawing the map in Bosnia. This was a remarkable démarche, given that the Serbs were holding hundreds of UN personnel hostage at the time. The West's courting of Pale did little to deter aggression, and by the summer of 1995, the safe areas had become "killing fields," a phrase used by Roger Cohen, who was drawing an obvious parallel with the slaughter that had occurred in Cambodia two decades earlier.[1]

Anthony Lewis chastised the UN for having "done precisely nothing" to stop "Serbian aggression," a display of inaction that had destroyed its "credibility." Lewis warned that by abandoning Bosnia, the West had jettisoned all it stood for, invited more "genocidal atrocities" by the Serbs, and caused Clinton considerable "military, moral and political trauma." Lewis believed that only U.S. leadership could protect the Bosnians from genocide and end the threat aggression posed to Western civilization.[2]

The *New York Times* published Lewis, but it also printed A. M. Rosenthal's scurrilous attack on those seeking to commit U.S. troops in Bosnia, his disingenuous assertion that the Serbs would be "an oppressed minority" in a Bosnian state, and his regret that Serb atrocities had "dwarfed their case." In mid-1995, his defense of the Serbs seemed gratuitous. They had won; Bosnia's polity was shattered. Joel Shapiro and Gordon R. Thompson urged Washington to press Bosnia to accept "the current confrontation lines as its new borders," and give the Serbs Srebrenica, Žepa, and Goražde.[3] The invitation to Pale to take the safe areas was as obvious as the West's lack of resolve was embarrassing.

While Karadžić threatened UN troops, an "old woman" complained that the West misunderstood the Serb cause and the stakes of the conflict. If so, nobody looked good when a Serb mortar round killed seven people in Sarajevo in June as UN officials celebrated the release of twenty-six peacekeepers. But the Serbs knew the UN was resolved to do nothing, and they ignored warnings that NATO would mount air strikes to halt their assault on Srebrenica in July.[4]

As Serb forces overran the safe area, Chris Hedges focused on the reactions of Dutch troops and UN complaints that Pale's "grave escalation of the conflict" had flouted UN authority and was "totally unacceptable."[5] Perhaps, but UN remonstrances mattered less than the Serb demand that the Muslims abandon the city within forty-eight hours. Although "serious consideration" was being given to air strikes and a "Pentagon official" assured Hedges that Srebrenica was secure, the Dutch were helpless and the city's mayor expected it to fall at any moment.[6]

Srebrenica's fall was a turning point even before confirmation that Serb forces had slaughtered the city's defenders. Silajdžić condemned the UN as "an accomplice to murder" because the West's "twisted policy of containment" had kept Muslims unarmed so as not to "endanger those Muslims living in the protected enclaves." There were reports of massacre, rape, and terror by Serb forces within two days of the enclave's surrender, but the West only lamented the limited uses of airpower and called a conference in London to discuss how to ensure the safety of the 23,000 UN "peacekeepers" in Bosnia.[7]

Roger Cohen's interlocutors in Sarajevo had warned in June that the conflict threatened Western values, and Western insensitivity and hypocrisy revolted Anthony Lewis, who ridiculed the "contact group" as a "bad joke," underscored the humiliation suffered by the UN and NATO, lamented the White House's passivity, and condemned neutrality as "morally sickening." Tired of Western appeasement, he urged the UN to end the embargo and withdraw, and NATO to bomb the Bosnian Serbs.[8]

Given that Bosnian Serbs had exploited weakness but stopped whenever any resistance was encountered, Robert Kagan, who had been with the State Department during Reagan's administration, wondered why Washington would "risk the lives of our troops in a retreat," but not to "restore American credibility and leadership" by intervening "to rescue a people from further slaughter." In fact, the West managed only feeble air strikes and planned to help the Dutch leave, not defend, the enclave—leading some to conclude that airpower was useless and Žepa and Goražde already lost.[9]

By 19 July, Žepa and the 10,000 Muslims there were clearly in grave danger, but the UN's concern was for the Ukrainian peacekeepers in the area, whom Chris Hedges implied were equally at risk from Serbs and Muslims. As the Serbs attacked Tuzla and Bihać, he could only allude to "what many writers say were killings and rapes" in Srebrenica because his UN and U.S. sources were reluctant to accept accounts of Serb atrocities.[10]

Although Hedges prematurely reported its fall, Žepa continued to resist, as did Bihać, triggering concern that Croatia might intervene. The UN and NATO, of course, would do nothing but fret, and Anthony Lewis again chastised them for allowing "genocidal aggression." Mladić had announced that he would take Goražde, Bihać, and Sarajevo by the fall, and Lewis saw what his forces did after taking Srebrenica as "a fair measure of his, and their humanity." Although the conferees in London already considered Žepa lost, it resisted for three weeks, and Hedges filed a report that painted its defenders in heroic colors and pointed a finger at Serbia for lending its buses to "evacuate people." He also noted that Mladić's forces had used gas (developed, he thought, in the United States).[11]

But anger was deflected from the West's negligent complicity and Belgrade's active complicity, and sympathy for the victims was diffused, by shifting focus. A Dutch private became a simple, anonymous hero for Alan Cowell, a NATO Forrest Gump. If the peacekeepers did nothing to stop the Serbian offensive, the Dutch commander still commended his men for having done "their best," and Cowell mused that peacekeepers were "soldiers but not warriors," defenseless "witnesses to outrages" that they were ordered to ignore. Burdened with "the hyperbole and hesitation of the world's diplomats," the privates of this world could only "learn not to feel pity for little things"—like mass murder and rape.[12]

Perhaps, but in August, the UN's special rapporteur on human rights violations in the former Yugoslavia, Tadeusz Mazowiecki, resigned over Boutros-Ghali's cover-up of the massacre carried out by Serbian forces in Srebrenica.[13] In a scathing editorial for the *Ottowa Sun*, Eric Margolis condemned the West for imposing an arms embargo, then blocking military aid to the victims of genocide. He excoriated Lewis MacKenzie and Russian leaders for their support of the Serbs, dismissed NATO as "a pathetic paper tiger," and labeled the UN "a tool of Serb aggression."[14]

Thomas Lippman thought that Serb cleansing of Žepa and Srebrenica, and Croatia's reoccupation of Krajina, had created the kind of ethnic states opposed by the United States and its allies. Yet both had stood by while the Serbs seized and cleansed the enclaves, Western peace plans were all based on ethnic division, and Lippman's sources, who included Warren Christopher, did not see "the Bosnian problem" as "a moral issue." It was "balance-of-power diplomacy." It was also domestic infighting that pitted Clinton's administration against a Congress pressing to lift the arms embargo on Bosnia.[15]

The media did not give the butchery in Srebrenica any detailed coverage until October. As William Perry announced that Pale had committed a "fatal error" by slaughtering Srebrenica's defenders, the Dutch blamed NATO for not providing air support and Clinton admitted that Washington had known of the massacres since July. Even so, no blame attached to anyone, evidently because these things happened in the Balkans, which had a "history of genocide and ethnic cleansing."[16]

Looking back from his chronological vantage point in November, Anthony Lewis concluded that Srebrenica had been crucial in convincing Western governments to act. But he believed Bush could have stopped "Serbian aggression at Vukovar."[17] Actually, he could have stopped it in June 1991, by recognizing and supporting Croatia and Bosnia. Milošević was an opportunist, who would probably have backed off if confronted with a firm stance by the West. But that was the one stance the West could not take.

A SURPRISE ENDING

The war's ending was foreshadowed in January 1993, when the Croats retook the Maslenica bridge connecting Zadar to the mainland, again in September 1993, when they overran Serb positions in the Krajina, and finally in May 1995, when they occupied western Slavonia in a quick "police operation." By mid-1993, Zagreb had 200,000 troops under arms, Pale and Knin only about 150,000.[18] Although Serbs took UN troops hostage, the media portrayed the Croats as sinister by reporting allegations of atrocities, repeating the refrain that "rebel" Serbs were fearful because Croatians had "massacred" their "forebears," and reciting the venerable cliché that the war would spread if anyone but Serbs conducted offensive operations.[19]

The allegations could not be confirmed, but UN sources repeated them, even though Akashi found nothing amiss in Pakrac on May 5. When "rebel" Serbs lobbed cluster bombs into Zagreb and shelled Pakrac and Novska, killing eight people and wounding 130, the Security Council urged Croatia to end its offensive. Polishing his new image as peacemaker, Milošević condemned both sides. A State Department official conceded that Croatia's action had been "legal," but condemned it as "highly provocative," and Roger Cohen reminded his readers that if Knin's attack on Zagreb was a "flagrant violation of the cease-fire," Croatian troops had illegally crossed UN lines.[20]

Aryeh Neier had already complained that Croats did not deserve the sympathy they were getting, and Rod Nordland had portrayed them as neofascists in *Newsweek*. So it was no surprise in late May that Mike O'Connor reported that UN monitors claimed that Croatian soldiers had mistreated civilians in western Slavonia, and 12,000 "rebel" Serbs had fled to "Serbian-controlled areas of Bosnia," because Zagreb failed to guarantee minorities "a safe, truly multi-ethnic environment." Like Neier, he equated Croat and Serb actions by noting that Bosnian Serbs were expelling Croats, and that Croats had "fled" [sic!] the same area when the "Serbs gained control" in 1991.[21]

In fact, only 940 Serbs had left Slavonia, and the Red Cross, UN officials, and reporters had access to areas occupied by Croatian forces. None found evidence of ethnic cleansing or atrocities. The U.S. ambassador condemned Knin's attack on Zagreb, and Robin Harris, a former adviser to Maggie Thatcher, ridiculed the UN for classifying the use of cluster bombs against civilians as legitimate retaliation. Serbs, he noted, had been guilty of "the great majority" of war crimes, and the Muslims and Croats had gained military parity despite the embargo.[22]

The last point was crucial, because UNCRO had failed to protect Croatians in its areas. The Croatian operation was well organized, well disciplined, and overwhelming. It had cost Croatia 42 dead and 162 wounded. The Serbs had taken 1,400 casualties, including hundreds of POWs who were interrogated and then sent home or handed over to the local prosecutor to be arraigned for war crimes. Whether or not Croatia's goal was peaceful reintegration of Serb-occupied areas, as Mate Granić, the foreign minister, announced, it was clearly reintegration, and Zagreb appeared to have the force needed to realize its goal. Whether the West would allow it to do so was another question.[23]

Pale's seizure of Srebrenica and Croatia's occupation of Krajina put Slavonia on the back burner until October, when Croatian forces seemed poised to retake the rest of the rich riverine plain. The usual UN sources warned that Serbs were "a politically insignificant minority," and not welcome in Croatia, which had become the greatest obstacle to peace, especially given reports Zagreb had expelled "over 120,000 Serbs" following its "ruthless capture" of the "Serb region known as Krajina."[24]

Incidents and atrocities had occurred, but most Serbs had fled; they had not been expelled. Croatian leaders had repeatedly reassured them that they would not be harmed, and they again opened their areas to international organizations and the press. Although may Croats wanted the Serbs to leave and their leaders often ignored actions against Serbs, their behavior was benign compared to that of the Bosnian Serbs who had kept northern Bosnia tightly sealed as they cleansed it in 1992–93 and had recently expelled thousands of Croatians and Muslims in Banja Luka.[25] Expulsion is not a synonym for flight, but past news frames overwhelmed current realities, and media accustomed to ethnic cleansing proved unable to recognize a conventional military operation or distinguish war crimes from genocide.

The debate over intervention had ignored other options, but it was obvious that achieving an "end state" to the war acceptable to all parties would only occur once the playing field in Bosnia was leveled. One way to do that was to lift the embargo; another was for Croats and Bosnians to cooperate, something the Serbs encouraged by attacking Bihać. Although a "Muslim" enclave, there were numerous Croats among the 160,000 residents and refugees in the city, which was strategically crucial to Zagreb.[26]

That the Croats would not entrust the enclave's safety to the UN was axiomatic, because the policy of safe areas was as bankrupt as the West's many peace plans. Allowing UN commanders to control air strikes had only given those opposed to the use of airpower a veto over acting decisively. This was unfortunate, because if not a panacea, airpower could have crippled Serb ground forces, cut their supply lines, and given Bosnian forces a chance to operate effectively, even with the embargo in place.[27]

Even without air support, the Croation army (HV), and the military arm of the Bosnian Croats (the HVO, Croatian Defense Council) advanced forty miles up the Livno valley between 27 and 30 July. By occupying Bosanko Grahovo and Glamoč, they secured Dalmatia, isolated Knin, and embarrassed Mladić, whose troops were committed at Goražde and Bihać. A UN official labeled the Croatian offensive "a very worrisome military buildup," but he conceded that only the Croats could save Bihać, which was besieged by 25,000 Bosnian and Croatian Serbs.[28]

The Croatian occupation of 700 sq. km. of territory prompted Yasushi Akashi to rush to save the Krajina, whose leaders and residents felt isolated and abandoned by Milošević. The media made the Croats appear intransigent and aggressive, but if Tudjman ignored Martić, ostensibly because he had been indicted for war crimes, Knin's leaders offered only to withdraw troops from Bihać. A determined Croatian government offered the Serbs the choice of being "peacefully reintegrated" or suffer the consequences of forcible occupation. They chose the latter, and on 31 July, AP reported artillery rounds falling near Knin, which the Serbs answered by shelling Gospić.[29]

Table 10.1
Strengths of Forces, August 1991

	Croat/HVO	Bosnia	Bos/Serb	Yugoslavia
Soldiers	135,000	70,000	80,000	120,000
- reserves	250,000	80,000	. . .	330,000
Tanks	700	20	350	1,100
AFVs	550	30	250	800
Mortars	1,900	200	800	2,500
Artillery	850	100	700	1,700
Rocket tubes	180	5	600	1,420
Aircraft	30	—	30	450
Helicopters	40	5–7	27	120

Source: *Globus* (Wittner, Croatian Net), 11 August 1995.

The UN had repeatedly placated the Serbs for fear they would retaliate, but the Croat and Bosnian armies were solid, whereas the combat efficiency of Serbian forces was uncertain. Moscow opposed a Croatian attack, but Serb arrogance had antagonized many outside Bosnia. The U.S. ambassador went to Brioni on August 1 to ask Tudjman for a cease-fire, but as one diplomat put it, many in the international community were "sick and tired of the Serbs."[30] He might have added that many were also sick and tired of the British-French policy of appeasing them.[31]

On August 1, "Operation Storm" was already well under way, as were efforts to discredit the Croatians and their Bosnian ally.[32] As the last UN forces left Žepa, Croatian units rolled over Serbian positions, taking as many as 4,000 POWs and occupying Knin and Benkovac. On August 5, "the jubilant invaders" linked up with the Bosnian V Corps at Bihać. By August 8, the Croats had relieved the embattled enclave and reintegrated the counties of the Serbian "Krajina," leading Muhammed Sacirbey to thank them and the UN's Carl Bildt to accuse them of genocide and aggression. Croatia's deputy foreign minister demanded an apology from Bildt, and Ivan Tolj, who headed the Defense Ministry's Political Department, announced that no civilians had been targeted, adding, "Any dreams about a 'greater Serbia' are past."[33]

Initial estimates set the number of Serbian dead at 750, to 174 Croatian dead and 1,430 wounded. Whether Serbian resistance had been "stubborn," as one report claimed, it had been brief. Zagreb tried to turn aside criticism by charging an officer who had used UN Danish peacekeepers as shields and hosting 150 journalists in Knin to prove that there had been little damage. Croatia's deputy prime minister noted that as many as 120,000 Serbs may have fled, but they had not been expelled like the 430,000 Croats whom the Serbs had chased from their homes in 1991. He also noted that there were over 100,000 Croatian refugees waiting to return to their homes.[34]

Unable to reverse Croatian and Bosnian successes on the ground, some sources and journalists sought to discredit Croatia. Reports of "atrocities" and "ethnic cleansing" multiplied as the offensive progressed, usually from anonymous UN officials, human rights activists, military analysts, and Western diplomats. On August 7, CNN reported that a quarter of a million Serbs had fled to Yugoslavia and carried an interview with a Serbian "colonel" who accused the Croats of attacking civilians.[35]

A simple check would have discovered that no more than 160,000 of the region's inhabitants had been Serbs, but CNN, PBS, and the major networks repeatedly inflated the number of refugees, broadly hinting at ethnic cleansing by Croatian forces. They also allowed Serb spokesmen easy access to the media, but largely ignored Croats and Muslims.[36] There was no careful analysis, no balance, no effort to check sources, only reports on the "humanitarian" tragedy created by the Croatian advance, leaving the impression that the Serbs had reason to fear that the Croatian "invaders" would harm them.

The *Washington Post* accused Croatia of ethnic cleansing, denounced it for refusing to "negotiate" with Knin, declared that its aggression had forfeited support by the West, and urged Washington, which had created the Croatian juggernaut, to bring "both sides" to the negotiating table.[37] The *Milwaukee Journal-Sentinel* echoed these sentiments. Evidently unaware that the areas occupied by Croatian troops were part of Croatia, its editors declared "military aggression [sic] by the Serbs or against them" to be "cruel and abhorrent," and urged it be stopped immediately. Although estimates of Serb "homeless" were down to 100,000, the editorial worried over "disturbing evidence [sic] of murder and other Croat atrocities against Serb civilians," and struck a familiar theme by blaming "Serbs, Croats and others [sic]" for genocide in Bosnia.[38]

Such editorials were understandable, if inaccurate, given bizarre reports that Tudjman had reassured Croatia's Serbs and then had his military attack them. The ubiquitous UN and Western officials speculated that the offensive might end the war, but worried that it would destroy any chance to realize an ethnically diverse Bosnian state, evidently because the Croats were racists, unlike the Serbs who had cleansed two-thirds of Bosnia and a quarter of Croatia. Some even claimed that the Croats had "used" mass graves in their attack, a baseless charge, but one that balanced the exposé of the Srebrenica massacres by Rohde.[39]

Page-one headlines of Serb atrocities in Srebrenica were quickly replaced by UN reports of Croatian atrocities in Krajina. On 6 August, AP reported that, although no one knew how many casualties there had been, a UN official in Knin claimed to have seen "quite significant numbers of bodies in the streets," including many women and children. This turned out to be untrue, but it undercut Ivan Tolj's remark that the Croatian army had "done what the world should have done"—saved Bihać.[40]

The usual Western diplomats and UN officials told James Rupert that Zagreb had "set in motion what they call[ed] the largest instance of 'ethnic cleansing' in the Balkan war." Croatia had supposedly been expelling its Serbs before August, and Croatian troops had purportedly shelled or bombed refugees during the offensive. A UN official, who asked not to be named, said the Croatians reassured the Serbs, then did "precisely the things to make the Serbs panic and run." What those things might be, the official did not say, and reporters on the scene did not find the damage reported by UN officials. It was clear that Serbs had fled advancing Croatian forces, not been expelled after they had arrived.[41]

Some Croatian forces had committed war crimes and Croat authorities had connived in harassment of Serbs in Croatia, but AP exaggerated when it reported that the Croats were "invading" (sic) Krajina, and, despite "appeals for restraint," the Croatians had deliberately "targeted civilian population centers and lightly armed international peacekeepers." The UN and the United States had predictably protested this "lack of restraint," and spokesman Chris Gunness announced that the UN deeply regretted that Zagreb had "abandoned the peace process" and "chosen the path of war."[42]

A "Western military analyst" told John Pomfret that the offensive would "end by complete ethnic partition," and AP claimed Zagreb had "mock[ed] a last-ditch bid by U.N. mediator Thorvald Stoltenberg" to get it "to respond to the first-ever Serb offer of peaceful reintegration of lands they had held since the six-month war of 1991."[43] Of course, Krajina was part of Croatia, and UN mediators had repeatedly proposed ethnic cantons, while Serbs had cleansed their areas under the watchful eyes of UN peacekeepers. But so muddled was the reporting that it was not clear whether Washington had given Zagreb a "green," an "amber," or a "red" light.[44]

Smearing Croats obscured news of Serb atrocities and offset the massacres in Srebrenica and UN and CIA reports that Serbs were responsible for most of the genocide and war crimes, including the destruction of 3,000 villages, the massacre of tens of thousands, and the rape and torture of 70,000 men and women. Roger Cohen believed such data made "nonsense of the view" that the conflict was "a civil war," but in August AP made it seem so by reporting UN claims that troops with Bosnian insignia had murdered five "elderly" Serbs in front of Danish peacekeepers, and that warplanes, "believed to be Croat," had dropped bombs near refugees during the offensive.[45]

Charles Krauthammer wondered why the West was "silent" when the victims of "ethnic cleansing" were Serbian. Blissfully unaware that Croatia's Serbs had cleansed Krajina of Croats, he claimed they had nothing to do with atrocities by "other Serbs," and that Croatia's fascist, genocidal past gave them a right to secede. Whether he really believed Zagreb had adopted the symbols and authoritarianism of the World War II "Nazi puppet state," the logic of his argument seemed to suggest that Serbs who were guilty of atrocities should indeed be cleansed.[46]

But logic was in short supply. Raymond Bonner described an "exodus" of "defeated and visibly frightened" "rebel" Serbs as "bitter Croats" advanced into Krajina. He conceded that in "a region accustomed to atrocities, there was little violence," but some Croats had "hooted obscenities" and UN officials had charged Croatia with "crimes against humanity" based on reports that five people had been murdered. Of course, hooting was not massacre, nor five murders genocide. Both Bonner and UN officials were indulging in hyperbole and applying a double standard. The latter even fretted that by helping Serbs to flee, they would further Croat ethnic cleansing, qualms they had not had in Žepa just a week earlier.[47]

Although Chris Gunness reported from Knin on August 6 that Croat troops were behaving professionally, and the U.S. ambassador dismissed reports of ethnic cleansing by Croatian forces, the Security Council called on the Croats to halt. Having treated the Serbian flight as ethnic cleansing of biblical proportions, confused media reported that 16,000 Croats and Muslims expelled between 14 and 30 August had "fled" Banja Luka and Vojvodina. Others were more cynical and believed that Serbia was evicting Croats to make room for Serb refugees. Others saw a swap in progress that involved both Zagreb and Belgrade. Few were interested in the 400,000 Croatian and Bosnian refugees in Croatia.[48]

Thomas Friedman was interested in maintaining a united NATO, containing hostilities, halting the Croat-Muslim offensive, heading off a "holy war" between Christians and Muslims, and assuring the Serbs half of Bosnia and union with Serbia.[49] That he worried about a holy war, given Muslim-Croat cooperation, was odd, but in line with A. M. Rosenthal's thinking and not far removed from the attitudes of Anthony Borden, who inflated the refugee figure to 200,000 and condemned

Croatian culture as "nationalist, militarist, and antidemocratic." Christopher Hitchens denounced Tudjman, the "Gauleiter of Zagreb," for the "mass expulsion of Serbian civilians from Krajina"; and Slavenka Drakulić called Tudjman a commissar.[50]

What seemed uncontestable was that the Croats had saved Bihać by a dazzling display of military efficiency. But after four years of fearing the invincible Serb, only a few cartoonists got the message. Others doubted the Croats capable of winning. Jack Mizes used Rebecca West, "who loved the Serbs as only a fellow romantic could," to argue that Serbs had a love affair with defeat and had "often" "chosen defeat" during the previous "six years." By defeating themselves, the Serbs made the West look foolish, because it had declared Bosnia prematurely deceased in its "haste to end the war." "Nothing," Mizes mused, "is so irretrievably humiliating as to abandon, in the name of realism, a loser who goes on to win." Mike O'Connor struck a similar chord by reporting that Serbs had voluntarily left areas they assumed would be given to "the Muslim-dominated government" during negotiations.[51]

So the Croatians and Muslims had not won after all; the Serbs had voluntarily yielded territory to avoid the humiliation of ceding it in negotiations. They thus remained a proud, if inscrutable, people, the victims of the whole world and of themselves. And yet, the image that emerged was of Serb "rebels" who made alibis for not fighting and retaliated against civilians when confronted with equal odds. On 23 August, as David Rohde uncovered mass graves near Srebrenica and the Serbs shelled Dubrovnik, Mike O'Connor reported a Serb attack that left six dead and thirty-eight wounded as "a firefight between two armies."[52]

Although David Binder later repeated the Serbian argument that the Bosnians had killed their own to gain sympathy, O'Connor criticized the UN for not reacting, and Roger Cohen saw the attack as part of a Serbian pattern that included the February 1994 shelling of the city's market in which sixty-eight people had died. Even so, he concluded that "all of the leaders in the region derive some benefits from a low-level war that cements their hold on power and privilege."[53]

Cohen dismissed Mladić's comparison of NATO air strikes to Nazi attacks on Belgrade in 1941, he chided Serbia's media for showing only the suffering of Serbian refugees, and he criticized its leaders for manipulating their fellows. But he also invoked Serbia's "war-ravaged history" and its "contribution to Allied victories" in the world wars, depicting Serbs as occasionally obstinate and given to self-pity, but "stoical," heroic, "proud and unpredictable." Cohen's view of the average Serb and "history" was Serbian, and he did not see that Serbs in

Pale, Belgrade, and Knin had used exactly this history to justify seizing and cleansing their neighbors' land.[54]

What people in America's heartland had learned from the media over four years became clearer in August. David Hekenlively wrote the local Milwaukee paper to warn that Bosnia was "the ultimate no-win situation" because the Serbs had been invincible in both world wars; and Edward Schneider wondered why the United States should bother with Bosnia. "Even if we were to go in and win the war," he wrote, "it would start up all over again as soon as we got out," because "centuries-old animosities" could not be overcome. Media coverage had obviously had an effect, and as Croatian and Muslims forces consolidated and expanded their gains, the Milwaukee paper published a bit of propaganda by a local Serb. It published no letters by local Croats in early August, although it ran a piece explaining why American Muslims were so bitter.[55]

Of course, rhetoric and baseless accusation could not undo military successes any more than hand-wringing and pious laments could bring back the victims of genocide. Operation Storm had shifted the balance of power in the region. Evidently unaware that Serbs had made up only 11.5 percent of Croatia's population before 1991, Pomfret and Spolar concluded that the flight of Serbs from Krajina had made Croatia "90% Croatian" (sic!) and urged sanctions against Croatia, which, like Serbia, was using ethnic cleansing to realize an ethnically pure state and employing "state-run" media to manipulate its citizens.[56]

Although Croatian support had been crucial to the relief of Bihać and to Bosnian advances in the fall, the threat posed by Croatia made arming and training Bosnia's army imperative, and in October, Cohen reported that U.S.-Croatia ties were "cooling."[57] In reality, the Croats and Bosnians had finally impressed the West, and Richard Holbrooke was furiously shuttling to and fro trying to cobble together some sort of viable peace.[58]

NATO also finally got serious. In late August and early September, after Operation Storm, its aircraft struck Serbian targets, from radar installations to command posts and ammunition dumps. Safire criticized the attacks for protecting Western troops, not Bosnians or Croatians, but they sobered up Pale's leaders, and Clinton shook up Belgrade by warning that Serbia would be next if peace was not reached. But if Izetbegović finally felt able to make demands, not merely accept them, the war was not over. In late August, Serbs dropped 5,000 shells on Dubrovnik in a single day, 2,000 less than they had fired daily at Vukovar in 1991, but 4,800 more than the Croats had supposedly dropped in the vicinity of Knin.[59]

PEACE?

In October 1995, Roger Cohen thought the Croats had "what they want," the Serbs were "exhausted," and the Muslims had "no better option." He compared the conflict to the 1948 war that had divided Palestine between Arabs and Jews, an apt comparison for the Balkan Lebanon. Cohen resorted to the passive voice to report that 200,000 "had been killed" and 3 million left homeless. Although he did not trust the Croats, because while Washington wanted a Bosnian-Croat federation, Zagreb wanted only eastern Slavonia, it was time for peace.[60] Further advances by the Bosnians and Croats would have forced Belgrade to react, and so peace talks were convened in Dayton, Ohio.

The media quickly cast the talks in familiar images, framing issues so Americans could grasp them and using individuals to symbolize countries and ideologies. As Holbrooke and his team set the table in Dayton, the administration began the hard sell. Equipping and training the Bosnian army became EAT, Karadžić became a loser, and the United States revived its old role of protecting Europe from the Europeans by concluding bilateral pacts reminiscent of those that had led to NATO.[61] Holbrooke even saw Bosnia as a potential model for future U.S. relations with NATO and Europe, and a "senior U.S. administration official" declared, "We've got to make the Balkans safe from Serbia." Pale's response was given by a retired military officer. "The arc of containment around us and this arms control pressure," he told Pomfret,"are not friendly acts." So the Serbs joined the Greeks to call for a "Balkan League."[62]

Elaine Sciolino recast complex issues as a simple confrontation between Americans by setting Richard Perle, the "bulldog" advising the Bosnians, against Richard Holbrooke, the "raging bull" responsible for the talks. Michael Dobbs transformed Dayton into a negotiation between a charming Milošević and a shrewd Tudjman, in which the Serbs got only 45 percent of Bosnia and the "Bosnian-Croat federation" 55 percent as a truculent and sullen Izetbegović demanded the Posavina Corridor.[63]

The media's Dayton was a drama interpreted by the leaders of Bosnia, Serbia, Croatia, and the United States. The Serbs of Bosnia and Croatia were noticeably absent. Zagreb's demand for eastern Slavonia and doubts as to whether Pale would acquiesce to Milošević's sacrifice of Sarajevo were overcome as leaders became caricatures—the devout Muslim, the bon-vivant Serb, the shrewd Croat. Complex issues were reduced to personalities and resolved by anecdote, with a surprise ending as the Americans discovered that the Serbs, not the Bosnians, would join them in a "fraternal Realpolitik" whose deals were cut over "slugs of whiskey." Americans and Serbs, both hard-working and convivial, thus saved the world, or at least the little corner known as the Balkans.[64]

Bruce Nelan saw Izetbegović as victim and Milošević as the cheery key to success. He ignored Tudjman, but praised Holbrooke for bringing the "locomotive of peace" to Bosnia. Holbrooke had pressed hard to make sure the Serbs kept half of Bosnia, and the photos illustrating his article seemed intended to drum up sympathy for the Serbs and portray the peace as a victory for the Muslims—as crowds cheered Izetbegović, Serbians wept at a grave. Michael Dobbs even quoted a U.S. official who described the peace treaty as a "fantastical deal" for the Muslims, even if it gave 49 percent of Bosnia to the Serbs, who were only a third of the population. It also lifted sanctions and the arms embargo on Belgrade, but it did not provide adequate guarantees to the 2 million refugees who were waiting to return to their homes. Izetbegović might have been forgiven his sullenness. As Thomas and Barny noted, Dayton was "a good, bad deal."[65]

Of course, CNN carried the signing of the treaty live. Judy Woodruff commented, and Warren Christopher began by proclaiming peace "a victory for all of us," the result of a combination of "Dick" Holbrooke's hard work and "Bill" Clinton's vision and leadership. Christopher, who had dithered since 1993, blamed no one, but implied that all sides bore a share of the guilt for the past five years by noting that all had decided to quit fighting. The real winners, he said, evidently without irony, were the civilians.[66]

Milošević followed, declaring that the conflict had been a "civil war" in which everyone had lost and "all sides" had been forced to make "painful concessions." Evoking the ethics of the '90s, he urged all sides to put the war behind them and get on with the future. His thanks to the United States, the EU, and Russia seemed appropriate.

Izetbegović gave the shortest speech. Given the state of the world, he doubted "a better peace" was possible, so he settled for something other than war that preserved Bosnia's "sovereignty and integrity." But what could he say? Tudjman followed and gave the longest, and the most poorly translated, speech. He stressed the need to strengthen the Croat-Bosnian federation, normalize relations with other states in the region, and peacefully integrate eastern Slavonia into Croatia.

The hero of the hour, Richard Holbrooke, then spoke. He began with a cliché, noting that fourteen weeks of shuttle diplomacy had seemed like fourteen years. He then completed Christopher's remarks by implying that everyone was, if not guilty, responsible, and he urged all sides to meet the "challenges" ahead by setting aside "their enmities, their differences." Carl Bildt ended the ceremony with the trite, and insensitive, observations that war was terrible, peace hard, and everyone would have to work to achieve "true peace," which all would recognize because there would be "free and fair elections" when it arrived.

The theme was clear: it's the nineties, guys, let's put it all behind us and get on with the future. No one was to blame, and only malcontents and embittered fanatics would worry about a past that was, well, past. That the peace was not equitable was obvious. "Pragmatism," as a Croatian minister put it, had "won over morality." Croatia's Serbs had not done well, but the consensus was that Bosnia's Muslims were the biggest losers. Who had won was trickier. Serbia was untouched by war, but hurt by sanctions, and Serbs held half of Bosnia. Croatia emerged with its borders intact, Dubrovnik and the Prevlaka Peninsula, a plan to reintegrate eastern Slavonia, a military reputation that had belonged to the Serbs, and billions in damage from the war and the Serbian occupation.[67]

Anthony Lewis reduced the terms of the treaty to questions of justice and U.S. leadership. He cited Richard Goldstone, who insisted the peace needed to be just and the Serbs come to realize and condemn what their leaders had done. Lewis doubted this would occur and saw the peace as flawed, but he declared his allegiance to the "party of hope," as if peace was an exercise in optimism. But he also quoted Izetbegović, who accepted the treaty not because it was "a just peace," but because it ended the war. For Lewis, U.S. leadership was the key to success, and he hoped that Washington would not "shirk" its responsibilities.[68]

Roger Cohen was not altogether with the party of hope. He saw the American-brokered peace—a favorite phrase—as containing the seeds of future conflict. It divided Bosnia on ethnic lines, it did not guarantee the extradition and trial of indicted war criminals, and Milošević might not be able to guarantee compliance by Pale. Like Lewis, he saw the United States as the key, and Sarajevo as forced to sign a peace it did not approve because Serbia and Croatia were ready to settle, putting the Bosnians in "an unenviable predicament."[69]

Branka Magaš believed Bosnia had been betrayed. Divided between antagonistic polities, the Republika Srpska and the Bosnian-Croat Federation, its economy was crippled and its structure resembled apartheid. The settlement had rewarded genocide by letting the results of ethnic cleansing stand, and closed Bosnia's internal borders while opening those to Serbia and Croatia. With three armies and a shared presidency, Bosnia was a structure courting collapse. And yet, it kept its borders, its capital, and a single legislature; refugees could return to their homes, albeit without guarantees; elections would be supervised; cooperation with the Hague was mandated; and the West had promised economic and military help.[70]

Jonathan Eyals, a "Balkan analyst at the Royal United Services Institute in London," predicted that as Bosnia armed, "neighboring countries" would "club together against it." Like John Pomfret, Eyals saw the Croats as a threat, largely because they might not disarm, and he noted that if the Islamic countries were ready to help arm and train Bosnia's "Muslim-led" forces, western European states were opposed to doing so.[71]

Once it was clear that the fighting had ended, the media focused on America's future role. Thomas Friedman admonished the administration not to go "beyond simple peacekeeping into nationbuilding," because the "American public," a.k.a. Friedman, would not approve. His argument for minimal U.S. involvement in the region was consonant with his earlier position and echoed Joe Klein, who thought Clinton was stupidly risking American lives.[72]

Concerns that Washington would arm and train the Bosnian Muslims were reasonable. After all, Belgrade was still arming the Bosnian Serbs, but with surprisingly little effect on Milošević's credibility. American and UN officials interviewed by Engelberg and Roane were indifferent, and J. McAllister thought that after years of atrocities, broken cease-fires, and abortive peace plans, Americans were just . . . bored.[73]

Like Mark Thompson and David Hackworth, the *New Republic* had qualms about sending troops, and, like Magaš, it saw Dayton as codifying ethnic cleansing—"a chilly, realpolitikal deal that enshrine[d] the balance of power in the Balkans [and] the domination of the region by Serbia and Croatia." Still, Washington had "acted wisely" by making peace in "our world" and saving a modicum of "pluralism, the American dispensation." Taking a swipe at Powellism as "a little insulting to the American soldier" and praising Clinton for "a rare act of political courage" in committing troops to the Implementation Force (IFOR), the magazine saw Americans returning to the Old World to save Europe from itself, assert American leadership, and affirm American values—just like 1945.[74]

But many Americans were leery, some still suffering from Vietnam syndrome, others from neoisolationism. Dana Priest quoted Holbrooke's observation that "leadership requires doing things in the national interest" no matter what the odds against you, but he also noted that smaller families and more married folks in the armed forces made Americans less willing to risk lives abroad. Easy victories against Iraq and Grenada had reinforced this feeling, prompting John Shalikashvili, U.S. chief of staff, to worry that Americans only wanted wars in which "nobody gets killed on our side" and there is no "collateral damage on the other side."[75]

If so, Bosnia seemed almost ideal. According to Chris Hedges, the Bosnians in Tuzla, especially the young women, were eagerly awaiting the arrival of American GIs. Of course, there were also mujahedeen, land mines, and the numb resignation of the Muslim who said, "Peace?

I don't care. I feel nothing." Like Congress, most Americans still had to be sold on the idea.[76]

A proponent of deployment, Anthony Lewis simply noted that since the United States maintained "the largest, most powerful military force on earth," it must meet "the new challenge" of "ethnic conflicts," which were "the great menace to peace today."[77] Clinton agreed, and the media echoed the notion that "America—and America alone—can and should make the difference" if called on to "defend our fundamental values as a people" and, of course, "serve our most basic strategic interests."[78]

Alan Cowell implicitly questioned the wisdom of deploying U.S. troops when he reported irreverent remarks by the children of American servicemen. One child wondered why the United States was playing "parent to the whole world" and solving others' problems, not its own, and another recalled that Clinton had not gone "to the war he was supposed to go to."[79] There were no easy answers to such questions.

But America's newspaper of record dutifully printed Pentagon press releases, among them a detailed description of the technical problems of transferring troops from Germany to Bosnia that included variables like bad weather. "The fact of the matter," Col. Douglas I. Walters announced, was that the U.S. Army had a plan that it was "executing in a very deliberate way with great precision." That was one answer. As NATO took over from the UN, the U.S. commander, Admiral Leighton Smith Jr., pronounced the change of control "a defining moment for the alliance" and expressed his faith that the "leaders" in the area would "ensure" the "implementation" of the peace accords.[80]

The United States was now "at bat" in Tuzla, a "Pittsburgh without a football team," and "commanders from lieutenant to general" assured Rick Atkinson that the "force's foremost objective [was] to safeguard itself." It wasn't clear whether this reassured "the locals," who weren't "used to dealing with Americans" and their "competitive pricing system." But it was clear that IFOR was in the tradition of UNPROFOR, and if "everything [took] a little longer in Bosnia," the troops were doing just fine. Even Bosnians were mobilized to reassure the American public. "You say you are from Bosnia," one man said, "and people think only it is crazy and dangerous." In fact, it was a "place where civilized ideas were accepted by all."[81]

By Christmas, the Americans had settled down, despite miserable weather, lack of infrastructure, interethnic incidents, mines, and, of course, mujahedeen. Although new dangers threatened, American technology and training would overcome any threat and all difficulties. As the treaty was signed in Paris, the media reported that all sides were laying mines and fighting had erupted in Sarajevo, discouraging Izetbegović and Tudjman, but leaving Clinton strangely optimistic. In fact, even the ubiquitous and fearsome mujahedeen never numbered above 300, and they were never much of a threat, despite what might be called the media's fundamentalist-fixation.[82]

Still, Raymond Bonner implied that problems in Bosnia would come from Muslims and Croats who wanted the Posavina area, a crucial corridor for the Serbs and a dangerous place for the GIs patrolling it. Its importance to Croats and Bosnians seemed not to count. Nor did Momčilo Krajišnik's warning that Serbs would "never accept Muslim authority" impress John Pomfret, who reported that Americans would have to figure out how to prevent Muslims and Croatians, not just Serbs, from exploiting international differences to undermine the peace plan.[83]

More intractable was the problem posed by the large number of refugees. As many as 2.5 million Bosnians, mostly Muslims, had been displaced, largely by Serbian ethnic cleansing. Unable to return home for various reasons, their plight seriously compromised the peace settlement, which tacitly approved ethnic cleansing by failing to guarantee safe return to Serb-held areas.[84]

Yet Mike O'Connor and Bradley Graham seemed to imply that Muslims were the major problem. Graham reported that the Bosnian government was filling former Serbian villages with Muslim refugees. O'Connor noted a "shootout" between "Islamic fundamentalist soldiers" and Croatian militia, and clashes between Muslim "fundamentalists" and British troops. Whether or not the British were muddying the ethnic waters, O'Connor did so by reporting that Croats beat and evicted Muslims while "mujahedeen" harassed Croats. He did not discuss Serbian actions at all.[85]

In December, John Goshko accused the Croats of murdering 230 Serbs in Krajina, and demanded that the Croatian government let Serbs return to their homes. The piece was both partisan and inaccurate. Among other things, Goshko claimed that 200,000 Serbs had fled in August.[86] But his was just one of several articles that depicted the Serbs as the big losers.

John Pomfret reported Serbian concerns over Bosnia's "Muslim-dominated" government and quoted General Bachelet, who had been sent home after announcing that Serbs could choose only the suitcase or the coffin. Pomfret also cited Izetbegović's overtures to the Serbs, but saw "his commitment to a multiethnic society as shaky at best," because Izetbegović had used "an Islamic greeting instead of Serbo-Croatian"[sic] during an "important speech."[87]

The degree of Serbian commitment to a multiethnic society was already well known. Those in doubt could look up Karadžić's comments on Serbian TV in July 1994 regarding a peace plan that partitioned Bosnia along ethnic lines. It was "astonishing," he had said, that "the international community would want people who hate each other to the point of extermination to live together again."[88] Given such comments, the odds of a Bosnian state in which the Republika Srpska maintained its own army becoming a multiethnic society were easy to calculate.

If the Croatian and Bosnian offensives had not led to a just peace, they had led to peace. They had also forced Washington to divulge information regarding Serb war crimes. John Pomfret believed they had dispelled three myths—that Serbs were invincible, that Croats and Muslims could not cooperate, and that mediation could end the war. He ended on a negative note, quoting the usual unnamed UN analysts and Western observers, who thought fighting in eastern Slavonia likely.[89]

Perhaps, but Croats and Bosnians had been cooperating—however reluctantly—ever since their offensive on the Kupreš Plateau in November 1994, and it was becoming clear that the Serbs were no more invincible than the West had been interested in brokering a peace before events forced them to do so.[90]

POSTMORTEM

As Croat troops advanced in August, Stephen Rosenfeld resurrected the concept of moral equivalency and the myth of a fascist Croatia. Like *The Nation*, he saw Croatia's occupation of Krajina as similar to Serb ethnic cleansing, but he implied that a "multi-ethnic" Serbia was morally superior to an "ethnically pure" Croatia. Rosenfeld blamed this sad state of affairs, which existed solely in his mind, on Washington, Berlin, and a war that had not been "a battle of good and evil but a tribal struggle," and "a savage one" at that.[91]

He was echoed by A. M. Rosenthal, who returned to the lists in September, insisting that Bosnia's Serbs deserved a "decent share" of Bosnia and "some hope of freedom from the imposition of Bosnian Muslim rule." After all, he insisted, the Bosnian Serbs had "long" been among America's "friends," and the Muslims had started the war.[92] Because "western diplomats" saw "Bosnian offensives" as undermining peace and NATO's efforts to maintain a "balance of power" in the region, the UN had urged restraint on Sarajevo and bombed only Serb supply routes, communications centers, ammo dumps, and air defense systems in eastern Bosnia.[93]

In December, Rosenthal enumerated the "lessons" of Bosnia. Foremost was that no country should be recognized unless it controlled its territory. He also thought it time Americans realize that using airpower inevitably forces deployment of ground forces, and he questioned

NATO's right to intervene when its members were not under attack.[94] Of course, what Rosenthal was really saying was what he had said all along, that the Serbs should have been allowed to dismember and digest Bosnia and Croatia.

Such frivolous, partisan, and uninformed pleading was supported by UN reports of "four" people shot in the back of the head, of "mass graves" in Krajina whose occupants might be Serbian, and of Croatian looting. Yet while Zagreb insisted that its soldiers had been ordered not to harm civilians and repeatedly reassured Serbs that their rights would be respected, the UN claimed it could give no evidence because its personnel had been fired on by someone while trying to investigate charges.[95] Hearsay, rumor, and allegation abounded; substantial evidence was rare.

This was clear to Holly Cartner, executive director of Human Rights Watch. But when her letter was published in late August, inaccurate reports had already done a lot of damage. In short, the *Washington Post* was not exactly balancing its coverage, and it is a measure of the media's impermeability that the one person who had the best knowledge of atrocities should have to resort to writing a letter to one of the nation's most influential newspapers.

Cartner stressed the differences in the degrees and types of guilt of the warring parties in Yugoslavia. If all sides had committed crimes, only Serbian forces in both Croatia and Bosnia had tried to eliminate "in whole or in part" a people on the basis of their ethnicity. If a single Croat commander had briefly hidden behind Danish peacekeepers, Serbs had used civilian refugees as shields. Nor were Serb conquests of territory in Bosnia and Croatia equivalent to Croatia's reoccupation of its own territory. While Zagreb allowed the Red Cross access to all occupied zones and POWs, Pale did not. She could find only two credible allegations of Croat atrocities, and neither even remotely comparable to Srebrenica.[96] In other words, Croats had committed war crimes, but the media had seen genocide.

Although R. Jeffrey Smith claimed that Washington was just playing down reports of Croatian atrocities, the CIA insisted that despite "instances of lack of discipline" by Croatian troops, nothing had occurred that "approached the scale and intensity" of Bosnian Serb atrocities. The CIA apparently had thirty months of photographic evidence to support its assertion. Unfortunately, it had not made it public when it might have swayed public opinion and helped halt the slaughter in Bosnia.[97]

But Chris Hedges quickly reported the murder of nine Serbs in Krajina as "the worst single act of killing since the Croat military authorities took control of the area." Of course, at this rate, the Croats would have needed years to cleanse the area, and Hedges was not even sure the killings had occurred. But he still quoted a UN official's complaint that "violence by the Croats" was "out of control" in the Krajina.[98] Lacking evidence of real atrocities, exaggeration and hyperbole did nicely.

So did baseless accusation. In early October, Robert Silk asserted that negotiations were a charade to give the Muslim-Croatian alliance time "to capture more territory." He did not note that the areas being occupied were parts of both states, but he did insist that "Croatian ethnic cleansing" was "as effective and often as brutal" as Serbian, and he accused Washington of encouraging "brutality" against Serbs. He wanted Banja Luka declared a "protected enclave" and urged the United States to intervene to end the "systematic campaign of arson, murder and looting by the Croatian military" in the Krajina, noting that "two armed American helicopters" should do the job.[99]

Silk could also have noted, but did not, that because the West had kept Croat and Muslim forces from occupying Banja Luka in August, by October, 5,000 Muslims and Croats were missing in the area and thousands more had been expelled. Arkan's men had been busy cleansing, and refugees related "gruesome stories" of rape and murder. Yet Hedges threw a stone at the Croats and made ethnic cleansing seem a venerable Balkan practice. Four years seem too few to establish a tradition, but in this age of instant obsolescence, perhaps they were enough. In addition to simple hyperbole, Hedges implied that the Bosnian Serbs had been next to invincible in 1991 as they "swept through Muslim and Croatian towns," and that the Croatians had preyed on the elderly and infirm in the Krajina after it somehow miraculously fell back into their "hands."[100] The passive voice has its uses.

As John Pomfret noted, not people, but the peace plan had legitimized ethnic cleansing, which in turn had created 2.5 million refugees and ethnic states. Rather than lay the blame on Serbia, which had started the whole process and committed most of the war crimes and genocide, Pomfret noted that Tudjman had promoted a general who had been indicted for war crimes, leaving the impression that the Croatians bore a major share of the guilt for the atrocities in Bosnia. In December, Pomfret insinuated that all sides were a danger to peace because an occupying army would have to contain the "vengeance of the warring parties." Lumping together recent genocide with crimes committed in the 1940s, he discerned a worrisome pattern, restated a Serb view of history, and tarred all sides with the same brush. Yet he knew that thirty-three of the forty indicted for war crimes by the Hague tribunal in 1995 were Serbs.[101] Of course, if 90 percent of all war crimes had been committed by Serbs, then the number of indictments was slightly misleading, because thirty-six of forty should have been Serb, to preserve the proportions. All sides had committed war crimes, but the scale was not comparable.

In October, Anthony Lewis, who approved deployment of U.S. troops, wondered why Clinton had suddenly discovered a vital American interest in Bosnia. Lewis believed that Clinton could have made the same case for intervention anytime, and Bush might have saved 200,000 lives by speaking out when Dubrovnik was shelled in 1991.[102]

Roger Cohen presented a counterargument steeped in technical musings from UN officials regarding peacekeeping and its hazards. His message was that "moral authority is not enough." Like Lewis, he saw the war as having "continuously flouted western values . . . and threatened a wider Balkan conflict," and, like Lewis, he saw Srebrenica's fall as crucial. But he let the UN off the hook by concluding that future UN missions operating in war zones would require good intelligence and credible firepower. Of course, NATO had had more than enough firepower, it simply did not use it; intelligence, including pictures of mass graves at Srebrenica, was simply suppressed. If Cohen thought an earlier use of force by the UN would have avoided deaths, he also praised the peacekeepers for feeding the victims of genocide rather than arming them, containing the conflict rather than opposing aggression, and creating defenseless safe havens.[103]

One of the more telling postmortems was published by *Time*, which juxtaposed Miloš Vasić, the West's favorite Serbian liberal, and Zletko Dizdarević, an obviously embittered Bosnian Muslim. True to form, Vasić laid the blame for the conflict on greedy politicians, the media, priests, and academics, casting Milošević as the archvillain and defining the war as a Serb-Croat conflict. Rejecting collective guilt as a barbaric notion, he favored individual culpability and urged all sides to prosecute their own war criminals. Since no one would do so, he encouraged everyone to learn to live together.[104] If Vasić savored peace, he had no taste for justice.

Dizdarević's appetite was different, and a bit less predictable. He believed that the real problems would start after the fighting ended. He saw Dayton as destroying both Bosnia and the dream of a multiethnic state. For Dizdarević, peace was a bad joke as long as Milošević—whom everyone knew had prepared and provoked the conflict, then directed ethnic cleansing and military aggression against Croats and Muslims—was free. Peace was merely duplicity, a deal approved by Tudjman and Milošević based on lies and grounded in injustice.[105] Nineteen eighty-four just arrived a little late in the Balkans.

Most could understand the Muslim shopkeeper who believed that "too much blood" had been shed for people to forget what had been done, but Karadžić's threat that the Bosnian Serbs would "continue to fight" rather than sign the peace was simply odd. Still, the *Washington*

Post had the bad taste to run a picture with the caption, "Peace will mean loss of home for some Serbs."[106] At best this was gratuitous, given the millions of Muslims and Croats driven from their homes, or murdered in them, and given that some of the homes Serbs would lose had belonged to their neighbors before 1991.

Nonetheless, George Church repeated some of the hoariest of myths regarding the conflict, possibly because his sources included Warren Christopher, UN officials, and U.S. military officers. Although he offered only the example of Muslims driven from Banja Luka by Serbs, Church thought that a legacy of "hate and fear" would continue to fuel ethnic cleansing, which all sides were still practicing. Even had a mechanism existed to punish the guilty, he believed the West lacked the will to do so.[107]

Why the wars ended is not clear, but it is clear that the Western powers and their Russian associate imposed a peace treaty in 1995 because successful military operations by Croatian and Bosnian forces during the summer and early fall had created a situation that threatened to strip the Bosnian Serbs of the territory that they had seized over the past four years and send them, like the Serbs from the Krajina, fleeing into more secure Serbian-held areas, including Serbia proper. Had this occurred, it would have put tremendous pressure on the fragile political structure of Serbia, inundated with embittered refugees demanding action by Milošević and Serbia's armed forces. The chances for an open clash between Croatians and Bosnians on one side and Serbians and Montenegrins on the other would have increased dramatically, especially if Zagreb had decided to occupy eastern Slavonia and if Sarajevo had attempted to reestablish its control of Banja Luka.

Had Croatian and Bosnian forces swept through Bosnia, the Yugoslav army would have had to intervene. But its morale was low, its command and control shaky, and its units needed in Kosovo and the Sandžak to look after the Albanians and Muslims there. Nor was Vojvodina secure. The end result might well have been similar to the outcome of the Turkish-Greek conflict of 1921–22, another bit of British handiwork. The end state might have seen more population transfers, the creation of a powerful Croatian-Bosnian federation, the emergence of an expanded Albania, and a much reduced, landlocked Serbia, shorn of Vojvodina, Kosovo, and possibly Montenegro.

Such a scenario was similar to those that the great powers had done their best to avoid since 1991, conscious of the risk that Serbia might disintegrate domestically under the weight of the number of casualties it would take in any direct conflict with Croatia and Bosnia. There had always been the danger that a conventional military conflict might alter the balance of power in the region should it result in the creation of a powerful Croatian-Bosnian bloc, which would enhance the positions of

Germany and Italy but leave Britain and France on the sidelines. Peace was therefore practically guaranteed once Croatia and Bosnia showed they could defeat the Serbs. If Zagreb and Sarajevo were too weak to face down the West, their offensives rang alarm bells in Paris, London, Washington, and Moscow; their successes seemed to convince Belgrade that it needed a deal quickly to keep what the JNA and its surrogates in Pale had gained. If the pro-Serbian orientation of Athens, Bucharest, and Sofia was obvious, what Berlin, Vienna, Budapest, and Rome thought was another question, and the conflict still awaits a definitive diplomatic analysis.

Certainly, Croatian and Bosnian military successes disconcerted the United States and its allies in Europe, whose message to the Croats and Bosnians in mid-September was "quit while you're ahead." Washington had flashed a red light when Croatian and Bosnian forces were poised to attack Banja Luka, which would probably have fallen, even if the media continued to depict it as a Serbian stronghold.[108] Western diplomats saw the Bosnian offensives as compromising both their peace effort *and* the success of their air strikes in September. The UN warned the Muslims to restrain themselves, evidently because it did "not want to tilt the military balance."[109]

So NATO air strikes, which came after Croatian and Bosnian successes in August, were confined to targets in eastern Bosnia and mounted only against supply routes, communications centers, ammunition dumps, and air defense systems. Claims that they were crucial to the success of Croatian-Bosnian forces were disingenuous or misinformed. William Safire more accurately viewed them as "bloodless fireworks" that made "the battlefield safer for aircraft." Whether NATO really lacked "the will to kill killers," it was clear that the Croatian and Muslim armies, not Richard Holbrooke, had turned the "tide of war," which Safire thought "would have turned long ago had we not embargoed arms to the Muslims and offered UN hostages to the Serbs." He urged NATO "to apply military muscle" and create a "local balance of power." In effect, he wanted a satisfactory end to the war, something the West's last-minute intervention failed to achieve.[110]

If military force finally determined the outcome of the war in Bosnia, it did so in a way that few understood or acknowledged. In its lead article on the Dayton peace talks, the *New York Times* noted that "reflecting battlefield reality," Bosnia was to be "divided into two sub-entities with about half governed by a Bosnian-Croatian federation and half by a Bosnian Serb republic."[111] The battlefield reality reflected Western policy and intervention, from the embargo to the imposed peace of December 1995, not the military capabilities of the warring parties, save to the extent that these were shaped and limited by Western governments, which had again intervened in the fall of 1995 to preclude a Croatian-Bosnian victory.

The success of the Croatian-Bosnian offensive was the best argument to have lifted the embargo long before, because it showed that Zagreb and Sarajevo knew how to use modern military equipment and that only military means could bring the Serbs to the bargaining table and realize an end state acceptable to the victims of aggression.

The unexpected prowess on the battlefield displayed by Croatian and Bosnian forces was not just an unpleasant surprise for the Western powers, but for Belgrade and Pale as well. Faced with an efficient and powerful Croatian-Bosnian military alliance, Pale was as powerless as Knin, and Belgrade had to make the choice to wage a real war, with all of the risks involved, or to find some way to salvage as much face and territory as possible. Given the poor command and control structure of the Yugoslav army, the questionable military efficiency of the Bosnian Serbs, internal feuding between political and military leaders in Yugoslavia, the lack of enthusiasm for the war among Serbs in general, and the likelihood of significant casualties, Belgrade and Pale did the only rational thing—they cooperated with the West to obtain a peace that would assure them those gains that they still held after Zagreb suspended Operation Storm.[112]

The West and Russia will continue to meddle in the Balkans, but what the peace will ultimately mean, and whether it will last, are for the future and the people of the region to decide. It seems to have polarized the states in the area along older religious lines, which reflect a complex set of contemporary nationalist beliefs. Whether the alignment will endure is hard to say. But the West and its Russian associate have already prejudiced the outcome and effectively approved aggressive warfare as an instrument of foreign policy by allowing the Serbs to keep the territory that they seized after June 1991. By refusing to press for the indictment, extradition, and trial of war criminals, the treaties tacitly accepted genocide as an instrument of national policy, and by transforming Milošević into a peacemaker, the West countenanced chauvinism and hatemongering as acceptable methods of conducting a state's internal and external affairs.[113]

The Dayton accords were a compromise by all of the parties concerned, a peace imposed by Western powers whose actions over the past years in fact seem to have been calculated not to end the war or mitigate the suffering, but, to paraphrase Mark Almond, to reduce the victims of aggression to helplessness and then declare peace.[114]

And the American media? Most will continue to seek out and report on troubled areas, reduce foreign policy to domestic frames, hang their stories on familiar news pegs, and parrot their sources. As routine and confidence-building replace conflict and genocide in the former Yugoslavia and politicians seek to put the events of 1991–95 behind them, reporters will move on to more interesting venues, academics will offer belated analyses, and diplomats will praise themselves for tidying up the mess. Compromise had already precluded a just end to the conflict before Dayton, just as the stereotypes trotted out by the media and their sources prevented our understanding the conflict. But unless the structure of the media and the nature of reporting change, such endings are inevitable.

NOTES

1. Roger Cohen, "Maps, Guns and Bosnia," "Rebel Serbs Trick U.N. on Captives," *New York Times*, 6, 7 December 1994, and "Search for Pilot," *New York Times*, 3 June 1995.

2. Anthony Lewis, "Clinton and Sarajevo," and "The Speech Not Given," *New York Times*, 19 May, 2 June 1995.

3. A. M. Rosenthal, "Bill Clinton's War," and "How to Succeed in Bosnia," *New York Times*, 2, 6 June 1995; Joel Shapiro and Gordon R. Thompson, "A Dead End in Bosnia," *New York Times*, 19 May 1995.

4. Christine Spolar, *Washington Post*, 9 June 1995; Roger Cohen, "Captives Free, U.N. Gives Up Effort to Shield Sarajevo," *New York Times*, 19 June 1995; Samantha Power, "UN Threatens Serbs with NATO Air Strikes," *Washington Post*, 10 July 1995.

5. Chris Hedges, "U.N. Warns Serbs of Bombing If They Attack Dutch Unit," *New York Times*, 10 July 1995.

6. Chris Hedges, "Serb Forces Fight Dutch UN Troops in Eastern Bosnia," *New York Times*, 11 July 1995.

7. Chris Hedges, *New York Times*, 12, 19, 21 July 1995. The CIA reported 151 mass graves in Bosnian Serb areas. Even the Bulgarian press, which had generally ignored ethnic cleansing, noticed Srebrenica. *Standard* of Bulgaria, 15 July, 11–12 August 1995, reported Karadžić's threat to cleanse the other Muslim enclaves, the discovery of a mass grave in Srebrenica, and reports that the Serbs had killed most of the 6,000 missing Muslims.

8. Anthony Lewis, "Weakness as Policy (Srebrenica and the Vacuum of U.S. Leadership)," *New York Times*, 14 July 1995; Roger Cohen, *New York Times*, 28 June 1995.

9. Robert Kagan, "The Risk of U.S. Inaction," *New York Times*, 18 July 1995; *Washington Post*, 10, 12, 13, 15, 18 July 1995.

10. Chris Hedges, *New York Times*, 19, 20 July 1995.

11. Chris Hedges, "Bosnian Troops Cite Gassings at Žepa," *New York Times*, 21, 27 July 1995.

12. Alan Cowell, "A Dutch Soldier Looks Back in Sadness and Frustration," *New York Times*, 25 July 1995.

13. Jeane Kirkpatrick, "A Matter of Principle at the UN," *Washington Post*, 18 August 1995.

14. Eric Margolis, "A World Deaf to Genocide," *Ottawa Sun*, 31 July 1995.

15. Thomas W. Lippman, "Senior Policy Advisers Regroup on U.S. Peace Efforts in Balkans," *Washington Post,* 22 August 1995; *Time,* 24 July 1995.

16. Michael Dobbs and Christine Spolar, "Anybody Who Moved or Screamed Was Killed," and M. Dobbs and R. Jeffrey Smith, "New Proof Offered of Serb Atrocities," *Washington Post,* 26, 29 October 1995.

17. Anthony Lewis, "Truth and Its Effects," *New York Times,* 13 November 1995.

18. John Pomfret, "Croatia Slips Closer to Renewed War," *Washington Post,* 14 November 1993. Typically, in September 1993, the Serbs retaliated by killing civilians in Zagreb. Pomfret's sources painted the Croats as aggressors and worried that Serbia might get involved.

19. Roger Cohen, "Croatia Hits Area Rebel Serbs Hold, Crossing UN Lines," *New York Times,* 2 May 1995.

20. Roger Cohen, "Rebel Serbs Shell Croatian Capital," *New York Times,* 3 May 1995; FPB Bulletin, 4, 5, 12 May 1995; Croatian News/Julie Busich, 5 May 1995; "The Other War in the Balkans," *Newsweek,* 15 May 1995.

21. Mike O'Connor, "Croatian Troops Said to Brutalize Serbs in Retaken Area," *New York Times,* 25 May 1995; Rod Nordland, "The Next Flash Point?," *Newsweek,* 22 August 1994; Aryeh Neier, *The Nation,* 9–16 January 1995.

22. FPB Bulletin, 12, 19 May 1995; Robin Harris, "The U.N. Prolongs the War in Ex-Yugoslavia," *Wall Street Journal,* 7 May 1995 (Bruna Sarić, 19 May 1995). FPB Bulletin and Josip Lončarić, NFCA Press Release, 3 May 1995. Patrick Moore, OMRI, 3 May 1995, was anti-Croatian.

23. FPB Bulletin, 4, 5, 12 May 1995.

24. Chris Hedges, "Croatia Reported to Move Troops to Disputed Serb Region," *New York Times,* 17 October 1995.

25. Chris Hedges, "Two Officials Report New Mass Killings by Bosnian Serbs," *New York Times,* 20 October 1995.

26. FPB Bulletin, 29 March, 3 April 1995. Bihać had doubled its population, owing to the influx of refugees.

27. Johnsen, *Deciphering,* 68–70, for the potential of airpower.

28. FPB Bulletin, 27, 28, 31 July, 4 August 1995; James Rupert, *Washington Post,* 29 July 1995.

29. Jovana Gec (AP), "Defeated Croatian Serbs Feel Abandoned by Comrades in Serbia," *Milwaukee Journal-Sentinel,* 8 August 1995; Bruna Sarić, 31 July 1995; "Croats Menace Rebel Serb City," *AP,* 31 July 1995; Julijana Mojsilović, *AP,* 31 July 1995.

30. FPB Bulletin, 1 August 1995; Raymond Bonner, "Croats Widen Threat to Rebel Serbs," *Milwaukee Journal-Sentinel,* 1 August 1995.

31. For Malcolm Rifkind and British policy, see Maggie O'Kane, "Look Here, Just Pack It In and Die Quietly," *Guardian Weekly,* 23 July 1995 (Bruna Sarić).

32. Mike O'Connor, "Investigation Concludes Bosnian Government Snipers Shot at Civilians," *Milwaukee Journal-Sentinel,* 1 August 1995.

33. FPB Bulletin, 4, 5, 6, 8, 12 August 1995; Bruna Sarić, 5, 6 August 1995; "Croatians Capture Serb Rebels' Strongholds" (AP/LAT), *Milwaukee Journal-Sentinel,* 6 August 1995.

34. FPB Bulletin, 8, 9, 12 August 1995; "Croats Take Key Town" (AP/LAT/NYT), *Milwaukee Journal-Sentinel,* 7 August 1995. Mario Profača, 10 August 1995, reported that a BBC reporter had died after the British had strayed into a battle area. Fifteen Croatian journalists had been killed or had disappeared since 1991.

35. Peter Arnett, *CNN*, 7 August 1995, 8:30 A.M. CST.

36. *Update, CNN*, 7 August 1996, 9:00 A.M. CST; Bernard Shaw, *CNN*, 5:00 P.M. CST. Peter Arnett interviewed Colonel Novaković from Pale.

37. *Washington Post*, editorial, 5 August 1995.

38. Editorial, *Milwaukee Journal-Sentinel*, 9 August 1995.

39. "U.N. says mass graves used in Croat attack" (WP/NYT/AP), *Milwaukee Journal-Sentinel*, 19 August 1995.

40. *Milwaukee Journal-Sentinel*, 6 August 1995.

41. James Rupert, "Croatia Accused of 'Ethnic Cleansing,'" *Washington Post*, 9 August 1995.

42. "Croats Attack Rebel Serbs with Heavy Artillery, Tanks" (AP), and "Croatia Launches Huge Attack" (AP/LAT), *Milwaukee Journal-Sentinel*, 4, 5 August 1995, and AP, *Wisconsin State Journal* (Madison), 4 August 1995. Human rights groups in Zagreb did not reply to my queries regarding atrocities by Croat forces during and after Operation Storm.

43. John Pomfret, "Battle Could Hasten Long War's Conclusion—on Fighters' Terms: Croatia's Invasion Signals Victory for Ethnic Dividers," *Washington Post*, 5 August 1995; FPB, 8 August 1995; *Wisconsin State Journal*, 4 August 1995.

44. AP stories, *Milwaukee Journal-Sentinel*, 1, 3 August 1995, and Chris Hedges, "Tensions Ease in Sarajevo," *New York Times*, 18 September 1995.

45. "U.N. Reports Intentional Killing of Civilians in Croat Offensive" (AP), and R. Jeffrey Smith, "U.S. Charges Serbs with War Atrocities" (WP), *Milwaukee Journal-Sentinel*, 10 August 1995; Roger Cohen, *New York Times*, 9 March 1995; Bruna Sarić, 7 April 1995; FPB Bulletin, 8 April 1995. According to the 3,500–page report by the UN Commission of Experts, 200,000 had perished in Bosnia, mostly Croats and Muslims; some 50,000 had been tortured and 20,000 raped in 800 Serbian concentration camps. Zagreb reported 2,820 missing, 197,000 refugees, including 12,000 expelled and 600 killed after UNPROFOR's arrival.

46. Charles Krauthammer, "Ethnic Cleansing That's Convenient," *Washington Post*, 11 August 1995; "The Devil Drives," *Newsweek*, 14 August 1995.

47. Raymond Bonner, "Frightened and Jeered At, Serbs Flee from Croatia," *New York Times*, 10 August 1995; Tracy Wilkinson and Dean Murphy, "Serb Refugees Flood Roads" (LAT), *Milwaukee Journal-Sentinel*, 9 August 1995.

48. "Croatians Capture Serb Rebels' Stronghold," "Croat, Muslim-led Armies Set New Offensives" (AP), and "Croats Continue Exodus from Serb-held Lands," *Milwaukee Journal-Sentinel*, 6, 13, 16 August 1995; FPB, 10, 12, 24 August, 1 September 1995; Vukusan, 27 August 1995. Ivica Misić accused the Serbs of encouraging the flight of Serbs in Croatia to gain sympathy. The shoe definitely was on the other foot.

49. Thomas L. Friedman, "Both Clinton, Congress Posturing about Bosnia," *Milwaukee Journal-Sentinel*, 2 August 1995. Rod Nordland, "Virtual Peace in Sarajevo," *Newsweek*, 9 October 1995, thought much of the land taken by the Croat-Muslim offensive was "traditionally Serbian."

50. *CNN*, 7 August 1996, 9:00 A.M. CST; Bernard Shaw, *CNN*, 5:00 P.M. CST. Peter Arnett interviewed Colonel Novaković from Pale. Anthony Borden, "Zagreb Speaks," and Christopher Hitchens, "Minority Report," *The Nation*, 28 August–4 September, 23 October 1995; Slavenka Drakulić, "A Tudjman Fantasy," *New Republic*, 11 September 1995.

51. Jack Mizes, "The Serbs Show Their Knack for Defeat," *New York Times*, 12 August 1995; Mike O'Connor, "Bosnian Serb Civilians Flee Joint Muslim-Croat Attack," *New York Times*, 14 September 1995.

52. Mike O'Connor, "Bosnian Serbs Hit Sarajevo and U.N. Force Fails to Act," *New York Times*, 23 August 1995; *CNN*, 17 August 1996; FPB Bulletin, 4 August 1995. Serb artillery killed three in Dubrovnik, two in Mostar.

53. Roger Cohen, "Shelling Kills Dozens in Sarajevo, U.S. Urges NATO to Strike the Serbs," *New York Times*, 29 August 1995; David Binder, "Bosnia's Bombers."

54. Roger Cohen, "Calling History to Arms: Serbs Invoke Their Past," *New York Times*, 8 September 1995.

55. David Hekenlively, Letter, Edward L. Schneider, "Why Are U.S. Troops 'Globocops' for U.N.?," and Stevan Pirocanac, "The War No One Will Report Honestly," *Milwaukee Journal-Sentinel*, 4, 10, 18 August 1995. Among other bits of misinformation, Pirocanac claimed that 200,000 Serbs had been cleansed in Croatia and that 700,000 had died in Jasenovac during World War II.

56. John Pomfret and Christine Spolar, "Croatian Drive Turns Tables on Serbians: Military Blitz through Krajina Marks Fundamental Shift," *Washington Post*, 22 August 1995; Samantha Power, "Finders, Keepers," *New Republic*, 4 September 1995.

57. Dana Priest, "In Shift, U.S. Should Arm Bosnian Muslims," and John Pomfret, *Washington Post*, 7, 14 October 1995; Roger Cohen, *New York Times*, 28 October 1995.

58. "Enough about Me," *Newsweek*, 25 September 1995; FPB Bulletin, 17, 22 August 1995.

59. FPB Bulletin, 17, 22 August, 1 September 1995; Vuksan, 31 August 1995.

60. Roger Cohen, "Clinton Seeks to Shore Up Muslim-Croat Federation," "Balkan Peace at Hand?" *New York Times*, 6 October, 3 November 1995.

61. Joe Klein, "Setting the Table" and "A Grip, but Not Grins," John Barny and Bob Clark, "Starting the Hard Sell," Bill Clinton, "Why Bosnia Matters to America," *Newsweek*, 16, 20 October, 13 November 1995.

62. Pomfret, *Washington Post*, 18 December 1995.

63. Elaine Sciolino, "At the Talks, Raging Bull Meets Bulldog, Cordially," *New York Times*, 18 November 1995; "Enough about Me," *Newsweek*, 25 September 1995, saw Holbrooke as the bulldog. Michael Dobbs, "After Marathon Negotiations, an Extra Mile to Reach Peace," *Washington Post*, 23 November 1995.

64. Elaine Sciolino, Roger Cohen, and Stephen Engelberg, "In U.S. Eyes, 'Good' Muslims and 'Bad' Serbs Did a Switch," *New York Times*, 23 November 1995.

65. Bruce Nelan, "A Perilous Peace," *Time*, 4 December 1995; Michael Dobbs, "Balkan Leaders Approve Bosnian Pact," *Washington Post*, 22 November 1995; Evan Thomas and John Barny, "Shipping Out," *Newsweek*, 4 December 1995.

66. CNN Transcripts, 21 November 1995 Internet.

67. For Croatian comments on the treaties, Mate Granić's remarks to *Veernji list*, reported by Bruna Sarić, 24 November 1995; also Lydia Nimac, 8 June 1996.

68. Anthony Lewis, "No Peace without Justice," *New York Times*, 20 November 1995, and "Modified Rapture," *New York Times*, 24 November 1995.

69. Roger Cohen, *New York Times*, 22 November 1995.

70. Branka Magaš, "A Dubious Deal in Dayton: A Nation Betrayed," and Phyllis Kaminsky, "Rewarding Serbian Aggression: The U.S. 'Piece' Plan for Bosnia," *Balkan Monitor* (Balkan Institute), 8 December 1995.

71. Michael Dobbs, "U.S. Starts Process of Army Aid," and John Pomfret, *Washington Post*, 18, 21 December 1995.

72. Thomas Friedman, "Keep It Simple," *New York Times*, 15 November 1995; Joe Klein, "A Grip, but Not Grins," and "Looking at the Big 'But,'" *Newsweek*, 13 November, 18 December 1995.

73. Stephen Engelberg and Kit Roane, "Yugoslav Army Reported to Aid Bosnian Serbs despite Promises," *New York Times*, 18 November 1995; J. F. O. McAllister, "Is Bosnia Worth Dying For?" *Time*, 27 November 1995.

74. *New Republic*, 9, 18 December 1995; David Hackworth, *Newsweek*, 4, 18 December 1995; Mark Thompson, "The Peacekeeping Paradox," *Time*, 11 December 1995.

75. Dana Priest, *Washington Post*, 2 December 1995.

76. Chris Hedges, "Bosnian Town Prepares for G.I.s and Switch from War to Peace," *New York Times*, 1 December 1995; Michael Kramer, "The Art of Selling Bosnia," *Time*, 11 December 1995; Michael Dobbs, "U.S. Gains Assurances on Troops," *Washington Post*, 24 November 1995.

77. Anthony Lewis, "What Is at Stake?" *New York Times*, 1 December 1995.

78. Ann Devroy and Helen Dewar, "U.S. Troops Vital to Bosnia Peace, Clinton Says," *Washington Post*, 28 November 1995.

79. Alan Cowell, "Army Children Express Their Doubts," *New York Times*, 2 December 1995.

80. Ian Fisher, "Peacekeeping Logistics: 600 Trainloads but Most Won't Be Rolling until Christmas," *New York Times*, 16 December 1995; John Pomfret, "UN Hands Over Its Bosnia Duties to NATO Force," *Washington Post*, 21 December 1995.

81. Pamela Constable, "Bosnians in Area Struggle to Regain Economic Status," Rick Atkinson, "U.S., NATO Now at Bat in Bosnia," and Bradley Graham, "GI's and Priorities: Logistics, Logistics, Logistics," *Washington Post*, 16, 27 December 1995.

82. George Church, "In Harm's Way," *Time*, 25 December 1995.

83. Raymond Bonner, "To G.I.'s, Disputed Corridor Will Test Path to Peace," *New York Times*, 18 December 1995; John Pomfret, "Bosnian Serbs Demand New Deal for Sarajevo," *Washington Post*, 27 December 1995.

84. Alan Cowell, "For Bosnia's Refugees, Return May Be Illusion," *New York Times*, 8 December 1995; John Pomfret, *Washington Post*, 20 December 1995.

85. Mike O'Connor, "Five Islamic Soldiers Die in Shootout with Croats," *New York Times*, 16 December 1995; Bradley Graham, *Washington Post*, 15 December 1995.

86. John Goshko, "Citing 230 Murders, UN Declares Serbs Victims of Croat Atrocities," *Washington Post*, 23 December 1995.

87. John Pomfret, "Sarajevo Serbs Prepare to Go," *Washington Post*, 23 December 1995.

88. "Shelling Shatters Bosnia Truce," *AP*, 14 July 1994.

89. John Pomfret, "Prescription for More War in Bosnia," *Washington Post*, 12 August 1995.

90. Jasmina Kuzmanović, *AP*, 3 November 1994.

91. Stephen S. Rosenfeld, "Arithmetic of Atrocity," *Washington Post*, 11 August 1995.

92. A. M. Rosenthal, *New York Times*, 15 September 1995.

93. *New York Times*, "Bosnian Muslims Said to Push Back Rebel Serb Forces," 13 September 1995.

94. A. M. Rosenthal, "The Missing Report," *New York Times*, 22 December 1995.

95. John Pomfret, "UN Reports Mass Graves in Krajina," *Washington Post*, 15 August 1995.

96. Holly Cartner, "Artificial Symmetry of Atrocity," *Washington Post*, 18 August 1995.

97. R. Jeffrey Smith, "Bosnian Serbs Guilty of Atrocities, U.S. Says," *Washington Post*, 10 August 1995.

98. Chris Hedges, "Nine Aged Serbs Found Slain in Croat Town," *New York Times*, 5 October 1995.

99. Robert H. Silk, *New York Times*, 5 October 1995.

100. Chris Hedges, "For Some, Hope of Peace Offers Little," and "More Expulsions by Serbian Force Reported by U.N.," *New York Times*, 11 October 1995.

101. John Pomfret, *Washington Post*, 22 November, 18 December 1995.

102. Anthony Lewis, "The Credibility Gap (Suddenly Bosnia Is a Key Issue)," *New York Times*, 20 October 1995.

103. Roger Cohen, *New York Times*, 20 December 1995.

104. Miloš Vasić and Zletko Dizderević, "Rage after Peace: Letters from the Balkans," *Time*, 11 December 1995.

105. *Ibid.*

106. Christine Spolar, "In Sarajevo Peace Can't Defeat Skepticism," *Washington Post*, 27 November 1995.

107. George Church, "Divided by Hate," *Time*, 18 December 1995.

108. Knin had also been depicted as a Serbian stronghold. Chris Hedges, *New York Times*, 18 September 1995.

109. *New York Times*, 13 September 1995.

110. William Safire, "The Phony Air War," *New York Times*, 18 September 1995. One could speculate that air strikes in Bosnia, like A-bombs in Japan, were intended to send a message not only to Pale, but to Belgrade and Zagreb as well. Otherwise, it is difficult to see why NATO waited so long to flex its aviation muscles.

111. *New York Times*, 15 December 1995, A1, A20.

112. The best analyses of the JNA and the ending of the war in Bosnia are by Cigar, "The Serbo-Croatian War," and "How Wars End: War Termination and Serbian Decisionmaking in the Case of Bosnia."

113. For a detailed indictment of Milošević, see Cigar and Williams, *War Crimes and Individual Responsibility*, passim.

114. Mark Almond, *Europe's Backyard War*, 326.

Selected Bibliography

MEDIA AND THEORY

Adler, Richard P., ed. *Understanding Television: Essays on Television as a Social and Cultural Force*. New York: Praeger, 1981.

Bagdikian, Ben H. *The Media Monopoly*. Boston: Beacon Press, 1983.

Biagi, Shirley. *NewsTalk II: State-of-the-Art Conversations with Today's Broadcast Journalists*. Belmont, CA: Wadsworth Publishing Co., 1987.

Bogart, Leo. *Press and Public: Who Reads What, When, Where, and Why in American Newspapers*. Hillsdale, NJ: Lawrence Erlbaum Associates, 1981.

Bolling, Landrum R., ed. *Reporters under Fire: U.S. Media Coverage of Conflicts in Lebanon and Central America*. Boulder, CO: Westview Press, 1985.

Buckingham, David. *Moving Images: Understanding Children's Emotional Responses to Television*. Manchester: Manchester University Press, 1996.

Cohen, Yoel. *Media Diplomacy: The Foreign Office in the Mass Communications Age*. London: Frank Cass, 1986.

Comstock, George, Steven Chaffee, Natan Katzman, Maxwell McCombs, and Donald Roberts. *Television and Human Behavior*. New York: Columbia University Press, 1978.

Čuvalo, Ante. "Croatian Nationalism and the Croatian National Movement 1966–1972, in Anglo-American Publications: A Critical Assessment." *Journal of Croatian Studies* (1989).

Downing, John, et al. *Questioning the Media: A Critical Introduction*. London: Sage, 1990.

Ellul, Jacques. *Propaganda: The Formation of Men's Attitudes*. New York: Vintage, 1973.

Ewen, Stuart. *All Consuming Images: The Politics of Style in Contemporary Culture*. New York: Basic Books, 1984.

Fallows, James. "Why Americans Hate the Media." *The Atlantic Monthly* (February 1996).

Fishman, Mark. *Manufacturing the News.* Austin: University of Texas Press, 1980, 1990.

Fiske, John. *Television Culture.* New York: Methuen & Co., 1991.

Gans, Herbert J. *Deciding What's News: A Study of CBS Evening News, NBC Nightly News, Newsweek, and Time.* New York: Pantheon, 1979.

Gaunt, Philip. *Choosing the News: The Profit Factor in News Selection.* Westport, CT: Greenwood Press, 1990.

Gitlin, Todd. *The Whole World Is Watching: Mass Media in the Making and Unmaking of the New Left.* Berkeley: University of California Press, 1980.

Goffman, Erving. *Interaction Ritual: Essays on Face-to-Face Behavior.* Garden City, NY: Doubleday, 1967.

Graber, Doris A. *Mass Media and American Politics.* Washington, DC: Congressional Quarterly Press, 1993.

Gross, Larry, John Stuart Katz, and Jay Ruby. *Image Ethics: The Moral Rights of Subjects in Photographs, Film, and Television.* New York: Oxford University Press, 1988.

Hachten, William A. *The World News Prism: Changing Media of International Communication.* Ames, IA: Iowa State University Press, 1992.

Haight, Timothy R. "The New American Information Order." *The Critical Communications Review* (Norwood, NJ: Ablex, 1984), II:101–117.

Herman, Edward S., and Noam Chomsky. *Manufacturing Consent: The Political Economy of the Mass Media.* New York: Pantheon, 1988.

Isaacs, Norman. *Untended Gates: The Mismanagement of the Press.* New York: Columbia University Press, 1986.

Kaplan, E. Ann, ed. *Postmodernism and Its Discontents: Theories, Practices.* New York: Verso, 1988.

Kellner, Douglas. *Media Culture: Cultural Studies, Identity and Politics between the Modern and the Postmodern.* London: Routledge, 1995.

———. *The Persian Gulf TV War.* Boulder, CO: Westview, 1992.

Klaidman, Stephen, and Tom L. Beauchamp. *The Virtuous Journalist.* New York: Oxford University Press, 1987.

Kroker, Arthur, and David Cook. *The Postmodern Scene: Excremental Culture and Hyper-Aesthetics.* New York: St. Martin's, 1988.

Lasswell, Harold D., and James Wechsler. *Propaganda Techniques in the World War.* New York: Knopf, 1927.

Lazere, David, et al. *American Media and Mass Culture: Left Perspectives.* Berkeley: University of California Press, 1987.

Lee, Martin A., and Norman Solomon. *Unreliable Sources: A Guide to Detecting Bias in News Media.* New York: Carol Publishing Group, 1990.

Lichter, S. Robert, Stanley Rothman, and Linda S. Lichter. *The Media Elite.* Bethesda, MD: Adler & Adler, 1986.

McLuhan, Marshall. *Understanding Media: The Extensions of Man.* New York: Mentor, 1964.

McQuail, Denis. *Media Performance: Mass Communication and the Public Interest.* Newbury Park, NJ: Sage, 1992.

Maier, Mark H. *The Data Game: Controversies in Social Science Statistics.* Armonk, NY: M. E. Sharpe, 1991.

Markel, Lester. *What You Don't Know Can Hurt You: A Study of Public Opinion and Public Emotion.* New York: Quadrangle, 1972.

Mattelart, Armand, and Jean-Marie Piemme. "Twenty-three Guidelines for Political Debate on Communications in Europe." *The Critical Communications Review* (1984), II:211–23.

Matthews, Loyd J. *Newsmen and National Defense: Is Conflict Inevitable?* Washington, DC: Brassey's Inc., 1991.

Merrill, John C., and Ralph D. Barney. *Ethics and the Press: Readings in Mass Media Morality.* New York: Hastings House, 1976.

Moscow, Vincent, and Janet Wasko, *The Political Economy of Information.* Madison: University of Wisconsin Press, 1988.

Myers, Garth, Thomas Klak, and Timothy Koehl. "The Inscription of Difference: News Coverage of the Conflicts in Rwanda and Bosnia." *Political Geography* (1996):21–46.

Nevitt, Barrington. *The Communication Ecology.* Toronto: Butterworths, 1982.

Newcomb, Horace, ed. *Television: The Critical View.* New York: Oxford University Press, 1987.

Olen, Jeffrey. *Ethics in Journalism.* Englewood Cliffs, NJ: Prentice-Hall, 1988.

Paletz, David L., and Robert M. Entman. *Media, Power, Politics.* New York: The Free Press, 1981.

Powers, Ron. *The Newscasters.* New York: St. Martin's, 1977.

Read, James Morgan. *Atrocity Propaganda, 1914–1919.* New Haven, CT: Yale University Press, 1941.

Ruehlmann, William. *Stalking the Feature Story.* New York: Vintage, 1977.

Said, Edward W. *Orientalism.* New York: Vintage, 1979.

Schiller, Herbert I. "Informatics and Information Flows: The Underpinnings of Transnational Capitalism." *The Critical Communications Review* (Norwood, NJ: Ablex, 1984), II:3–29.

Severin, Werner J., and James W. Tankard, Jr. *Communications Theories: Origins, Methods, Uses.* New York: Longman, 1988.

Soley, Lawrence C. *The News Shapers: The Sources Who Explain the News.* Westport, CT: Praeger, 1992.

Spirova, Maria. "Razpaddaneto na iugoslavia v bulgarskata presa (1991–1995)." *Balkaniistichen Forum* (1996).

Stoler, Peter. *The War against the Press: Politics, Pressure and Intimidation in the '80s.* New York: Dodd, Mead, 1986.

Tester, Keith. *Media, Culture, and Morality.* London: Routledge, 1994.

Thompson, Mark. *Forging War: The Media in Serbia, Croatia and Bosnia-Herzegovina.* London: Article 19/International Centre against Censorship, May 1994.

Tichi, Cecelia. *Electronic Hearth: Creating an American Television Culture.* New York: Oxford University Press, 1991.

Tuchman, Gaye. *Making News: A Study in the Construction of Reality.* New York: The Free Press, 1978.

Vanderbilt TV New Archives. *Television News Index and Abstracts* (Nashville, TN).

Weber, Ronald. *The Literature of Fact: Literary Nonfiction in American Writing.* Athens, OH: Ohio University Press, 1980.

Whittemore, Hank. *CNN: The Inside Story.* Boston: Little, Brown, and Co., 1990.

LAW, WAR, AND GENOCIDE

Amnesty International. *Bosnia-Herzegovina: Rape and Sexual Abuse by Armed Forces*. London: January 1993.

Best, Geoffrey. *War and Law since 1945*. Oxford: Clarendon Press, 1996.

Briggs, Herbert W. *The Law of Nations*. New York: Appleton-Century-Crofts, 1952.

Brownlie, Ian. *Basic Documents in International Law*. Oxford: Clarendon Press, 1983.

Buergenthal, Thomas, and Judith R. Hall, eds. *Human Rights, International Law and the Helsinki Accord*. New York: Allanhead, Osmun, & Co., 1977.

Butterfield, Herbert, and Marin Wight, eds. *Diplomatic Investigations: Essays in the Theory of International Politics*. Cambridge, MA: Harvard University Press, 1966.

Cigar, Norman. *Genocide in Bosnia: The Policy of Ethnic Cleansing*. College Station, TX: Texas A&M University Press, 1995.

———. "How Wars End: War Termination and Serbian Decisionmaking in the Case of Bosnia." *South East European Monitor* (Vienna, 1996).

———. "The Right to Defence: Thoughts on the Bosnian Arms Embargo." *Institute for European Defence and Strategic Studies* (1995).

———. "The Serbo-Croatian War." *Journal of Strategic Studies* (1994).

———. "War Termination and Croatia's War of Independence: Deciding When to Stop." *Journal of Croatian Studies* (1991–92).

Cigar, Norman, and Paul Williams. *War Crimes and Individual Responsibility: A Prima Facie Case for the Indictment of Slobodan Milosevic*. Washington, DC: The Balkan Institute, 1996.

Cohen, Marshall, Thomas Nagel, and Thomas Scanlon, eds. *War and Moral Responsibility*. New Brunswick, NJ: Princeton University Press, 1974.

Crkvencic, I., and M. Klemencic. *Southern Croatia and Dalmatia, Borders and Population*. Washington, DC: Croatian Democracy Project, 1992.

Cullen, Robert. "Human Rights Quandary." *Foreign Affairs* (Winter 1992–93).

Eknes, Åge. "The United Nations' Predicament in the Former Yugoslavia." In *The United Nations and Civil Wars*, edited by Thomas G. Weiss. Boulder, CO: Lynne Rienner, 1995.

Falk, Richard A. *Law, Morality, and War in the Contemporary World*. Westport, CT: Greenwood, 1963.

Falk, Richard A., et al. *Crimes of War: A Legal, Political, Documentary, and Psychological Inquiry into the Responsibility of Leaders, Citizens, and Soldiers for Criminal Acts in War*. New York: Random House, 1971.

Forestier, Patricia. "The Use of Social Sciences to Stir Up Ethnic Conflict." *International Conference on Bosnia-Herzegovina*, Ankara, April 1995.

Freedman, Lawrence, ed. *Military Intervention in European Conflicts*. Oxford: Blackwell, 1994.

Friedrich, Carl Joachim. *The Philosophy of Law in Historical Perspective*. Chicago: University of Chicago Press, 1958, 1963.

Gilpin, Robert. *War and Change in World Politics*. New York: Cambridge University Press, 1981, 1991.

Gow, James. "Nervous Bunnies: The International Community and the Yugoslav War of Dissolution." In *Military Intervention in European Conflicts*, edited by Lawrence Freedman. Oxford: Blackwell, 1994.

Gray, J. Glenn. *The Warriors: Reflections on Men in Battle*. New York: Harper, 1986.

Gutman, Roy. *A Witness to Genocide*. New York: Macmillan, 1993.

Helsinki Watch. *Human Rights in a Dissolving Yugoslavia*. Washington, DC, 9 January 1991.

———. *Increasing Turbulence: Human Rights in Yugoslavia*. Washington, DC, October 1989.

———. *Letter to F. Tudjman*, 13 February 1992.

———. *Letter to S. Milošević and B. Adžić*, 21 January 1992.

———. *Violations of the Helsinki Accords: Yugoslavia*. Washington, DC, November 1986.

———. *War Crimes in Bosnia-Hercegovina*. New York, August 1992, April 1993, vols. I, II.

———. *Yugoslavia: Crisis in Kosovo*. Washington, DC, March 1990.

———. *Yugoslavia: Human Rights Abuses in the Croatian Conflict*. Washington, DC, September 1991.

Henkin, Louis, et al. *The International Bill of Rights: The Covenant on Civil and Political Rights*. New York: Columbia University Press, 1981.

Holmes, Richard. *Acts of War: The Behavior of Men in Battle*. New York: Harper, 1986.

International Court of Justice. *Reports of Judgements, Advisory Opinions and Orders: Case Concerning Application of the Convention on the Prevention and Punishment of Genocide (Bosnia-Herzegovina vs. Serbia-Montenegro)*. The Hague, 13 September 1993.

Kačić, Hrvoje. "Recognizing Croatia's Independence: The Role of the United States and the European Community." *Journal of Croatian Studies* (1991–92).

Kočović, Bogoljub. *Žrtve Drugog svetskog rata u Jugoslaviji*. London: Naše delo, 1985.

Kraljic, John. *Belgrade's Strategic Designs on Croatia*. Washington, DC: Croatian Democracy Project, 1991.

Kuper, Leo. *Genocide: Its Political Use in the Twentieth Century*. New Haven, CT: Yale University Press, 1982.

Kuzmanović, Tomislav Z. "Croatia's Constitution: A Blueprint for Democracy in Croatia." *Journal of Croatian Studies* (1991–92).

Lael, Richard L. *The Yamashita Precedent: War Crimes and Command Responsibility*. Wilmington, DE: Scholarly Resources, 1982.

Lemkin, Raphael. *Axis Rule in Occupied Europe: Laws of Occupation, Analysis of Government, Proposals for Redress*. Washington, DC: Carnegie Endowment for International Peace, 1944.

Letica, Slaven. "The Post-Communist Balkan's Wars: Could They Be Avoided and How Can They Be Stopped." Paper delivered at *A Symposium on the Question of Multilateral Military Intervention*, University of North Carolina at Chapel Hill, 13–14 April 1993.

Levi, Werner. *Contemporary International Law: A Concise Introduction*. Boulder, CO: Westview, 1979, 1991.

Lipstadt, Deborah. *Beyond Belief: The American Press and the Coming of the Holocaust.* New York: The Free Press, 1985.

McCoubrey, Hilaire, and Nigel D. White. *International Organizations and Civil Wars.* Brookfield, NH: Dartmouth, 1995.

McDougal, Myres S., and Associates. *Studies in World Public Order.* New Haven, CT: New Haven Press, 1987.

Maugham, Viscount. *U.N.O. and War Crimes.* Westport, CT: Greenwood, 1951/1975.

Mazlish, Bruce, Arthur D. Kaledin, and David B. Ralston, eds. *Revolution: A Reader.* New York: Macmillan, 1971.

Meštrović, Stjepan, ed. *Genocide after Emotion: The Post-Emotional Balkan War.* London: Routledge, 1996.

Meštrović, Stjepan, and Thomas Cushman, eds. *This Time We Knew: Western Responses to Genocide in Bosnia.* New York: New York University Press, 1996.

North, Robert C. *War, Peace, Survival: Global Political and Conceptual Synthesis.* Boulder, CO: Westview Press, 1990.

Pick, Daniel, *War Machine: The Rationalisations of Slaughter in the Modern Age.* New Haven, CT: Yale University Press, 1993.

Rieff, David. *Slaughterhouse: Bosnia and the Failure of the West.* New York: Simon & Schuster, 1995.

Sereni, Angelo Piero. "The Status of Croatia under International Law." *American Political Science Review* (1941).

Sieghart, Paul. *The International Law of Human Rights.* Oxford: Clarendon Press, 1983.

Stiglmayer, Alexandra, ed. *Mass Rape: The War against Women in Bosnia-Herzegovina.* Lincoln: University of Nebraska Press, 1994.

Walzer, Michael. *Just and Unjust Wars: A Moral Argument with Historical Illustrations.* New York: Basic Books, 1977.

Wells, Donald A. *War Crimes and Laws of War.* Washington, DC: University of America Press, 1984.

Žerjavić, Vladimir. *Yugoslavia—Manipulations with the Number of Second World War Victims.* Zagreb: Croatian Information Centre, 1993.

HISTORY AND POLITICS

Adamić, Louis. *My Native Land.* New York: Harper and Brothers, 1943.

Ali, Rabia, and Lawrence Lifschultz, *Why Bosnia? Writings on the Balkan War.* Stony Creek, CT: The Pamphleteer's Press, 1993.

Almond, Mark. *Europe's Backyard War: The War in the Balkans.* Toronto: Mandarin, 1994.

Auty, Phyllis, and Richard Clogg, eds. *British Policy towards Wartime Resistance in Yugoslavia and Greece.* London: Macmillan, 1975.

———. *Tito: A Biography.* Harlow: Longman, 1970.

Banac, Ivo. *The National Question in Yugoslavia: Origins, History, Politics.* Ithaca, NY: Cornell University Press, 1984.

Barker, Elisabeth. *British Policy in South-East Europe in the Second World War.* London: Macmillan Press, 1976.

Beard, Charles, and George Radin. *The Balkan Pivot: Yugoslavia: A Study in Government and Administration.* New York: Macmillan, 1929.

Bennett, Christopher. *Yugoslavia's Bloody Collapse: Causes, Course and Consequences.* New York: New York University Press, 1995.

Borden, Anthony, Ben Cohen, Marisa Crevatin, and Davorska Zmiarević, eds. *Breakdown: War and Reconstruction in Yugoslavia.* London: Institute for War and Peace Reporting, 1992.

Cohen, Lenard J. *Broken Bonds: The Disintegration of Yugoslavia.* Boulder, CO: Westview, 1993.

Cohen, Philip J. *Serbia's Secret War: Propaganda and the Deceit of History.* College Station, TX: Texas A&M University Press, 1996.

Crnobrnja, Mihailo. *The Yugoslav Drama.* Montreal: McGill-Queen's University Press, 1994.

Čučić, Ljubomir. *U.S. Foreign Policy and Croatia.* Zagreb: European Movement, 1995.

Dizdarević, Zlatko. *Sarajevo: A War Journal.* New York: Fromm International, 1993.

Djilas, Aleksa. *The Contested Country: Yugoslav Unity and Communist Revolution, 1919–1953.* Cambridge, MA: Harvard University Press, 1991.

Djordjević, Dimitrije, ed. *The Creation of Yugoslavia, 1914–1918.* Santa Barbara, CA: ABC–Clio, 1980.

Donia, Robert, and John Fine. *Bosnia and Herzegovina: A Tradition Betrayed.* New York: Columbia University Press, 1994.

Dragnich, Alex N. *The First Yugoslavia: Search for a Viable Political System.* Stanford, CA: Hoover Institute Press, 1983.

———. *Serbs and Croats: The Struggle in Yugoslavia.* New York: Harcourt, Brace, Jovanovich, 1992.

———. "The Anatomy of a Myth: Serbian Hegemony." *Slavic Review* (1991).

Drakulić, Slavenka. *The Balkan Express: Fragments from the Other Side of the War.* New York: HarperCollins, 1993

Duncan, W. Raymond. "Yugoslavia's Break-up." In *Ethnic Nationalism and Regional Conflict: The Former Soviet Union and Yugoslavia,* edited by W. R. Duncan and G. Paul Holman, Jr. Boulder, CO: Westview, 1994.

Eterovich, Francis, and Christopher Spalatin, eds. *Croatia: Land, People, Culture.* Toronto: University of Toronto Press, 1964.

Fogelquist, Alan F. *The Breakup of Yugoslavia, International Policy, and the War in Bosnia-Hercegovina.* Los Angeles, CA: Institute of South Central European and Balkan Affairs, 1993.

Glenny, Misha. *The Fall of Yugoslavia: The Third Balkan War.* New York: Penguin, 1992.

Gow, James. *Legitimacy and the Military: The Yugoslav Crisis.* London: Printer Publishers, 1992.

Guldescu, Stanko, and John Prcela, eds. *Operation Slaughterhouse: Eyewitness Accounts of Postwar Massacres in Yugoslavia.* Philadelphia: Dorrance & Co., 1970.

Hall, Brian. *The Impossible Country: A Journey through the Last Days of Yugoslavia.* David Godine, 1994.

Hehn, Paul N. *The German Struggle against Yugoslav Guerrillas in World War II: German Counter-Insurgency in Yugoslavia, 1941–1943.* New York: East European Quarterly, 1979.

Hoptner, J. B. *Yugoslavia in Crisis, 1934–1941.* New York: Columbia University Press, 1962.

Irving, Jill. *The Croat Question: Partisan Politics in the Formation of the Yugoslav Socialist State.* Boulder, CO: Westview Press, 1993.

Jelavich, Charles. "The Nationality Problem in Austria-Hungary." *Austrian History Yearbook* (1967).

Jelavich, Charles and Barbara, eds. *The Balkans in Transition: Essays on the Development of Balkan Life and Politics since the Eighteenth Century.* Hamden, CT: Archon Books, 1974.

———. *The Establishment of the Balkan National States, 1804–1920.* Seattle: University of Washington Press, 1977.

Johnsen, William T. *Deciphering the Balkan Enigma: Using History to Inform Policy.* Strategic Studies Institute, March 1993.

Kaplan, Robert J. *Balkan Ghosts: A Journey through History.* New York: St. Martin's, 1993.

Karchmar, Lucien. *Draža Mihailović and the Rise of the Četnik Movement, 1941–1942.* New York: Garland, 1987.

Kerner, Robert J., ed. *Yugoslavia.* Berkeley: University of California Press, 1949.

Lederer, Ivo J. *Yugoslavia at the Paris Peace Conference: A Study in Frontier Making.* New Haven, CT: Yale University Press, 1963.

Maček, Vladko. *In the Struggle for Freedom.* New York: Robert Speller & Sons, 1957.

Magaš, Branka. *The Destruction of Yugoslavia: Tracking the Break-up 1980–92.* New York: Verso, 1993.

Malcolm, Noel. *Bosnia: A Short History.* New York: New York University Press, 1994.

Mamatey, Victor S. *The United States and East Central Europe, 1914–1918: A Study in Wilsonian Diplomacy and Propaganda.* Princeton, NJ: Princeton University Press, 1957.

Martin, David. *Allies Betrayed: The Uncensored Story of Tito and Mihailovich.* New York: Prentice-Hall, 1946.

———. *The Web of Disinformation: Churchill's Yugoslav Blunder.* New York: Harcourt, Brace, Jovanovich, 1990.

Mestrović, Matthew, and Radovan Latković. *The Croatian Response to the Serbian National Program.* Saddle River, NJ: The Croatian National Congress, 1988.

Meštrović, Stjepan, Slaven Letica, Miroslav Goreta. *Habits of the Balkan Heart: Social Character and the Fall of Communism.* College Station, TX: Texas A & M University Press, 1993.

Mihailovic, Dražha. *The Trial of Dragoljub-Draža Mihailović: Stenographic Record and Documents from the Trial of Dragoljub-Draža Mihailović.* Belgrade, 1946/Salisbury, NC: Documentary Publications, 1977.

Milazzo, Matteo J. *The Chetnik Movement and the Yugoslav Resistance.* Baltimore: Johns Hopkins Press, 1975.

Pattee, Richard. *The Case of Cardinal Aloysius Stepinac.* Milwaukee: Bruce Publishing, 1953.

Pavlowitch, Stevan K. *The Improbable Survivor: Yugoslavia and Its Problems, 1918–1988.* Columbus, OH: Ohio State University Press, 1988.

Petrovich, Michael Boro. *A History of Modern Serbia, 1804–1918.* New York: Harcourt, Brace, Jovanovich, 1976.

Polonsky, Antony. *The Little Dictators: The History of Eastern Europe since 1918.* London: Routledge & Kegan Paul, 1975.

Pozzi, Henri. *Black Hand over Europe.* London: F. Motto, 1935.

Prpić, George. In O'Grady, Joseph P., et al. *The Immigrant Influence on Wilson's Peace Policies.* Lexington, KY: University of Kentucky Press, 1967.

Ramet, Sabrina P. *Balkan Babel: Politics, Culture, and Religion in Yugoslavia.* Boulder, CO: Westview Press, 1992.

———. *Nationalism and Federalism in Yugoslavia, 1962–1991.* Bloomington, IN: Indiana University Press, 1984, 1992.

———. "Serbia's Slobodan Milosević: A Profile." *Orbis* (1991).

———. *Social Currents in Eastern Europe: The Sources and Consequences of the Great Transformation.* Durham, NC: Duke University Press, 1995.

Ramet, Sabrina Petra, and Ljubiš S. Adamovich. *Beyond Yugoslavia: Politics, Economics, and Culture in a Shattered Community.* Boulder, CO: Westview, 1995.

Roberts, Walter R. *Tito, Mihailović and the Allies 1941–1945.* New Brunswick, NJ: Rutgers University Press, 1973.

Rothenburg, Gunther E. *The Military Border in Croatia, 1740–1881: A Study of an Imperial Institution.* Chicago: University of Chicago Press, 1966.

Rothschild, Joseph. *East Central Europe between the Two World Wars.* Seattle: University of Washington Press, 1977.

Rusinow, Dennison. *The Yugoslav Experiment, 1948–1974.* Berkeley: University of California Press, 1977.

Sadkovich, James J. *Italian Support for Croatian Separatism, 1927–1937.* New York: Garland, 1987.

———. "Objectivity and Bias: The First Yugoslavia, by Alex Dragnich." *Journal of Croatian Studies* (1986).

———. "Serbian Hegemony Revisited, or Blaming the Perpetrator, not the Victim." *Association of Croatian Studies Bulletin* (Oct. 1992).

———. "Terrorism in Croatia, 1929–1934." *East European Quarterly* (March, 1988).

———. "The Use of Political Trials to Repress Croatian Dissent, 1929–1934." *Journal of Croatian History* (1987–88).

———. "War, Genocide, and the Need to Lift the Embargo on Bosnia and Croatia." *Journal of Croatian Studies* (1991–92).

Sckelj, Laslo. *Yugoslavia: The Process of Disintegration.* Boulder, CO: Columbia University Press, 1993.

Seton-Watson, Hugh. *Eastern Europe between the Wars, 1918–1941.* New York: Harper and Row, 1962/1945.

———. *The East European Revolution.* New York: Praeger, 1956.

Seton-Watson, Robert W. *The Rise of Nationality in the Balkans.* London: Constable & Co., 1917.

Silber, Laura, and Allan Little. *The Death of Yugoslavia.* London: Penguin/BBC Books, 1996.

Singleton, Fred. *Twentieth-Century Yugoslavia.* New York: Columbia University Press, 1976.

Stokes, Gale, ed. *From Stalinism to Pluralism: A Documentary History of Eastern Europe since 1945.* New York: Oxford University Press, 1991.

———. *The Walls Came Tumbling Down: The Collapse of Communism in Eastern Europe.* New York: Oxford University Press, 1993.

Sugar, Peter F., ed. *Ethnic Diversity and Conflict in Eastern Europe.* Santa Barbara, CA: ABC–Clio, 1980.

Thompson, Mark. *A Paper House: The Ending of Yugoslavia.* London: Hutchinson Radius, 1992.

Tomašević, Jožo. *Peasants, Politics and Economic Change in Yugoslavia.* Stanford, CA: Stanford University Press, 1955.

———. *War and Revolution in Yugoslavia, 1941–1945: The Chetniks.* Stanford, CA: Stanford University Press, 1975.

United States, Department of the Army. *German Antiguerrilla Operations in the Balkans (1941–1944)* (August, 1954).

Vucinich, Wayne, ed. *Contemporary Yugoslavia: Twenty Years of Socialist Experiment.* Berkeley, CA: University of California Press, 1969.

Vuilliamy, Ed. *Seasons in Hell: Understanding Bosnia's War.* New York: St. Martin's, 1994.

West, Rebecca. *Black Lamb and Grey Falcon: A Journey through Yugoslavia.* New York: Viking, 1941/53.

Wheeler, Mark C. *Britain and the War for Yugoslavia, 1940–1943.* Boulder, CO: East European Monographs, 1980.

Wolff, Robert Lee. *The Balkans in Our Times.* Cambridge, MA: Harvard University Press, 1956.

Woodward, Susan L. *Balkan Tragedy: Chaos and the Dissolution of Yugoslavia after the Cold War.* Washington, DC: Brookings Institution, 1995.

Zametica, John. *The Yugoslav Conflict.* London: IISS/Brassey, 1992.

Živojinović, Dragan. *America, Italy and the Birth of Jugoslavia (1917–1919).* Boulder, CO: East European Quarterly, 1972.

REPORTERS AND NEWS SHAPERS*

Jim Adams, *Reuters,* 1994
Charles Aldinger, *Reuters,* 1994
David Andersen, *Wall Street Journal,* 1992
Rick Atkinson, *Washington Post,* 1995
Russell Baker, *New York Times,* 1995
Tony Baker, *The Independent,* 1995 (Bruna Sarić).
Jean Baudrillard, *Libération,* 1993, 1995

*Please note that the following citations for 1994 were taken from CD News Bank: AP, Reuters, *Christian Science Monitor, Hartford Courant, Philadelphia Inquirer, Montreal Gazette, Ottawa Citizen, Ottawa Sun, Chicago Tribune, Guardian Weekly, Calgary Herald, Detroit Free Press, Toronto Sun,* and *San Diego Union-Tribune.*

Nora Beloff, *National Review*, 1992
——, *New York Review of Books*, 1992
Richard K. Betts, *Foreign Affairs*, 1994
David Binder, *New York Times*, 1991
Laura Blumenfeld, *Washington Post*, 1993
Celestine Bohlen, *New York Times*, 1991
Farhan Bokhari, *Christian Science Monitor*, 1994
Raymond Bonner, *Milwaukee Journal-Sentinel*, 1995
——, *New York Times*, 1995
Anthony Borden, *The Nation*, 1992
Boutros Boutros-Ghali, *Foreign Affairs*, 1992–93
——, *International Herald Tribune*, 1995
Charles G. Boyd, *Foreign Affairs*, 1995
——, *New York Times*, 1995
Holly Burkhalter, *Washington Post*, 1995
John Burns, *New York Times*, 1992
Mark F. Canciar, *Parameters*, 1993
Holly Cartner, *Washington Post*, 1995
Marc D. Charney, *New York Times*, 1994
Yigal Chazan, *Christian Science Monitor*, 1994
George Church, *Time*, 1995
Francis X. Clines, *New York Times*, 1995
Roger Cohen, *New York Times*, 1994, 1995
Matthew Daly, *The Hartford Courant*, 1994
Dan De Luce, *Reuters*, 1994
Barbara Demick, *Philadelphia Inquirer*, 1994
Ann Devroy, *Washington Post*, 1994
Ann Devroy and Helen Dewar, *Washington Post*, 1995
Zlatko Dizdarević, *Time*, 1995
Aleksa Djilas, *New Republic*, 1993
Michael Dobbs, *Washington Post*, 1995
—— and Fred Babash, *Washington Post*, 1995
—— and Ann Devroy, *Washington Post*, 1995
—— and Jeffrey Smith, *Washington Post*, 1995
—— and Christine Spolar, *Washington Post*, 1995
Nicholas Doughty, *Reuters*, 1994
Boro Dropulic, *New York Times*, 1991
William Drozdiak, *Washington Post*, 1995
Giles Elgood, *Reuters*, 1994
Stephen Engelberg, *New York Times*, 1991
—— and Kit Roane, *New York Times*, 1995
Moina Farrow, *Montreal Gazette*, 1994
Ian Fisher, *New York Times*, 1995
Thomas L. Friedman, *New York Times*, 1991, 1995
——, *Milwaukee Journal-Sentinel*, 1995
Charles Gati, *Washington Post*, 1995
Jovana Gec (AP), *Milwaukee Journal-Sentinel*, 1995
Carol Giacomo, *Reuters*, 1994

Misha Glenny, *New York Times*, 1994, 1995
——, *New York Review of Books*, 1992, 1995
Globus (Zagreb), 1995
Peter Glynn, *New Republic*, 1992
David Gompert, *Foreign Affairs*, 1993
Anthony Goodman, *Reuters*, 1994
Michael R. Gordon, *New York Times*, 1993
Michael R. Gordon, Douglas Jehl, Elaine Sciolino, *New York Times*, 1994
John Goshko, *Washington Post*, 1995
James L. Graff, *Time*, 1993
Bradley Graham, *Washington Post*, 1995
Steven Greenhouse, *New York Times*, 1994
Peter Grier, *Christian Science Monitor*, 1994
Robert Guskind, *National Journal*, 1992
Roy Gutman, *Newsday*, 1992
—— (Bruna Sarić), 1995
David Hackworth, *Newsweek*, 1993, 1995
Lee Hamilton, *Washington Post*, 1992
Blaine Harden, *Washington Post*, 1993
Robin Harris, *Wall Street Journal* (Bruna Sarić), 19 May 1995.
Richard Harwood, *Washington Post*, 1995
Chris Hedges, *New York Times*, 1995
Mark Heinrich, *Reuters*, 1994
Gerald B. Helman and Steven R. Ratner, *Foreign Policy*, 1992–93
Christopher Hitchens, *The Nation*, 1993, 1994, 1995
John Hoey, *The Nation*, 1995
Stanley Hoffman, *New York Times*, 1994
David Hujic (Davor Hudžić), *Reuters*, 1994, 1996
Joseph Joffe, *Foreign Affairs*, 1992-93
Paul Johnson, *National Review*, 1992
Robert Kagan, *New York Times*, 1995
Elizabeth Kastor, *Washington Post*, 1994
George Kenney, *New York Times*, 1992
——, *Washington Times*, 1994
Stephen Kinzer, *New York Times*, 1991, 1995
Jeanne Kirkpatrick, *Washington Post*, 1995
Joe Klein, *Newsweek*, 1995
Miki Prific Knezevic, *New York Times*, 1995
Erwin Knoll, *The Progressive*, 1993
Michael Kramer, *Time*, 1995
Charles Krauthammer, *International Herald Tribune*, 1995
——, *Washington Post*, 1996
Jasmina Kuzmanović, *AP*, 1994
Bruce Lambert, *New York Times*, 1991
Jane A. Lampmann, *Christian Science Monitor*, 1994
Jonathan Landay, *Christian Science Monitor*, 1994
Charles Lane, *New Republic*, 1993
——, *Newsweek*, 1995

Evelyn Leopold, *Reuters*, 1994
Paul Levine, *The Nation*, 1995
Anthony Lewis, *New York Times*, 1994, 1995
Flora Lewis, *New York Times*, 1991, 1992
Michael Lind, *New Republic*, 1992
Thomas W. Lippman, *Washington Post*, 1995
R. C. Longworth, *Chicago Tribune*, 1994
Donatella Lorch, *Ottawa Citizen*, 1994 (CDN).
J. F. O. McAllister, *Time*, 1995
Doyle McManus, *Los Angeles Times*, 1994
Noel Malcolm, *National Review*, 1991
Eric Margolis, *Ottawa Sun*, 1995 (CD/World Net)
Robert Marquand, *Christian Science Monitor*, 1994
Charles William Maynes, *Foreign Policy*, 1992–93
Walter Russell Mead, *Los Angeles Times*, 1993
Alfred Meyer, *Psychology Today*, 1992
Peter Millership, *Reuters*, 1994
Peter Millionig, *New York Times*, 1991
Jack Mizes, *New York Times*, 1995
George Moffett, *Christian Science Monitor*, 1994
George Moffett and Peter Grier, *Christian Science Monitor*, 1994
Julijana Mojsilovic, *AP*, 1994
Patrick Moore, *OMRI*, 3 May 1995
Lance Morrow, *Time*, 1993
Lucia Mouat, *Christian Science Monitor*, 1994
Aryeh Neier, "Watching Rights," *The Nation*, 1992, 1993, 1995
Bruce Nelan, *Time*, 1992, 1993, 1995
Aleksandar Nenadović, *New York Times*, 1991
Elizabeth Neuffer, *Boston Globe*, 1996
David Newhouse, *New Yorker*, 1992
Rod Nordland, *Newsweek*, 1995
Joseph Nye, *Foreign Affairs*, 1992
Mike O'Connor, *Milwaukee Journal-Sentinel*, 1995
——, *New York Times*, 1995
Maggie O'Kane, *Guardian Weekly*, 1995 Bruna Sarić.
Frederick Painton, *Time*, 1993
Jane Perlez, *New York Times*, 1995
William Pfaff, *New York Review of Books*, 1992 (originally *LA Times* 1992)
John Pomfret, *Washington Post*, 1993, 1995
—— and Christine Spolar, *Washington Post*, 1995
Dave Pommer, *Calgary Herald*, 1994
Srdja Popović, *New York Times*, 1991
Colin Powell, *Foreign Affairs*, 1992-93
Samantha Power, *New Republic*, 1995
——, *Washington Post*, 1995
Dana Priest, *Washington Post*, 1995
Igor Primorac, *Journal of Croatian Studies*, 1991–1992
Max Primorac, *National Review*, 1992

Sabrina P. Ramet, *East European Politics and Societies*, 1994
——, *Foreign Affairs*, 1992
Tom Raum, *AP*, 1994
Alan Riding, *New York Times*, 1991
David Rieff, *New Yorker*, 1992
Sara Rimer, *New York Times*, 1995
Stephen S. Rosenfeld, *Washington Post*, 1995
A. M. Rosenthal, *New York Times*, 1994, 1995
James Rupert, *Washington Post*, 1995
William Safire, *New York Times*, 1995
Michael Scammell, *New York Times*, 1991
Kurt Schork, *Reuters*, 1994
Elaine Sciolino, *New York Times*, 1993, 1994, 1995
Elaine Sciolino, Roger Cohen, and Stephen Engelberg, *New York Times*, 1995
Radek Sikorski, *National Review*, 1991
R. H. Silk, *New York Times*, 1995
Marlise Simons, *New York Times*, 1994
Alison Smale, *AP*, 1994
R. Jeffrey Smith, *Washington Post*, 1995
Christine Spolar, *Washington Post*, 1995
Alessandra Stanley, *New York Times*, 1994
Stephen John Stedman, *Foreign Affairs*, 1992–93
Ronald Steel, *New Republic*, 1992
Alexandra Stiglmayer, *Time*, 1995
Warren Strobel, *Washington Times*, 1994
Chuck Sudetic, *New York Times*, 1991, 1994
John Tagliabue, *New York Times*, 1991
Paul Taylor, *Reuters*, 1994
Allan Thompson, *Toronto Star*, 1994
Mark Thompson, *Time*, 1995
Gregory F. Treverton, *Foreign Affairs*, 1992
Neely Tucker, *Detroit Free Press*, 1994
Miloš Vasić and Zlatko Dizdarević, *Time*, 1995
Craig R. Whitney, *New York Times*, 1991, 1993, 1994
Tracy Wilkinson and Dean Murphy, *Milwaukee Journal-Sentinel*, 1995
Carol J. Williams, *Los Angeles Times*, 1994
Dov S. Zakheim, *New York Times*, 1995
Warren Zimmerman, *International Herald Tribune*, 1995

NEWSPAPERS, WIRE SERVICES, AND INTERNET

ABC (Spain), 1992
Associated Press, 1991, 1994
Bosnia Internet Forum, 1996
Foreign Press Bulletin, 1995
International Herald Tribune, 1995
International Intelligence Report, 1994 (CD News Bank)

Los Angeles Times, 1991–93
Milwaukee Journal-Sentinel, 1995
New York Newsday, 1994
New York Times, 1991–95
Reuters, 1991, 1994
San Diego Union-Tribune, 1994
Bruna Sarić, 1995, 1996
Standard (Bulgaria), 1992–95
24 Chasa (Bulgaria), 1991–95
Washington Post, 1991–95
Washington Times, 1992
Wisconsin State Journal, 1995

TELEVISION AND RADIO

"ABC Nightly News," *ABC*, 1992, 1995
"All Things Considered," *NPR*, 1993
"America's Talking," *NBC*, 1995 (CD News Bank)
Peter Arnett, *CNN*, 1995
Stephen Cassidy, *CNN*, telephone interview, 20 July 1993
"CBS Nightly News," *CBS*, 1995
CNN, 1993, 1995
"Day 1/one," *ABC*, 1993 (Journal Graphics)
Gail Evans, telephone interview, 19 July 1993
Frontline, *PBS*, 1994 (Journal Graphics)
"Inside Washington," *Federal News Service*, 1994 (CD News Bank)
Peter Jennings, specials, *ABC*, 1993, 1994
MacNeil-Lehrer Newshour, *PBS*, 1993-95, interviews with David Owen, Mile
    Akmadžić, Radovan Karadžić, Bianca Jagger, Ann Fleming, José Maria
    Mendiluce, Warren Christopher, Joseph Biden, Vaclav Havel, Lee Ham-
    ilton, Nancy Kassebaum, George Mitchell, Lawrence Eagleburger, Tom
    Lantos, Tom Foley, Michael Elliott, Anthony Lewis, Jacqueline Gropin,
    Sakato Ogata, Madeleine Albright, Bill Odom, Brent Scowcroft, Laurie
    Mylroie, Mohamed Hakki, Thomas Pickering, Joseph Liberman, John
    McCain, Pat Schroeder, Hank Brown, Bob Springer, John Galvin, Gregory
    Vuksich, William Perry, Bill Hyland, Vitaly Churchin, Richard Lugar,
    John Warner, Elizabeth Furse, Joseph Biden, William Hyland, Jeanne
    Kirkpatrick, Jim Hoaglund, W. R. Mead, Holly Burkhalter
"John McLaughlin's 'One on One,'" *Federal News Service*, 1994 (CD News Bank)
Meet the Press, *NBC*, 1994, interview with Samuel R. Berger (CD News Bank)
Nightline, *ABC*, 1991–95, interviews with Dimitrij Rupel, Darko Silović, Mark
    Wheeler, Slobodan Milošević, Radovan Karadžić, Anthony Lewis, Ilara
    Zorić, Mike Nicholson, Elie Wiesel, Robert Dole, Dave Marash, Tony
    Birtley, Joseph Biden, Frank McCloskey, Henry Kissinger, Leon Wiseltier,
    George Schultz, Jim Wooten, Lewis MacKenzie, John McCain, Jeane
    Kirkpatrick, Barry Dunsmor, Mike Lee, Jim Wooten, John McQuethy,

David Owen, Jim Bitterman, Kate Adic, Susan Woodward, Newt
    Gingrich, William Styron, Letty Cottin Pogrebin
Juan Señor, telephone interview, 16 July 1993
This Week with David Brinkley, ABC, 1993, reports by Jack Smith and Tony Birtley
    and interviews with Madeleine Albright, Robert Dole, Brent Scowcroft,
    Radovan Karadžić, Muhammed Sacirbey, Jack Smith, Tony Birtley
Today, NBC, interviews with James Rawson, William Crowe, J. H. Binford Peay
    III, 1994 (CD News Bank)

Index

ABOUT THE AUTHOR

JAMES J. SADKOVICH is an independent scholar. He is the author of *The Italian Navy during World War II* (Greenwood, 1994).

ISBN 0-275-95046-8

90000>

EAN

9 780275 950460

HARDCOVER BAR CODE